The Italians
and the Holocaust

THE ITALIANS AND THE HOLOCAUST

Persecution, Rescue, and Survival

SUSAN ZUCCOTTI

Basic Books, Inc., Publishers

NEW YORK

Library of Congress Cataloging-in-Publication Data

Zuccotti, Susan, 1940–

   The Italians and the Holocaust.

   Includes bibliographic references and index.
   1. Jews—Italy—Persecutions.   2. Holocaust, Jewish,
(1939–1945)—Italy.   3. World War, 1939–1945—Jews—
Rescue—Italy.   4. Italy—Ethnic relations.   I. Title.
DS135.I8Z83   1987   940.53'15'03924045   86–47738
ISBN   0–465–03622–8   (cloth)
ISBN   0–465–03621–X   (paper)

To Emilia Levi, three years old,

a "curious, ambitious, cheerful, intelligent child,"

whose parents managed to find water on the deportation train

to bathe her on the eve of her arrival at Auschwitz,

and

to all the other children who shared her fate

CONTENTS

Contents

ACKNOWLEDGMENTS

THIS BOOK could not have been written without the help of two outstanding scholars at the Centro di Documentazione Ebraica Contemporanea (CDEC) in Milan. Liliana Picciotto Fargion, director of research, shared with me the most recent results of her work in Holocaust statistics, much of it still unpublished. She brought documents, books, articles, and photographs to my attention, read my nearly completed manuscript, and offered invaluable suggestions. I have never met as generous a scholar, and I am profoundly grateful.

At an earlier stage in my research, Michele Sarfatti brought me the hundreds of documents of survivor testimony on file at the CDEC, and helped me understand the dimensions of the story. Some of the testimony was written immediately after the war. More was written in 1955, on the occasion of the tenth anniversary of the liberation. Italian Jewish Community leaders at that time wanted to honor Italian non-Jews who had rescued Jews during the German occupation, and they asked survivors to write their stories and nominate potential honorees. Additional testimony was written between 1955 and the present, as more survivors were contacted and encouraged to record their experiences for posterity. Altogether, the documents offer precious insight into patterns of rescue and survival in Italy, and I am grateful to Liliana Picciotto Fargion, Michele

Acknowledgments

Sarfatti, and the entire staff at CDEC for making them available to me.

Historians, archivists, and librarians at many other institutions were also helpful. I would like to thank Professor H. Stuart Hughes at the University of California, San Diego, for his encouragement and attention to my manuscript. Professor Robert O. Paxton at Columbia University I thank for his teaching and support. Raleigh Trevelyan kindly answered my questions, even though I was a total stranger. Archivists and librarians assisted me in a variety of ways. I would like to express my gratitude to the many men and women, most of whose names I never knew, who placed at my disposal the resources of the New York Public Library, Columbia University libraries, the YIVO Institute for Jewish Research, and the Leo Baeck Institute in New York City; the Holocaust Memorial Council and the National Archives in Washington, D.C.; the Wiener Library in London; the Associazione nazionale ex-deportati politici in Milan; and the Associazione nazionale partigiani italiani and the Istituto Luce in Rome.

Many individuals agreed to speak with me, reviving old memories and opening old wounds. Among these, I especially thank Laura Erbsen, formerly of Trieste but now living in New York City; Giorgina Nathan and her husband Winston Burdett in Rome; Massimo Medina in Genoa; and Gastone Orefice, from Livorno but in New York at the time of our interview. Also, many friends thought enough of my work to refer me to these sources. I am grateful to Tobi and Max Frankel for putting me in touch with Laura Erbsen; to Don Hewitt for his trans-Atlantic telephone call to Giorgina and Winston Burdett; to Giovanna and Andreina Zuccotti for the introduction to Massimo Medina. All of these people believe that the story of the Holocaust in Italy must be remembered.

The kindness and consideration of many other friends and family members contributed to this book. Barbara and Donald

Zucker made possible my trip to Yad Vashem, and I thank them for their generosity. Israel and Elli Krakowski and Ulo and Ethel Barad shared with me their unbearably painful memories of the Holocaust in Poland and Austria, and focused my attention on similar horrors in Italy. Paul Selver and Lloyd Kaplan carefully read my manuscript, to its great benefit. Lenora Silvers performed numerous technical tasks of manuscript preparation, always cheerfully. Anna DeLaney typed and retyped. I am very grateful to these good friends and special people.

My parents Jane and Ralph Sessions, my mother-in-law Gemma Zuccotti, my aunt Barbara Dill, and my aunt by marriage Rina Mandaro deserve particular thanks, for without their help I could never have completed my research. My children Gianna, Andrew, and Milena have been long-suffering and patient with a mother who was often harassed and preoccupied. Above all, I thank my husband John Zuccotti. He read and studied my manuscript as carefully as any editor and gave me his support and encouragement when I most needed them. He spent days and weeks alone while I was doing research and writing. I know he did it out of love, and I am grateful. But he did it also because he shares my determination that the story of the Holocaust be told and retold, that we who were young then shall not forget, and that new generations of children like our own shall learn, reflect, and try to understand the inconceivable.

PROLOGUE

THE FAMILY NAME Nathan is familiar to most Italians. Students still read of Sara Levi Nathan, devoted admirer, friend, and correspondent of Giuseppe Mazzini, the leader, with Cavour and Garibaldi, of Italian unification. Students still learn of Sara's even more famous son, Ernesto Nathan, the first Jewish mayor of Rome, elected in 1907.[1] But Italians know little about Giuseppe Nathan, Ernesto's son and Sara's grandson. His is a story they may prefer to forget.[2]

During the 1920s and most of the 1930s—the era of triumphant fascism in Italy—Giuseppe Nathan was a prosperous and respected Roman banker. He lived in London for many years, representing the Bank of Italy, marrying an Australian woman, and raising his children to be bilingual. But his heart belonged to Italy. It was an allegiance that nearly cost him his life.

Unlike his father, Giuseppe Nathan had no interest or time for politics. He was neither favorable nor opposed to fascism. He was too busy with his young family, his travels, and his career. The career flourished until 1938. In that fateful year, Mussolini's racial laws suddenly decreed that Giuseppe Nathan could no longer work for the Bank of Italy. His children could not attend public schools. He could not have a Catholic maid in his house. He could not even list his name in the telephone directory. The illustrious name of Nathan now scarcely existed, because it was a Jewish name.

In desperation, Giuseppe Nathan moved his young family to Australia late in 1938. Restless and nostalgic for both work and Italy, he set out alone for Europe, via the United States. In San Francisco, his reputation and experience as a banker held him in good stead, and he received excellent career offers. He had arrived at the turning point of his life. Yet late in 1939, as war was breaking out in Europe, he decided to refuse all offers, return to Italy, and send for his family. He missed the land of his forefathers. He did not want to make his way outside it.

The Nathans lived in wartime Italy for several years, under constant police surveillance. Their passports were confiscated. Giuseppe's career was finished and his income vastly reduced. Sorrow and anxiety turned to terror on September 8, 1943, however, when the Germans occupied the country of their former ally. Immediately aware of the danger of arrest and deportation, Giuseppe fled with his family to a village in the Abruzzi.

After the Allied landings at Anzio in January 1944, the Nathans returned to Rome, believing that the city would soon be liberated. They even managed to hitch a ride home on a German truck. The Nazis and their Italian Fascist cronies were arresting all Jews, but despite their fanatic racism, they could not recognize their victims by sight.

The Nathans naturally could not live at home in Rome. Giuseppe hid his wife, an enemy national, and his children in private homes or convents. He himself found refuge in a monastery. In the spring of 1944, an Italian spy informed the Nazis that fugitives were hiding in the monastery. During the raid that followed, Giuseppe hid behind heavy draperies. His shoes protruded, and he was caught. He spent four days under relentless interrogation at Gestapo headquarters in the Via Tasso. He was then transferred to the infamous Roman prison of Regina

Coeli. He was fortunate to have arrived there after the Ardeatine Caves massacre on March 24, 1944. Regina Coeli had
been emptied of its male Jewish prisoners at that time, to help
fill the SS order for victims to be shot in reprisal for the killing
of 33 German SS police during a partisan attack in Rome's Via
Rasella. The Nazis demanded a ratio of 10 Italians to be killed
for every German. They executed 335 men and boys—5 more
than ordered. Of the 335, 77 were Jewish.[3]

Giuseppe Nathan remained at Regina Coeli, awaiting transport to Auschwitz. Again he was fortunate. The Allies arrived
in June, before enough Jewish prisoners could be assembled to
make a new transport worth the effort. Liberated, shaken, and
in need of care, he checked into the Grand Hotel. On the
registration form, he wrote his previous address: Regina Coeli.

The Nathan family survived the war and eventually resumed
a semblance of normal life. Giuseppe Nathan was reemployed
at the Bank of Italy. He died in 1952, at the age of sixty-five.

The adventures of Giuseppe Nathan typify, in almost every
respect, the experiences of Jews in Italy during World War II.
Italian Jews were rarely as famous as Giuseppe's father, but
most were assimilated middle-class professionals. Most had
lived in Italy for generations and were profoundly patriotic. All
were devastated by the racial laws in 1938, and many emigrated
or converted. All were forced into hiding during the German
occupation, although the majority did not recognize the danger
as quickly as the Nathans. Most, like Giuseppe, survived with
the help of Italian rescuers, often men and women of the
Church. But more than 6,800 did not survive.[4] Like Giuseppe,
they were betrayed by informers. Unlike him, they were forced
into cattle cars and shipped to the gas chambers and ovens of
Auschwitz.

About 85 percent of the 45,200 Jews in Italy during the
German occupation lived to see liberation.[5] This book exam-

ines the nature of the Holocaust in Italy, where the survival rate was among the highest in occupied Europe. The statistic cannot be taken for granted. After all, as late as the second half of the nineteenth century, Italy hosted some of the most oppressive Jewish ghettos in the world. After a few decades of unification, emancipation, and democratic government, the country fell under authoritarian Fascist rule in 1922. Then in 1938, Italy became officially anti-Semitic, and non-Jewish Italians were informed that Jews were their enemies and the cause of all evil. Furthermore, Italy became Hitler's willing ally in war in June 1940, and a full partner in a crusade that included, among other objectives, the goal of making Europe *Judenrein* —free of Jews.

After the German occupation of Italy, Benito Mussolini's puppet regime continued to cooperate fully with the Nazis. The political manifesto of the new regime declared in November 1943, that Italian Jews were enemy aliens. A police order in December 1943, called for the internment of all Jews. Adolf Eichmann sent highly experienced teams of Jew hunters to Italy, as he did to all occupied nations. Thousands of Italian Fascists, from conviction, careerism, or sheer greed, were eager to help them. The Holocaust in Italy was executed with ferocious determination. How did so many manage to survive it?

Yet, strangely enough, quite the opposite question might be asked. About 15 percent of the Jews in Italy during the German occupation did not survive the Holocaust. This book asks how more than 6,800 people could have been rounded up and deported to be gassed from a country that, despite its nineteenth-century ghettos and the promptings of its Fascist rulers, had no significant anti-Semitic tradition. Jews had lived in Italy since before the Christian Era. In 1943, they were proportionately few, thoroughly assimilated, and physically indistinguishable from their Christian countrymen. It should not have been difficult for them to hide. They lived in the shadow of the

Vatican, in close proximity to the moral and spiritual leader of the Catholic world and the supreme teacher of Christian precepts of brotherly love and the sanctity of human life. And the Holocaust began much later in Italy than in most other European countries, so that Jews should have been aware of the danger and quick to flee. In Rome, the danger period from September 1943 to June 1944 lasted only nine months; in most of central Italy, it continued three or four months longer; in northern Italy, it existed until April 1945. A maximum of twenty months, yet 15 percent of Italy's Jews were destroyed. How could it have happened?

The answers to both questions lie with the people involved. The majority of Jewish Italians were brave, resourceful, individualistic, nonsubmissive, and determined to survive. A tiny minority were terrified, unimaginative, passive, and unable to act to save their own lives. Many non-Jewish Italians were anti-German, anti-Fascist, and prepared to help all fugitives who came their way. Italian men and women of the Church stood in the forefront of the rescue effort, even while the man in the Vatican resolved not to be involved. Sympathetic priests and nuns were joined by doctors, lawyers, government officials, peasants, and housewives. Meanwhile, a small minority of non-Jewish Italians served the Nazi occupiers of their country, hunted fugitives at the side of the Gestapo, and betrayed their Jewish neighbors.

This book examines the behavior of men, women, and children, Jewish and Christian alike, living in the shadow of death. Jews who survived owed their lives to their own personal initiative, Christian help, and large doses of good luck. The tragedies of those who died can be traced occasionally to lack of initiative, but more often to betrayal by Christian neighbors. In occupied countries where the Nazi goal was total Jewish extermination, survival rates were determined by the personal decisions of Jews, the responses of Christian countrymen in both their public and private capacities, and luck. In Italy, those factors determined that 38,400 Jews would survive while more than 6,800 would die.

The sad but ultimately favorable balance suggests that, for the most part, the decisions of Jews in Italy were wise and correct. The responses of many Italian non-Jews, in the absence of support from their government, were decent and courageous. We cannot explain why individuals are good or bad, wise or foolish, courageous or cowardly. We can, however, try to understand the context in which decisions are made. We can also ask ourselves whether we, in our country essentially free from anti-Semitism, might, under similar pressures, make decisions as wise and courageous as many Italians did.

The Italians
and the Holocaust

1

The Holocaust
Comes to Italy

EVEN before the Italian declaration of war against the Allies on June 10, 1940, sixty-eight-year-old Marshal Pietro Badoglio, chief of the General Staff, had warned that the army was not prepared. Events confirmed his judgment. Only a few days after the Italian attack on Greece on October 28, 1940, the army was in retreat. In January 1941, the British defeated Marshal Rodolfo Graziani in North Africa, advancing three hundred miles into Libya and taking more than 100,000 prisoners. Italy lost Eritrea, Somalia, and Ethiopia by April, along with another 250,000 prisoners. Prime Minister Benito Mussolini, the individual most responsible for reckless military decisions and poor planning, unceremoniously retired both Badoglio and Graziani.

In March 1941, the Germans bailed out the Italians in North Africa. In April, they conquered Greece, where Italians

The Italians and The Holocaust

had been bogged down for five months. Mussolini in turn sent 200,000 men to fight beside the Germans in Russia in June. A euphoric year and a half of Axis victories followed. Defeats at El Alamein and Stalingrad at the end of 1942, however, abruptly ended illusions of victory, and Italians began to perceive the truth. Anglo-American troops landed in Morocco and Algeria in November 1942, and the pincers closed tightly around Axis forces in Tunisia. Meanwhile, 115,000 Italians died and 60,000 were captured on the frozen Russian steppes. Those who straggled home again spread demoralizing tales of defeat and German abandonment of their Fascist ally on the battlefield.

Conditions deteriorated rapidly in Italy. Food shortages and rationing made the war highly unpopular. Allied bombing took an increasingly devastating toll. Thousands of urban refugees sought safety in the countryside, disrupting production and straining resources. Disgruntled workers staged frequent work stoppages. Finally, in March 1943, a strike of Fiat workers in Turin spread across northern Italy despite vicious police efforts to stop it. It ultimately affected more than 100,000 workers. The strike convinced industrialists and businessmen that Mussolini was no longer in control. Allied landings in Sicily in July brought military leaders to the same conclusion. Mussolini's fate was sealed.

On July 25, 1943, the diminutive and indecisive King Victor Emmanuel III finally heeded the advice of businessmen, military officers, and Fascist moderates. All hoped to disassociate themselves from Mussolini and salvage their lives, property, and a shred of honor from the wreckage of dictatorship. Emboldened by a Fascist Grand Council vote of no confidence in Mussolini the previous day, the king summoned the prime minister to his villa, stripped him of authority, and arrested him. In a broadcast to the people that evening, the king announced that Badoglio was returning from retirement and would head the new government. He added that the war would continue.

The news stunned the Italian people. Benito Mussolini had, after all, ruled Italy since October 1922, when thousands of Fascist thugs had threatened to tear Rome apart unless the young Victor Emmanuel III appointed their leader prime minister. Twenty-one years later, many Italians could remember no other government. Yet, after three years of an unpopular war, most greeted Mussolini's fall with jubilation. Huge crowds cheered in the streets. Eager young men destroyed Fascist symbols and monuments and searched out petty Fascist tyrants for beatings, imprisonment, or worse.

But not everyone rejoiced during that confused July. Many Fascist sympathizers remained lurking in the shadows. They knew that a permanent transition from dictatorship to democracy would not be easy. They consoled themselves with schemes for a future reckoning of accounts. Meanwhile, the war continued.

Among those who greeted the fall of fascism with jubilation and immense relief was a community of about 37,100 Italian and 7,000 foreign Jews.[1] Their number had been considerably larger—the census of 1938 recorded more than 47,000 Italian Jews, or slightly more than one-tenth of 1 percent of a population of forty-five million. It also listed more than 10,000 Jews of foreign nationality.[2] But the fascism that in 1922 seemed remarkably free of anti-Semitism had not, in the end, done well by its Jews. The racial laws introduced in 1938 required, among other things, the expulsion of all foreign Jews. While this objective was never achieved, the outbreak of war in 1940 resulted in the arrest and detention of thousands. Foreign Jews in miserable internment camps were "permitted" to build their own huts and dig their own wells, if they could secure tools and materials.

The Italians and The Holocaust

For Italian Jews, the racial laws decreed that they could no longer practice their professions, own property over a certain value, send their children to public schools, or marry or employ non-Jews. Throughout the country, thousands of doctors, lawyers, teachers, and civil servants were suspended. Military officers with a lifetime of service were suddenly retired. Children were withdrawn from school. With the outbreak of war, many Italian Jews were also subjected to forced labor. [3] Under the pressures of the racial laws, at least six thousand Italian Jews had emigrated and about the same number had converted by July 1943. [4] Those remaining hoped for better days.

Their optimism was not unjustified. Badoglio was expected to restore the full rights of all Italian citizens and release foreign Jews from internment camps. He would end harassment, anti-Semitic posters, graffiti, and the sacking of synagogues. But Badoglio was still at war. His dangerous and suspicious ally needed to be reassured, or deceived, about Italy's intentions. While he did release most political prisoners, excepting Communists but including Italian Jews, he did little to mitigate the racial laws. The Jews—and the nation—waited. Through the hot summer of 1943, as the Allies raced across Sicily and approached the Italian mainland, the Germans waited as well, and prepared for the day they knew was not far off.

Badoglio, in fact, would have only forty-five days. The real turning point in the lives of all Italians was not July 25 but September 8. At 6:30 that evening, Allied Commander in Chief General Dwight D. Eisenhower announced Italy's unconditional surrender. At 7:45, Badoglio confirmed the armistice and instructed the Italian army to lay down its arms before the Allies but to "react" to attack "from any other quarter." Because the U.S. Fifth Army was not scheduled to land at Salerno until the next day, Allied forces on the Italian mainland on September 8 were limited to General Bernard Montgomery's British Eighth Army disembarking at the

Straits of Messina, at the southernmost tip of the peninsula. There were virtually no Allies available before whom the Italian army could lay down its arms. There were, however, at least eighteen German army divisions throughout Italy, with more poised on the frontier awaiting the Italian surrender.[5] The entire Italian army found itself abandoned without realistic instructions on how to deal with its former ally. Because the Germans were naturally determined that no Italian territory, manpower, or weaponry should fall to the enemy, armed confrontations occurred throughout the country.

Some heroic Italian officers after the September 8 armistice resisted German capture. On the island of Cephalonia, thousands of officers and men followed Badoglio's instructions and "reacted" to attack. When they finally surrendered to the Germans, they were all summarily executed. In Corfu, after an equally heroic three-day resistance, seven thousand surrendering Italian soldiers were killed. Nor was resistance limited to distant fronts. General Don Ferrante Gonzaga, commanding Italian forces at Salerno, refused to surrender his weapon to the Germans and was immediately shot down.[6] And there were others.

In the absence of instructions and a declaration of war against the Germans who surrounded them, however, most Italian officers and men decided that their best option was to disappear. Throughout Italy, hundreds of thousands of young soldiers abandoned uniforms and weapons, put on civilian clothes, and went home. Many ultimately joined the partisans, particularly after it became clear that the Germans and their Fascist sympathizers would hunt them down and treat them as deserters. Many others were captured immediately. About 640,000 Italian officers and men spent the remainder of the war in German prison camps, where 30,000 died.[7]

* * *

The Italians and The Holocaust

Italian civilians greeted the events of September 8 with mixed emotions. Official hostilities, at least, were over, but Italy was an occupied country. Germans were much more formidable as conquerors than as allies, particularly for the Jews. For despite the hardships and degradations of the racial laws, it must be remembered that until September 8, 1943, the Jews in Fascist Italy had fared better than Jews in almost any other country in Nazi Europe. Even in unoccupied France, laws in 1940 and 1941 similar to the Italian racial laws of 1938 had limited or banned Jews from most professions and expropriated their property. Foreign Jews in unoccupied France were systematically thrown into wretched internment camps. Then in July 1942, fully four months before the Germans entered the unoccupied French zone, Vichy agreed to release foreign Jews to the Nazis for deportation. At least seven thousand were delivered by August. [8] Such a thing never happened in Fascist Italy before the German occupation. On the contrary, Jewish refugees continued to seek and obtain sanctuary in Mussolini's Italy until the very day of the armistice. In addition, Italian army officers and diplomats occupying Croatia, Greece, and parts of southern France protected Jews from German demands for deportation.

In German-occupied countries, the nightmare of the Holocaust was in full swing. Deportations began in Belgium, the Netherlands, and occupied France in 1942. In a single action in Paris, on July 16 and 17, 1942, French police rounded up 12,800 foreign Jewish men, women, and children. Deported to Auschwitz, about 30 returned after the war. [9] By the end of 1942, about 42,500 Jews had been deported from France to Auschwitz, including 6,000 children. [10]

Even during the Badoglio interlude, Italian Jews dependent on censored news services knew little of these horrors, or regarded radio reports from the BBC and neutral countries as Allied propaganda. At the very worst, they thought, deportation to the East meant work camps and hard labor. Such a fate was certainly undesirable, but it could never happen in Italy. Italy had been Germany's ally. Indeed, after the Germans rescued Mussolini on September 12 and set him up at Salò on Lake Garda as the titular head of the new Italian Social Republic, Italy became Germany's ally again. Italian Jews were enlightened, educated, and assimilated. They were good and patriotic citizens. Why would anyone bother them?

Within a few days, the Jews had their answer. On September 16 in Merano, a beautiful mountain resort town near Bolzano, twenty-five Jews, including a child of six and a woman of seventy-four torn from her sick bed, were arrested by Nazis, interrogated, beaten, and deported. Only one of the twenty-five survived the war.[11] On September 18 in small northern Italian villages near the French border, about 349 Jewish refugees from France were also caught by the SS. These men, women, and children, originally from countries throughout occupied Europe, had fled to France before 1940, then to Vichy France, then to the Italian-occupied French zone, and finally, after the Italian armistice, to Italy itself. About 330 of the prisoners were deported back to France and ultimately to Auschwitz. Nine survived the war.[12]

Elsewhere that tragic September, SS troops invaded the tranquil shores of beautiful Lago Maggiore, on the Swiss frontier. In idyllic villages like Stresa, Arona, Baveno, and Meina, they hunted Jews as one might track wild game. They murdered forty-nine victims on the spot, throwing their bodies into shallow graves or into the lake. They raped one young girl in front of her mother, before shooting both.[13]

The worst atrocities occurred in Meina, a village on the lake between the more famous tourist towns of Arona and Stresa. The train between Milan and the Simplon Pass leading to Switzerland stops there today, and the traveler can see quiet streets and vine-covered hills dropping to the water's edge. But in 1943 Meina's tourists were refugees, Jews and non-Jews, Italians and foreigners, fleeing the bombed-out cities of northern Italy. The tiny village, beautiful, full of vacant hotel rooms off-season, and conveniently near the Swiss border, was a perfect haven. Sixteen Jews, many from war-torn Greece, took lodgings in the Hotel Meina. They sought safety in the very nation that, with significant German help, had defeated their own. Someone informed the Nazis.

On September 16, one week after the German occupation, the SS stormed the hotel. They seized a family of six from Salonika, including the mother and father, the seventy-six-year-old grandfather, and the children aged fifteen, twelve, and eight. They kept this family and ten other victims under guard for a week, debating, apparently, what to do with them. Finally, on the night of September 22, they marched out three separate groups of four people each. They shot each victim in the back of the neck and tossed the bodies into the lake.

At dawn, only the elderly grandfather and his three grandchildren remained under SS guard at the hotel. The parents had already been taken away. The four terrified victims waited that entire day. During the afternoon, one of the children found the courage to go onto a balcony and call to a woman below, "Where are Mommy and Daddy?" The woman replied gently that she thought they had been taken away for an interrogation. Finally, at nightfall, the SS came for the remaining prisoners. A witness at the hotel later reported hearing the grandfather scream and beg for the lives of the children. The children died as brutally as their elders. The SS auctioned the belongings of the victims on Meina's public square. Lago Maggiore gave up only one of the sixteen corpses. [14]

And so the Holocaust came to Italy. The war that began in June 1940 had caused young men to be drafted and sent to die in Russia or Africa or the Balkans. With that war had come air raids, and civilians killed in their beds. But three years later, the war acquired a new dimension. After the German occupation of Italy, children and grandparents could be shot in the back of the neck merely because of their religion.

A non-Jewish Italian maid seeking information about the fate of her Jewish employer, just murdered by the SS near Meina, was told she would never see them again. She objected timidly that they were good people. An SS man replied, "Not good people. Jews, who are the ruin of Europe." [15] This was the war that came to Italy on September 8.

2

Italy's Jews

THE JEWS of Italy trace their roots back hundreds of
years before the barbarian invasions that contributed so much
to the "mixed blood" of their persecutors. In fact, if one wishes
to speak of "pure blood" in Italy at all, one thinks first of the
Jews. Long before the destruction of the Temple in Jerusalem
by Titus in A.D. 70—indeed, long before the heirs of Saint
Peter proclaimed Rome the holy city of Christendom—a Jewish colony had settled along the banks of the Tiber. The historian Josephus records at least eight thousand Jews living there
in the year 4 B.C. The synagogue well preceded the Vatican.
Many more Jews arrived during the imperial period, when the
community peaked at about fifty thousand.[1] This population
exceeded the entire Italian Jewish community in 1943.

During the Christian Era and the Middle Ages, Jews in Italy
experienced a grim succession of restrictions and persecutions,
relieved by brief interludes of calm. The Italian Renaissance,
from roughly the early fifteenth to the mid-sixteenth century,
offered some respite. Jewish scholars worked with Christian

humanists in an atmosphere of mutual tolerance and respect. Jews exiled from Spain and Spanish-controlled territories settled in Italy at this time, bringing rich variations of liturgy, language, and customs which they carefully preserved apart from their Italian coreligionists.

The Counter-Reformation shattered tolerance and introduced the phenomenon of the ghetto. The word "ghetto" is said to derive from the Italian word "getto," meaning metal casting and referring to the iron foundries in the part of Venice where Jews were first confined in the sixteenth century. From there, ghettos quickly developed in most major Italian cities and throughout Europe. Jews were confined to these ghettos, with few exceptions, for over two hundred years.

Ghetto life was difficult and degrading. [2] In many cities, Jews could work only as street peddlers, hawkers, ragpickers, dealers in second-hand merchandise, and pawnbrokers. Women, not allowed to make and sell new clothes, mended old clothes for their men to sell. Poverty was endemic. The housing was wretched, and the stench appalling. Scarcely able to contain an ever-growing population, the walled enclaves became festering labyrinths of dark and narrow streets lined with tall, rickety structures. Buildings soaring upward to meet the pressure for shelter sometimes collapsed altogether.

Ghetto Jews faced the problems of poverty, malnutrition, and disease by organizing self-help associations for every category of daily life. There were societies to help the poor, provide dowries, aid in childbirth, tend the sick, finance funerals, and provide for orphans. Jews dealt with problems of isolation and despair by educating themselves. Illiteracy was unusual in the ghetto at a time when it was the general rule outside. But ghetto residents could not so easily resist the threat from beyond their walls.

Jews in Italy paid crushing taxes and tributes, with no hope of appeal. Police could enter their homes and confiscate household goods at will. Incited by perpetual charges of ritual murder, police could search the ghettos for missing children. On Saturdays, they could look for and punish friendly Christians lighting the Sabbath fires and thus illegally "working" for Jews. In the Papal States, where the ghetto system was most repressive, police also sought out Jews evading their obligation to attend lengthy conversionist sermons, where earnest priests, sometimes themselves converted Jews, lectured for hours. Christian churchmen regularly examined their captive audiences to determine that no one had stopped his ears or fallen asleep.

If a Jew of any age expressed, or even seemed to evidence, an interest in conversion, the outside threat magnified itself a hundredfold. The "convert" could be held indefinitely in a special house of catechumens, regardless of his age or the wishes of his family. On the contrary, if the "convert" was head of a household, his whole family could be held as well, or children could be taken from their mother. Such stories may help explain why Italian Holocaust survivors, when writing of priests who helped them, invariably add, "and they made no attempt to convert me." The current reader would take that for granted, but not so in 1943.

Involuntary baptism was another terror for ghetto Jews until well into the nineteenth century. Any Catholic layman or laywoman was qualified to perform a valid baptism. If he or she baptized a Jew, regardless of age or ability to consent, that person was a Christian and could not live in a non-Christian community. As recently as 1858 in Bologna in the Papal States, a seven-year-old boy baptized at age one by a servant girl was seized from his family, paraded through the ghetto, baptized again, and not returned, despite appeals from his desperate parents and protests from around the world.[3]

The Enlightenment sounded the death knell of the ghetto, but in some parts of Italy the ancient institution took nearly a century to pass away. In Hapsburg-controlled Lombardy and Trieste, the Grand Duchy of Tuscany, and the Duchy of Parma, reforms began well before the French Revolution. In nearly all Italian cities, Jews were temporarily emancipated during the Revolutionary and Napoleonic Eras, only to be sent back to the ghettos during the Restoration. Full permanent emancipation did not come until the unification of Italy: in 1848 in Piedmont, in 1859 or 1860 in the states that joined Piedmont to form Italy, and in 1870 in Rome. Jews correctly attributed their new-found freedom and equality to the House of Savoy, secular nineteenth-century Liberalism, and their new nation. In gratitude, they firmly endorsed all three institutions.

Many Jews contributed to the struggle for Italian unification. In Venice, the famous patriot Daniele Manin, elected president of the new republic when it tried to rid itself of Hapsburg rule in 1848, was half Jewish. Many Venetian Jews eagerly supported him. In Rome, the city with the most repressive ghetto in Italy, three Jews were elected to the National Assembly of the new republic proclaimed after Pope Pius IX fled in 1849. Three others sat on the City Council, and two served on the Committee for Defense.[4] Jews fought and died in the unsuccessful defense of Rome against French and papal troops in 1849, in battles against the Hapsburgs in Lombardy in 1848, 1849, and 1859, and with Garibaldi's gallant Thousand against the Bourbons in Sicily in 1860. They served with the Italian troops who breeched the walls of Rome at the Porta Pia Gate and seized the city from its papal defenders in 1870. In the process, they helped unify the peninsula and opened the last ghetto remaining in Western Europe.

After emancipation, Italian Jews immediately began to appear in positions of prominence and distinction. Isacco Artom, for example, served as private secretary to Prime Minister Camillo di Cavour in Piedmont in the 1850s. He later became the first Jew in Europe to fill a high diplomatic post outside his own country. Giacomo Dina directed Cavour's official publication, *Opinione*. Two Jews became city councilors in Rome in 1870, as soon as the ghetto was dissolved. Three Jews were elected to the first parliament of a nearly united Italy in 1861. Nine sat in 1870, after Venice and Rome were included. Eleven sat in 1874.[5]

The prompt appearance of Jews in prominent positions after emancipation suggests that a large segment of the Italian population had not shared the prejudices of its Old Regime rulers. Discrimination in the nineteenth century had indeed been an artificial imposition, intimately tied to broader attempts to restore pre-French Revolutionary regimes. Many Italians, and particularly those anticlerical Liberals who became the governing elite in the newly united nation, had disapproved. Each time revolutionary crowds assaulted ghetto walls and opened gates between 1820 and 1848, witnesses described mass jubilation by Jews and non-Jews alike. But the rapid integration after emancipation also testifies to the character of the Italian Jewish community itself. Italian Jews were not foreigners. They looked, dressed, and spoke like everyone else. And above all, they were educated. In 1861, only 5.8 percent of all Italian Jews over the age of ten were illiterate; the figure for the Catholic community was 54.5 percent.[6] Italian Jews were well prepared for the opportunities that emancipation offered.

Complete integration was nevertheless not without its difficulties. In 1873, for example, the possibility of the appointment of a Jew as minister of finance aroused so much fear of a revival of Catholic anti-Semitism that the candidate quietly withdrew.[7] By 1891, however, Luigi Luzzatti, a member of a prominent and highly patriotic Venetian Jewish family, was appointed to the same position without protests. He served until 1892, and then from 1896 to 1898 and again from 1903 to 1906. In 1910, he was appointed prime minister. This, it might be noted, occurred twenty-six years before the first Jewish prime minister served in France.

Luzzatti was not the only Jew to reach a pinnacle of power. Salvatore Barzilai, a fiery Irredentist orator and journalist from Trieste, was elected to the Chamber of Deputies in 1890, remained for eight terms, served in the cabinet before and during World War I, and was a member of the Italian delegation to the peace conference at Versailles after that war. Claudio Treves and Giuseppe Emanuele Modigliani, elder brother of the painter Amedeo Modigliani, served as Socialist deputies for many years before, during, and after World War I. Ernesto Nathan, a Freemason, became mayor of Rome in 1907, only thirty-seven years after the ghetto had been opened. Leopoldo Franchetti, sociologist and author of numerous foreign colonization schemes, served as a conservative senator for many years before committing suicide in despair after the Italian debacle at Caporetto. And Baron Sidney Sonnino, the converted (Protestant) son of a Tuscan Jewish landowner, served as finance minister and foreign minister, and finally in 1906 (and again from 1908 to 1910) as prime minister. These are only the best-known Jewish politicians; there were many others. By 1902, the Italian Senate of about 350 notables appointed by the king included six Jews. By 1920, there were nineteen. [8]

The Jewish contribution to the military during the late nineteenth and early twentieth centuries was also outstanding, particularly in contrast to other European nations. One might compare the fate of Captain Dreyfus to the glittering career of Giuseppe Ottolenghi, Italy's first Jewish general appointed in 1888. Ottolenghi served as an instructor to the future Victor Emmanuel III. In 1902, at a time when in Germany no professing Jew could even hold a commission, he became a senator and the minister of war.

A few years later, fifty Jewish generals served in World War I. Among them, General Emanuele Pugliese became the most highly decorated general in the Italian army. General Roberto Segre, an artillery commander, designed the artillery defenses on the Piave that checked the Austrian offensive there in June 1918 and decisively shattered enemy morale. General Guido Liuzzi was commander of the War School. General Angelo Modena distinguished himself in the Libyan War and in World War I, concluding his career with an appointment in the late 1920s as president of the Supreme Army and Navy Tribunal. These generals were joined by thousands of other Jewish officers and enlisted men. More than a thousand won medals for valor.[9] The nation's youngest gold-medal winner, Roberto Sarfatti, killed in combat at the age of seventeen, was Jewish, as was the oldest, volunteer Giulio Blum.

Italian Jews also made significant contributions in business, banking, and insurance, in the professions, and in education and the arts. Lodovico Mortara, for example, was president of Italy's highest court in the 1920s. Vittorio Polacco was a highly respected professor of law at the Universities of Padua, Modena, and Rome from 1885 until the 1920s. In 1930, 8 percent of all university professors were Jewish.[10] And in literature, two of Italy's finest novelists before World War II, Italo Svevo, born Ettore Schmitz, and Alberto Moravia, born Alberto Pincherle, were Jewish and half Jewish respectively.

Not only had many Italian Jews reached positions of prominence by the early years of the twentieth century, but most others had assimilated and were leading full and varied lives. In his perceptive memoirs, a prosperous Modenese lawyer named Enzo Levi follows the transition from isolation to integration through several generations of his own family, from 1858 until World War II.[11] In the process, Levi reveals changes in the society as well.

In 1858, Enzo Levi's great-grandfather was forced to flee the Duchy of Modena with all his worldly goods in the back of a wagon. He had refused the duke's demands to change his name and convert to Catholicism. Enzo's own father, then a one-year-old child, rode in the wagon. The Levis returned a year later, when the duke was in turn expelled and the duchy was united to Italy.

In keeping with the new age of opportunity, Enzo's father became a successful lawyer and a fervent patriot and monarchist. "In my family," the son remembers, "as in many bourgeois families, especially Jewish ones, there really existed a blind veneration for the House of Savoy." During the Dreyfus Affair, Levi's parents assured him that such a thing could never happen in Italy, where Jews were protected by the king and the constitution. After the assassination of King Umberto by an anarchist in 1900, the Levi family grieved as if the loss were personal. They seemed much like any other middle-class Italian family, with slight differences.

Enzo Levi's parents were religious, and they observed the Sabbath, the holidays, and the dietary laws. Their friends were mostly Jewish. Their son recalls how difficult it was immediately after the abolition of the Modena ghetto for Catholics and Jews to get to know each other. They did not share the same holidays, and they could not even eat together easily. Of about fifteen marriages in Enzo's family in the 1880s, only one was mixed. That one was much criticized even though it was a civil marriage requiring no conversion.

Enzo Levi was born in 1889. Like most middle-class children, whether Jewish or Catholic, he attended public elementary and high schools. Unlike the Catholic students, however, Levi has vivid memories of being tormented by a group of boys, always the same ones, because he was Jewish. He reluctantly learned to fight, but he could not understand either how they knew he was Jewish or why they disliked Jews. He adds that the boys were "from a bad element," and that he had many Catholic friends.

By the time Levi was approaching adulthood around 1910,

The Italians and The Holocaust

Jews and Catholics began mixing much more easily. The appointments of Luzzatti as prime minister and Ottolenghi as minister of war were taken by Jews as signs of the end of anti-Semitism. Levi's own children suffered virtually none of the anti-Semitism that he himself had known. At the same time, however, Italian Jews began to abandon their heritage. Mixed marriages in Levi's generation were more common than Jewish ones. The children of mixed marriages generally became Catholics. Levi himself married a Jewish girl, but they had a civil ceremony and did not circumcise their son. Levi became an atheist. He did not go to the synagogue or believe in the religious institution, but he retained, like so many, a profound belief in the relevance of the ethical concepts of Judaism to modern life.

Levi's account of his drift away from Judaism is echoed in the writings of many middle-class Jews who were young in the 1920s and 1930s. Emanuele Artom, for example, the twenty-nine-year-old Jewish partisan captured by the Germans and tortured horribly until he died in 1944, recorded in his famous diary that he had little interest in Judaism until he was about eighteen.[12] Sion Segre Amar, a young Jewish anti-Fascist arrested and tried before the Fascist Special Tribunal in a much-publicized case in 1934, remembers that Yom Kippur was the only holiday he respected and observed.[13] Carlo Modigliani, an industrial engineer, mathematics professor, talented amateur pianist and composer, and air force pilot in World War I, records that until the racial laws he "had forgotten completely about being Jewish."[14] His father, a successful musician, was an atheist; his mother was religious. Carlo went to the synagogue irregularly in Ferrara, learning to read Hebrew and say the prayers as a child, but he ceased all participation when he moved to Milan at the age of eighteen.

In an amusing reminiscence in 1962, Salvatore Jona summed up what it meant to many to be Jewish in the 1920s:

"For the young it was a matter of going to the temple a couple of times a year, of not eating pork *at home,* and of not telling one's good mother that one would willingly marry a nice Catholic girl." [15] And what did one do to avoid displeasing one's mother with the prospect of a mixed marriage? "As long as mamma lived, a Christian girl remained only the beloved. After mamma died, sometimes, a decent period of mourning having passed, the beloved became a spouse." Under such circumstances, Italian Jewry seemed destined to decline and disappear within a few generations.

The high degree of assimilation and the decline of religious observance by the mid-1930s should not be misconstrued as an abandonment of Jewish values. Italian Jews were Italians through and through, but many remained aware and proud of their Jewishness. Enzo Levi, even as an atheist, retained a deep respect for Jewish ethical concepts. Emanuele Artom, in some of the most moving entries of his diary, expressed the same respect, even reverence, for his cultural and ethical heritage. Ora Kohn from Turin, whose parents did not work on Saturday but allowed their children to ride the streetcar and attend school that day, nevertheless remembers that her family "had this sense of values, a sense of tradition." She adds, "Our sense of Jewish identity came from the family. It was not from observing holidays, because we weren't holiday-observing people." [16] Gastone Orefice, the only Jew in his class at the public school in Livorno, says the same. "My grandfather didn't care very much [about religion] and my father didn't care and my mother as well. But we were Jews. This was important to us. Our culture, our talking at home was Jewish." [17]

The most impressive proof of Italian Jews' ties to their heritage came after the racial laws, when conversion became a tempting method of avoiding discrimination. The racial measures of 1938 did not apply to offspring of mixed marriages baptized before the promulgation of the laws (or if born after the laws, within ten days of birth). Individuals with two Jewish parents but baptized before October 1938 were not automatically exempt from persecution, but they could hope for preferential treatment, Vatican protection, and a change in the law. Compounding the temptation, the Church was very cooperative in back-dating baptismal certificates. Under these circumstances, roughly six thousand Italian Jews, particularly those in mixed marriages, converted. [18] Most Jewish families had some relatives who were baptized. But tens of thousands did not yield, although doing so would have allowed them to continue their careers or educations and retain their businesses or lands. They were not observant, but they would not deny their heritage.

If Levi's memoirs err in any way, it is in the portrayal of Italian society as entirely free of anti-Semitism by the 1920s. Levi is not alone in this respect; most Jewish writers confirm his description almost too readily, as if they wanted to convince themselves. Upon reflection, however, and perhaps with the benefit of hindsight, the situation seems more complex. Could a society that had tolerated ghettos as late as 1870 have changed so totally in half a century—in less than a single lifetime? Could Catholics, whose holy mass contained a reference to Jews as the killers of Christ until the reforms of Pope John XXIII, remain entirely immune to such rhetoric? Did the virulent anti-Jewish press campaign and the violent cruelty of Fascist fanatics during the German occupation of Italy come from nowhere, from a society previously free of anti-Semitism? A closer look seems necessary.

Indications of anti-Semitism are rare, but they exist. Ora Kohn, born in Turin in 1921, says, "Most of my friends were not Jewish. . . . Religion had nothing to do with making friends. Occasionally you might find someone who was anti-Semitic, who would be cold when he found out you were Jewish, but it was a big world. There were lots of other people." [19]

Renata Lombroso from Milan, born in 1903, has more unpleasant memories. "My parents had taught me not to say that I was Jewish," she remembers, "but I . . . said it in a loud voice, provoking anti-Semitism. In elementary school, having refused to participate in the Christian religious lessons [refusal was her legal right], I had my first fights with my schoolmates, who waited for me by the exit. . . . Even the teachers showed anti-Semitism, although I was one of the best pupils." One publicly called her "the rotten pear among the good pears," a phrase that she says stayed with her all her life. [20]

If Renata Lombroso's experiences were unusual, other Jewish writers mention being taunted occasionally, especially on Good Friday. Augusto Segre, the son of a rabbi from Casale Monferrato in Piedmont, sums up the situation:

> If, even in my times, when I was a boy [he was born in 1918], sporadic unpleasant episodes occurred involving us, and some religious or laic anti-Semite stumbled upon us . . . many of us were always ready to pass over these little incidents, to minimize them, maintaining that it was not wise . . . to argue with Christians and that it was instead much more important and useful, for the good of all, to keep quiet, pretend nothing had happened, avoid responses that were useless and stupid because they were always damaging to us. In short, we were taught it was necessary to do everything possible not only to avoid being noticed, but to demonstrate always more, through work, through charity, through participation in the political life of the country if possible, that the liberty conceded us was simply justified by so much fervor of Italian patriotism. [21]

The years of Jewish assimilation in Italy extend well into the years of fascism. Mussolini's rise to power in 1922 brought not the slightest change in the process. Indeed, many Jews were loyal Fascists from the start. At least five Jews were included among the 119 Italians who met in a small hall on the Piazza San Sepolcro in Milan on March 23, 1919, to found the *Fasci Italiani di Combattimento,* Mussolini's first national organization and the precursor of the Fascist party. Cesare Goldman, one of these *sansepolcristi,* as they were called, had helped secure the hall. Among the Fascist "martyrs" who died in violent conflicts with Socialists between 1919 and 1922, there were three Jews—Duilio Sinigaglia, Gino Bolaffi, and Bruno Mondolfo. By the time of the Fascist march on Rome in October 1922 and Mussolini's ascent to the office of prime minister, 746 Jews belonged to either the Fascist or the Nationalist party (the two merged in March 1923). Over two hundred Jews claimed to have participated in the march, and officially received special honorary status to prove it. [22] And in addition to the activists, many Jewish businessmen, like their non-Jewish counterparts, helped finance the fledgling Fascist movement.

Jewish involvement with Italian fascism is not surprising. With the exception of many in Rome, most Italian Jews were solidly middle-class, and by late 1921, fascism had become a basically middle-class, antiworker movement. Early revolutionary aspects had declined, leaving as primary goals anti-socialism, union busting, strike breaking, and the restoration of law and order at workers' expense. These objectives pleased both the Jewish and non-Jewish middle classes—conservative men and women who had loyally supported the war and suffered from war-induced inflation, and who now felt threatened by industrial and agricultural workers with their powerful trade unions, their inflation-adjusted wages, and their antipatriotic revolutionary rhetoric. In addition, many middle-class Jews felt more comfortable with fascism's anticlerical strain, a remnant of its radical origins, than with Catholic conservative factions.

Obviously not all, or even most, middle-class Jews were Fascists, any more than most non-Jews. A majority of all thoughtful, educated adults understood the danger of an authoritarian regime that employed violence to convince doubters and intimidate opponents. A majority of Jewish adults understood the particular danger of such a regime to themselves, agreeing quietly with Augusto Segre's father, the local rabbi of Casale Monferrato, who told his son in the 1920s that "whoever considers himself truly Jewish will not mix with those people who are against justice and liberty." [23]

Most doubters and opponents kept their opinions to themselves, but some courageously spoke out. Eucardio Momigliano, for example, one of the original Jewish *sansepolcristi,* abandoned fascism almost immediately, proclaimed his opposition, and founded the anti-Fascist Unione Democratica. Pio Donati, an anti-Fascist Jewish deputy, was twice beaten and finally driven into exile, where he died alone in 1926. Other anti-Fascist Jews in exile in the 1920s and early 1930s included Claudio Treves, Giuseppe Emanuele Modigliani, and Carlo Rosselli. There were many anti-Fascist non-Jews in exile as well.

If the presence of Jews among the Fascists indicates again the thorough integration of Jews into Italian society, it also suggests that Mussolini's movement was as free from anti-Semitism as any other political party in Italy. There were, it will be noted, no full Jews who remained in the Nazi party after Hitler came to power. In this respect, fascism was a reflection of the society at large. Prejudiced individuals existed, but they remained a vocal few. Fascism did not become officially anti-Semitic until Mussolini chose to make it so, with the racial laws in 1938.

During the 1920s and 1930s, a number of Jews held important positions in the Fascist government. Aldo Finzi, a pilot with Gabriele D'Annunzio in Fiume and the only Fascist among the nine Jews elected to the Chamber of Deputies in

The Italians and The Holocaust

May 1921, became an undersecretary at the Ministry of the Interior and a member of the first Fascist Grand Council. Dante Almansi, a prefect before the march on Rome, served as a vice-chief of police under Emilio De Bono until his forced retirement after the racial laws. Guido Jung served as minister of finance from 1932 to 1935.

These three were only the most important. There were many others. Maurizio Rava was a vice-governor of Libya, governor of Somalia, and a general in the Fascist militia. Renzo Ravenna, a lawyer, friend of Italo Balbo, and former *squadrista* (the name given to fanatical Fascist thugs who in 1920 and 1921 roamed the countryside in armed groups beating up Socialist workers and peasants) was the *podestà*, or appointed mayor, of Ferrara for fifteen years. Ugo Foà, captain in World War I, winner of a silver medal for military valor, lawyer, and Fascist party member after 1932, served as magistrate from 1939 until, like Almansi, he was forced into retirement. And Giorgio Del Vecchio, an eminent professor of international jurisprudence and philosophy, became the first Fascist rector of the University of Rome in 1925.

On a less elevated plane but nonetheless indicative of the Duce's attitudes, Margherita Sarfatti, Mussolini's mistress and influential associate for many years, was also Jewish. Margherita was the editor of the art and literature page of Mussolini's *Popolo d'Italia* and a coeditor of *Gerarchia,* the Fascist party's monthly ideological review. She presided over a fashionable salon of Fascist *prominenti* in Milan for many years, and she liked to think that she had made Mussolini fit for polite society. She was ousted by Clara Petacci, quite another type, about 1936.

The prominent Jewish Fascists were joined by thousands of their more humble coreligionists. Gastone Orefice recalls his grandfather, a successful pharmacist in Livorno, as "a very nice honest person, a very old-style person, and until 1938 he was sure that fascism and Italy were one. When the Fascists told him he wasn't a good Italian anymore and that he couldn't be a Jew and an Italian at the same time, he had problems with himself." [24] There were many honest, nonpolitical Italian Jews who felt the same. Between October 1928 and October 1933, 4,920 of them joined the Fascist party. [25] They represented slightly more than 10 percent of the Italian Jewish population as a whole. The membership percentage of the non-Jewish population was roughly the same.

3

The Racial Laws

ON MARCH 11, 1934, Sion Segre Amar, a young man from Turin, was caught at the frontier town of Ponte Tresa smuggling anti-Fascist literature into Italy from Switzerland. His friend Mario Levi escaped by swimming back across an icy river to safety. According to the hostile press, the dripping wet Levi shouted anti-Fascist and, the newspapers added significantly, anti-Italian insults from across the frontier. [1]

Segre Amar and Levi were Jewish. They were also members of the well-known Giustizia e Libertà (Justice and Liberty), the largest non-Marxist anti-Fascist organization of the period. Giustizia e Libertà had a large proportion of well-educated and high-minded Jewish members—so many, in fact, that Segre Amar later recalled that when he informed Carlo Levi, subsequently famous as the author of *Christ Stopped at Eboli*, of his interest in the group, Levi's comment was, "Alas, another Jew." [2]

Segre Amar's arrest was followed by a roundup of thirty-nine suspects, including Mario Levi's brother Gino, an engineer at the Olivetti Typewriter Company in Ivrea, and his elderly father Giuseppe, a biology professor at the University of Turin. Most detainees were soon released, but of the seventeen held at length, eleven were Jewish. Carlo Levi, then a doctor, painter, and writer in Turin, was held, as was Leone Ginzburg, a future Resistance hero who died in prison during the German occupation. The newspapers covered the Ponte Tresa "conspiracy" with gusto, emphasizing Mario Levi's alleged anti-Italian insult. Also, for the first time in their coverage of anti-Fascist activities, the press stressed the fact that many of the conspirators were Jewish. [3]

None of those arrested were Zionists. Giustizia e Libertà, in fact, had no active Zionist members. [4] The press was not concerned with facts, however, and the Ponte Tresa affair became the focus of a vicious anti-Zionist campaign. The equation anti-Fascist = anti-patriot = Zionist = Jew was repeated over and over again. "Next Year in Jerusalem; This Year at the Special Tribunal" was a headline in Telesio Interlandi's newspaper *Il Tevere* on March 31. "It is necessary to decide," said Roberto Farinacci in his newspaper *Il Regime fascista*. "Whoever calls himself a Zionist has no right to try to retain obligations, honors, benefices, etc., in our country." [5]

The Ponte Tresa affair could hardly have come at a worse moment. Adolf Hitler had become chancellor of Germany a year earlier, on January 30, 1933. Mussolini was proud of his protégé, whose success was another demonstration of the decadence of Liberal democracy. He was disturbed, however, by Hitler's undisguised ambitions in Austria and among German minorities in Italy's own Trent and Trieste. In 1934, Mussolini still regarded Austria as within his own sphere of influence, and he had every intention of resisting German expansion there. He was nevertheless reluctant to alienate Hitler.

One obvious method of mollifying Hitler while yet resisting him was to instigate an anti-Semitic campaign in Italy. Thus in January 1934, Mussolini unleashed his anti-Semitic journalist friends, led by Telesio Interlandi. A series of anti-Zionist articles appeared. Into that maelstrom came the Ponte Tresa affair. Mussolini must have been rather pleased.

And yet, as quickly as it began, it was over. Austrian chancellor Engelbert Dollfuss was assassinated by Nazis on July 25, 1934, and Mussolini mobilized troops at the Brenner Pass to defend Austria from German attack. Better relations with Britain and France now seemed desirable, and an anti-Semitic campaign was no longer expedient. In September, Mussolini made his wonderful comment, "Thirty centuries of history permit us to regard with supreme pity certain doctrines supported beyond the Alps by the descendents of people who did not know how to write, and could not hand down documents recording their own lives, at a time when Rome had Caesar, Virgil, and Augustus."[6] Anti-Zionist articles ceased. By the time the Ponte Tresa conspirators appeared for trial in November, they were virtually forgotten. Only three—Sion Segre Amar, Leone Ginzburg, and Mario Levi (in absentia)—were actually tried and convicted. They received light sentences and little publicity.

While the reaction to the Ponte Tresa affair revealed the intimate connection between Mussolini's Jewish and German policies, it also unmasked an unexpectedly vocal and vicious anti-Semitic presence in Italian society. Italians who took pride in the religious and racial tolerance of the regime were surprised, but others recalled warning signs that had existed even in the good years. Some remembered, for example, a brief incident in 1928 when an article entitled "Religione o nazione?" in the November 29–30 issue of *Popolo di Roma* criticized a recent Italian Zionist congress and questioned the patriotism of its participants. While the article was unsigned, its author was generally recognized as Mussolini himself. The article prompted a flood of letters from Jews protesting their loyalty to the Duce and the nation. It was a sad harbinger of things to come.[7]

By the early 1930s, skeptics of Mussolini's benevolence toward Jews began to point out that despite the high number of accomplished Jewish scholars and scientists in the country, none had been appointed to the Italian Academy. Mussolini made light of the criticism, assuring an interviewer in 1932 that he was at that very moment considering a Jewish appointment. None occurred.[8]

More alarming was the shadowy existence of obscure anti-Semitic fanatics hovering in the wings awaiting their cue. Chief among these was Giovanni Preziosi, renegade priest, nationalist, and Fascist since 1920. Preziosi published his anti-Semitic newspaper *La Vita Italiana* throughout the 1920s. In 1921, he translated and circulated throughout Italy the infamous "Protocols of the Elders of Zion," a forged document proporting to prove a Jewish conspiracy to dominate the world. Mussolini seems to have detested Preziosi, but Roberto Farinacci was his protector. He also cultivated German Nazi friends who later became useful. As most Fascists considered him a crank throughout the 1920s and early 1930s, however, his role remained minimal until the war.[9]

Among the Fascist rank and file too, there were anti-Semitic elements even in the 1920s. In his memoirs, Augusto Segre remembers several early incidents in his town of Casale Monferrato, east of Turin. In one case, someone put two old rusty gates against a wall facing a café frequented by Fascists, with a sign "Put the Jews back in the ghetto." In another incident, one of the best-known Fascists in town approached Segre's twenty-year-old brother in a café, grabbed his jacket, and called him and all Jews "subversives and Freemasons." Segre himself was also harassed on occasion by Fascist thugs.[10]

On another level, Mussolini's persistent suspicion of Zionism also disturbed many perceptive observers. He regarded

The Italians and The Holocaust

Zionists as "internationalists" or as people with "dual loyalties" —both unacceptable in his increasingly monolithic state. With more justification, perhaps, he also saw them as tinted with Liberal democracy, socialism, and, consequently, anti-fascism. As a result, he was always more sympathetic to Vladimir Zwed Jabotinsky's brand of authoritarian Zionist revisionism than to the official democratic Zionist mainstream. Mussolini also viewed Zionists as instruments of British imperial policy who would facilitate the division and rule of the Palestinian mandate. Only sporadically did he consider that support of Zionism might help extend Italian influence in the Mediterranean. Finally, he feared that support of Zionists would alienate the Arabs, whose good will he hoped to cultivate as part of his anti-British policy in the Middle East.

Throughout the good years, Mussolini's anti-Zionist suspicions remained dormant. Between July 1934 and the middle of 1936, while he cultivated the Stresa front, hoped for a British and French blessing upon his Ethiopian endeavor, and remained wary of Nazi Germany, Mussolini actually made pro-Zionist statements and held several friendly meetings with Zionist leaders. In December 1934, with the temporary idea that support for Zionism might increase his international influence, he even permitted young Jews from Jabotinsky's revisionist Zionist organization (but not those from official Zionist circles) to study at the Italian Maritime School in Civitavecchia. Jewish students from all over Europe and from Palestine formed a special section at the school, pursuing Hebrew, Palestinian geography, and other related subjects in addition to their maritime courses. Years later, Jewish graduates of the Maritime School became the basic cadres of the fledgling Israeli navy. [11]

In mid-1936, after the Ethiopian sanctions and Italian intervention in the Spanish Civil War, Mussolini decided to burn all his bridges. Soon after the appointment of his pro-German son-in-law Galeazzo Ciano as foreign minister, Mussolini allied Italy unequivocably with Hitler. Anti-Zionism was immediately rekindled with a vengeance. This time, the flames grew into an intense, undisguised anti-Semitism. One of Italy's first profoundly anti-Semitic pamphlets, Alfredo Romanini's *Ebrei-Cristianesimo-Fascismo*, appeared in 1936. Later that year, Farinacci's newspaper *Il Regime fascista* began to attack not only Zionists but all Jews, claiming that they had not done enough for their country and must put fascism before Judaism. Anti-Semitic graffiti appeared for the first time on the walls of Jewish homes in Ferrara in the summer of 1936. [12] And in April 1937, Paolo Orano's famous book *Gli ebrei in Italia* appeared. The transition from anti-Zionism to anti-Semitism seemed complete as Orano called upon Jews to reject, not just "foreign loyalties," but their entire cultural heritage. They should withdraw from all local Jewish social, educational, cultural, or athletic associations and blend entirely into the anonymous Fascist masses.

While a chronological connection between Mussolini's Jewish and German policies is undeniable, the causal connection is subtle. Mussolini was isolated and anxious for a German alliance after the Ethiopian War and the Italian intervention in Spain, but there is no evidence that Hitler or his top aides ever demanded an anti-Semitic program as the price of German friendship. [13] Mussolini alone bears responsibility for the racial laws. On the other hand, he did not have to be told that an Italian racial policy would please the Führer by demonstrating that the Fascists had cut all ties with Britain and France. Mussolini introduced the racial laws, in part, as a token of the sincerity of his bid for an alliance.

By 1936, an increasingly racist political and intellectual climate at home also influenced the formation of Fascist Jewish policy. To some extent, Mussolini controlled that climate by unleashing his anti-Semitic cronies at appropriate times. But other factors remained beyond his control, and here again German influence appears. Nazi agents operating in Italy in the early 1930s frequently stirred up local anti-Semites and encouraged young pro-Nazi government officials. Bureaucrats who hoped to build their careers on a German alliance were quick to understand the value of an anti-Semitic policy, and tried to push the prime minister in that direction.

Apart from the German influence, many right-wing associations as well as elements within the Church became increasingly anti-Bolshevik during the Spanish Civil War. These forces tended to equate Bolsheviks with Jews. Publications like the Jesuit newspaper *La Civiltà cattolica* and the Catholic University of Milan's journal *Vita e pensiero* began to warn the public of the Jewish danger. [14] At the same time, government officials, ever more conscious of racial issues after the Ethiopian War, began to penalize Italians for sexual contact with blacks. [15] Racism was clearly growing in Italy, independently of the Nazis. Mussolini's decision to adopt a racial policy was consistent with the times.

Once decided, Mussolini mobilized a vast press campaign to marshal public support for the racial laws. Early in 1938, the standard anti-Semitic press became increasingly shrill. Small local newspapers and youth organization publications, especially those most in need of funds and subject to government influence, promptly followed the new line. In August 1938, Telesio Interlandi began his particularly vicious newspaper *La Difesa della razza*, which appeared throughout the country every two weeks until July 1943. Eventually, almost every national newspaper picked up the anti-Jewish theme. [16] Fascist spokesmen, bureaucrats, and rival journalists made life difficult for publications that seemed reluctant to toe the line. Very few resisted for long.

Many press attacks focused on foreign Jews, cited as the cause of housing shortages, high rents, high prices, food scarcities, unemployment, low wages, crowded schools, crime, and every other conceivable social and economic ill. Articles emphasized the pro-British aspects of Zionism, anti-Semitic measures in other countries, and Jewish support for the Loyalists in the Spanish Civil War. The press denigrated all Jewish contributions to cultural and intellectual life, past and present, in Italy and beyond. Indeed, considering the extent of the attacks and the complete absence of published dissent, it is remarkable that Italians remained as skeptical and disapproving of the racial laws as they did.

Radio programs also reflected the anti-Semitic theme throughout 1938. Associations ranging from the Italian Academy and the National Institute of Fascist Culture to university student clubs and local party groups held conferences, seminars, and study sessions. Finally, on July 14, 1938, the infamous *Manifesto degli scienziati razzisti* (Manifesto of the Racial Scientists) was published. The scientists claimed that "the population and civilization of Italy today is of Aryan origin. . . . [and] there exists a pure Italian race. . . . [but] Jews do not belong to the Italian race." The manifesto attempted to provide a scientific justification for the coming racial laws. [17]

The manifesto was a fraud in every respect. Even Mussolini, who understood all too well the German definition of the term Aryan, did not believe its content. Furthermore, the manner of its proclamation was farcical. It was signed by ten "experts," of whom at least four were young university assistants just beginning their careers and vulnerable to political pressure. Only one of the ten had national stature. [18] Worst of all, the original Manifesto of the Racial Scientists appeared with no signatures at all. The list of ten followed several days later!

As a final step in the preparation for the racial laws, the Ministry of the Interior announced in July that the Central Demography Office would become the far more sinister Office of Demography and Race. The new agency was immediately ordered to conduct a census of all Jews in Italy—a task it performed in August.

After Mussolini's softening-up campaign, the actual anti-Semitic measures surprised no one. The first restrictions involved education. Just before the autumn term, the government announced that no Jews could study or teach in public schools during the coming academic year. Elementary schools with more than ten Jewish students were required to establish separate sections and facilities for them. Secondary schooling was not provided, but individual Jewish communities were empowered to organize their own schools if they wished. Jewish students, both Italian and foreign, already enrolled in universities could complete their program, but no new students would be admitted.

Other early restrictions concerned the more than ten thousand foreign Jews recorded by the August census. On September 2 and 3, the government announced that foreign Jews could no longer establish residence in Italy, Libya, or the Dodecanese Islands. Those already in residence were to leave within six months. Worst of all, Jews who had been nationalized after January 1, 1919, lost their citizenship and were regarded as foreigners.

The bulk of the racial laws became official on November 17, 1938.[19] Marriage between Jews and non-Jews was prohibited. Jews were not permitted to own or manage companies involved in military production, or factories that employed over one hundred people or exceeded a certain value. They could not own land over a certain value, serve in the armed forces, employ non-Jewish Italian domestics, or belong to the Fascist party. Their employment in banks, insurance companies, and national and municipal administration was forbidden.

The original November laws also wrestled with the elusive problem of exactly who was Jewish. In a country where intermarriage and religious conversion were common, the inevitable result was confusion. First, in ostensibly the easiest cases, the law decreed that children of two Jewish parents were themselves Jewish, even if they belonged to another religion. That provision, denying as it did the possibility of conversion, antagonized the Church. Next, those with one Jewish and one foreign parent were also declared Jewish, as were the offspring of a Jewish mother and an unknown father. In cases of obvious mixed marriages between Jewish and non-Jewish Italian citizens, children were Jewish if they practiced Judaism or were inscribed in the community. They were not Jewish only if, in addition to having one non-Jewish Italian parent, they had been baptized before October 1, 1938. Furthermore, that non-Jewish parent had to be "pure Aryan," for according to the law, children of a mixed marriage were Jewish if they had "more than fifty percent Jewish blood."[20]

The law ultimately provided for other cases. Children of mixed marriages born between October 1, 1938 and October 1, 1939 were given time for baptism; those born after October 1, 1939 had to be baptized within ten days. Those baptized before October 1938 but subsequently compromised through marriage to Jews were subject to various intricate provisions.[21]

In the attempt to appease opponents of the racial laws, the original November regulations also defined a policy of exemptions for certain categories. The immediate families of Jews killed, wounded, or decorated while fighting in Libya, World War I, Ethiopia, and Spain, along with the families of men who volunteered for service in those wars, might secure exemptions. Individuals and their families who had participated in Gabriele D'Annunzio's occupation of Fiume in 1919, had joined the Fascist party between 1919 and 1922 or during the second half of 1924 (after the murder of Socialist deputy Giacomo Matteotti by Fascist thugs), or had been wounded in the Fascist cause, were also included as eligible exemptees. Finally, individuals with exceptional merit of a "civic nature" (a quality left undefined in the statutes) might secure exemptions for themselves and their families.

All exemptions, however, were subject to limitations. First, they were not awarded automatically, but on a case-by-case basis determined by a special commission of the Ministry of the Interior. Decisions were capricious, to say the least. The family of Memo Bemporad, for example, was denied an exemption despite the fact that his grandfather had supported Garibaldi, his mother's brother had died in combat in World War I, his mother had directed a hospital during the same war and received a silver medal, and his father-in-law had been decorated for service as an officer in two wars. Denial was based on the grounds—accurate, Bemporad hastens to add—that the family had shown no enthusiasm for fascism.[22]

Decisions were usually determined, not on the merits, but by the greed, envy, fanaticism, and, occasionally, good will of those in power. It was not unusual to wait for hours, be forced to return several times, have to pay bribes, and have announcements of decisions delayed for months while the bribes continued.[23] After all that, a favorable decision might be granted to one individual but not extended to the family. Exemptions could also be revoked at any time, without reason or explanation.[24]

Even when secured, exemptions did not cover all the restrictions defined in the racial laws. Exemptees still could not hold a job in a bank or in public administration. They could not teach, and their children could not study in the public schools. They could, according to the November laws, still serve in the armed forces, but on December 22, 1938, military authorities themselves decided to retire all Jewish officers in permanent active service, regardless of their exemption status.[25] Exemptees could, however, hold property without limitation and continue in most professions. By January 15, 1943, the Office of Demography and Race at the Ministry of the Interior had examined 5,870 applications. Of these, they had granted 2,486 and refused 3,384. [26]

The exemption policy may be seen as a reasonable, if badly executed, attempt to recognize Jews who had rendered some special services to their country or to the Fascist cause. Indeed, Italo Balbo, Emilio De Bono, and some other Fascist Grand Council members who disliked the racial laws had argued that exemptions should be granted to the families of all who had served in Italy's wars, and not merely to those who had been killed, wounded, or decorated. A subsequent exemption program, however, had no justification of any kind, and was starkly symptomatic of overall Fascist cynicism and corruption.

On July 13, 1939, the government introduced an Aryanization program, by which a special commission could simply declare arbitrarily that a Jew was not a Jew. Because applicants for Aryanization did not have to prove any personal service record, bribery became the primary determinant of decisions. [27] Even worse, Aryanized individuals received privileges that far exceeded those awarded exemptees under the earlier program. Because Aryanized Jews were no longer Jews, they suffered no disabilities at all. The Aryanization program promptly fulfilled the purpose for which it had been designed, honoring the most corrupt and penalizing by default the most worthy.

In addition to the Aryanization law, scores of other laws, regulations, and decrees appeared in 1939 to supplement the original November program. On June 29, for example, all Jews were prohibited from working as notaries, and only exemptees were allowed to work as journalists, doctors, pharmacists, veterinarians, lawyers, accountants, engineers, architects, chemists, agronomists, and mathematicians. The vast majority without exemptions could practice their professions only among other Jews. Another law prohibited all personal service by Aryans for Jews. Many other 1939 decrees constituted pure and simple harassment. For example, Jews could not own radios, place advertisements or death notices in the newspapers, publish books, hold public conferences, list their names and numbers in telephone directories (operators could give the information orally), or frequent popular vacation spots. The last measure appeared in the summer, when many were already away. They had to come home.

In many cases, local anti-Semitic initiatives exceeded even the national program. Local ordinances frequently denied licenses to small Jewish businesses, shops, restaurants, and cafés. A local decree in Rome revoked the licenses of rag pickers and second-hand clothes dealers. Supplies could be withheld even from legitimate shops. Jewish employees not officially affected by the racial laws could nevertheless be fired on unofficial orders from above. The zeal with which these measures were executed varied from place to place, but the suffering was widespread and acute. [28]

Advocates of the Italian racial laws liked to claim that their brand of anti-Semitism differed from the Nazi variety in two respects. First, they maintained, it was based on spiritual and cultural, rather than biological, concepts. As such, it was consistent with Italian traditions and the teachings of the Church. The truth was rather different. Provisions that refused to recognize conversions, either because both parents were Jewish or because baptism had not occurred before a certain date, clearly treated Jews as a race. [29] On the other hand, provisions that treated the children of mixed marriages differently depending only upon their religion ignored the concept of race. So, too, did provisions granting exemptions on the basis of service or even bribes. In fact, Italian anti-Semitism had no ideological base, but was the product of mindless and cynical opportunism.

Second, advocates of the laws liked to claim that their goal, unlike that of Nazi anti-Semites, was to discriminate, not persecute. The government did not interfere with freedom of worship, Fascists pointed out, and education in principle was not prohibited—the state simply ceased to provide it. Jews retained their right to protection under the law, and they could practice their professions among themselves. The state merely demanded their separation from the rest of society. In fact, however, this was a specious distinction. Inability to practice a trade or profession freely, or even to operate a shop, constituted economic persecution for thousands of unfortunates. It could have been worse, but it was severe enough.

The racial laws immediately affected thousands of people. The more than ten thousand foreign Jews were the hardest hit, for they had been required in September 1938 to leave the country altogether. A mitigating clause in the November laws stipulated that those aged sixty-five and over by October 1, 1938, and those married to Italian citizens by the same date could remain, but all others had to leave by March 1939. By then, 933 had won the right to stay and 3,720 had left—a number that increased, often through threats of expulsion, to 6,480 by September. [30]

Emigrants were simply replaced, however, by thousands of Jewish refugees entering from even less hospitable countries. Italy closed her frontier to German, Polish, Hungarian, and Rumanian Jews in August 1939, but sympathetic Italian border guards often looked the other way. By October 1941, there were 7,000 foreign Jews in Italy, of whom more than 3,000 were fairly recent arrivals. [31] They had no official status, no means of sustenance, no right to remain in the country, and no place to go. Many were placed in internment camps or enforced residence after Italy entered the war.

Among Italian Jews, the racial laws caused, first of all, the abrupt end of jobs and educations. Within a few weeks, about 200 teachers at all levels, 400 public employees, 500 private employees, 150 military personnel, and 2,500 in the professions lost their positions. At the same time, 200 students in universities, 1,000 in secondary schools, and 4,400 in elementary schools were affected. [32]

To ease the economic impact of the racial laws, special clauses provided that pensions, and in cases of brief employment, partial pensions, be paid to those who would have received them upon normal retirement. Also, confiscated property was partially compensated. Professional people could continue to practice within the small and now impoverished Jewish community. Teachers could teach in Jewish schools. These provisions helped many in middle-income groups but were no consolation to small shopkeepers, artisans, and workers —the less affluent lower classes, particularly numerous in Rome. Without economic resources or the means to emigrate, many existed almost entirely on charity from the Jewish communities. Clustered in old ghetto neighborhoods and lacking the money and contacts to secure hiding places, they were the first to fall into the clutches of the SS in 1943.

Many non-Jews benefited financially from the elimination of professional competition and sales of Jewish property and shops. More than 2,500 non-Jews suffered, however, when they lost the personal service jobs they had held with Jewish families. Their complaints went unheeded. Again fascism succeeded in serving the strong and harming the weak.

If the economic impact was harshest among the lower classes, however, the emotional shock was probably greater among the more affluent and assimilated—among those who thought they belonged to Italian society. Nearly 6,000 Italian Jews had emigrated by October 1941—a particularly poignant statistic in light of their veneration for country and king before 1938—and another 6,000 had converted. [33] There were also several suicides among the middle classes. The most dramatic case was that of Angelo Fortunato Formiggini, a highly respected author, journalist, publisher, and early critic of fascism. On November 29, 1938, Formiggini threw himself from the

Ghirlandina Tower in his native Modena, in the expressed hope of demonstrating to all his countrymen the horror of racial laws that persecuted a few. [34] Fabio Della Seta, a young high school student in Rome, also recalled the suicide of a distant relative who had served in World War I and had been unable to bear the racial laws. His regimental band had played a beautiful funeral march, which the Jewish community thought to be a good sign. [35]

The vast majority of assimilated and nonpolitical Italian Jews reacted to the racial laws with shock and disbelief. Particularly poignant is the story of General Ugo Modena, a gold medal winner in World War I and the son of General Angelo Modena, president of the Supreme Army and Navy Tribunal in the late 1920s. In 1938, Ugo Modena, along with twenty-four other Jewish generals and five admirals, was abruptly dismissed. He refused to apply for an exemption and retired quietly to the country. When his children were forced to leave school, however, he could no longer bear it. He wrote a courteous letter to his king, requesting that, if his medals and service had any meaning, his children be reinstated. The king promised to try, but General Modena obtained no results. Quietly and without publicity, he returned his medals. [36]

Every Italian Jew was affected. Giorgio Bassani, who later wrote *The Garden of the Finzi-Continis,* had to break off his engagement to a Catholic girl. [37] Rita Levi Montalcini, a 1936 graduate from the University of Turin Medical School, had to leave her job at a research institute. She moved her laboratory into her home—and went on to win the Nobel Prize in Physiology or Medicine in 1986. Carlo Modigliani, who had, in his own words, "forgotten completely about being Jewish," was given one hour's notice to resign his teaching position. Also a talented musician and composer, Modigliani had belonged to a Society of Authors since 1915. In 1919, an operetta he had written was performed in Rome. After the racial laws, he received a letter informing him that he was no longer a member of the society. He received no explanation. At about the same time, in accordance with the racial laws, the non-Jewish maid who cared for Modigliani's sick and nearly totally deaf eighty-six-year-old mother had to leave. He could not find a Jewish replacement. After much difficulty, he finally found a Catholic woman who was willing to ignore the law and work for him. In the years that followed, she took many risks and proved to be devoted to her charge. [38]

Enzo Levi, a lawyer from Modena mentioned earlier and, like Modigliani, a proud veteran of World War I, also found many individuals willing to take a chance. Racial decrees limited Levi's law practice to Jewish clients. He recalls, however, that many non-Jewish clients came to him secretly, and lawyer friends often let him use their names. In this respect, Levi was more fortunate than many. In other towns, even Jewish clients were pressured to use non-Jewish professionals.

For Enzo Levi and his wife, the educational constraints were the most painful aspect of the racial laws. The Levis lived near the elementary school, which their younger children could no longer attend. At the close of every day, the grieving youngsters could hear the voices of their friends in the school yard. The older Levi children were also excluded from the secondary school. They could enter it only for state examinations, for which they prepared in their Jewish schools. They took the written portions in a separate room and were always questioned last in the oral examinations. The Levis finally left Italy in 1942. As Enzo Levi wrote in his memoirs, "At least five centuries . . . of life of my family in Italy, my own passionate participation in the war, a lifetime of honest work on my part and on the part of my ancestors . . . were not valid in identifying me as a citizen of my country." [39]

Carlo Modigliani survived for a time by teaching at the newly constituted Jewish School of Milan. Giorgio Bassani, fresh from the university and seeking his first job, did the same in Ferrara. Enzo Levi also solved one problem by sending his older children to the Jewish School in Modena. Before 1938, not even the most religious families sent their children to Jewish secondary schools unless they wanted to become rabbis. After 1938, special schools played a major role in the lives of thousands of teachers, students, and parents.

Fabio Della Seta's Jewish high school in Rome was located near the old ghetto, on the other side of the Tiber River. About 350 middle-class students were thus brought back to the very streets their parents and grandparents, with so much effort, had left behind. Della Seta expected all the students at the Jewish School to be brilliant because, as he says, "it is known that in every class there is a 'first,' and almost always it is a Jew." His image of his people was as stereotyped as that of non-Jews. "What is a Jew?" he asks. "Someone who [in the public schools] does not go to the religious lessons." [40]

Della Seta's experience at the Jewish School changed his life. Not all the students were brilliant, but most of his teachers were. They had recently lost jobs in universities and other secondary schools. [41] For the teachers, it became a point of honor to prepare students to excel on state exams. As a result of the school, Della Seta remembers, "one was no longer ashamed to be Jewish. Even those, and they were perhaps the major part, who came from families with Risorgimento traditions—laic, therefore, with a clear strain of anticlericalism, naturally also anti-Jewish—began to sense a strange, unmotivated pride in being Jewish." [42] Students developed a great interest in Jews who were famous—Einstein, Freud, Spinoza, Kafka. Some even began to attend religious services.

Of course Della Seta's memories are not all positive; he poignantly describes the isolation and despair of the period. As the Holocaust approached, students drew away from their families, where catastrophe was the main subject of conversation. They focused entirely upon themselves, on research and polemics, acting, he says, as if all the world's problems could be solved by mathematics or reduced to a correct reading of Kafka or Dostoevsky. In their bewilderment, helplessness, and isolation, they resemble the characters in Bassani's *Garden of the Finzi-Continis.* [43] Bassani clearly understood the desperate attempt, when one is helpless to influence big events, to pretend that only small ones matter.

Jewish schools also functioned in Trieste, Milan, Venice, Florence, Turin, and other major cities, employing the cream of the recently unemployed Jewish professional classes. They continued heroically until the German occupation. Modigliani describes the last examination period at the Milan Jewish School, in the autumn of 1943. The Germans were already in Milan, and neighbors warned teachers and students assembled at the school that Nazis had come looking for them two days before. Exams on the first day were held in the cellar, with an escape route planned and with teachers and students guarding the main entrance. According to regulations, a government supervisor, in this case a non-Jewish woman, was present. She suggested that, for safety, examinations on the following days be held in her apartment. Upon their conclusion, the school closed its doors, and students and teachers alike spent the next year and a half in hiding. [44]

The Jewish schools and, more generally, the racial laws themselves often had the effect of instilling a new sense of Judaism into a highly assimilated and previously indifferent community. In addition to Della Seta's testimony, we have that of Gastone Orefice, the young man from Livorno. Orefice remembers endless discussions with fellow students on the subject of conversion. Their Jewishness seemed such a remote influence in their lives that a refusal to convert often appeared mere stubbornness. A closer examination of their special heritage helped them appreciate its role and meaning. Without

the racial laws, most would never have made such an evalua-
tion. [45]

While Jews were considering, and usually rejecting, conversion, Catholic priests took various positions on the issue. Many
were willing to backdate baptismal certificates for the children
of mixed marriages to qualify converts for exemption from the
racial laws. Others interpreted their role much more broadly,
however, and used the possibility of racial persecution as a
means of gaining converts. They encouraged false rumors: only
Catholics could emigrate to South America; the Vatican soon
would be able to protect all Catholics, whether of mixed parentage or not; the government was about to Aryanize all Catholics, regardless of parentage. While Levi rightly condemns
such methods, he speaks admiringly of other priests, who
refused to sanction conversions under false pretenses. One
priest told a friend of Levi's, who believed that conversion
would lead to Aryanization and save his wife and children, that
the rumor was not true. He refused the conversion, but promised the man a false date on a baptismal certificate if the
rumor ever became fact. [46]

The racial laws broke the great popular consensus that Mussolini had created with the Ethiopian War. After 1938, the
prime minister's popularity declined each year until the end.
While most Italians could accept claims that Zionists were
disloyal, that Jewish refugees caused price increases and
crowded facilities, or that Leon Blum was a natural enemy of
Mussolini, they could not accept persecution of the family next
door. Furthermore, with the racial program, average Italians
realized more clearly than ever that Fascist laws did not demand unquestioning obedience; they could be and were being
broken every day. They saw Fascist notables bend the rules for
or against the Jews, depending on circumstances, and they
began to do the same.

Carlo Modigliani found a Catholic maid to care, illegally,

for his mother. Enzo Levi found supportive colleagues and friendly priests. A young university graduate in Turin named Emanuele Artom could not use the library for research on a book, but he found a former teacher who allowed him to take books home. [47] A young mother in Trieste named Laura Erbsen received phone calls from friendly shopkeepers asking her not to come near their shops. They were ashamed that she would see the signs they had been forced to put in their windows: "No Jews or dogs allowed." [48]

An industrialist named Giuseppe Segre, later deported with his wife to Poland, had to fire two faithful non-Jewish servants —two elderly women, who cried and said they had no place to go, but had to leave nevertheless. The next day, two servants from a family in the same building knocked on Segre's door and asked if they could serve him, naturally without pay. [49]

Such attitudes extended to public officials as well. In 1938, Laura Erbsen received a dreaded knock on the door. Policemen told her they had terrible news. She was terror-stricken. The news, they said, was that she would have to let her maid go. She was immensely relieved, but they were crestfallen and deeply ashamed. "How will you manage? You have a new baby, an elderly mother, and a big house." She assured them that the news could have been worse.

The next news was clearly worse. The Erbsens were expelled from Italy in 1939 because the husband was a foreign Jew. When they left the country, many friends came to the train station to see them off. Among them was the father of Mrs. Erbsen's childhood friend, who was a retired general and an official in the Fascist party section in Trieste. After the train was underway, officials charged with seeing expelled persons across the border began their customs inspection. One inspector knocked on Mrs. Erbsen's compartment door and saw that she was wearing jewelry. Only a small amount of jewelry could be taken out of the country, and she had been told that it was safest to keep it on her person. "Put your baby to sleep," he said, "and I will return. And why don't you change and prepare for your journey?" She understood that he did not want to see the jewelry. He never asked for it. [50]

Many others had similar experiences. Frontier guards allowed illegal Jewish immigration (after 1943, some would allow illegal Jewish emigration to Switzerland). Police searched Enzo Levi's house for an illegal radio, and he had the distinct impression that they did not want to find it. [51] But perhaps the best story is that told by Carlo Modigliani of his eighty-six-year-old, nearly deaf mother. Seeking refuge from Milanese air raids in a small village near Varese in February 1943, she had to register with a local official and declare her religion. "I am of the religion that does no evil to any living soul," she declared. "Well then, you are an Aryan," he replied, and thus she was registered. When the Germans arrived a few months later, she survived because of that registration. [52]

Even the most important Fascist leaders occasionally showed a lack of enthusiasm for the racial laws. Roberto Farinacci, Fascist boss of Cremona and one of the country's most vocal Jew baiters, long resisted firing his Jewish secretary. Later, during the German occupation, he turned a list of fifty-three Jews of Cremona over to the Nazis, who were demanding it, but he first warned the individuals on the list that they should hide. [53] Dino Grandi, former *squadrista*, foreign minister, and ambassador to London, passed Giancarlo Sacerdoti's father in the street in Bologna and, when Sacerdoti delicately tried to ignore him to spare him embarrassment, Grandi greeted him jovially with the words, "Ciao, Sacerdoti, don't you recognize an old friend?" [54] Tullio Tamburini, a vicious Fascist *squadrista* from Florence who became chief of police during the German occupation, wrote a letter of recommendation for an exemption for Memo Bemporad's family, his former employers. Mario Piazzesi, Fascist party secretary in Lucca and

Bemporad's former schoolmate, did the same, loudly telling a crowd waiting near his office, "We will make them hear our voice in Rome: we pure Fascists are not anti-Semites, those are German matters."[55]

There is broader, less personal evidence of popular disapproval of the racial laws within the Fascist party. Between 1938 and 1943, over one thousand Fascists lost membership cards because of "pietism," the name given to the crime of sympathizing with Jews.[56] Plans for university chairs on racial studies never materialized. Local Fascist party sections in the largest cities were instructed to establish Centers for the Study of the Jewish Problem, and by 1942 most had done so. Popular participation, however, was negligible. By the fall of Mussolini in July 1943, only 864 Fascist party members out of a total of over 4,000,000 were enrolled as participants. In Milan alone, of 10,000 Fascist party members, 65 were enrolled.[57]

However, the record is uneven. Bemporad's family ignored the law one summer and took lodgings in a beach hotel where they were well known. The hotel management was willing, but someone complained and they had to leave.[58] Police had not wanted to find Levi's radio, but someone—he suspected a competitor—had reported the radio in the first place. Revenue collectors were accommodating with Laura Erbsen and her jewelry, but other officials mercilessly demanded bribes from desperate refugees trying to leave Trieste.[59] Friendly shopkeepers apologized for their "No Jews allowed" signs, but the existence of such signs in the first place was a national disgrace. Bureaucrats processing exemption applications often deliberately humiliated applicants. Many employers were more zealous in firing Jewish employees than the law required. Businessmen were sometimes eager to grab Jewish property. Non-Jewish Italians were showing symptoms of an already deadly disease.

Perhaps the saddest indictments, however, are those that

must be directed against the Church and the king. Pope Pius XI himself had condemned atheistic Nazi anti-Semitism in the papal encyclical *Mit brennender Sorge* in March 1937, but a year and a half later he offered few objections to the Italian racial laws. His protests and those of Pius XII, who succeeded him in March 1939, primarily concerned the treatment of Jews who had converted. The Church strongly objected to Fascist interference with the sacrament of marriage and to Fascist denials of valid conversions. The Church as an institution objected, in other words, to biological racism, but was less strongly opposed to anti-Semitism.[60]

While most Jews may have expected little from the institutional Church, they expected far too much from the monarchy. Jewish veneration of the House of Savoy cannot be overemphasized. Dating from the Jewish emancipation, it was an irrational and deeply embedded attitude that united individuals who managed to disagree about almost everything else. Nearly every Jewish home, shop, and place of worship had a portrait of King Victor Emmanuel III. Yet when Mussolini, before the racial laws, made discreet inquiries about the king's position, Victor Emmanuel expressed no objections. The laws were issued in his name.[61]

Augusto Segre has written an amusing account of his father's disillusionment with the king. Years earlier, the elder Segre, rabbi of Casale, had come under considerable pressure to include Mussolini's name in the traditional blessing of king and country. As the rabbi did not like Mussolini, he tried for a time to claim forgetfulness. Eventually, however, he had to tack on the prime minister's name at the end of his blessing, followed by some words in Hebrew. His congregation, not understanding Hebrew, was satisfied. After 1938, the rabbi shifted the name of the king from the middle of the blessing to the end, linking it with Mussolini. He repeated the same Hebrew words. Segre leaves us to imagine what those words actually were.[62]

4

The War Years:
June 1940–September 1943

THE MORNING after Mussolini declared war on the Allies, Italian police began to arrest foreign Jews. At first they seized only men between the ages of eighteen and sixty. They held their victims for weeks in major city prisons—places like San Vittore in Milan, Marassi in Genoa, and Regina Coeli in Rome, which were to become dreaded household names in the years to come. Conditions were appalling. Toilet facilities were virtually nonexistent, and overcrowding compounded the filth. Eventually the men, in manacles, were sent by train to wretched internment camps at Ferramonti Tarsia in the province of Cosenza, Campagna in the province of Salerno, and others, usually in remote areas of southern Italy. By September 1940 there were fifteen such camps. At Ferramonti and Campagna, there were already about four hundred prisoners each. [1] Men lived in unfinished huts, without electricity or water. Malaria was endemic. [2]

Although Italy was officially a racist country, the primary purpose of the arrests of foreign Jews was not to persecute them as Jews but to intern them as presumably anti-Axis refugees. For the same reason, police also arrested many enemy nationals living in Italy. Most Italian Jews, on the other hand, were not bothered, unless their political pasts suggested potential anti-Fascism to the increasingly paranoid authorities. By the same token, the poor treatment of foreign Jewish prisoners was not a result of deliberate cruelty or racism. All prisoners were similarly treated in Fascist Italy—with indifference and supreme contempt.

From sheer necessity, the prisoners at Ferramonti organized themselves to provide facilities. They completed the huts and dug wells. Eventually, they did much more. Women and children began to arrive. Left without economic means, some actually joined their men voluntarily. More elaborate facilities were required. Prisoners organized a nursery, library, school, theater, and synagogue. They held concerts and athletic events. They established baths, medical offices, and even a pharmacy. Life became bearable, and the initially harsh attitude of most Fascist guards softened into one of trust and respect.

By 1942, about 1,400 people were interned at Ferramonti. [3] Most were German refugees, with smaller numbers of Czechs, Poles, Hungarians, and Yugoslavians. Most were from the middle classes, for the poor could rarely afford to leave their countries. Those with special skills found work in the camp as artisans, gardeners, cooks. Some became food vendors, wandering about the camp selling pastries or hot tea. The general atmosphere was peaceful but efficient. With neat rows of white huts looking out over barren hills and cultivated fields, Ferramonti reminded one visitor of Israel. [4] Unlike Israeli settlements, however, the Italian camp was surrounded with barbed wire and watchtowers.

The Italians and The Holocaust

Fascist policy was often directed toward breaking up families, as in the case of Arthur Frankel. Frankel had lived in Italy since 1912, becoming a citizen in 1923. The racial laws had revoked his citizenship. On July 19, 1940, he and his family were arrested—police were no longer limiting their arrests to men. Frankel was sent to Cosenza, his wife to Potenza, and two other relatives to Avellino. Their three-year-old daughter was left in Milan.[5]

In addition to internment camps, the government maintained a second system of detention known as enforced residence or confinement, in which individuals or whole families were held under light surveillance in private houses in small villages. Before the war, anti-Fascists convicted of minor offenses had often been held in this way. In *Christ Stopped at Eboli*, Carlo Levi describes his experiences of confinement in the 1930s.[6] For the war years, a Jewish woman from Galicia, whose account bears only the initials K. L., offers a brief description.[7]

Mrs. L. lived in Merano, near Bolzano, with her husband, also a foreigner, and their three-year-old child. They operated a large wholesale textile outlet. Mrs. L.'s ordeal began even before Italy entered the war. In August 1939, the government demanded that all Jews not born in Merano leave that town so near the Austrian frontier. Mrs. L., expecting to be away only a short time, put all her belongings in storage and left with her family for Lake Garda.

On July 6, 1940, at 6 A.M., Mrs. L. and her family were arrested. After many delays, lies, and attempts to separate the parents from their child, Mrs. L. and her child were sent to Trea, in the province of Macerata, and her husband, typically, was sent elsewhere. Perhaps because she became very ill, she was reunited with her husband after several weeks. The family was then sent to Orsogna, in the province of Chieti, where they remained until September 1943.

In Orsogna, Mrs. L. and her family lived in a normal house. They received an allowance of thirteen and a half lire a day, which she says was enough to live on. They also probably received a monthly housing allowance of about fifty lire. While they could move freely around the village, they could not leave it. They were not constantly guarded, but they had to report regularly to the police. They could send and receive mail. Mrs. L.'s was only one of ten Jewish families confined in Orsogna. She says that, at least in her case, the villagers all knew she was Jewish but never troubled her. Also in Orsogna were about fifty non-Jewish families—enemy nationals similarly confined.

The famous Italian Jewish author Natalia Ginzburg, from Turin, also recorded a period of enforced residence.[8] Natalia was the sister of Mario Levi, who escaped to Switzerland at the time of the Ponte Tresa affair in 1934. In 1938, she married Leone Ginzburg, son of a wealthy family from Odessa but raised and educated in Italy. Leone, a young university instructor of Slavic languages, had established his anti-Fascist credentials early in 1934 by refusing to sign the oath of loyalty to the Fascist regime demanded of all professors since 1931. He promptly lost his first job. Soon after, he was arrested for complicity in the Ponte Tresa affair and, with Sion Segre Amar, given a light sentence. A year later, he was arrested and sentenced again for his activities as a leader of Giustizia e Libertà.

Leone Ginzburg became an Italian citizen, but the racial laws revoked that status. In June 1940, as a foreign Jew and a known anti-Fascist, he was arrested again. He was sent to enforced residence in the small town of Pizzoli in the Abruzzi, where Natalia and their two sons were allowed to join him two months later. They remained there together until the fall of Mussolini. Natalia remembers those years as among the best in their tragically brief life together. Leone somehow managed to continue his work as a director of the new Einaudi publishing company. They were able to walk in the countryside beyond the village, and they began to appreciate rural life for the first time. Their third child, a daughter, was born early in the summer of 1943.

After Mussolini's fall in July 1943, Leone Ginzburg returned to Rome to resume political activity with Giustizia e Libertà. It is an indication of his feeling for the village of his enforced residence that he left Natalia and his children there. When the Germans invaded in September, his family joined him in Rome —Natalia simply climbed aboard a German truck, telling the driver they were war refugees and had lost their papers. They all went into hiding, but Leone intensified his Resistance work. He was arrested in November. In February 1944, Natalia learned that he had died mysteriously in the infirmary of Regina Coeli prison. The period of enforced residence became, for her and the children, a memory of enforced tranquillity.[9]

Internment camps for civilians, whether Italian for Jews, British for Boers, or American for Japanese Americans, are in all cases abhorrent. They become even more inexcusable when the interned individuals have demonstrated their loyalty through years of residence, hard work, and, often, citizenship in their adopted country. They become nightmares when internees suffer, as in Italy, from lack of food, shelter, and medicine, and from official neglect and indifference. As bad as the camps were, however, life for Jews there was better than in other countries in occupied Europe. As discussed earlier, about 6,500 of Italy's 10,000 foreign and denationalized Jews had left the country by September 1939—also disgraceful, but nevertheless true. Of the 7,000 foreign Jews known to be in Italy in October 1941, at least 3,000 were new arrivals.[10] It is a tragic index of the times that most refugees were grateful for whatever they found in Italy.

As the war progressed, Italian treatment of Jewish refugees softened, and enforced residence became more common than internment. Enemy nationals joined the Jewish families under surveillance. Nor was enforced residence limited to the harshest southern mountain villages. Refugees were housed throughout northern and central Italy as well. Augusto Segre recalls that in 1942, about four hundred Yugoslavian Jewish refugees lived as enforced residents around Asti in northern Piedmont. He was able to visit and assist them on a regular basis.[11] If those four hundred people had remained in German-occupied zones of Yugoslavia, they would have been deported by the Nazis or murdered by the Croatian terrorists whom the SS allowed to operate with impunity. Italy was one of the few countries to grant them asylum.

Primo Levi, survivor of Auschwitz and prize-winning author today, also remembers a beneficiary of Italian refugee policy. Olga, a young Croatian Jew, fled to Piedmont with her entire family in 1942. While in enforced residence, she learned to speak Italian. She belonged, Levi remarks, "to that flood of thousands of foreign Jews who had found hospitality, and a brief peace, in the paradoxical Italy of those years, officially anti-Semitic."[12] Hospitality is a strange word for enforced residence, but those were strange times. Olga lived gratefully in Italy until the German occupation. Left without protection, she and her family were then deported to Auschwitz. Primo Levi met her there after the liberation. Of her entire family, only she survived.

Finally, it must be noted that until the German occupation, Mussolini's government did not release a single Jew to the Nazis for deportation. The Germans were unable to secure even the German refugees on Italian soil. Dr. Carltheo Zeitschel from the German Embassy in Paris reported after a visit to Rome:

The German Embassy in Rome has for years the strictest orders from Berlin not to do anything that might in any way disturb the friendly relations between Italy and Germany. It is unthinkable, it seems, for the German Embassy in Rome to touch such a burning subject as the Jewish question in Italy. [13]

Also, as will be seen, Italian government officials protected both indigenous and refugee Jews in Italian-occupied territories in Croatia, Greece, and southern France, despite considerable German pressure there. [14] In contrast, the Vichy French authorities agreed to deliver foreign Jews to the Nazis for deportation in July 1942, several months before German armies entered unoccupied France, and actually handed over seven thousand by August. [15] They withdrew the protection that Fascist Italy never denied its refugees.

While Jews in Fascist Italy were free from the danger of deportation, and while conditions were worse in other countries, daily life during the war remained difficult. First of all, arrests, internment camps, and enforced residence were not limited to foreigners. About two hundred Italian Jews were also arrested in the early days of the war, and by 1943, their number had grown to over a thousand. [16] A few victims were charged as anti-Fascists, although most active anti-Fascists had been arrested or had emigrated long ago. Others were described as Socialists, Republicans, former radicals, anarchists, Zionists, Freemasons, defeatists, subversives, or spies. One was described simply as leading a "mysterious life." [17] In fact, these Italian citizens were victims of the paranoid suspicion the racial laws had created. Their coreligionists lived in constant apprehension of similar suspicion and arrest.

In addition, as the war fanned popular emotions, ugly anti-Semitic violence began to occur in Italy. By far the worst cases took place in Trieste, where Jewish shops had been vandalized and signs reading "No Jews allowed" had appeared in store windows even before the war. Germans, Italians, Slavs, and

Jews lived side by side in Trieste and heartily disliked one another. About 4 percent of the population was Jewish—much more than the national average—and Jews played a visible role at the highest levels of society. The city always had a stronger anti-Semitic element than the rest of Italy. Furthermore, Italian tolerance and skepticism of government had never prevailed there. Trieste shared the Austrian tradition of taking laws seriously, and the laws sanctioned anti-Semitism.

After Italy entered the war, attacks on Jewish individuals and shops in Trieste increased significantly. Fascist thugs raided cafés frequented by Jews, beating up anyone they could catch. In October 1941, they assaulted the local synagogue, writing curses on the outer walls and shattering windows. Teachers allegedly let children out of school to participate. On July 18, 1942, a second assault reached inside the synagogue. Vandals destroyed sacred scrolls and books, lamps and furniture. The dates of these incidents are significant because, it must constantly be recalled, the German occupation of Italy did not occur until September 1943. Anti-Semitic violence in Trieste cannot be blamed on the Nazis. [18]

Similar but less frequent incidents occurred in many other Italian cities. In Ferrara, particularly vicious anti-Semitic tracts were distributed to the public in July and September 1940. Then on September 21, 1941, vandals destroyed the synagogue of Ashkenazi rite and beat a rabbi. [19] At about the same time in Turin, anti-Semitic graffiti began to appear on walls, especially in neighborhoods near the synagogue. On the night of October 14, 1941, incendiaries with gasoline tried unsuccessfully to ignite the synagogue itself. Then on October 15, 16, and 17, vicious posters calling for death to Jews, accompanied by long (and according to Emanuele Artom, often inaccurate) lists of local Jewish names and addresses, appeared along Turin's main streets. [20] Artom twice suggested in his diary that German agents may have been responsible for these outrages, but he had no proof.[21] Certainly a brilliant university graduate from a family distinguished for generations of service in Italy would have preferred to believe that outside agitators, not Italians, were the guilty parties.

In fact, foreign provocateurs seem to have played a negligible role in the anti-Semitic violence of the early war years. Many incidents were purely spontaneous, as, for example, the attack on the synagogue in Casale Monferrato, which Augusto Segre witnessed and described as an escapade of Fascist youths who had just viewed an anti-Semitic movie at a local theater.[22] Other acts, such as the synagogue attacks in Trieste and Ferrara, were more carefully planned. They seem, however, to have resulted not from foreign provocateurs or even from Fascist pressure at high levels, but from petty rivalries between local party sections or individuals, all attempting to appear more Fascist than their comrades.[23] Police response to incidents was equally unpredictable. In his own small city, Segre found that the local police chief ignored his complaints and said he could do nothing. On the other hand, the *carabinieri* chief, a friend of his parents, was outraged and provided immediate protection.[24]

Most Italian Jews, however, not directly affected by either the political arrests or the anti-Semitic incidents, probably suffered most during the war from their sense of isolation and irrelevance. Jewish men, of course, could not be drafted for military service, nor could they contribute to military production. Indeed, in one of the most pathetic demonstrations of the absurdity of the racial laws and the depth of Jewish patriotism, some Italian Jews wrote Mussolini, begging to be allowed to fight for their country. They were refused. The government made only one exception, in the case of Umberto Pugliese, inspector general of the Naval Engineer Corps. In 1938, the racial laws had forced General Pugliese into early retirement at the age of fifty-eight. In November 1940, his desperate government summoned him as the man most qualified to raise the fleet sunk by the British at Taranto. When asked what payment he would require, he replied that he wanted nothing more than a round-trip ticket to Taranto and the right to wear his uniform with his decorations during the performance of his duty. General Pugliese completed his assignment and then quietly returned to retirement. [25]

As another example of the absurdity of the racial policy, Augusto Segre tells the story of his cousin, Bruno Jesi. Jesi's father had died from wounds received at the front during World War I. Jesi himself had lost a leg as a result of valiant service in the Ethiopian War. His military record was most impressive. Not only had he saved, at great personal risk, the lives of several wounded men in his unit in Ethiopia, but he had crossed enemy lines on horseback to bring a Catholic military chaplain to attend a dying man. On the insistence of a Catholic cardinal, Bruno Jesi received a gold and a bronze medal in January 1941, with the racial laws in full effect and with Italy at war. He was honored in a fine ceremony at an army base at Turin, in the presence of the highest military, civil, and religious authorities. He received his medals for military valor at a time when no Jews could serve in the armed forces. He died in 1943 from the delayed effect of his wounds. [26]

While many Jews might have liked to serve, many more non-Jews deeply resented the fact that they did not. Ugly accusations began to circulate that Jews were (somehow) getting rich while other boys were dying for their country. Partly to counteract such complaints, a new decree appeared on May 6, 1942. All Italian Jews between the ages of eighteen and fifty-five were required to register for labor service. Even Jews with exemptions were to be included.

Emanuele Artom's experience with forced labor in Turin was probably typical. [27] Presumably, he and his father registered immediately, as required, but they were not summoned until October. At that time, 180 men were called, divided into three equal groups, and assigned to unload wood, work on roads, and handle coal. With his customary humor, Artom describes a convert, apparently not recognized as such by the Fascists, whom the other Jews scrupulously avoided. He also remembers a man who protested that he had not been called and insisted upon enlisting immediately as a volunteer. Artom and his highly educated middle-class friends debated the possibility of formally requesting the larger bread, pasta, and rice rations to which factory workers (but not Jewish forced laborers) were entitled. The Fascists would undoubtedly not have enjoyed the joke.

The actual work was long and hard. Those in Artom's group were not accustomed to manual labor. They could not rest, drink, or smoke while working. They received only a token hourly wage. They had to wear workmen's overalls. Many victims of the forced-labor program allege that primarily middle-class Jews were called, in a deliberate effort to harass and humiliate them. Artom makes no such suggestion, but he was vividly aware of the dramatic role reversal between workers and supervisors. "I was a street cleaner," said one supervisor to Artom, "and I have passed from the street to the office." "We, instead," Artom replied, "have passed from the office to the street." After a day's hard labor, the Jews, anxious to return to their libraries or their offices, would say, "See you later. We are going to work." The guards would reply, "We, instead, are going home."[28]

Not all those eligible for forced labor were called. Women were usually not called, and the work itself rarely lasted more than a few weeks. There were exceptions, however. Artom heard that in nearby Alessandria, notorious until liberation for its fanatic Fascist section, everyone was called—men and women alike. Medical exemptions, however, could be requested in all cities. In Turin, at least, municipal officials and doctors considered these requests with elaborate attention, courtesy, and surprising concurrence.

Other personal accounts of forced-labor service generally resemble Artom's. During the autumn of 1942, Marcello Morpurgo of Gorizia worked for a time in a sawmill. He realized that the owner needed workers and had applied to the new forced labor program for them. Like Artom, Morpurgo approached the situation with an ironic sense of humor. For his first meeting with the sawmill owner, he dressed in his best suit and presented his calling card. The confused owner called Fascist headquarters, complaining that he wanted workers, not university graduates.

Work at the sawmill was hard, and Morpurgo was not a skilled laborer. He says he deliberately worked badly and wasted wood, as his little contribution to the war effort. He was soon transferred to a factory that made tiles. There he did light work in the morning, ran errands, and tutored the owner's children in the afternoon. The owner and his family were kind to him. Morpurgo also reports that medical exemptions were easy to obtain and doctors were very understanding, particularly after the first weeks when Fascists turned their attention elsewhere. Like so many Fascist endeavors, he says, the forced-labor program finally just petered out. It never ended by actual decree. [29]

In Ferrara in September 1942, Gianni Ravenna was required to load heavy boxes of fruit. Jewish women worked also, sorting the fruit. Ravenna confirms that the program slowly fell apart, but he provides an interesting twist. Many people in Ferrara, he claims, did not approve of the racial laws and regarded the forced-labor program with extreme distaste. Jews in the program began to be regarded with more favor than ever—a reason, perhaps, for ending it. [30]

Actual statistics on the forced-labor program confirm that,

in most areas, it was not executed with vigor. On July 31, 1943, a few days after the fall of Mussolini, an official report declared that 15,517 people had registered for labor. Of these, 2,410 had received temporary exemptions and 1,301, permanent ones. Of the remaining 11,806 people, 2,038 had actually worked—only 13 percent of the total registered. [31]

For most Italian Jews during the war, life simply went on, a little harder and a little sadder than before. Everyone knew families with members who had converted, emigrated, or been arrested. Many endured unpleasant anti-Semitic incidents and noticed that certain Christian friends no longer recognized them. But as the war continued and grew increasingly unpopular, Augusto Segre, among others, noticed that other old friends made a point of being seen with him. Segre's friend, a soldier home on leave, deliberately and publicly walked with him while in uniform. [32] Such an act in Germany would have put the friend in prison.

With the restrictions of the racial laws, jobs were hard to find. Carlo Modigliani eked out a living teaching at the Jewish School in Milan. When British bombing raids drove many Milanese to the country, he added to his earnings by private tutoring, and not only in Jewish families. He reached his pupils by train, by bicycle, and often on foot. [33] Augusto Segre's job was similarly extra-legal. A university graduate, he worked in the office of a small winery near Asti. His employers wore black shirts faithfully on all public occasions. Privately, they disliked the war and the racial laws. They were perfectly aware that Segre was Jewish. Most of the Piedmontese peasants Segre met at work had never known a Jew before, just as he had scarcely known a peasant. When the Germans arrived, these new friends saved his life. [34]

In addition to the difficult task of earning a living, many Jews became involved with charitable service agencies. Segre worked with an organization that recruited, trained, and supplied documents to young people wishing to emigrate to Palestine.[35] Others devoted themselves to education. Some of the most extensive relief work, however, was directed toward foreign refugees in Italy. That work was largely conducted by the Delegazione Assistenza Emigranti Ebrei, or Delasem, a most remarkable Jewish service agency for an officially anti-Jewish state.

Dante Almansi, newly designated president of the Union of Italian Jewish Communities, was the single individual most responsible for securing government permission for the founding of Delasem in 1939. It will be recalled that Almansi had been, until the racial laws, a Fascist party member and vice-chief of police. He was well connected. In 1939, he called upon former friends and acquaintances to convince them that an agency like Delasem was in Italy's best interests. It would, he argued convincingly, not only relieve the government of the onerous task of caring for unwanted refugees, but would also bring in much-needed foreign exchange. Delasem amply fulfilled both promises.

In the months before the Italian entry into the war, Delasem helped about 2,000 Jewish refugees emigrate abroad, spending about eight million lire on their behalf. During the same period, before the wartime policy of internment, Delasem also provided food, clothing, medicine, and living allowances to about 9,000 other refugees, spending another three and a half million lire. A Delasem report in July 1940 stated that about two and a half million lire came from the contributions of Italian Jews, and the balance—roughly nine million lire—came from abroad. The American Joint Distribution Committee provided about $15,000 a month for assistance programs, and the Hias-Ica Emigration Association (HICEM) supplied funds for emigrants. The Italian government must have been pleased.

The Italians and The Holocaust

After Italy entered the war, Jewish emigration became more difficult, but not impossible. Special trains and planes carried Jews to Spain and Portugal, and, with the tacit consent of the police, special guides conducted them across the frontier into Vichy France. Another 3,000 people managed to leave by the time of the armistice. Of the total of 5,000 Delasem emigrants, about 2,000 went to Spain and Portugal, 800 to North America, 600 to Shanghai, 500 to Tangiers, 400 to France and England, and smaller numbers to Argentina, Cuba, Paraguay, and Palestine.[36]

Delasem also continued to assist thousands of refugees in Italy during the war. Many of these were interned, but Delasem tried, among other things, to encourage enforced residence instead—often to the point of actually providing living quarters. Delasem workers supplied refugees with vital food, clothing, and medicine, and, whenever possible, with books, religious materials, and gifts for children. They tried to reach Jews in every remote area, helping them to locate and communicate with relatives and friends.[37] Funds continued to arrive from the American Joint Distribution Committee by way of Switzerland, and Delasem managed to function with ever-increasing difficulty even during the German occupation.

Young Mario Finzi may well be representative of the quality and dedication of Delasem workers. Finzi was the only child of two secondary school teachers in Bologna. He was just beginning to practice law in Milan when the racial laws ended his career. A highly talented musician, he moved to Paris to attempt a new career as a pianist. High praise from his teacher, invitations to give concerts, and a French radio contract all indicated future success in his new endeavor. In August 1939, however, he returned to Italy to renew his visa and could not leave. The Germans had invaded Poland. Mario Finzi began to teach in Bologna's Jewish School, and became involved with refugees. In 1940, he became the Delasem representative in his native city.

Arrested in Bologna by the Fascist government early in 1943, Finzi remained in prison until Badoglio freed him. After the German occupation of Italy, he continued his work, helping Italian Jews in hiding as well as foreigners. Giancarlo Sacerdoti, one of his students, recalls that he never carried a gun, feeling that it would be wrong to shoot another human being. In March 1944, Mario Finzi was recognized during a routine document check in his home city. He was arrested and deported to Auschwitz. There, according to Sacerdoti, unwilling to brutalize his sensibilities in order to survive, he threw himself on the high-tension wire that surrounded the camp. He left a message for his parents, begging their forgiveness. He was thirty-one.[38]

The story of the children of Villa Emma stands out as Delasem's finest achievement.[39] The spectacular rescue effort began with Lelio Vittorio Valobra, a lawyer from Genoa, vice-president of the Union of Italian Jewish Communities, and national director of Delasem. In the spring of 1942, Valobra learned from Eugenio Bolaffio, his Delasem representative in Gorizia, that a number of children had survived the terrible massacres of Jews in German-occupied parts of Yugoslavia and were hiding in the countryside around Ljubljana. He traveled to Ljubljana, then in the Italian-occupied zone. There he learned that a large group had sought refuge in a castle in no man's land, in an area overrun by partisans and not clearly occupied by either Italians or Germans. With the help of a woman who was president of the Slovenian Red Cross, Valobra obtained a car and reached the castle. He found forty-two Jewish children between the ages of nine and twenty-one. Some were Yugoslavian, but most were refugees from Germany, Poland, Rumania, and Austria. Their parents had been murdered.

Somehow Valobra managed to transport the children to safety in Ljubljana, where they stayed for a few months. During that period, he secured permission from his officially anti-Semitic government to move them into Italy. In the little village of Nonantola, about ten kilometers from Modena, the president of the local Jewish community found a suitable nineteenth-century villa called Villa Emma. Spared the agonies of internment, the children were installed there as enforced residents. The community doubled in size when about fifty more children between the ages of four and twenty-two arrived, mostly from Croatia, in March and April 1943.

Delasem workers and ordinary Modenese residents took responsibility for the support, education, and supervision of the children. School-aged children studied academic subjects, agriculture, carpentry, and tailoring. A local peasant family named Leonardi taught farm methods to children who would later apply their skills in Israel. A town doctor named Giuseppe Moreali provided free medical care. Another neighbor named Aristide Barani helped with provisioning, and took two of the smallest children into his own home. The local rabbi from Modena celebrated seven marriages.

The already remarkable story of Villa Emma became little short of miraculous after the arrival of the Germans. Shortly after the occupation began, Nazis led by a local Fascist fanatic approached the villa. It was completely empty. Approximately ninety-two children had simply disappeared. Within twenty-four hours, before most Italians were even aware of the Nazi danger, they had found shelter with local residents. They remained in hiding until liberation. Not one was ever caught.

The story of the survival of the Villa Emma children involved a whole cross section of provincial Modenese society: many children were taken in by priests at the local seminary at Nonantola; others went into the homes of local peasants; sharecroppers at one estate took about fifteen; agricultural day laborers took others into their poor homes; artisans like the carpenter Erio Tosatti took still others. In addition to homes, all the children had to have false documents. Dr. Moreali and two priests from the seminary helped solve this problem. They located an old artisan named Primo Apparuti, who made a false seal out of gratitude to a Jew who had once been kind to him. They obtained blank forms from several sources: a sympathetic communal employee in Nonantola, friends at Modena's military academy, a municipal functionary who sold them in exchange for clothes from the Delasem stocks.

Dr. Moreali, the two priests, and all who provided shelter, food, or documents for Jews, risked their lives daily. If caught and found guilty, rescuers were occasionally shot on the spot. If not executed, they were usually deported to German concentration camps, where many died from starvation, disease, hard labor, and the sadism of their guards. [40]

Similar events were occurring all over Italy. The ratio was the same everywhere: A handful of Fascist fanatics, like the one who led the Germans to Villa Emma and the others who arrested local priests and tried unsuccessfully to make them talk, were countered by hundreds who took in Jews, assisted them, or, at the very least, knew exactly where they were and kept quiet. But nowhere else in Italy were the results so spectacular. The problem of disguising ninety-two orphans, none of whom spoke flawless Italian or were familiar with Catholic ritual (essential to those hiding in the seminary), must have seemed insuperable. And yet, somehow, it was done. At least two adults involved in the story—Eugenio Bolaffio, Delasem representative in Gorizia, and Mario Finzi, Delasem representative for Emilia with jurisdiction in Nonantola—disappeared in the death camps, but all the children survived.

By the summer of 1943, Italy's independent war effort was clearly drawing to a close. On July 10, U.S. and British troops landed in Sicily, and the race for Messina began. Sicilian villagers welcomed them loudly, trampling pictures of Mussolini in the dust. On July 19, when the Allies bombed Rome for the first time, thousands who had believed the Holy City to be immune from air attack felt the fear that had become common in northern cities. A local Fascist club asked Romans for contributions to aid the bombing victims. A friend of Fabio Della Seta from the Jewish School gave some linens, and when thanked, told them he was Jewish. No one cared. [41]

At 10:45 P.M. on the hot night of July 25, 1943, Luciano Morpurgo, a Jewish author and editor prohibited by the racial laws from publishing or working, was sitting on the balcony of his apartment in Rome. He was drinking wine with a neighbor and watching the stars in the clear sky. From the streets below, he began to hear shouting and laughing. Are the people always happy, he wondered, even in these terrible times? Then cries of *"Evviva* Badoglio!" began to pierce the night air. He ran to his forbidden radio and heard the great news. [42] Mussolini had been removed. Badoglio was the new prime minister. Fascist leaders were in hiding; it was now their turn to be hunted. Badoglio announced that the war would continue, but no one noticed. Italy was in an uproar.

The next day, joyous crowds assembled everywhere. They broke windows at Fascist party headquarters. They marched on prisons in Rome and Turin, releasing political prisoners. Morpurgo noted in his diary:

On all the public buildings, swarms of workers removed the Fascist symbols; those of plaster fell quickly, those of marble and travertine had to be chiseled with difficulty. Through the streets passed flocks of boys . . . who with the same mouths that once had shouted "Duce, Duce!" were now shouting . . . "Death to Mussolini, Viva Badoglio." [43]

While most Italians celebrated, Morpurgo was among the few who understood what was coming. He quietly prepared a secret room, a hiding place, just in case.

In the days that followed, the Fascist party was dissolved, the militia was incorporated into the army, and some Fascist leaders were arrested. The Jews, jubilant at the new developments, waited for the racial laws to end. On July 27, Antonio Le Pera, director of the infamous Office of Demography and Race which had rigorously enforced the racial laws, was arrested and placed in a prison cell recently vacated by anti-Fascists freed from Regina Coeli. Telesio Interlandi, the virulently anti-Semitic newspaper editor, was also arrested. These seemed like good signs.

And yet, during his forty-five-day regime, Badoglio did almost nothing more for the Jews. After the war, he explained that an abrogation of the racial laws had been impossible—it would have resulted in violent German opposition. Badoglio not only retained the racial laws, however. He failed even to send a circular to his prefects suggesting that they ease enforcement. He did not officially end forced labor. He did not dissolve the Office of Demography and Race. With regard to the thousands of Italian and foreign Jews in prisons, internment camps, and enforced residence, he sent out a series of vague orders sanctioning the release of those not accused of political activities and those accused of mere anti-fascism. Communists, anarchists, and spies were to be held. In fact, the guidelines were imprecise and confusing. Many Jews, like Leone Ginzburg and Mario Finzi, were released, but most recent refugees remained confined. [44]

Even more serious in the long run, Badoglio took almost no measures to safeguard Jews from the possibility of a German invasion. In this regard, the Jews were not unique, for Badoglio took almost no measures to protect anyone except the king and himself. The consequences of his neglect, however, were particularly disasterous for the Jews. Despite appeals by Jewish leaders and others, Badoglio's bureaucrats refused to destroy their many lists of Jewish names and addresses. Nearly all these lists fell into German hands after September 8.

Badoglio also did nothing to warn Jews in the Italian colonies of Rhodes and Cos and in Italian-occupied Corfu of any impending danger. [45] Hiding places were not easy to secure on the islands, and the occupying Nazis rounded up and deported thousands. [46] The new prime minister did somewhat better in two cases. After considerable pressure from military and diplomatic officers, he issued instructions prohibiting the release of interned Jews to the Croats and, later, allowing Jews in Italian-occupied France to follow the retreating army into Italy. In the days just before the armistice, he also promised to help Jews in France emigrate to North Africa. The fact that Badoglio's promise came too late to save lives was only partially his fault. [47]

Despite any real change in Italy's racial policy, however, most Jews during the Badoglio period sensed that things were improving. Emanuele Artom wrote in his diary on August 7, 1943, "The other day the *Gazzetta del Popolo* [of Turin] cited the honesty of the [Jewish] Minister Luzzatti as exemplary; today his monument has been restored and on the radio the works of Jews are again presented." [48] On September 3, five days before the German occupation that would ultimately destroy his life, he noted that Jews could again publish funeral notices, hire non-Jewish domestics, go to summer resort areas, and have radios. [49] Like most Italians, Jewish and non-Jewish alike, Artom assumed that Badoglio would soon end the war, and he was willing to wait patiently until then for the end of the racial laws.

In fact, for Jews and non-Jews alike, Badoglio's forty-five days constituted a period of unwarranted hope that blinded them to a fearful reality. Very few thought about the six German divisions with one hundred thousand soldiers already in Italy in July, or about the additional troops that had poured in by September, bringing the total to at least eighteen divisions.[50] During the same period, the seven effective Italian divisions in the country did not increase. And very few noticed the unemployed Fascists, bitter, desperate, and ignored. Nursing their grievances, hard-core Fascists were becoming far more fanatical than in their days of glory. Searching for scapegoats, they were becoming more anti-Semitic than ever. Like the Germans, the Jews, and all Italians, they were simply biding their time.

5

Italians and Jews in the Occupied Territories

I N HIS MEMOIRS, Primo Levi recalled Olga, the Yugoslavian Jewish refugee who found temporary peace in "paradoxical Italy, officially anti-Semitic." [1] He did not exaggerate. Wartime Italy was indeed a paradox. Italian Jews could be arrested for no apparent cause in their own country, while their government did everything in its power to protect them in German-occupied areas. Italian Jewish doctors, lawyers, and teachers could not practice and were forced to perform manual labor, yet foreign Jewish refugees received rudimentary shelter and living allowances from the same government. Synagogues were sacked with impunity, while Jewish relief agencies were allowed to collect funds abroad and aid refugees.

Nothing demonstrates the paradox more clearly than the exceptional measures of the Italian army, Foreign Ministry, and entire diplomatic corps to protect all Jews in Italian-occupied territories. Italy occupied much of Greece in 1941, part of Croatia at about the same time, and eight departments in southern France in November 1942. In all three areas, military and diplomatic personnel, often without instructions or coordination, acted similarly. They resorted to every imaginable scheme and subterfuge to resist repeated German demands for the deportation of Jews. They ignored Mussolini's directives, occasionally with his tacit consent. They neglected to pass on instructions, made orders deliberately vague and imprecise, invented absurd bureaucratic excuses, lied, and totally misled the Germans. If the subject had not been so serious and the stakes so desperately high, the story might have acquired the dimensions of a comic opera, with befuddled Germans concluding, as usual, that Italians were blatant liars and hopelessly incompetent administrators. But thousands of lives were at stake, and the game was stark and deadly.

The game was also unique, for the behavior of the players bore little resemblance to activities in other nations. In most European countries, but especially in Denmark and in Italy itself somewhat later, individuals tried to save local Jews who were their friends, neighbors, and compatriots. Even in areas friendly to Nazi Germany such as Vichy France, Bulgaria, and Rumania, local authorities resisted German demands for the deportation of native Jews. But they rarely extended their protection to foreign Jews. In complete contrast, the occupying forces in the Italian-controlled territories of Croatia, Greece, and southern France protected total strangers—neither Italian citizens nor, in many cases, even citizens of the occupied country. The only link between protector and victim was their common humanity.

Chronologically, the story of the Italian rescue of foreign Jews begins in Croatia. After a military resistance of eleven days, the kingdom of Yugoslavia capitulated on April 17, 1941, to the invading German army and its Italian, Bulgarian, and Hungarian allies. The Germans immediately occupied Serbia, with its capital at Belgrade, and the Italians seized most of the Dalmatian coast. In Croatia, a nominally independent government was established at Zagreb under the leadership of Ante Pavelíc, chief of the Ustasha, or Croatian Fascist party. Because Pavelíc had close ties with Italian Fascists, Croatia was expected to remain within the Italian sphere of influence. In fact, independent Croatia was almost immediately divided into an Italian and a German military occupation zone, to last for the duration of the war.

During the terrible summer of 1941, Ustasha assassins ran wild in Croatia, destroying entire villages and murdering thousands of Jews and Serbs. Italian policy toward Jews began in response to this rampage. While the Germans tended to give the Ustasha free rein in their zone, individual Italian soldiers refused to look the other way. Without instructions from above, they simply gathered up Jews in military trucks, cars, and even tanks, and moved them to protected areas. Their officers, soon aware of events, did nothing to interfere. Many lives were saved, and the infuriated Ustasha ceased operations in most of the Italian zone. Meanwhile, word spread, and thousands of other Jews and Serbs fled from German to Italian territory. [2]

Julia Hirschl, a Croatian Jew, and her Viennese husband were among the many refugees who came under Italian protection. Desperately fleeing Croatian terrorists, the Hirschls found themselves in a burned-out village in Herzegovina, 1,100 meters above sea level, in the middle of a battle between the Ustasha and Tito's partisans. "Fortunately the Italians arrived," she recalls, "naturally to help the Ustasha, but at the same time they helped us refugees." The Italians protected them and helped them reach Kupari, near Dubrovnik, in the Italian zone.[3]

Of a prewar total of about thirty thousand Jews in Croatia, only a few thousand remained alive in 1942. These survivors faced a new threat that summer, when Ante Pavelíc agreed to restrain his Ustasha terrorists and allow the Germans to deport the Jews instead. The Croatian leader even promised to pay thirty marks for every Jew deported. This grisly deal had one serious drawback, however, for three to five thousand Jews had taken refuge in the Italian zone, where the authorities refused to give them up. Croatian and German officials were more than a little embarrassed. Italian occupying forces were playing the role of noble savior, amid much popular approval.

For the first time in the history of Nazi-Fascist relations, the Germans began to interfere with Italian policy toward the Jews. They had not pressed for anti-Semitic measures in Italy itself, but now, in Croatia in 1942, they did. Italians at all levels of command refused to budge. Finally in August 1942, the frustrated Germans appealed to Mussolini himself. The obliging prime minister replied that he had no objections to the deportations. He communicated this position to the Army General Staff clearly, but without detailed instructions or a timetable. Nothing happened.

The Italian response to Mussolini's communication was masterful. Foreign Ministry officials concerned with Croatia met and decided to ignore it. They made careful arrangements with army liaison officers to delay and obfuscate matters as much as possible. Bureaucratic reports began to flow, explaining that while military authorities would hand over some Jews as soon as possible, the matter was immensely complicated.

The Italians and The Holocaust

Croatian Jews subject to deportation had to be separated from foreign Jews who were exempt. Criteria needed to be established. Was place of birth to be the defining characteristic of a Croatian Jew, or should place of residence, citizenship, and family connections be considered? The army needed time.

Such evasion was not easy. With Croatians and Germans constantly complaining, most high-level Italian officials were anxious to avoid personal responsibility for the delay. A reputation as a "pietist," after all, was not good for one's career. Furthermore, military and diplomatic officers wanted to prevent the involvement of Ministry of the Interior personnel, notoriously less sympathetic to Jews than themselves. In October, the Italian Army General Staff finally decided that some concrete action was needed.

Without warning and within a very few days, soldiers rounded up about three thousand Jews in the Italian zone, settled them in a confined area, and began a census.[4] The roundup was traumatic for the victims, who were certain that they were about to be delivered to the Nazis. Tragically, there were even a few suicides. The roundup also prompted a furious response from many Italian army officers who similarly misunderstood the policy. Everyone soon realized, however, that the roundup and census were simply another ruse. The Italians could now show the Germans they were trying, and the Germans could no longer argue that the Jews constituted a security risk.

Diplomatic pressure did not cease with the roundup. After many less formal appeals, Foreign Minister Joachim von Ribbentrop himself met with Mussolini in Rome in late February 1943. The prime minister again agreed to deliver the Croatian Jews. When he conveyed that decision to General Mario Robotti, commander of the Second Army in Yugoslavia, however, Robotti protested strongly. Mussolini's response, confirmed by several sources, is classic. "O.K., O.K.," he is reported to have told Robotti, "I was forced to give my consent to the extradition, but you can produce all the excuses you want so that not even one Jew will be extradited. Say that we simply have no boats available to transport them by sea and that by land there is no possibility of doing so."[5]

As the spring and early summer of 1943 passed, the Italian problem became less one of German diplomatic pressure than one of the physical inability to protect Jews in Croatia. An Allied invasion of Italy itself seemed imminent, involving the probability that many Italian troops based in Yugoslavia would be withdrawn for defense of the homeland. Foreseeing disaster, Italian authorities again did everything in their power to save the Jews in their zone. By July 1943, roughly three thousand people had been transferred to the Island of Arbe in the Gulf of Carnero, just a few miles from the Italian mainland. After the fall of Mussolini on July 25, the Foreign Ministry repeatedly instructed the General Staff that the Jews on Arbe should not be released unless they themselves requested it. The same ministry also began desperate negotiations with other Italian agencies to arrange for the transfer of the Jews to Italy itself.

Fortunately, because Jews in Italy were soon to be hunted and deported also, those negotiations proceeded too slowly. On September 8, 1943, General Eisenhower announced the armistice, and the Italian army in Yugoslavia laid down its arms. In the resulting confusion, all but 204 mostly sick or elderly Jews on Arbe were able to go into hiding or join Tito's partisans before the Germans occupied the island. The 204 were immediately deported to Auschwitz. Roughly 275 of those who joined the partisans also died before liberation. The rest survived—roughly 2,200 out of 2,661 according to one set of figures; about 3,000 out of 3,500 according to another. The numbers are not high relative to other Holocaust statistics. Perhaps for that very reason, the exceptional effort of Italian officials to protect so few Jewish refugees in their Croatian zone of occupation was indeed impressive. [6]

Julia Hirschl and her husband were among the Jews transferred to Arbe. She relates that after the armistice, partisans helped her move to the island of Lissa. From there, a British convoy took her and many others to a huge refugee complex in the Sinai. Twelve hours after she left Arbe, the Germans arrived there and deported all remaining Jews—the men, women, and children the Italians had been protecting for so long. [7]

On his long journey home from Auschwitz after liberation, Primo Levi traveled for a time with a Greek Jewish survivor. They spent two nights at a monastery in Cracow that was sheltering Italian soldiers who had been in Greece and had been captured by the Germans at the time of the armistice. Levi remembers:

> They spoke Greek, some of them with ease, these veterans of the most compassionate military occupation that history records; they talked of places and events with colorful sympathy, in a chivalrous tacit recognition of the desperate valor of the invaded country. [8]

Levi sensed something special in these former occupying forces, but he could not have learned of the finest chapter in their story until later. He could not have known that, like their colleagues in Croatia, they had helped thousands of Jews who were total strangers to them.

Like Yugoslavia, a defeated Greece had been divided into occupation zones in the spring of 1941. Bulgaria received most of Thrace. Germany controlled Crete, Macedonia, a narrow strip of Thrace bordering Turkey, and the city of Salonika with its 53,000 Jews. Italy occupied what remained: the Ionic islands and much of the Greek peninsula, including Athens. The

German zone contained a total of 55,000 Jews. The much larger Italian zone had only 13,000.[9]

The brutal Nazi roundup and deportation of the Jews of Salonika began early in 1943. At that time, officers of the German General Staff invited the Italian General Staff to follow the Nazi example. The Italians not only refused, but insisted that the Germans spare all Jews of Italian origin. In a brief comic scene in an otherwise tragic setting, Italian consulate officials in Salonika then proceeded to define "Italianness" in the broadest possible way. They issued naturalization papers to Jews married to Greeks in the Italian zone and to their children—"minors" often as old as thirty. Any remote relationship to an Italian was sufficient, as was an Italian-sounding name. Indeed, they often demanded no pretext at all.[10] All this was done by representatives of the same government that, at home, had revoked the citizenship of Jews who had lived in Italy for years and had been nationalized as long ago as 1919!

During the Salonika roundups, Italian consulate officials presented the Nazis with daily lists of newly naturalized Italian subjects being detained awaiting deportation. In most cases, detainees were promptly released. Furthermore, scores of Italian soldiers went to detention areas each day to insist that particular female detainees were their wives. These, too, were often released.[11] The Nazis were undoubtedly not fooled. Perhaps they already assumed they would soon reach into Italian-occupied Greece as well. In any case, they were obliging. Italian military trains carried the released Jews to Athens, where they were fed, sheltered, and protected.

Their respite was short. Unlike the Jews in Italian-occupied Croatia, most Greek Jews did not survive. When the Germans occupied all of Greece after the Italian armistice, brutal manhunts began immediately. Nearly half of the 3,500 Jews in Athens were deported in 1944. Over 5,000 from the remaining Greek mainland, and several thousand from Rhodes, Corfu, and Crete soon joined them.[12] The Italians who had protected them until the armistice were gone. There was no one to help.

In France, the story of the Jews and the Italian occupation began about a year and a half later than in Croatia and Greece. Vichy France before occupation was, like Croatia and Italy, an anti-Semitic state. French Jews could not hold public office, teach, or participate in banking, real estate, or military service. Their share in the professions was restricted by quota. Their properties and businesses were subject to expropriation by the General Commissariat of Jewish Affairs.

Foreign Jews in Vichy France fared even worse. Before the occupation, thousands of refugees, mostly from Germany and Austria, were interned in abominable concentration camps where many died. On July 2, 1942, a full four months before the German and Italian occupying forces arrived, Vichy authorities agreed to deliver foreign Jews to the Germans for deportation. Police were to conduct roundups, with the understanding that French Jews would be spared. By the end of August at least seven thousand people had been delivered to the Germans, including, after Prime Minister Pierre Laval's pious insistence in July that families remain united, children under sixteen.[13]

On November 11, 1942, shortly after the Allied landings in Morocco and Algeria, the German army moved into southern France. The Italians, in turn, occupied eight French departments east of the Rhône. Technically, as in "independent" Croatia, the indigenous government remained in place, but in fact, occupying forces controlled events. In the German zone, the French police were encouraged to continue their manhunts for foreign Jews, while the Nazis watched. In the Italian zone, arrests ceased, and Jews already captured but not yet deported were released. Jews actually found themselves better off than before the Italian occupation.

The first direct confrontation between Italian occupation authorities and Vichy administrators occurred in December. The prefect of Alpes-Maritimes, a close friend of Vichy chief of state Henri Philippe Pétain and an ardent collaborator, ordered that all foreign Jews in his department be sent for security reasons to enforced residence in the departments of Drôme and Ardèche. Drôme was partially occupied by the Germans, and Ardèche, west of the Rhône, was entirely in the German zone. Jews sent there would certainly be deported. Italian Foreign Ministry officials immediately canceled the order, explaining that non-French Jews including Italians, of whom there were comparatively few, were under Italian, not French, jurisdiction. By implication, the Vichy administrators could do what they liked with French Jews, but they could not touch the foreigners. [14]

Laval immediately protested. He could understand, he said, why the Italians might want to protect Italian Jews, but why were they concerned about foreigners? [15] Why, indeed, he might have added, after having interned foreign Jews at home? The Italians, however, had placed Laval in an untenable position. He had promised to protect French Jews; how could he arrest them while allowing foreign Jews to go free? As in Croatia, but even more so in a nation with stronger pro-Jewish sympathies, native authorities did not wish to place the Italians in the role of noble savior. The Italian action, soon extended to all eight occupied departments, in effect protected French and foreign Jews alike.

In the weeks that followed, Italian occupying forces prevented other anti-Jewish measures. They refused to allow foreign labor camps in their occupation zone. They forbade the stamping of identification papers or ration books with the word "Jew," as required by a recent French law. In March, they

ordered the French government to annul all arrests and internments of Jews in their zone, including French Jews. French
police had arrested well over a hundred Jews in February and
were holding them for deportation. In Grenoble and Annecy,
Italian soldiers actually surrounded the prisons where they were
being held to insure their release.

As in Croatia and Greece, reports of Italian policies toward
the Jews spread rapidly, and thousands of refugees fled into the
Italian zone. According to a German report, an area that before
the war had contained 15,000 to 20,000 Jews held 50,000 in
July 1943.[16] Of these, 20,000 to 30,000 were foreigners. Most
refugees gravitated to Nice, where they received the necessary
residence permits and ration cards. From Nice, many were sent
to enforced residence in villages in the interior.

Enforced residence was not necessarily unpleasant. Refugees
were sent to villages in all the Italian-occupied departments,
but the largest numbers went to lovely resort areas where hotel
space and vacation homes were available because of the war.
The most frequently mentioned villages include Mégève,
Saint-Gervais, Chambéry, Vence, Saint-Martin-Vésubie, and
Barcelonnette, which all had the added advantage of being
near the Swiss and Italian frontiers, "just in case." Refugees in
enforced residence had to report to the Italian authorities twice
a day, observe a 9:00 P.M. curfew, and remain within the limits
of their village. Social contacts were not limited, and they were
free to visit restaurants and cafés and organize schools, cultural
centers, and clubs.

For Jews who had been eluding the Nazis for years, enforced
residence in the Italian zone seemed almost like freedom. Before the winter of 1942–43, the young refugee Alfred Feldman,
who lives today in Washington, had spent many months hiding
in Vichy France. His mother and sister had been caught and
deported. His father had escaped from a French labor camp for

foreign Jews and had eventually been sent to Saint-Martin-Vésubie. His son joined him there. Alfred Feldman remembers:

> I arrived at Saint-Martin toward evening and I saw something that I had not been accustomed to seeing for a long time; Jews were passing peacefully through the streets, sitting in the cafés, speaking in French, German, some even in Yiddish. I also saw some *carabinieri* who passed through the narrow streets of the town with their characteristic Napoleonic hats, and even a group of *bersaglieri* [Italian elite light infantry] with their black plumes. Everything seemed to be happening freely, there were no particular regulations concerning relations between refugees. Discussion flourished with the greatest liberty. [17]

Another survivor recalled Saint-Martin years later, and mused, "All in all, the people were not unhappy, and it would have been beautiful if that state of things could have lasted until the end of the war, but it was too beautiful to last." [18]

Needless to say, Italian protection of the Jews in their zone enraged the Nazis, and the German Foreign Ministry exerted considerable pressure for the delivery of refugees for deportation. Foreign Minister Joachim von Ribbentrop added the issue to his discussion of Croatian Jews when he met Mussolini in Rome in late February 1943. Hans Georg von Mackensen, German ambassador to Italy, also had at least two conversations with the prime minister on the subject. As with the Croatians, Mussolini apparently told the Germans everything they wanted to hear. In a telegram on March 18, 1943, Mackensen reported that Mussolini had said:

> This is a question with which the [Italian] Generals must not meddle. Their attitude is the result not only of lack of understanding, but also of sentimental humanitarianism, which is not in accord with our harsh epoch. The necessary instructions will there-

fore be issued this very day to General Ambrosio, giving a completely free hand to the French police in this matter. [19]

As proof of his intentions, Mussolini subsequently sent Guido Lospinoso, a former police inspector from Bari, to establish a Commissariat for Jewish Affairs at Nice. Lospinoso was a personal acquaintance of the prime minister, with a reputation for efficiency and energy. The Italian message to the Germans was clear. If Italian Foreign Ministry and military officials were reluctant to cooperate with German demands, the Italian police and the notoriously more anti-Semitic Ministry of the Interior would simply bypass them. The Germans were delighted. Heinrich Müller, chief of the Gestapo, stated from Berlin on April 2 that Lospinoso would "regulate the Jewish problems . . . in accordance with the German conception, and in the closest collaboration with the German police." Lospinoso had, Müller added, already been in France for several days. [20]

Another brief comedy began. On April 5, SS Colonel Dr. Helmut Knochen, chief of German security police in Paris, informed Berlin that "nothing is known of [Lospinoso's] journey." [21] On April 7, Müller in Berlin insisted that "Lospinoso has been in France for some days." [22] By April 8, Knochen had finally learned that Lospinoso had been in Menton for three days, but had returned to Rome. [23] A month and a half later, on May 24, Knochen was still complaining that "we know nothing of [Lospinoso's] possible presence in the Italian zone." [24]

On May 26, relieved SS agents in France finally discovered that Lospinoso had set up headquarters in a villa near Nice. The man himself, however, remained elusive. As late as June 23, Knochen complained that Lospinoso was still "evading a visit to the Supreme Chief of the SS . . . yet at the same time establishing contact with the Chief of the French Police about the application of the anti-Jewish measures."[25] Then on July 7, Lospinoso failed to appear at an arranged meeting with German security police in Marseilles. He sent a representative, who immediately declared that he had no authority to make decisions about the Jewish question. The Germans would have to speak with Lospinoso himself![26]

As in Croatia, however, Italian authorities realized that some action was required to appease German wrath. Thus between May and the September 8 armistice, they intensified their efforts to send Jews away from coastal areas to enforced residence in the interior. The Nazis were far from satisfied. They complained that the transferred Jews were lodged in luxury hotels in fashionable spas, while the thousands remaining along the Côte d'Azur dined in the best restaurants, lived comfortably, and attempted to undermine Italian-German friendship. There was an element of truth in their charges, but Italian authorities could again claim that they were trying.

Mussolini's fall in July did not alter Lospinoso's official status, but it did provide him with a welcome excuse for further delay. He carefully informed the Germans on August 18 that he would have to return to Rome for new instructions. In fact, however, the nature of his problems had changed, for the Badoglio government, anticipating the still secret armistice, decided in August to withdraw from most of occupied France. The Italian army would attempt to hold only a vastly reduced area around Nice. On August 28, Italian officials agreed that the Jews should be allowed to accompany the army when it withdrew. Jewish relief agencies hired fifty trucks to bring refugees in Haute Savoy back to Nice and, they believed, to safety.

The Badoglio period also witnessed the Herculean efforts of Angelo Donati, a Jewish Italian from Modena, to organize a massive rescue operation. Donati had served as a liaison officer between the French and Italian armies during World

War I. After the war, he had helped found and direct a French-Italian bank in Paris. He became involved with German Jewish refugee relief after 1933. When the Germans occupied northern France in 1940, he moved to Nice and dedicated his considerable talents to refugee assistance. [27]

Donati's activities span the entire period of Italian occupation in southern France. In December 1942, when the prefect of Alpes-Maritimes wanted to evacuate foreign Jews into a German-occupied department, Donati first alerted Italian authorities. In March 1943, when Lospinoso arrived in Nice to begin his duties as commissar for Jewish affairs, Donati met, befriended, and advised him. Donati cooperated fully in the transfer of foreign Jews from Nice to enforced residence in Haute Savoy—a move that temporarily stalled the Germans and located Jews near the Swiss and Italian frontiers. Donati subsequently petitioned the Badoglio government to permit those same Jews to withdraw with the Italian army back into the soon-to-be reduced occupation zone around Nice.

Donati knew that thousands of Jews could not remain permanently concentrated around Nice, practically surrounded by Germans and totally dependent on the protection of the crumbling Italian army. During the last days of August and the first week of September, he made a last heroic effort to save his people. On the morning of September 8, after desperate negotiations with Italian officials, British and U.S. representatives at the Vatican, and the American Joint Distribution Committee, he established a rescue plan: the Badoglio government agreed to provide four ships, the British and Americans agreed to permit thirty thousand Jews from France to land in North Africa, and the "Joint" agreed to finance the vast move. The armistice, signed by Badoglio, was not scheduled to be made public until the end of the month. The ships would sail well before then. [28]

The premature announcement of the armistice caught everyone but the Germans unprepared, destroying all hope of implementing Donati's plan. The Italians clearly could not hold Nice, or even keep the Germans out of their own country. The army immediately disintegrated and Italian soldiers scrambled back across their frontier. As in Croatia and Greece during the same period, the Jews were left unprotected.

The Nazis entered Nice on September 9, angry and determined to take revenge for the ten months of Italian interference with their Final Solution. In addition to more than five thousand French Jews living in Nice at the time, there were at least sixteen thousand Jewish refugees in the city officially, and probably another two thousand there unofficially. At least another two thousand had left their enforced residences and descended on Nice in the early days of September, as rumors of the reduced Italian zone and Donati's escape plan filtered through the countryside. Most of the refugees were foreigners. They did not speak French. They knew no one in Nice. They had no plans, no hiding places, and with the disintegration of the Jewish relief agencies, no money. They were totally helpless.

The Jews of Nice, French and foreign alike, were caught in the most ruthless manhunt of the war in Western Europe. For more than a week, the Nazis searched every hotel and boarding house in the city, room by room. They also searched all trains leaving the city, so no one could escape. They ignored even valid documents, arresting and beating people who simply "looked Jewish." They physically searched every male, and sent every circumcised victim, together with all the men, women, and children in his household, to the notorious French holding camp at Drancy. From there, the trains left for Auschwitz. For 1,326 desperate refugees and 494 Jews born in France, a long odyssey of escape reached a terrible conclusion. The Italians had given them only a brief respite. [29]

Jews still in the French countryside on September 8 fared

somewhat better. While many were caught and deported when the Germans entered the Italian zone, some escaped into the mountains and joined the French partisans. Others hid with French families or crossed the border to Switzerland. About 1,100 others, too far from Switzerland, followed the retreating Italian army across another frontier, hoping to find an Italy at peace. They entered, instead, a country as strictly occupied as the one they had left. In the next year and a half, their fate became linked with that of the Jews of Italy.

Many of the Jews to follow the Italian army after the armistice left from Saint-Martin-Vésubie, a French village located 60 kilometers north of Nice and just a few kilometers from two mountain passes leading into northern Italy. Saint-Martin lay at an altitude of 1,000 meters above sea level. The nearby passes were both over 2,400 meters. At least 225 Jews lived in enforced residence in Saint-Martin, but over a thousand panic-stricken refugees collected there as the news of the Italian collapse spread. [30]

Between September 8, the date of the Italian armistice, and September 13, when the Germans arrived to stop the exodus, about 1,000 men, women, and children fled from Saint-Martin over the rugged passes into Italy. For the strongest, the flight lasted five or six hours; for the old and the very young—and there were many—it was much longer. One man, who later died of a heart attack in an Italian hospital, was eighty-four, and several babies, born in Saint-Martin, were under a year. Some refugees traveled in groups and some in small family units. Many accompanied the hundreds of Italian soldiers who had chosen the same flight. Soldiers helped carry their luggage and even their babies. [31]

The exhausted refugees and soldiers came out of the passes into two little Italian villages, Valdieri and Entraque, in the province of Cuneo southwest of Turin. They were treated kindly, fed bread and coffee, and given two large rooms where they could sleep on straw on the floor. One survivor remembers, "Our hearts filled again with hope: the Italians were so good, everything would work out for the best." [32] As their panic eased, they began to wonder why they had come. Alfred Feldman explains that they had vaguely expected the Germans to occupy France and the Americans, Italy. [33] But in Valdieri and Entraque, the Americans were not to be seen. Ominously, the Germans had occupied nearby Cuneo on September 12.

Most refugees finally realized that Valdieri and Entraque, however friendly, were dangerous traps. The Nazis, aware of the mountain passes, would soon come looking for them there. The youngest and strongest quickly left the two villages to hide in the mountains. Many others could run no longer. Winter was coming. Children and old people, with no money and no heavy clothing, could not survive in the wilderness. They found lodgings in the two villages.

On the morning of September 18, a poster appeared in villages near the passes, demanding that all foreigners present themselves to the German SS occupying forces by 6:00 P.M. that night, on pain of death. Italians protecting foreigners, the poster added, would also be shot. [34] The original text of the poster apparently used the word "Jew" instead of foreigner. The SS realized, however, that most local residents had never seen a Jew and would scarcely understand the term. Foreigners were more easily recognizable.

To encourage surrender, one SS soldier was sent to Valdieri and one to Entraque. Together they arrested about 349 Jewish refugees from southern France. These 349 included at least 119 Poles, 56 French, 42 Germans, 34 Hungarians, 25 Austrians, 22 Belgians, and 20 Rumanians. [35] Many had been eluding the Nazis for years. In country after country, they had found the courage to give up homes or temporary refuges to flee again. Now the Nazis reached them even in the remote mountain valleys of northern Italy. They had no more strength to run.

Natan Frankel, a thirty-three-year-old engineer from Warsaw, personally led a group over the Alps. On September 18, he learned that his entire group planned to give themselves up. The local family sheltering him and his wife urged him to remain in hiding. He insisted that his place was with his people. He and his wife surrendered. They both died at Auschwitz. [36]

The 349 were taken to an old army barracks in Borgo San Dalmazzo, the nearest town. There they were held under guard for two months. A few managed to escape, and many fell ill and were taken to nearby hospitals. On November 21, 1943, about 330 were deported. Their sealed boxcars carried them back to Nice, then to Drancy, and finally, in December and January, to Auschwitz. No more than 9 are known to have survived. [37]

On the gray November morning when the prisoners marched to the boxcars that were to carry them back to France and ultimately to Auschwitz, parish priest Don Raimondo Viale of Borgo San Dalmazzo stood on his church steps with a friend, watching helplessly. The priest had recently been imprisoned as an anti-Fascist. He was at that moment hiding about thirty Jews from France in his church, and he could not endanger them. His friend was freer to act. A mother with two young daughters, ages five and seven, marched past. The man recognized them, for their father, also a prisoner, had been in the local hospital. Profiting from a moment of inattention on the part of the SS guards, the man tried to lure the two children away from the group. The mother had spent years eluding the Nazis in France. Now she saw the attempt, failed to understand, and began to scream. She reclaimed her daughters, and they marched on to their deaths. [38]

About 750 refugees remained in the mountains of the province of Cuneo. Their story during the year and a half that followed is a replica of the experiences of Jews in occupied Italy generally. Many received help in one form or another from the exceptional Don Viale. The parish priest found hiding places, provided false documents, and distributed funds essential for survival. He and trusted assistants, many of them local parish priests, also accompanied many refugees to Genoa. There they introduced them to Don Francesco Repetto, secretary to the archbishop, Cardinal Pietro Boetto. Don Repetto lodged the refugees in seminaries, monasteries, and convents throughout the city, where they waited for guides to take them to Switzerland or south to the Allied lines. [39]

Most of the funds that Don Viale distributed came originally from the American Joint Distribution Committee. Deposited first in London, they were transferred to Rome with the help of the British ambassador to the Vatican. Those destined for the Jews from Saint-Martin-Vésubie were sent first to Don Repetto in Genoa, then to Don Viale in Borgo, and finally to parish priests in tiny villages throughout the province of Cuneo. [40]

Some money was also distributed by Delasem delegates under conditions that defy the imagination. Most early Delasem couriers were Jewish, and they had to travel on trains where control agents demanded to see their false documents. Body searches were not infrequent. Couriers needed explanations for their large amounts of money and for their presence in remote areas. They also needed nerves of steel. Not surprisingly, as networks of courier-priests developed, they tended to replace Jewish couriers. The priests pretended the funds were for the distribution of parish news bulletins in isolated areas.

Don F. Brondello, assistant parish priest of tiny Valdieri, tells the story of a distinguished-looking, elderly gentleman named Guido De Angeli who appeared at his church one autumn day with Delasem funds. De Angeli asked the priest if, when he distributed the money, he would remind the recipients that the next day was Yom Kippur. "I didn't know exactly what that word meant," Don Brondello relates, "But I obeyed the request precisely. In every case, at the word Kippur I saw many faces brighten, and I heard many affectionate words directed toward De Angeli."[41]

In addition to the priests and the Delasem delegates, many other Italians offered assistance to the Jews of Saint-Martin. Giuseppe Tiburzio, an Italian officer, convinced a Belgian Jewish father that his nine-year-old daughter, Paola Gotlieb, could not survive the winter in an open mountain hut at an altitude of 1,700 meters. After promising the father to raise the girl in the Jewish faith, he took her to his parents in Venice. The father was caught and died at Auschwitz. Paola survived, and the Tiburzio family, despite their love for her, gave her up to an aunt living in England after the war. In 1955, Giuseppe Tiburzio wrote, "What I did appeared then, as now, perfectly natural, and I believe that in my place, many others would have done the same."[42]

Other Italians tried to escort Jews into Switzerland. Luciano Elmo, a Milanese lawyer, recalls the supreme difficulty of trying to move foreigners through public places in a country teeming with Italian and German police. Elmo had taken refuge from the bombing of Milan in his wife's house in Borgo. When the Jews of Saint-Martin came down from the mountain passes, thirty found lodgings with him. He provided them with false documents and then, in groups of five or six, took them by train to Milan, en route to Switzerland. He remembers:

We used to leave Borgo on the 4:15 morning train. I distributed one Jew in each car, with instructions to pretend to sleep; thus if a control agent came, they could produce their false identity cards with a sleepy air. Not one of them spoke a single word of Italian. [43]

In some cases, even government bureaucrats from Mussolini's puppet regime at Salò seem to have treated Jewish refugees with consideration. Letters of thanks from the Jews of Saint-Martin who hid in the commune of Demonte during the last year of the war expressed gratitude to officials of the prefecture and even to the local marshal of the *carabinieri*. [44]

Not all Italians, of course, acted with courage or even common decency, and not all refugees survived. Several were caught and deported. Several others were executed in the province of Cuneo as real or supposed partisan activists. Sometimes the executioners were Germans; sometimes they were Italians. The last and perhaps most terrible atrocity to befall the Jews from Saint-Martin occurred at the very end of the war, and was a purely Italian affair. On the evening of April 25, 1945, Fascist militiamen seized six Jewish refugees from a prison at Cuneo, where they had been held since their arrests that spring, and murdered them in cold blood. The oldest was fifty-three; the youngest, only seventeen. They had crossed the Alps in September 1943. Italy had represented their last hope of survival, and Italy had, in the end, failed them. [45]

Leaving aside for the moment the many Italians at home who aided or failed to aid Jews, the behavior of Italian officials in occupied territories remains to be explained. Why did they act as they did? The Jews they helped were not friends, neighbors, or even co-nationals. Their own government was officially anti-Semitic. They themselves had shown no heroic tendency to protest when Italian Jews were forced out of the army or the Foreign Ministry. They had stood by when police shipped foreign Jews in Italy to internment camps. Why, when Germans tried to deport foreign Jews, did they behave differently?

The Italians and The Holocaust

It should be noted that most Italians dealing with Jews abroad probably had no direct experience with anti-Semitism at home. The tiny size of the Jewish community—one-tenth of 1 percent of the population—and its concentration in larger cities meant that most Italian soldiers and diplomats, like most Italians generally, knew almost no Jews at all. They may or may not have found the racial laws distasteful and the Ministry of the Interior bureaucrats who enforced them reprehensible. But one rarely risks a career to protest something one has not directly experienced.

On the other hand, Italians in the occupied territories faced an enormous "Jewish problem" every single day. They could not ignore the massacres of Jews and Serbs in Croatia, the roundups and deportations in Croatia and Greece, or the manhunts for thousands of destitute refugees in southern France. Furthermore, the implications of the problem were overwhelmingly different, for if in Italy Jews were being persecuted, in the occupied territories they were clearly being murdered. In 1941 and early 1942, Italian soldiers in Croatia acted spontaneously to save Jews and Serbs from murder on the spot. By mid-1942, when Nazis began to demand Croatian and Greek Jews for "resettlement in the East," most Italian diplomats and officers understood that deportation also meant murder. [46] The distinction between internment camps in southern Italy and "resettlement in the East" was a distinction between hardship and death. While Italians might overlook the first, they would not abet the second.

The peculiar blend of little direct experience of anti-Semitism at home and daily contact with persecution and murder abroad explains statements by Italian officials that would otherwise smack of hypocrisy or outright lying. For example, an Italian chief of staff in Mostar, near the Dalmatian coast, refused to permit deportation of Jews from that city on the grounds that Italians granted full equality to all residents. [47]

Italians and Jews in the Occupied Territories

After 1938, that clearly was not true. An Italian consul general in southern France, when denying a similar demand, stated that he would apply the same legislation as at home, for it was "a humane legislation."[48] It is hard to label internment camps, expulsion from professions and schools, and denial of nationality "humane," but that official may never have seen his country's racial laws at work. He had surely seen victims of anti-Semitism in southern France.

Nevertheless, Italian officials might have stood aside. After all, French bureaucrats, German army officers, and thousands of frightened, ambitious, or merely indifferent public officials in other occupied countries simply pretended they did not know about, or could not influence, events. Even most Italians, when the Germans in turn occupied their country, chose to ignore the deportations. Why did Italians abroad act differently?

The Jewish question in the occupied territories was intricately related to Italian perceptions of their own honor, prestige, and independence in the Axis partnership. That image had suffered greatly since the beginning of the war and the revelation of Italian military weakness. The German army had bailed out the Italians twice, in Greece in April 1941, and in North Africa later the same year. Italian pride had been hurt, and public officials were sensitive to challenges to Italian sovereignty.

Nor were the challenges imaginary. In all areas where Italians ultimately resisted German demands for the Jews, they already nursed grievances against their ally. In Croatia, Italians had expected to occupy the entire new state, only to be forced to divide it with the Germans. Adding insult to injury, the Germans and the Croats then made a deal to deport Croatian Jews without even consulting the Italians. In Greece, the Germans had easily taken Athens in April 1941, after the Italian military stalemate. They then delivered it to the Italians for occupation. Humiliating Nazi interference in Athens continued, and German-sponsored groups of Greek students attacked Jews there throughout the period of Italian occupation. In southern France after November 1942, Italy had occupied most of the region east of the Rhône with little difficulty, but actual jurisdiction in the departments nearest the German zone was often unclear. Significantly, it was in this border area, in Ardèche and Drôme, that Italian, German, and French differences over the treatment of Jews in France first emerged.

Italian diplomats and military officers, with their injured pride and their grievances against the Germans, were determined to resist any demand that appeared as an encroachment upon their sovereignty. German demands for the Jews clearly fell into that category. Furthermore, Italians feared that submission to those demands would weaken their authority over the occupied peoples and complicate the job of maintaining order. In both Croatia and southern France, they were dealing with nominally autonomous governments that wanted to cooperate with German deportation decrees. Italian acquiescence would have reduced their own role to that of a mere accomplice. In addition, in Greece and southern France where a majority of the population remained mildly sympathetic to the Jews, Italian opposition to deportations could serve as a wedge between citizens and local pro-Nazi contenders for power. In all areas, Italian submission to German deportation demands would have made them look like weak junior partners in the Axis alliance, unworthy of the respect of those they meant to rule.

To some extent, their first spontaneous responses to the Jewish question also committed Italians to consistent resistance to German demands. Thus, in Croatia, after Italian soldiers rescued Jews from Ustasha terrorists, it would have been difficult for Italian officers to deliver them up for deportation later. Local Croatians would have concluded that the Italians were afraid of the Germans. Similarly, in southern France, after Italian officials publicly opposed the transfer of foreign Jews from the Italian to the German-occupied zone for internment—a decision probably made as much to insure Italian authority over Nazi and French police as to safeguard Jews—it was difficult to alter that policy. Concessions or changes would appear as weakness.

Finally, some evidence exists that with regard to Jews in the occupied territories, Italian officials acted with an eye on a future reckoning of accounts. By early 1943, many knew the horrors that resettlement in the East entailed. By about the same time, German defeats at Stalingrad and in Africa left little doubt about the outcome of the war to all but the most fanatic. Italy shared with Germany an ideology and a responsibility for an aggressive war. Many of her less fanatic leaders did not wish to share responsibility for the Holocaust as well.

But when all is said, something still seems missing. Bureaucrats in other nations suffered wounded pride, yet often hastened to ingratiate themselves with those in power. As late as 1944, Hungarian bureaucrats who knew the war was lost and were not yet implicated in Nazi atrocities did not hesitate to deliver their own, not foreign, Jews for deportation. Furthermore, from the Italian point of view there were often good reasons why protection of the Jews was not in the best interest of officials or of the country at large. Resistance to German demands not only jeopardized personal careers, but weakened the whole alliance on which Italian security during the war depended.

When all the logical reasons for and against cooperation in the Holocaust are weighed and measured, it is apparent that decency, courage, and humanity often tipped the balance. The soldiers who instinctively saved Jews and Serbs from the Ustasha did not act merely from calculation or a dislike of Germans.

The Italians and The Holocaust

Italians who issued passports to Greek Jews with Italian-sounding names in Salonika or went to internment camps to claim their "wives" were not motivated by threats to their nation's sovereignty, for Salonika was clearly in the German zone. Italian officials during the confused Badoglio period who remembered to instruct authorities on Arbe not to release interned Jews to the Croats unless Jews themselves requested it, and who negotiated frantically to find places for those same Jews in Italy, were no longer motivated by injured pride or concerns of sovereignty. They were preparing to abandon Croatia, and were acting to save lives. Italian peasant soldiers who carried Jewish children over the Alps from France to Italy would not have understood complicated behavioral analysis. They too were acting to save lives. Not the lives of friends, neighbors, coreligionists, or countrymen. Just lives.

Italian soldiers, officers, and diplomats in Croatia, Greece, and southern France restored a glimmer of honor to the shabby history of Fascist Italy. They proved that many Italians had not succumbed to twenty years of Fascist rhetoric. In the darkest hours of the Holocaust, they proved that some Christians in public positions cared about the fate of the Jews and were willing to act. They were brave, decent, and far too few.

6

Rome, 1943:
The October Roundup

ROMANS venturing into the streets near the old Jewish ghetto in the early hours of Saturday, October 16, 1943, must have understood instantly that the relative tranquillity of the first six weeks of German occupation had ended. In the rainy darkness, German SS security police were surrounding an area of several blocks lying adjacent to the ancient Roman Theater of Marcellus and across the Tiber from Trastevere. The area housed about four thousand of Rome's twelve thousand Jews. After blocking passages in and out of the ghetto, the SS struck. It was 5:30 A.M., and most people were still asleep.

As armed guards outside every building fired indiscriminately to keep residents inside, two or three SS men pounded on doors. On entering apartments, they immediately cut any existing telephone wires. Then they ordered inhabitants into the street. Foggy with sleep and often still in their night clothes, the terrified victims had no choice but to obey.

The Italians and The Holocaust

Despite the darkness and the confusion, few escaped. Some young men, believing the raid to be a labor conscription, fled along the rooftops. Two courageous mothers, together in an apartment with four young children, barricaded the door with a heavy marble table and crouched behind it. In silent terror, they waited while the SS tried to break in. Finally convinced that no one was home, the police left and the women and children were safe. [1] There were few other fortunate exceptions that tragic morning. More common was the case of forty-four-year-old Settimio Calò. He had left his home before dawn to queue for cigarettes. When he returned, he discovered that his wife and nine children were gone. Their beds were still warm. [2]

Once in the streets, many were immediately herded into waiting trucks. Such was the case with the family of Marco Miele, a baby of about eighteen months. As the truck drove off, the cries of an old aunt who had been left behind aroused the pity of an unknown Catholic woman passing by. She screamed to the Nazis that the baby was hers, and a Catholic. They believed her, and Marco Miele was saved. [3]

Many other victims in the old ghetto were herded toward the ruins of the Theater of Marcellus, where they waited in their night clothes in the rain and the cold. The old and the sick could barely stand. Children wailed. Families, trying to stay together, clung to each other desperately. SS guards pushed and shoved. An employee at a nearby government ministry on his way to work that morning described it as a scene out of purgatory. "Everywhere the pleas and heartrending cries of the victims could be heard, while their captors, whether violent or impassive, performed their sorry task without showing any sign of human pity." [4] Eventually trucks carried off the last of the waiting groups, and the deserted streets were silent.

Other SS police armed with lists of the names and addresses

of Jews living outside the ghetto methodically visited individual apartments. They also began early, about 5:30 A.M. They usually handed their victims written instructions, printed in German and Italian. The orders explained that the Jews had twenty minutes in which to pack food for eight days, two blankets, money, jewelry, and valuables. They were going on a long trip. Meanwhile, a police car or truck waited outside.

Twenty-nine-year-old Arminio Wachsberger, his wife Regina, and their five-year-old daughter lived just across the Tiber from the old ghetto. His neighborhood, Trastevere, housed another three thousand Roman Jews. When the SS knocked on Wachsberger's door, his two-year-old nephew was also with him. All were forced into a truck. As the truck stopped in front of his brother-in-law's building, Wachsberger took advantage of a brief moment of SS inattention to hand the boy over to the janitor's wife. "Thus," he remembered later (he was one of the handful of survivors), "the child was saved, while my daughter would die with her mother in the gas chambers at Auschwitz." [5]

As the SS police ventured away from the predominantly Jewish neighborhoods of the old ghetto and Trastevere, arrests became more difficult. Emanuele Sbaffi, a Methodist minister, was working in his office on the fourth floor of his apartment building when he saw two SS police with fixed bayonets guarding the outside door. Descending to his apartment on the second floor, he intercepted two Jewish women whose elderly father had just been arrested in front of the building. He pushed the women into his living room. The SS knocked on his door to ask about the Jewish tenants on their list. He replied evenly that he thought they had all gone away. His two fugitives were saved. Meanwhile, two other Jewish women in the next apartment jumped from their back window and also escaped. [6]

Piero Modigliani and his family were equally fortunate. At

8:30 A.M., Piero received a telephone call from a close, non-Jewish friend giving him a prearranged word of warning. After alerting his mother and brother in another apartment in the same building, he and his wife left immediately. His mother and brother, not quick enough, were still at home when the German SS police arrived. They simply did not open the door, and their doorman convinced the Nazis that they had left town. Afraid that the police, still waiting in the street, might return to break into the apartment, they descended to the ground floor and entered a typing school by an interior doorway. There, with the full knowledge of the students, they joined the class![7]

Many were not so lucky. Admiral Augusto Capon, the seventy-one-year-old father-in-law of Enrico Fermi, was captured that morning. Half paralyzed from an illness incurred in military service, he had to be carried to the car.[8] Alina Cavalieri, a distinguished sixty-one-year-old woman who had won a silver medal in World War I for nursing services at the front, was also taken.[9] The wife of Commendator Giuseppe Segre, about eighty, was seized from her sick bed.[10] Lionello Alatri, owner of one of Rome's largest department stores and prominent member of the Jewish Council, was arrested with his wife and her ninety-year-old father.[11] Arminio Wachsberger remembers many doctors and professors among the prisoners. The October 16 roundup had reached well beyond the ghetto into all social and economic groups. Altogether, 365 German SS police had arrested 1,259 people before the action ended nine hours later.[12]

Why were so many people caught asleep in their own apartments in the sixth week of the German occupation of Rome? They knew the 1938 government census of Italian Jews, constantly updated by Fascists during the war, had fallen into German hands. Were they unaware of the fate of Jews in other occupied countries? Wachsberger explains, "From Radio London we had learned about the existence of concentration camps and the provisions against the Jews but, to tell the truth, we did not believe much: we thought all these stories were matters of Allied propaganda against the Germans." [13] Stories of German atrocities during World War I had turned out to be untrue, and so, it was hoped, would these.

But had no one heard of the massacres of Jews around Lago Maggiore, or the arrests of Jewish refugees escaping into Italy from France? Surely some had. Perhaps they dismissed the stories as actions against foreign, not Italian, Jews. Since September 23, after all, most of Italy had been reorganized as the Italian Social Republic (RSI), under the nominal leadership of Mussolini himself. Freed from an Italian prison by German SS commandos on September 12, Mussolini had become a Nazi tool and ally. But he had not released Jews for deportation in the past, and they now hoped he would continue to protect them. They overlooked the limited nature of Italian autonomy.

The fears of Roman Jews were also lulled by the presence of the Pope in Vatican City. They knew, of course, that Pope Pius XII was hardly their staunch defender. [14] He had not opposed the Italian racial laws. He had not condemned occasional Catholic press articles and bishops' speeches approving religious, if not racial, discrimination. He had not tried to protect Jews in other European countries. But in Rome itself, Vatican officials had often been quietly sympathetic.

Every Roman Jew could cite cases of Vatican good will. Some individuals who had lost jobs because of the racial laws found employment there. Others who wished to emigrate received assistance. Jewish high school graduates interested in law but rejected by Italian universities for racial reasons were accepted at the Pontificium Institutum Utriusque Iuris. Fabio Della Seta remembers it as "the only Roman university institution where, in those days [1938–43], a language of almost absolute liberty could be spoken." [15] The language was Latin. Surely the Pope, a world-wide symbol of benevolence who offered employment, aid, and education to all Romans, would not allow Jews to be arrested and deported under his very windows.

Even more reassuring were the attitudes and behavior of the leaders of the Roman Jews. Dante Almansi, national president of the Union of Italian Jewish Communities, and Ugo Foà, president of the Jewish Community of Rome, have appeared earlier in this book. The former had been a vice-chief of police under Mussolini; the latter, a high-ranking magistrate. Both were conscientious civil servants whose private lives were above reproach. Both were well-connected Fascist party members who nevertheless lost their jobs because of the racial laws. Both decided then to dedicate themselves to the Italian Jewish community. Almansi served the union brilliantly, restoring order to an organization torn by dissent on the question of reconciling fascism with Zionism. With his many connections in high places, he was also instrumental in obtaining government permission to establish Delasem for the aid of foreign Jewish refugees. Foà, too, won concessions for his people, and with his integrity and dedication, he won their respect. [16]

After the German occupation, Almansi and Foà decided that Rome's Jewish Community should continue to function exactly as before. They refused to close the synagogue, or to stop or even reduce the number of services. They discouraged the circulation of alarming information. They had certainly heard rumors of the Holocaust. Settimio Sorani, local Delasem representative, later testified that "I knew then [mid-1943] as much as is known today. Everything." [17] He had listened to the refugees he was assisting, and he pleaded with Almansi and Foà to warn the Jews of Rome. They refused.

The motivation of Almansi and Foà remains a matter of speculation. Critics say they were reluctant to disperse the community upon which their power and status depended, without clear cause. The more charitable suggest that their decision was a natural product of their personalities and careers. They were conservative, cautious, rational men conditioned to believe that deals were always possible, that everything could be manipulated, and that the ruling class, at least in the short run, usually kept its word. Their apologists explain that they were determined to avoid provoking the Nazis, as the closing of the synagogue and the disappearance of the Jews might have done. They also stress the difficulty of finding hiding places so early in the occupation, before Christian rescuers understood the full depth of the danger and before false documents were available. [18]

Perhaps there is some truth in all three explanations. Like so many others, Almansi and Foà retained their faith in Mussolini and the Pope, and they feared the consequences of panic and disorder. They knew that hiding places were not easy to secure, especially for the poor, and that people caught hiding where they did not live could be arrested. Also, they knew that abandoned property could be confiscated. Hiding seemed premature. And in any case, they thought, the Allies would soon reach Rome.

To their faith in Mussolini, the Pope, and their leaders, Roman Jews added another dimension common to European Jews everywhere. The memoirs of survivors constantly echo the same phrases: "We thought it could never happen here. We had done nothing wrong. We were always loyal citizens." Polish Jews thought it could only happen in Germany. German Jews thought it could only happen in Poland. Dutch and Belgian Jews thought it could only happen in the East. French Jews thought it could only happen to foreigners in France. Italian Jews, who looked, spoke, and worked exactly like their Christian neighbors and who had known so little anti-Semitism in the past, thought it could happen anywhere but in civilized

Italy. They had always been loyal Italians, and the concept of undeserved punishment was inconceivable. To some extent, they were simply believing what they desperately wanted to believe. On the other hand, the reality of the Final Solution defied the imaginations of all pre-Holocaust Europeans, often until the gas began to flow.

Throughout September and October 1943, Roman Jews made the private, agonizing decisions upon which their lives would soon depend. Silvana Ascarelli Castelnuovo, with her five children and her parents, went from convent to convent until she found places for everyone. She and her family would survive the October roundup and the war. [19] Author and publisher Luciano Morpurgo quietly stored food and blankets in a room in a distant neighborhood, and remained at home as long as possible. [20] He, too, would survive. Piero Modigliani rented a room in a modest pension, but delayed moving until he narrowly escaped the October 16 roundup. Several of his friends, most of them affluent Jews who could afford it, acted similarly. On September 29, Modigliani noted in his diary a joke that was circulating in Rome. Tourists ask their guide where Michelangelo's statue of Moses is. The guide replies, "For some days now, he has been in the home of friends." [21]

Despite the impression conveyed by the joke, many Roman Jews, perhaps the majority, did not hide at first. Like Arminio Wachsberger, most probably considered hiding, but ruled it out as inconvenient, expensive, and premature. The Germans were behaving in exemplary fashion. Surely warning signals would precede a roundup. Wachsberger's daughter was frail and sickly. He and his wife did not want to submit her to the rigors and deprivations of hiding. He would remain alert but at home. [22] His family did not survive.

For people like Wachsberger, not privy to inside information, respectful of their elders, anxious to survive, and in no way fatalistic, a warning from the Jewish leaders might have made all the difference. So, too, might a Papal condemnation of Nazi atrocities. The unbelievable might then have become real, and the step their instincts urged might have appeared essential. Some would not have fled under any circumstances—well after the October roundup, a few shattered, bewildered souls were caught still living in the old ghetto. But for the majority, official confirmation of their fears could have saved their lives.

While Roman Jews resolved to be watchful, the signs remained difficult to read. German soldiers treated civilians with courtesy and respect. They bought watches, cameras, and souvenirs from ghetto shopkeepers, paying the full price without quibbling. Jews were reassured, as the SS intended them to be. For the fate of the Jews had been decided. On September 12, SS Major (soon to become Lieutenant Colonel) Herbert Kappler, chief of the German security police in Rome, had received a telephone call from the Berlin office of SS Chief Heinrich Himmler, informing him that the Jews were to be deported. On September 25, Kappler received another message that said in part:

> All Jews, regardless of nationality, age, sex, and personal conditions must be transferred to Germany and liquidated. . . . The success of this undertaking will have to be ensured by a surprise action and for that reason it is strictly necessary to suspend the application of any anti-Jewish measures of an individual nature, likely to stir up among the population suspicion of an imminent action. [23]

Deception was the order of the day.

The first blow fell the following evening, when Almansi and Foà were summoned to a meeting in Kappler's office at 6:00 P.M. Kappler did not mince words. He informed the two men that the Germans considered Jews among their worst enemies, and would treat them as such. But, Kappler added, according to Foà:

> It is not your lives nor those of your children we will take, if you fulfill our demand. It is your gold we want to provide new arms for our nation. Within thirty-six hours you must bring me fifty kilograms of gold. If you do so, nothing bad will happen to you. If you do not, two hundred of you will be taken and deported to Germany. . . . [24]

Fifty kilograms of gold is the equivalent of more than 110 pounds. Kappler extended his deadline to forty and eventually to forty-four hours. During that period, Foà collected donations at his office at the synagogue. At first, word spread slowly, but by the afternoon of the first day, a long line had formed. Most of the richest Jews were in hiding or otherwise out of touch. Donations came mainly from Jews in the ghetto and Trastevere. Individuals gave a ring or two, or perhaps a single chain. Foà later recalled that the people "deprived themselves of every dear remembrance, every precious jewel to avoid the gigantic massacre." [25] Most receipts were for an eighth of an ounce. The line moved slowly; the gold accumulated still more slowly.

As word of the extortion spread, non-Jews, including some priests, joined the line. A Roman Jew present at the time later remembered:

> Circumspectly, as if fearing a refusal, as if afraid of offering gold to the rich Jews, some "Aryans" presented themselves. They entered that place adjacent to the synagogue full of embarrassment, not knowing if they should take off their hat or keep their head covered, according to the well-known Jewish custom. Almost humbly, they asked if they too could—well, if it would be right to. . . . Unfortunately, they did not leave their names. [26]

By 4:00 P.M. on Tuesday, September 28, fifty kilograms of gold had been delivered to Gestapo headquarters in Via Tasso, carefully weighed, and accepted. The Jews breathed a sigh of relief. The Germans had, after all, said they only wanted the gold, and the Germans were, most agreed, men of honor. The Jews were reassured, and the noose tightened another notch.

The idea to extort Jewish gold seems to have originated with Kappler, but his motives are subject to interpretation. In a deposition filed at the time of the trial of Adolf Eichmann, Kappler claimed that he had disapproved of the order to deport the Roman Jews. He never claimed opposition on moral grounds. Rather, he regarded the Jews as politically insignificant, and he was reluctant to risk popular and Vatican opposition unnecessarily. A police officer by profession, he preferred to use his victims as a source of money to finance espionage activities. He also believed them to be in contact with the Allies, and thus a source of valuable information. His gold extortion scheme, Kappler claimed, was intended to convince Himmler of the great potential in Jewish exploitation. [27]

A second interpretation of Kappler's motives is distinctly less charitable. Kappler knew that the unequivocal top-secret order for liquidation of the Jews had been intercepted by German army and diplomatic personnel in Rome. He had no idea how much farther the word had spread, but he knew that the Jews, once warned, would seek sanctuary in the hundreds of churches, monasteries, and convents throughout the city. His assigned task of capturing them would become much more difficult. He conceived of the gold extortion scheme with the specific intention of reassuring the Jews, until his preparations for a roundup were complete. [28]

The less charitable theory seems the more probable. Kappler may well have regarded deportation as a tactical error, but it is unlikely that he would have questioned his orders. It is equally unlikely that by September 1943, Kappler did not know that Himmler's SS fanatics were totally uninterested in mere exploitation of the Jews. The SS in Western Russia had demanded the systematic destruction of Jewish workers, farmers, artisans, and middle-class professionals—the only elements in an otherwise unskilled population who could effectively supply and sustain the German war effort there. Did Kappler really think they would act otherwise in Italy? Did he think Himmler would be impressed by fifty kilograms of gold when he had not recognized the labor potential of millions? After the war, the fifty kilograms of Roman gold were found in the office of Ernst Kaltenbrunner, chief of the Reich Security Main Office (RSHA). The box had never even been opened. [29]

The response of Pope Pius XII to the gold extortion is also subject to various interpretations. Apologists maintain that he was so outraged by the news that he immediately offered a gift of gold. Others go so far as to say that the gift was accepted. The facts as related by Foà, who was nothing if not respectful, deferential, even obsequious to all authority, are somewhat different.

> The Holy See, learning immediately of the fact [of the extortion], spontaneously made it known to the President of the Community [Foà himself] through official channels that if it was not possible to collect all the fifty kilograms of gold within the specified thirty-six hours he would place at his disposition the balance, which could be paid back later without hurry when the Community was in a condition to do so. [30]

This "noble gesture of the Vatican," Foà went on to say, was not needed, for he was able to collect the fifty kilograms of gold from other sources.

The Vatican offer, then, constituted a loan, not a gift, and even that contribution was contingent on the failure to collect gold from other sources. Furthermore, many individuals even question Foà's assertion that the offer was spontaneous. Renzo Levi, businessman and president of the Roman section of Delasem, related that he and another Jewish leader actually requested a Vatican loan during the first hours of the collection, when contributions were coming in slowly. The Pope authorized the loan, which was never needed.[31] Whether spontaneously offered or requested, the Vatican gesture was commendable, for it relieved Jewish leaders of their terrible fear of failure. As word of the offer spread, it also reassured Roman Jews and made them feel less alone. Unfortunately, it also confirmed their hope that, in the final analysis, the Pope would stand up for them.

If the extortion of gold temporarily eased Jewish fears of something worse, events the very next day revealed the emptiness of Kappler's promises. Early Friday morning, September 29, Kappler's security police surrounded the main synagogue, which also housed the Jewish Community's administrative offices. The Nazis claimed to be searching for compromising documents and correspondence with enemy agents. They found nothing of the sort, but they seized two million lire from the safe as well as vast archival materials. The Community's documents, registers, minutes of meetings, and records of contributors found their way to Gestapo headquarters. Entire file cabinets were transported intact. "A great truck," Foà recalled, "was scarcely sufficient for loading all the material."[32]

After the war, Foà insisted that the SS police had not obtained the detailed Community lists of members' names and addresses because he had hidden them elsewhere. Several witnesses have challenged this allegation; one man claimed to have found the lists at Gestapo headquarters after the liberation of Rome.[33] But even Foà admitted that the Nazis had seized records of contributors, and these in all likelihood included addresses as well as names. The details of September 29 are less important than the fact that all lists of names should have been destroyed. And the fact that the Nazis were interested in documents at all should have constituted a warning—the very sign of pending trouble that Roman Jews were looking for. Yet still no warning issued from the shambles of the Community offices. Instead, services went on as usual in the synagogue by the Tiber. It was the eve of Rosh Hashana.

During the days that followed, the pretense of normalcy continued. The actions of some might even be labeled active deception. Many of Rome's best-informed Jews went into hiding, but their decisions were never communicated to the masses around the old ghetto. The controversial chief rabbi of Rome, Israel Zolli, disappeared from view as early as September 18, after trying in vain to convince Foà to close the synagogue and warn the people. Born in Eastern Europe in 1881, the year of great Russian pogroms, Zolli had personal memories of anti-Semitism. As a rabbi in Trieste for nearly thirty years before coming to Rome in 1940, he had talked with hundreds of Jewish refugees from northern Europe during the 1930s. He was much more wary of the Nazis than most of his native Italian colleagues. His absence from Sabbath services on September 18 and from the observance of Rosh Hashana was vaguely attributed to illness. It was not allowed to constitute a warning. [34]

Almansi himself quietly changed apartments during the first week of October. No one was told. On October 10, the day following Yom Kippur, he also closed the office of the national Union of Italian Jewish Communities and removed the archives. Not wishing to cause alarm, he carefully explained that the war had disrupted communications between Jewish communities and made his office temporarily unable to function. [35] Excuses were similarly found for the individual, unexplained arrests of several Jews on October 9. These were "special cases," everyone agreed. The victims were anti-Fascists. The implication was clear. The innocent had nothing to fear.

Renzo Levi and Settimio Sorani, directors of Delasem in Rome, also went into hiding in early October. Again no one knew, although Sorani tried in vain to convince Foà of the danger. Delasem offices closed by October 10. As the main Delasem responsibility had always been the care of foreign Jewish refugees, however, Sorani took advantage of the lull before the storm to organize hiding places and clandestine assistance networks. He began in September 1943, with just over 100 refugees, all totally helpless without money, friends, or knowledge of Italian. By the time of the liberation of Rome nine months later, his "clients" numbered 1,500 foreigners, as well as 2,500 Italian Jews, often not Romans, who had abandoned their homes and needed help and support.[36]

Sorani's fugitives hid in churches, convents, and apartments throughout the city. They received identification cards, ration books, food, and money on a regular basis from secret visitors, usually priests mobilized after Sorani was forced to go underground and directed by a remarkable French Capuchin monk named Father Maria Benedetto.[37] Thanks to the efforts of Sorani, Father Benedetto, and the dedicated Italians who helped them, only about 100 of the approximately 1,800 Jews known to have been deported from Rome during the occupation were refugees.[38] Overall, foreign Jews fared better than the Roman Jews who had lived beside the Tiber for centuries.

On Wednesday, October 13, another blow struck the Jewish community. Two railroad cars rolled up on the trolley tracks and stopped in front of the synagogue. An Italian shipping company employee informed Foà that the Germans intended to seize the contents of his two libraries. Foà was not surprised. Several German scholars and soldiers had visited the libraries during the preceding days, confiscating catalogues and indexes and warning Foà that he must remove nothing, on pain of death. Now German soldiers carefully removed everything.

The loss of what Foà rightly called "Italian cultural patrimony" was staggering. The Library of the Roman Jewish Community contained, in his words, "manuscripts, incunabula,

. . . Eastern prints from the sixteenth century, unique copies of Jewish books, numerous important documents concerning the life of the Roman Community under papal domination from the first dawn of Christianity until 1870, etc. . . ."[39] Much material had been brought to Rome by Jews expelled from Spain and Sicily in the fifteenth century. The contents of the Rabbinical Library were less precious, but still significant. Now all this material of incalculable value was heading north in two fully loaded freight cars marked "Munich."

Three days after the plundering of the library, Rome's Jewish community was violated again. As previously described, the attackers this time consisted of 365 SS police and Waffen SS men, and they did not want gold or documents or books, but human beings.[40] By the time the October 16 action ended at 2:00 in the afternoon, 1,259 people, including 896 women and children, had been transported to a temporary detention center in the Italian Military College, only six hundred feet from Vatican City. There they remained under armed guard, while a crowd of curious onlookers gathered outside.

Because Arminio Wachsberger spoke German, the SS guards at the Military College immediately enlisted his services as an interpreter. His first assignment was to calm the terrified prisoners arriving in the college courtyard. Guards were pushing and shouting words that no one could understand. Wachsberger had to explain that the prisoners were all to be sent to a labor camp in the north. Those who were young and strong would have to work hard. The sick and the weak, the elderly and the children, would be assigned light jobs to earn their keep. The prisoners were soothed and became more manageable. By his own testimony after the war, Wachsberger himself believed the story.[41]

Among the prisoners at the Military College were numerous non-Jews, rounded up by mistake. Wachsberger helped the

Germans separate them from the others. All non-Jews, Wachsberger explained, were to present themselves to the SS guards. The penalty for lying would be immediate death. [42] Eventually, the special claims of 252 people were accepted. According to Kappler's report to Berlin, these consisted of the children of mixed marriages, spouses in mixed marriages including the Jewish partners, foreigners from neutral countries including one citizen of the Vatican, and "Aryan" servants and boarders who had been caught in Jewish homes. Because SS deportation measures at the time did not apply to individuals in these categories, they were released at dawn the following day. [43]

At least seven Jews also managed to slip into the non-Jewish group. Giuseppe Durghello, his wife Bettina, and their son Angelo, enjoyed the luxury of a "non-Jewish" last name. So did Enrico Mariani and, to a lesser extent, Angelo Dina. Wachsberger knew the truth, but he did not share it. Apparently the Nazis did not check claimants against their Community lists. The lucky ones were released. So, too, were Bianca Ravenna Levi and her daughter Piera. The sources do not explain their good fortune. Bianca had not one but two typically Jewish names! [44] Among those who remained, however, there was at least one non-Jew. A nurse charged with the care of a young epileptic Jewish boy chose not to abandon her charge. She died with him in the gas chambers at Auschwitz. [45]

Wachsberger remained busy throughout that Saturday afternoon and evening. He helped the guards record the names of the remaining 1,007 prisoners. Then he was ordered to inform them that because they were going to a labor camp where many would not be able to work, they must surrender their money and valuables to help support the weaker members. The penalty for refusal would be death. A long line formed. At first the prisoners gave up everything, for the welfare of all. Gradually, however, they observed that the most valuable items were disappearing into the guards' pockets. Word spread quickly down the line, and some prisoners managed to withhold a few treasures. [46]

By now it was nearly evening, and the lack of food became a problem. Many prisoners had brought nothing with them, and the Nazis had nothing to give. Some non-Jews and many courageous relatives of the prisoners had brought packages of food and clothing to the Military College, but the guards would allow no contributions. Instead, Wachsberger was instructed to collect the prisoners' apartment keys and go to their homes under armed guard to gather food. He thought that quite reasonable until he arrived at the apartments. Then he realized that his guards had no interest in food, but focused instead on thoroughly looting every home. [47]

At the college, hunger remained a problem, for many prisoners had not eaten all day. Wachsberger was given some of the money collected from the prisoners and sent again under guard to a nearby bakery. He was also allowed to buy medicines. [48] That must have reassured him and his people. Would the SS guards bother with medicine if they intended to murder their prisoners?

As night fell, the prisoners settled down and tried to rest. They had been assigned to various rooms, with the men apart from the women and children. A thin layer of straw covered the bare floor. Sanitary facilities scarcely existed. At least one young woman went into labor during the night, with her two children at her side. The Nazis summoned an Italian doctor, but they did not allow the mother to be transferred to a hospital. The baby was born in the courtyard. [49]

The thoughts of the prisoners that night can scarcely be imagined. To the sturdy poor, the prospect of a labor camp and regular employment was not totally negative. On the other hand, the old and the weak had few illusions about the rigors of life in a German camp, or about their ability to survive there.

Nevertheless, the promise of work offered at least a possibility of survival, and a thousand desperate minds focused eagerly on that slender hope.

The consequences of that hope cannot be exaggerated. In the days that lay ahead, several young people who might have escaped declined. One young man discovered an unbarred door in the Military College, left to buy cigarettes, and then returned to his wife and child. A group of young boys found themselves unguarded at a rest stop during the trip to Auschwitz. Several others rode north in a freight car with an unbarred window. Many more succeeded in breaking the lock on a freight car door, and rode for miles with the door open. Yet among all of these, only one young man chose to escape. [50]

Why did so many others not flee? Usually their decisions centered around their families. They did not want to be separated. They thought their families would need them in the labor camp. They did not wish to subject their families to collective reprisals for their own flight. Only the certainty of death for everyone at the end of the line could have convinced the young and the strong to attempt a break-out. But, as the Nazis intended, the Jews of Rome rejected that certainty despite everything they had heard about the fate of Jews in other countries.

Nor, on reflection, were their last illusions surprising. Why would the Nazis transport Jews hundreds of miles merely to kill them? Why would the Nazis kill them when they needed workers? Why would civilized people want to kill them in the first place? These questions have no rational answers, and the Jews were rational men and women. They could not conceive of the inconceivable.

Sunday, October 17, passed much like the afternoon and evening of the previous day. The non-Jewish prisoners were released at dawn. For the others, food and space remained in short supply. The questions, the rumors, and the fear continued.

At least one question was answered the following morning. Before dawn on October 18, trucks began to collect the Jewish prisoners at the Military College. As the trucks filled, they left to drive quickly across the city. Their destination was the cargo-loading platform at Rome's Tiburtina Station. The Jews did not pass through the normal passenger terminal.

At the station, a train with about twenty empty freight cars was waiting. As the trucks arrived, guards loaded their prisoners into the cars. As each car was filled to its capacity of fifty or sixty people, its door was slammed shut and locked from outside. The prisoners waited in darkness and terror while the trucks returned to the college for more victims. The earliest arrivals waited eight hours. Finally at about 2:00 P.M., the dreadful journey north began.[51]

Most prisoners on the train continued to believe they were going to a work camp. Arminio Wachsberger found himself in a car with Admiral Capon, who had a different opinion. "We are certainly going to our deaths," he declared, but no one believed him. "You don't know the Germans," he insisted. "I saw them in the First World War."[52]

Inside the crowded freight cars, conditions barely sustained human life. For light and air, most cars had only a single narrow window, barred and high up on the wall. The prisoners were so crowded they could scarcely all sit at the same time. Sanitary facilities did not exist. Desperate prisoners usually agreed to use one small area of the car as a toilet, and then struggled among themselves to find a place as far from that spot as possible. In many cars, people tried to shield the toilet area with some sort of covering for privacy, but most efforts were futile. Grown men and women wept from shame.

There was little food and no water. The first day of the

journey was very hot, and the prisoners' thirst soon became unbearable. The train stopped briefly at Orte, one hour out of Rome, where prisoners were allowed to descend to relieve themselves along the tracks. Only fifty did so; the others did not yet realize that no better arrangements would occur. After another hour, the train stopped briefly again, to remove the first dead prisoner. No one was allowed to descend.

The train reached Florence at 8:00 P.M., but the cars remained sealed. The hot day turned into a cold night as the train crossed the Appennines. Prisoners still in pajamas or light clothes shivered miserably. Finally at noon on Tuesday, October 19, the train crawled to an unscheduled stop at Padua. One car had mechanical problems and needed to be replaced. The other cars remained sealed. Prisoners, with nothing to drink for two days, began pleading for water.

A group of Fascist railroad militiamen who heard the cries asked why the prisoners could not be allowed to drink from several nearby fountains. "They are Jews," Wachsberger heard the SS guards replying, as if that explained everything. "Yes, but they are also people," insisted the Fascist militiamen. [53] An argument ensued. Finally, one of the Fascists raised his submachine gun and settled the issue. If the Jews were not allowed to get out and drink, he would shoot. [54] The Nazis submitted.

During the next two and a half hours, the freight cars were unsealed and several people from each car were selected to bring water to the others. Women from the Italian Red Cross were permitted to visit the cars and distribute food and medicine. At least two more dead bodies were removed. No one tried to escape. On the contrary, as the cars were closed and locked, several men and boys undetected in the confusion rushed to get back on the train. They did not want to be separated from their families. [55]

The death train left Padua on Tuesday afternoon and reached the Brenner Pass in the early hours of Wednesday,

The Italians and The Holocaust

October 20. In the frigid darkness, a German crew replaced the Italian one, the cars were opened, and the prisoners were carefully counted. The train then proceeded into Austria and Germany. Late Wednesday, it stopped outside Nuremberg. Women of the German Red Cross distributed hot barley soup to exhausted prisoners who had not eaten since noon of the previous day. One wonders what those women thought.

The train continued to roll eastward all day Thursday and Friday. At sunset on Friday, as the Sabbath began, the prisoners crossed their last frontier and entered Poland. Several more had died, including a young pregnant woman, but their bodies remained in the cars. Finally, about 11:00 P.M. Friday night, the train lurched to its last stop. It had reached Auschwitz too late for the prisoners to be admitted that night. They had been in captivity for almost a week. They had been on the train for five days and nights. Now they would wait until the morning of the Sabbath for the final chapter.

As the first morning light appeared over the camp, Arminio Wachsberger peered through the small barred window and saw huge barrage balloons over the camp. He lifted his five-year-old daughter up to see the balloons. An SS guard outside the train saw her little face at the window and threw a large rock straight at her. "After such an act of barbarity against that tiny, harmless human being," her father recalled, "I finally understood that we had arrived on the threshold of Hell." [56]

An hour or two later, the freight cars were unsealed, and the Jews of Rome were ordered to descend. Stiff, weak, and famished, many could hardly move. The infamous Dr. Josef Mengele himself was waiting for them on the platform. He addressed them through Wachsberger.

Mengele explained that the strongest were to walk to a work camp, where they would perform heavy labor. The sick and the weak, the elderly, and all young children and their mothers would be driven to a light labor camp to rest. All families,

Mengele explained, would be reunited each evening. The prisoners lined up, and Mengele himself made the selection.[57] He chose about 450 for heavy labor, and directed the others to the waiting trucks.

Then Mengele introduced a new factor. He explained to the 450 people chosen for labor that the walk to the work camp was about ten kilometers. Those who wanted to ride could join the others on the trucks. About 250 did so. At the conclusion of this second selection process, 149 men and 47 women remained.[58] They were duly admitted to the camp, disinfected, tattooed, and assigned prison garb. They never saw their loved ones again.

An entry in the Auschwitz log for October 23, 1943, one week after the roundup in Rome, states the situation precisely:

> RSHA—Transport, Jews from Rome. After the selection 149 men registered with numbers 158451–158639 and 47 women registered with numbers 66172–66218 have been admitted to the detention camp. The rest have been gassed.[59]

The rest, more than eight hundred people, were driven from the railroad platform directly to the Auschwitz killing center. Still mercifully unaware of their fates, they were divided into two large groups and forced to undress and enter a large sealed room where they would shower. There they died slowly in pools of blood, vomit, and defecation, as poison gas destroyed their respiratory systems.

By evening, over eight hundred people had disappeared in the roaring crematoria of Auschwitz. Only their hair and the gold from their teeth remained behind to serve the German war effort. Among the eight hundred were the wife of Arminio Wachsberger and the daughter who had not been allowed to enjoy the balloons. Among them also were the baby born at the Military College, its mother, and her other two children. Among them were the wife and nine children of Settimio Calò, the boys who had rejoined the train to save their families from reprisals, the father-in-law of Enrico Fermi, and many, many others. They never had time to wonder why they had to die, but even with time, they would have found no reason. There was no reason. They were Jews.

Several days later, Wachsberger asked Mengele about his wife and child. Incredibly enough, no one in the huge labor camp had told him about the gas chambers, and he had continued to hope that they were well. Mengele told him his family no longer existed. Weeping, Wachsberger asked him why. Mengele gave him the standard answer. "You are Jews." [60]

On a different occasion, Wachsberger asked Mengele another question. At the time of the selection on the railroad platform, Mengele had refused to allow Wachsberger to join his family on the trucks, explaining that he was needed as an interpreter. He set out on the ten-kilometer walk to the labor camp, only to discover that it was but half a kilometer. He asked Mengele why he had allowed so many strong young people to ride to their deaths when they had already passed the initial selection. They would have been capable of solid work. "They were lazy if they were afraid of a ten-kilometer march," Mengele replied. [61]

Apart from the fact that those young people had just completed a five-day trip in crowded freight cars with little food, water, or sleep, many of them chose to ride because they did not want to be separated from their families. Mengele's policies obviously had nothing to do with obtaining good workers for Germany. Workers were expendable; they could always be replaced. The same Nazis who were spending time and money in all the occupied nations to obtain non-Jewish laborers for work in Germany, and who were, in the process, driving young men into the Resistance, were murdering strong Jewish workers in the death camps. The Holocaust was a process beyond control: it was even against Germany's immediate material interests.

The 196 men and women who remained alive that Sabbath evening now addressed themselves to the problem of survival. They had been deliberately stripped of every personal possession—clothing, photographs, letters, books, mementos—that might tie them to their pasts. They had no families and no nationality; no past and no future. They had no identity but the numbers burned into their arms.

One man died almost immediately. Of the 148 remaining men, about half went to work at the coal mines of Jawiszowice, where the average life span for slave laborers was three months; 11 survived. Forty-two went to recover bricks from the rubble of the Warsaw ghetto; 3 survived. The rest stayed to work at Auschwitz. Of these, none seems to have survived.[62]

Even less is known of the women, for only 1 of the 47 who entered the labor camp survived. Settimia Spizzichino, age twenty-two, was separated from the other women and sent to Dr. Mengele's laboratories. She was subjected to so-called medical experiments until the end of the war. The Allies liberating Bergen Belsen found her still alive among a pile of corpses. Years later she told Robert Katz, "I felt more comfortable with the dead than with the living."[63]

In his excellent book about the October roundup published in 1969, Katz listed fifteen survivors with their professions and cities of residence.[64] One had since died and one had emigrated to Montreal. The remaining thirteen lived in Italy; all but one of these (Arminio Wachsberger, a chemical executive in Milan) still lived in Rome. The youngest boy to return was fifteen in 1943; three others were sixteen and three were seventeen. The oldest survivor was forty-four at the time of his arrest. He defied all odds, for men over forty rarely survived the first selection. A French Jewish inmate on the railroad platform at

Auschwitz whispered a warning to Wachsberger. "Tell the Nazis you are under thirty." [65]

News of the October 16 roundup spread through Rome quickly, even before the prisoners departed for Auschwitz. On Sunday, October 17, the day after the arrests, the Italian Resistance newspaper *L'Italia libera* informed Romans with remarkable prescience that "the Germans during the night and all day long went around Rome seizing Italians for their furnaces." [66] Nevertheless, not a single regular newspaper carried the story. Not a single Italian government official seems to have publicly protested the German action against Italian citizens. Worst of all, not a single word of public protest issued from the Vatican. Like other Italians, priests, monks, and nuns throughout Rome, and indeed, throughout the country, were hiding Jews at great personal risk to themselves. But from the Pope himself, there was only silence.

In fact, the Pope seems to have learned about the pending roundup by at least October 9, one week before it actually occurred. Eitel Friedrich Möllhausen, acting German ambassador to Rome during the temporary incapacity of Ambassador Rudolf Rahn, learned in September that Kappler had been ordered to arrest and deport the Roman Jews. He also knew that Kappler's orders said that the Jews were to be "liquidated." Möllhausen was horrified, both because he abhorred mass murder and because he believed that the action would provoke a public papal condemnation, with adverse consequences for the German war effort.

Among other steps, Möllhausen on October 6 informed Foreign Minister Joachim von Ribbentrop of the pending action and actually used the word "liquidated." He suggested that the Jews instead be kept in Rome and be used to build fortifications. [67] On October 9, Möllhausen received the answer he should have expected. He was told, in no uncertain terms, to mind his own business. [68] At that point, if not before, Möllhausen informed the German ambassador to the Holy See, Baron Ernst von Weizsäcker, who in turn told officials at the Vatican about Kappler's orders. [69] Those officials surely notified the Pope.

Apparently both Möllhausen and Weizsäcker believed that Vatican pressure behind the scenes could forestall the SS roundup. They were soon enlightened and disappointed. There is no evidence that Pope Pius XII ever acted on his knowledge. Before the roundup, he never threatened, suggested, or even hinted that he would publicly condemn any SS action to deport the Jews of his own city.

According to Möllhausen, Vatican officials learned of the pending roundup from Weizsäcker. Even if this account were untrue, however, it is unlikely that the Pope did not learn of the Nazi plan from other sources. Too many people knew. German diplomats attached to the embassy and to the Holy See, many of whom were Catholics and acquainted with German priests in Rome, knew. Some Italian police knew. Many Italian bureaucrats responsible for census data and ordered to provide the names and addresses of Roman Jews during the week before October 16 knew. It is inconceivable that the Pope himself, with his vast information network of priests and active Catholic laymen throughout Rome, did not know.

Furthermore, the Pope had been informed of the specific fate awaiting all deported Jews long before October 1943. Diplomatic representatives to the Holy See from several Allied nations and leaders of international Jewish organizations sent him reports of the Holocaust as early as September 1942. Like everyone else, he at first regarded the reports as wildly exaggerated Allied propaganda, and he was unwilling to become an Allied tool. But the reports kept coming in from different sources, and each new one confirmed the others. The truth was inescapable. [70]

The Italians and The Holocaust

By the end of 1942, the Pope had almost certainly received the graphic and detailed report of SS Colonel Kurt Gerstein, a disinfection officer who personally witnessed a mass gassing at Belzek in August. Gerstein had first attempted to contact Monsignor Cesare Orsenigo, the papal nuncio in Berlin, but he was turned away. He then delivered his report to a Dr. Winter, the coadjutor of Cardinal Count Preysing, archbishop of Berlin, with the request that it be forwarded to the Vatican.[71] Vatican spokesmen never denied receiving it.

Gerstein, a religious Protestant who joined the SS in the late 1930s solely to investigate rumors of the gassing of German mental patients, was a strange and enigmatic figure. His report, if unconfirmed by other sources, might have sounded like the ravings of a madman. But his report was not unconfirmed. It simply repeated, with more terrible precision, the information already given the Pope by diplomats and Jewish leaders.[72]

Eventually, churchmen from all of Europe also confirmed the reports. There were, after all, millions of German Catholics, many of whom served in the army and were aware of the massacres of Jews in the East. Thousands of Catholic priests also served in the army. What the priests did not learn for themselves, Catholic soldiers told them. Thousands of other Catholic priests lived and worked throughout Europe, in close contact with the people. They too learned part of the truth, both from their own experience and from at least some conscience-stricken parishioners. They passed information along to their superiors, and ultimately it reached the Vatican. New reports reaffirmed those already received.[73]

What might the Pope have done before October 16? A private threat to condemn publicly any SS action against Roman Jews probably would not have forestalled the roundup, but it would certainly have placed the Pope on sounder moral ground. In addition, the Pope might have made use of his knowledge by warning unsuspecting Jews who felt secure in part because of his very proximity. Either publicly or privately through the good will of thousands of priests, he might have sounded an alarm and saved thousands of lives. He, of all people, would have been believed.

Pope Pius XII, however, did not just fail to speak out or exert private pressure before October 16. He also failed to issue a public protest after the roundup had actually occurred. When the news of the raid reached him, he limited himself to permitting Bishop Alois Hudal, rector of the German Catholic Church in Rome, to write a mild letter to General Rainer Stahel, German army commander of occupied Rome. The letter, delivered in the early evening of October 16, said in part:

> A high Vatican dignitary in the immediate circle of the Holy Father has just informed me that this morning a series of arrests of Jews of Italian nationality has been initiated. In the interests of the good relations which have existed until now between the Vatican and the German High Command . . . I earnestly request that you order the immediate suspension of these arrests both in Rome and its vicinity. Otherwise I fear that the Pope will take a public stand against this action which would undoubtedly be used by the anti-German propagandists as a weapon against us. [74]

Here at last was a private warning of the possible public condemnation that so many Germans dreaded. Weizsäcker believed the possibility to be very real, and in a message to the German Foreign Ministry in the earliest hours of October 17, he said so. He also declared, "People say that when similar incidents took place in French cities, the bishops there took a firm stand. The Pope, as supreme head of the Church and Bishop of Rome, cannot be more reticent than they." In the same message Weizsäcker suggested that the Pope's reaction to the arrests "could be dampened somewhat if the Jews were to be employed in labor service here in Italy." [75]

The Italians and The Holocaust

If the Pope ever had a chance to help Roman Jews, however, by October 16 it was too late. Bureaucracies react slowly. Eberhard von Thadden, a German Foreign Ministry official, sent a routine description of Hudal and Weizsäcker's communications to Adolf Eichmann, chief of the Gestapo section dealing with Jews, on October 23.[76] That day, over eight hundred Roman Jews were gassed and cremated at Auschwitz. Furthermore, the Pope never carried out his private threat. He never publicly condemned the deportation of the Jews who lived beneath his very windows.

Pope Pius XII's only public comment on the events of October 16 appeared in the Vatican newspaper *L'Osservatore Romano* on October 25–26, after most deportees were dead. The article said in part:

> As is well known, the August Pontiff, after having vainly tried to prevent the outbreak of the war . . . has not desisted for one moment from employing all the means in His power to alleviate the suffering which, whatever form it may take, is the consequence of this cruel conflagration. With the augmentation of so much evil, the universal and paternal charity of the Supreme Pontiff has become, it might be said, ever more active; it knows neither boundaries nor nationality, neither religion nor race.[77]

Ambassador Weizsäcker assessed the article in a message to the Foreign Ministry on October 28. Obviously relieved by the mildness of the Pope's comment, he wrote:

> Although under pressure from all sides, the Pope has not allowed himself to be drawn into any demonstrative censure of the deportation of the Jews of Rome. Although he must expect that such an attitude will be resented by our enemies and exploited by the Protestant circles in the Anglo-Saxon countries for the purpose of propaganda against Catholicism, he has done all he could in this delicate matter not to strain relations with the German Government and German circles in Rome.[78]

After a brief analysis of the *L'Osservatore Romano* article, Weizsäcker concluded, "There is no reason whatever to object to the terms of this message . . . as only a very few people will recognize in it a special allusion to the Jewish question."

Weizsäcker was wrong in that last conclusion, for many people undoubtedly understood the reference to "paternal charity" regardless of "religion or race." But he was right in feeling relieved. Pope Pius XII had hardly condemned a specific German action or warned others of pending danger.

Even a strong and immediate papal condemnation of the October arrests would have been too late for the 1,007 prisoners awaiting deportation and death. The Pope could not have saved them. For most Roman Jews still free after October 16, a papal warning to hide was no longer necessary. They now understood that they could be arrested at any time. Nor did hundreds of priests, monks, nuns, and Catholic laymen need the Pope to tell them to take in the Jews, because they were already acting. For most Romans, then, a papal condemnation after the event would have made little difference.

Outside Rome, however, the situation was different. Surprisingly enough, many Jews did not immediately learn about the October 16 roundup, or about raids in Milan, Turin, and Trieste during the same month. As will be seen, organized arrests of Jews in Florence, Genoa, Venice, and other cities with small Jewish populations did not begin until November or December. Many Jews continued to live at home or, at the very least, frequent Jewish institutions until that time. If the Pope had publicly said what he knew—if he had declared, clearly and unequivocally, that the Nazis were systematically deporting all Jews, without exception, in every country they occupied, and that once they had begun in any individual country, there was no reason to believe that they would limit their raids to just a few cities—many more people would have abandoned their homes and hidden. If he had added what he also knew—that the deportation trains were carrying Jews not to labor camps, as was the case with other Italians, but to certain death—people might have taken even greater precautions, and abandoned their jobs, their synagogues, and, if possible, even the cities where they could be recognized. After all, strong and healthy parents are much more likely to subject fragile grandparents and small children to the rigors of hiding if the alternative is annihilation rather than "resettlement."

Furthermore, while many courageous Italian Catholics sheltered Jews with no word of guidance from the Pope, still more might have done so if the head of the Church had clearly led the way, or if they had understood the full significance of the Holocaust.[79] In recognition of that fact, many Italian priests told parishioners, falsely, that the Pope had asked them to protect Jews. Also, a papal threat of interdict or excommunication might have led a few Italian Catholic policemen, militiamen, and bureaucrats serving Mussolini's Republic of Salò to think twice before arresting Jews. Even a few German Catholics might have hesitated. If only a few hundred lives had been saved, the effort would have been worthwhile.

Outside Italy, a strong papal condemnation of the Holocaust could have had an even greater impact. The Jews of Hungary, for example, were still free at the end of 1943. During the spring and summer of 1944, hundreds of thousands were arrested and deported by Hungarian officials who might have been influenced by the Pope. Even if he were not heeded, however, Pope Pius XII would, again, have been believed. His statement would not have been dismissed as enemy propaganda. Why did he not make the statement?

Several explanations of the Pope's behavior may be dismissed as unworthy and without foundation. Suggestions that he was in some way anti-Jewish and therefore insensitive to Jewish suffering are reprehensible. The Pope may have shared the prejudices of many Christians against Judaism as a religion, but there is no evidence that he did not grieve at the violence and horror of the Holocaust. Charges that he acquiesced out of personal fear are equally unworthy and lacking in evidence. A third explanation, that the Pope so feared bolshevism that he refused to condemn nazism, comes closer to the truth. Pope Pius XII was almost pathologically afraid of bolshevism. He loudly condemned Russian aggression in Finland, while ignoring German aggression in Catholic Poland. In Rome itself, he so feared a Communist takeover that on October 19, three days after the roundup, he actually requested the Germans to put more police on the streets. German police, who would also arrest Jews and, for that matter, anti-Fascist Christians, were the last thing the Romans wanted or needed.

But the Pope's anti-bolshevism does not adequately explain his reaction to the Holocaust. In fact, as he decided what to do that terrible October, Pope Pius XII faced several overwhelming problems. He knew that a strong public definition and condemnation of the Holocaust—the only reaction that might save lives—might cause the Germans to occupy the Vatican and invade churches and monasteries throughout Italy. In Rome alone, more than 450 Jews eventually hid in the enclaves of the Vatican, while more than 4,000 others found shelter in churches, monasteries, and convents. [80] Many thousands more hid in religious institutions throughout the country. Serious disintegration of German-Vatican relations could place these lives in jeopardy, without necessarily, in the Pope's view, saving others.

Second, the Pope feared that a condemnation of the Holocaust might provoke Nazi reprisals against Catholics in German-occupied countries, as well as even more terrifying persecution of the Jews. While it is difficult to imagine any more ferocious persecution than that already existing, it must be remembered that Catholic churchmen in several countries had been able to secure temporary exemptions from deportation for converted Jews and the children and Jewish spouses of mixed marriages. The Nazis sometimes granted these exemptions in order to buy silence from leaders of the Church, only to rescind them when all other available Jews had been deported. The Pope, however, did not want to jeopardize these private arrangements, especially when it remained unclear how many lives his condemnation of the Holocaust might save.

Third, Pope Pius XII was as concerned about his responsibility to preserve and protect an institution as he was about his moral leadership. He was well aware that Hitler toyed with the idea of establishing a rival papacy in Germany. He knew that the Vatican was completely at the mercy of the German troops occupying Rome. Above all, he had reason to believe that a large majority of German Catholics would reject any papal denunciation of the Holocaust. He feared that a threat to excommunicate Catholics who murdered Jews or to place Nazi Germany under interdict would result in a large-scale defection of German Catholics from the Church. Such a reaction certainly does not speak well of German Catholics, and perhaps it would not have occurred. The point here is that the Pope apparently believed it, and his belief influenced his policy. [81]

The fact that Pope Pius XII did not publicly condemn the Holocaust does not mean that he did nothing to help the Jews. The thousands of Jews hidden in religious institutions throughout Italy were there with his knowledge and consent, if not at his instigation. The hundreds of priests and even bishops in Italy who risked their lives to feed and shelter Jews were not discouraged by the head of their Church. But neither, apparently, were they particularly encouraged. The Pope seems to have chosen not to be involved even with priests inside the Vatican who were helping and supplying the persecuted. The best that can be said of him is that he allowed others to take great risks and that he fulfilled his institutional mandate at the expense of moral leadership.

And what of the Pope's most immediate flock—the Catholic population of Rome? What did they do after October 16? It is a twisted legacy. Hundreds of testimonies exist describing the revulsion and horror that ordinary Romans felt at the spectacle of the roundup. Most of these testimonies were written later, however, when the war was over and the truth of the Holocaust was known to everyone. They may be self-serving. Most people wanted to remember that they cared. It is difficult to know how many did.

Gestapo chief Kappler had no reason to distort the reaction of the Roman people when he composed his report of the roundup on October 17. He wrote:

> The behaviour of the Italian people was clear passive resistance which in some individual cases amounted to active assistance. In one case, for example, the police came upon the home of a Fascist in a black shirt and with identity papers which without doubt had already been used one hour earlier in a Jewish home by someone claiming them as his own. As the German police were breaking into some homes, attempts to hide Jews were observed, and it is believed that in many cases they were successful. The anti-Semitic section of the population was nowhere to be seen during the action, only a great mass of people who in some individual cases even tried to cut off the police from the Jews. In no case was there any need to use fire-arms. [82]

Kappler's report accords with the testimony of many Jewish survivors who remember the non-Jews who helped them. Several families received phone calls from non-Jewish friends on October 16, warning them of the danger that had not yet reached their buildings. [83] Others hid in non-Jewish homes and passed from home to home for the duration of the war. Non-Jews provided food, money, and false documents. [84] Luciano

The Italians and The Holocaust

Morpurgo remembers how his Catholic neighbor even fabricated false bills of sale to prove that Morpurgo's valuable furniture belonged instead to him, saving it from confiscation and returning it after the war. [85]

And yet, as always and everywhere, there was another side. Official newspapers not only failed to report the roundup, but avoided all mention of the sealed train winding its way north to the Brenner Pass, filled with Italian citizens. Fascist Italian diplomatic personnel, before the German invasion of their country, had tried to protect Jews throughout occupied Europe, but now bureaucrats at home seem to have done little for Jews on native soil. During the forty-eight hours that the prisoners were in the Military College, no one tried to free them. No one attempted to stop the deportation train as it crept slowly north toward the Brenner Pass. Perhaps if someone credible like the Pope had declared that for Jews deportation meant the gas chambers and crematoria, the public reaction would have been different. But perhaps it would not.

The lack of overt resistance was a measure of the Nazi terror, the disintegration of Italian authority, the difficulty of daily life for everyone in occupied Italy, and public ignorance about the Holocaust. Large-scale resistance to the deportations may have been too much to expect, and certainly the Italian record of passive resistance and spontaneous informal assistance to Jews is impressive. But here again, there was another side. Italian police did not participate in the October 16 roundup, in part because the Germans did not trust them and in part because of the still uncertain position of the new Italian national government at Salò. But as will be seen, at least 835 more Roman Jews were arrested before Rome was liberated in June 1944, and most of these were caught by Italian police. [86] Many were betrayed by Italian informers—individual citizens motivated by general anti-Semitism and pro-nazism, private quarrels and vendettas, their own personal involvement in illegal activities, or just plain greed. The Nazis offered rewards for information leading to the arrests of Jews, and several Italians collected. More often, the Germans received anonymous letters, such as the following:

> The Jew Benedetto Veneziano . . . a very rich textile merchant and real estate owner, is the owner of the following [three] automobiles [then listed with license plate and engine numbers].
>
> These cars have not been turned in at the proper collection center; on the contrary, with the tricks and corruption which only Jews know about, the owner has succeeded in obtaining permission to drive from the German command. . . .
>
> For more than a month the above-mentioned Jew has traveled the length and width of Italy to escape capture, using up gasoline and weaving intrigues. [87]

After providing more details, the informer signed his letter "A friend of Germany."

When the Germans finally retreated from Rome after nine months of occupation, at least 1,700 Jews arrested in Rome had been deported. [88] Over 10,000 had survived. Every survivor owed his life to one, and usually to several, heroic non-Jewish supporters. But except for those caught in that first, unexpected roundup in October, most deportees could also trace their tragedy to non-Jews who had, in the last analysis, failed to provide support.

The old buildings and narrow streets of the former ghetto still simmer beneath the hot sun, in the shadow of classical Roman ruins. Tiny shops still bear the same family names: Di Porto, Di Veroli, Spizzichino, Piperno, Limentani. The names evoke painful memories. Fifty-three men, women, and children named Di Porto, including three babies of six and seven months and fourteen other children ten and under, were deported to Auschwitz after the October 16 roundup. They were joined by forty-five Di Verolis, thirty-three Spizzichinos, thirty-one Pipernos, and sixteen Limentanis. None returned.[89]

The main synagogue in Rome still sits beside the Tiber adjacent to the ghetto, as it did when Foà's offices were there, and when Nazis seized its gold, archives, and library.[90] A plaque outside the synagogue and a room of prayer inside commemorate the Holocaust. After October 1982, a commemorative wreath marked another spot by the fence outside. Arab terrorists had launched an attack there, killing a two-year-old boy and wounding at least thirty-four others. Nazis had marched on that spot, and their Jewish victims had waited nearby for the trucks that would carry them on the first leg of their final journey. Forty years had passed, but hatred and fear had not entirely ceased.

7

Autumn 1943: The Nightmare Begins

DR. GIUSEPPE JONA, president of the Jewish Community of Venice since 1940, had been a well-known doctor, director of hospitals in Venice, and professor at the University of Padua before the racial laws. Denied the right to teach or hold a public position after 1938, he helped found a secondary school for Jewish students barred from government schools. He also worked with the thousands of refugees passing through Venice.

On Friday, September 17, only nine days after the unilateral Italian armistice with the Allies and the beginning of the German occupation, an unknown agent called upon the seventy-three-year-old Dr. Jona. The visitor demanded the lists of Community members. Dr. Jona, evidently well informed about the Holocaust in other countries, stalled for time. Perhaps he had learned the truth from the many refugees he knew, for little enough had yet occurred in Italy. The massacres of Jews around Lago Maggiore were underway, but he could hardly have known about them. German SS in Borgo San Dalmazzo had not yet demanded that all refugees from France surrender themselves on pain of death—they would do so the following day. Perhaps Dr. Jona had heard that the SS in Merano, a resort town near the Brenner Pass, had arrested twenty-five Jews, including a child of six, on September 15, but he could not have known that they would all be deported. Yet somehow Dr. Jona understood what lay ahead.

Calmly, Dr. Jona explained to his visitor that he needed time to collect the lists. Could he please return tomorrow? The man agreed. During the night, Giuseppe Jona collected and burned all documents bearing Jewish names and addresses. He never sought Italian police assistance. Instead, he injected himself with a lethal dose of morphine. Italy lost a distinguished public servant. She would lose more, many more. [1]

For most Italian Jews, September was a month of deadly quiet. As the German occupation forces solidified control and Mussolini's new Republican government (the king and Badoglio having become the traitors who signed the armistice) struggled to define its authority, hundreds of Jews silently abandoned their homes. Those with something special to hide usually went first. The Jewish American art critic Bernard Berenson left "I Tatti," his beautiful villa near Florence, a few days after the armistice. He found refuge with friends nearby. He somehow hid most of his vast art collection, along with about twenty thousand of his most valuable books. Another twenty thousand volumes remained behind. [2]

Letizia Morpurgo in Fano, with her husband and young children, left home in Trieste on September 10. Letizia's husband Giuseppe Fano had been director of Delasem in Trieste, and they believed that his position would make him a leading target for arrest. The Fano family fled to Venice, where they stayed for a time in hotels. They were not yet aware of the threat to all Jews, regardless of wealth or position, but they understood their own danger. That early knowledge, combined later with incredible good luck and heroic assistance from several sympathetic Italians, saved their lives. [3]

Like the Fano family, Pino Levi Cavaglione also left home in September because he feared he was a special target. Levi Cavaglione believed he was endangered as a Communist, rather than as a Jew. He had spent six years in prison and confinement during the Fascist regime. Released by the Badoglio government at the end of July 1943, he had returned to live with his parents in Genoa. The announcement of the armistice on September 8 was a cause for rejoicing, but the following day, German troops began disarming Italian soldiers.

On the evening of September 15, the chief of the political bureau of the Genoa police department came to call on the Levi Cavaglione family. He was, Pino recalls, the same agent who had arrested him six years before. This time his purpose was quite different. He warned Pino's father that the Germans intended to arrest the son the next morning.

Pino Levi Cavaglione promptly left home and found temporary refuge in a monastery. The monks, he remembers, were fully aware of his politics. Several days later, he traveled to Rome and joined a team of partisans in the Castelli Romani. He was still unaware of his vulnerability as a Jew. His parents remained at home for at least another month. By October 27, however, they too had changed names and moved to another house. They may have learned of the October 16 roundup in Rome from their partisan son or from their other son who was hiding with his family in a Roman convent. But despite their precautions, they did not survive. They were arrested on November 11, at the height of the Nazi manhunts in Genoa, and they disappeared in the vast inferno to the north. [4]

Another who went immediately into hiding in September

1943, for private reasons, was Ettore Ovazza, a fervent patriot, veteran of World War I, *squadrista,* participant in the march on Rome, and wealthy Turinese banker. During the late 1930s, Ovazza made a name for himself as a Jewish Fascist and anti-Zionist. In his newspaper *La nostra bandiera,* he constantly echoed the government's position that Zionists were disloyal and called upon all Italian Jews to condemn them. The official government favor he thus acquired enabled him and his followers to obtain leadership roles in the Jewish Community organizations, at the expense of Jews who were reluctant to disassociate themselves from Zionism.[5]

Unlike most others who fled early, Ovazza's move was not enough to save him, his wife, his twenty-year-old son, and his fifteen-year-old daughter. The family took refuge in the Valle d'Aosta, northwest of Turin and within view of the Swiss border. Early in October 1943, the German SS caught the son as he attempted to flee to Switzerland, and somehow discovered the family's hiding place. The SS murdered the boy and arrested his parents and sister. On the morning of October 11, in the cellar of an elementary school in Intra, north of Stresa, Ettore Ovazza, his wife, and daughter were shot. Their bodies were chopped into pieces and burned in the school furnace. The odor of burning flesh filled the air for days. Much later, a child playing near the furnace found a single human tooth.[6]

All who write of Ovazza agree that he was an honest man who acted in good faith. He understood what was happening in Germany in the 1930s. He sincerely believed that Italian Jews could prevent a similar fate only by demonstrating total devotion to fascism. It is true that, in the end, he died as a Jew under German, not Italian, domination. But the Duce he so loyally supported had abandoned him and his people several years before. Mussolini had used the Jewish question as a diplomatic tool. He had issued the racial laws, formed the alliance

Nazi, Fascist, and anti-Semitic graffiti on the walls of the synagogue in Trieste in December 1938, shortly after the onset of the racial laws. *CDEC, Milan.*

An official certificate of exemption from most provisions of the racial laws, awarded to Giacomo Tedesco "of the Jewish race" in 1941.
Reasons for the exemption, unstated on the certificate, may have included voluntary military service, decoration for bravery, or wounds received in combat in Libya, World War I, Fiume, Ethiopia, or the Spanish Civil War; enrollment in the Fascist Party between 1919 and 1922 or during the second half of 1924; or wounds received while fighting for the Fascist cause in Italy. *CDEC, Milan.*

A store in Trieste in 1942, covered with graffiti declaring it "Closed forever. Jewish shop." *CDEC, Milan.*

CITTÀ DI TORINO

DIVISIONE DELLO STATO CIVILE

L'Ufficiale dello Stato Civile sotto-
scritto certifica che TEDESCO Giacomo fu Emilio
e fu Husai Sara nato in Ancona il 11-6-1889, di
razza ebraica è stato DISCRIMINATO con provvedi-
mento ministeriale n. 2637/15051 in data 23-8-941.
Torino, 3 Ottobre 1941-XIX°

L'UFFICIALE DELLO STATO CIVILE

Jewish forced laborers in 1942 working along the banks of the Tiber River in Rome, in the shadow of the Castel Sant'Angelo. *Publifoto, Rome.*

Forced labor card issued to "the Jew" Ada Levi in Cividali, of Bologna. The recipient was fifty-one years old and the mother of two children, both of whom were still minors. *CDEC, Milan.*

CONSIGLIO PROVINCIALE DELLE CORPORAZIONI
IN BOLOGNA

Cartolina-precetto N. 307

IL PREFETTO
Presidente del Consiglio Provinciale delle Corporazioni

Ai sensi delle disposizioni vigenti in materia di precettazione del lavoro;
Per delega del Ministero delle Corporazioni;

PRECETTA

l'ebreo **Levi Ada in Cividali**

In attesa dell'avviamento al lavoro che sarà successivamente comunicato il suddetto ebreo deve tenersi a disposizione del C. P. C.

Ogni cambiamento di domicilio dovrà essere tempestivamente notificato al suddetto Consiglio Provinciale delle Corporazioni.

Bologna, 14/9/42 XX°.

p. IL PREFETTO
Presidente del Consiglio Provinciale delle Corporazioni

COMANDO GERMANICO
DI BORGO S. DALMAZZO

Entro le ore 18 di oggi tutti gli stranieri che si trovano nel territorio di Borgo S. Dalmazzo e dei comuni vicini devono presentarsi al Comando Germanico in Borgo S. Dalmazzo, CASERMA DEGLI ALPINI.

Trascorso tale termine tutti gli stranieri che non si saranno presentati verranno immediatamente fucilati.

La stessa pena toccherà a coloro nella cui abitazione detti stranieri verranno trovati.

Borgo S. Dalmazzo, 18 settembre 1943.

q.

IL COMANDANTE GERMANICO DELLE S. S.
Capitano Müller

German SS announcement posted on September 18, 1943, in Italian villages near the mountain passes which led into southern France. The poster demands that all "foreigners" in the area around Borgo San Dalmazzo turn themselves in by 6 P.M., on pain of immediate death to themselves and all who might help them. About 349 Jewish refugees from France surrendered and, of these, 330 were deported to Auschwitz. *CDEC, Milan.*

Barbed wire and guard tower at Fossoli, the main internment camp in Italy for Jews awaiting deportation to Auschwitz. *CDEC, Milan.*

Site of the crematorium in the prison of La Risiera di San Sabba, in Trieste. German soldiers trying to destroy evidence blew up the structure before abandoning the prison. *Italian postcard.*

Death cells in the internment camp at Gries, near Bolzano. Jews were held at Gries after the Nazis abandoned Fossoli in late July 1944. *CDEC, Milan.*

An anonymous informer's letter to Nazi or Fascist police. The text, full of errors, reads, "The Jew Joshua [Giosuè] who was at the Monti's house can be found hidden at Dottoressa Gentile's house in via Doria 9 [the Jew Joshua] has a wholesale shoe business in Milan." This letter led to the arrests of Augusta Menasse Voghera and her mother Giulia Voghera Leoni. Both were murdered at Gries in March 1945. *CDEC, Milan.*

Virginia and Leone Bondì with the three youngest of their six children. The entire family was caught in the Rome roundup on October 16, 1943, and gassed at Auschwitz a week later. *CDEC, Milan.*

Carlo Rosselli, world-famous anti-Fascist leader and organizer in the 1930's, and his brother Nello, a noted Italian historian. The brothers, from a prominent Italian Jewish family, were murdered by French Cagoulards in Italian Fascist pay on June 9, 1937, at Bagnoles-de-l'Orne in Normandy. *CDEC, Milan.*

Fiorella Anticoli, age 12. The child was captured in the Rome roundup with her mother, siblings, grandparents, and several aunts and uncles. She alone survived Auschwitz and was evacuated by the Nazis to Bergen-Belsen in November 1944. American troops who liberated that camp in April 1945 circulated a group photograph that included her. Her father Marco saw it in Rome and hoped for her survival, but Fiorella died in a hospital at Bergen-Belsen on May 31, 1945. *CDEC, Milan.*

Leone Ginzburg, brilliant son of a Jewish family from Odessa, raised and educated in Italy. A university instructor, author, journalist, editor, and Resistance hero, he died under torture at Regina Coeli prison in Rome during the German occupation. The writer Natalia Ginzburg was his wife. *CDEC, Milan.*

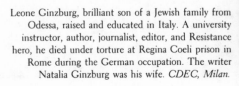

Enzo Sereni (with glasses), and his brother Emilio (in the dark jacket), from a highly respected Roman Jewish family. Enzo, a Zionist who settled in Israel in 1927, joined a British parachute unit in World War II, was captured in Italy, and died at Dachau. Emilio, a Communist Resistance leader, survived the war and became a senator. At the far left, Emilio's wife Marina. *CDEC, Milan.*

False identity card of the Jewish partisan Vittorio Finzi, issued in the name of Vittorio Rossi. *CDEC, Milan.*

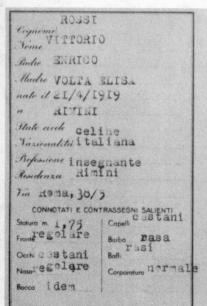

Italian Jewish anti-Fascists during the German occupation. *Clockwise from upper left:* Franco Cesana, killed on a scouting mission just before his thirteenth birthday; Rita Rosani, the only known Italian woman killed in combat; Mario Finzi, deported and died at Auschwitz; and Primo Levi, survivor of Auschwitz and famous writer today. *CDEC, Milan.*

Jewish Resistance heroes. *Clockwise from upper left:* Eugenio Colorni, murdered by Italian Fascists in Rome; Eugenio Curiel, murdered by Italian Fascists in Milan; Emanuele Artom, tortured to death by Nazis; and Mario Jacchia, tortured and executed by Nazis. *CDEC, Milan.*

with Nazi Germany, gone to war, and ultimately allowed the Germans to rule Italy in his name. Like so many others, Ovazza never understood that the denial of the legal rights of a few dissenters in the 1920s, which he enthusiastically endorsed in the sacred name of law and order, would inexorably lead to the denial of an entire people's right to exist.

While some Jews hid for economic or political reasons, others left urban residences simply to avoid enemy air raids. By pure chance, then, they no longer lived at the addresses on the Community lists that the Nazis were seizing throughout Italy. As seen, Carlo Modigliani moved to a small village near Varese in February 1943 to escape air raids in Milan. His prescient mother then managed to register as an Aryan. [7] Similarly, Giancarlo Sacerdoti, age fourteen in 1943, remembers that his father moved his family out of Bologna in July. They moved again in August. In both cases, sensing that they might need real hiding places in the future, they did not inform new acquaintances that they were Jewish. [8] The whole family survived.

Jews in the heavily bombed industrial and port city of Livorno are the best large-scale example of this phenomenon. Like nearly everyone else in the city, hundreds escaped air raids by moving to remote mountain villages where no one knew them. Presumably, they did not register themselves as Jews, although cases where an entire village knew of Jewish families and did not report them were not unknown. As a result of their mobility, only about ninety-three Livornese Jews were deported during the entire occupation period. [9] Tragically, those who were caught were usually too poor, too old, or too sick to escape enemy air raids and, ultimately, the Nazis and Fascists.

Some Jews who changed residence that ominous September were not just trying to protect valuable possessions, avoid arrest for past activities, or escape enemy air raids. Some immediately understood the danger of arrest and deportation that threatened all Jews. Silvana Ascarelli Castelnuovo of Rome was one of these. Immediately after the armistice, she began to contact every convent she could find, going from door to door. Finally on September 30, just two weeks before the Rome roundup, the Convent of the Sacred Heart of the Infant Jesus accepted her, four of her children, and her mother. With false documents, they could pass as Sicilian refugees in the event of a search. Only the Mother Superior knew they were Jewish.

Mrs. Ascarelli Castelnuovo had more difficulty hiding her thirteen-year-old son and her father, for they could be identified during a search because they were circumcised. She finally lodged her son with a priest and her father at the Università Gregoriana, a Vatican institution technically safe from Nazi searches. Primarily because of her intelligence and foresight, her entire family survived the war. The pressure for hiding places increased every day of the occupation. Mrs. Ascarelli Castelnuovo herself notes that she found lodgings because she was among the first to look. [10]

Unfortunately, however, the vast majority of Italian Jews with no particular reason to hide adopted an often fatal wait-and-see attitude. Typical of this majority was Sylvia Lombroso, who noted her growing awareness of danger in her diary on September 17, but did nothing about it until October 18. [11] Similarly, Luciano Morpurgo in Rome prepared a hiding place in September but did not move in until October. [12] By the end of October, very few Jews still lived at home. But by then, it was too late for many. Roundups not only in Rome but in Trieste, Milan, Turin, and other smaller cities had caught hundreds still in their homes. Even Jews who had changed residence usually continued to work and shop where they were known, leaving themselves open to denunciation by informers. It took still more time for many to learn that they had to disappear completely. As Sylvia Lombroso wrote at the time,

"People who do not or aren't able to leave their own city are virtually lost." [13]

The 8,100 foreign Jewish refugees in Italy (a number that includes about 1,100 who crossed from France at the time of the armistice) were generally much quicker than Italian Jews to recognize the terrible danger. [14] Personal accounts frequently cite foreign Jews telling Italians, both Jewish and non-Jewish, "You don't know what these Germans are capable of." The foreigners knew, and they usually acted accordingly.

Shortly after the onset of the German occupation, Nazis guided by a Fascist fanatic from Nonantola arrived at the Villa Emma, the home for Jewish orphan children from Yugoslavia. As seen in chapter 4, not one of the approximately ninety-two residents could be found. They had needed only a twenty-four-hour notice of the occupation to hide. Elsewhere, a group of fifty or sixty Polish, Czech, Austrian, and other foreign Jews assigned to enforced residence in a mountain village near Vicenza had disappeared entirely within forty-eight hours. They fled on September 10, despite the fact that they had no identity papers, no ration books, and no contacts. A few were caught; a father and son captured in Rome were subsequently murdered during the Ardeatine Caves massacre in March 1944. But most survived, in part because they understood the danger early. [15]

The most fortunate foreign Jews were those residing near the frontiers. In the north, for example, a group of about forty mostly Croatian Jews in enforced residence in Castellamonte, north of Turin, escaped into Switzerland immediately after the armistice. The Olivetti Typewriter Company in nearby Ivrea, owned in fact if not in law (because of the racial laws) by the Italian Jewish Olivetti family, provided transportation. [16]

In the south, refugees benefited from lower population densities in mountain areas, lower degrees of politicization, and greater disorganization near the front. Most quietly headed for the Allied zone as soon as they learned of the armistice. Many reached it, or survived until it reached them. In one instance, Mrs. K. L., born in Galicia and interned with her husband and three-year-old child near Chieti in 1940, lived in a hole in the ground for four weeks in December until a sympathetic mayor gave them false papers. [17]

However, despite their early awareness of danger, the readiness of many Italian non-Jews to help them, the fact that their names and addresses were on no Community lists, and the nonexistence of former acquaintances who could identify them as Jews, Jewish refugees in Italy seem to have fared less well, over all, than Italian Jews. If currently accepted statistics are correct, the 1,915 refugee deportees represent 23.6 percent of the 8,100 foreign Jews in Italy at the time of the occupation, while the 4,439 Italian deportees represent only 12 percent of the 37,100 Italian Jews (the combined figure, including the 210 deported Jews of unknown origins and the 237 recently ascertained deportees from Trieste, is 6,801 Jewish deportees from the Italian peninsula, or 15 percent of 45,200). [18] For the most part, foreign refugees in Italy, half of whom had arrived after 1938, existed without money, documents, or acquaintances, and without any capacity to pass themselves off as Italian Catholics because of the language barrier. They were totally vulnerable and dependent upon non-Jews. In 23.6 percent of the cases, they did not find the help they needed.

If September was a month of planning, maneuvering, and uncertainty for Jews, it was the same for Germans and for Italian Fascists. The Germans needed time to establish their authority, restore order, resist expected Allied invasions, and deal with thousands of bewildered Italian soldiers. The SS also needed time to collect lists of Jewish Community members, quietly and efficiently, without arousing apprehension. Given their other problems, the speed with which the Nazis directed their attention to Jewish lists is impressive, demonstrating their determination with terrifying clarity. They usually began within a week of their occupation of any given city. By the end of September, they had everything they were going to get.

Sometimes, as in Venice, searchers for Jewish lists encountered problems. Sometimes non-Jews, and even Fascist bureaucrats, created obstacles. In Ancona, for instance, the prefect repeatedly informed the SS, falsely, that all Jews had already left town, that their goods had been confiscated, and that the Community lists had been destroyed in an air raid. [19] In fact, the Nazis rarely obtained all the population data they wanted, for cases of name scrambling in municipal records offices were not unusual. But by the end of September, they had enough to begin their fearful purge.

Italian Fascists were the most disoriented of all. They needed time to establish a government, define their authority, and organize a military force. On an individual level, every former Fascist had to make a personal decision upon which his very survival might depend. Would he support Mussolini's newly constituted government and party, or would he quietly retire to some hidden lair until the storm passed?

The new Italian Social Republic was announced in the middle of September. Denied even a capital, most of the republic's offices were scattered throughout the province of Verona, an area conveniently located, for German purposes, on the direct rail line to the Brenner Pass. While commonly called the Republic of Salò, only the Foreign Ministry and the Ministry of Popular Culture were located in that small town on the western side of Lake Garda. The more important offices of new Fascist party Secretary Alessandro Pavolini and Minister of the Interior Guido Buffarini Guidi were in Maderno, just north of Salò. Mussolini himself lived under German SS guard at the Villa Feltrinelli in Gargnano, a few kilometers north of

Maderno. Less important offices were as far away as Brescia, Venice, Padua, Cremona, and even Milan.[20]

The Republic of Salò governed a vastly reduced Italy. The Germans denied the *Repubblichini*, or little Republicans, as many Italians contemptuously (and privately) called them, any meaningful authority in or south of Rome. In the northeast, eight provinces were simply annexed to the Third Reich. Udine, Gorizia, Trieste, Pola, and Fiume were incorporated into the Adriatisches Kustenland and assigned to the Gauleiter of Styria, Friedrich Rainer, an Austrian. Bolzano, Trent, and Belluno were grouped together to form the Voralpenland and placed under the Gauleiter of the Tyrol, Franz Hofer, also Austrian. Italy's northern frontier now actually touched Lake Garda. These eight provinces were the same territories "redeemed" from Austria after Italy's victory in World War I. They were the justification for the war itself, and symbols of the completion of unification. Their loss in 1943, along with the loss of Rome as the capital of Italy, were a profound blow to Mussolini's prestige. They were dramatic evidence of the legacy of twenty years of fascism.

If the *Repubblichini* scattered along Lake Garda seemed like harmless puppets, however, the semi-autonomous militarized squads of Fascist fanatics that sprouted up throughout the country in September were far more dangerous. Their very names would spread terror among Jews and anti-Fascists for the next year and a half. In Milan, the Muti Legion, organized and led by Francesco Colombo, numbered about 2,300 men—idealists, opportunists, sadists, ex-convicts, adventurers, and adolescents.[21] In Florence, Major Mario Carità's band of about two hundred thugs operated without restraint against Jews and anti-Fascists. A German officer inspecting its headquarters found it so drenched with the blood of torture victims that he insisted the unit leave town. Carità transferred operations to Padua. In Rome, Pietro Koch, the tall, thin, elegant son of a former German naval officer who had established a wine and marsala business in Avellino, also organized a band of Italian Fascists that bore his name. Koch, too, established "offices" later remembered as rooms stained with the blood of partisans and Jews. When Rome fell to the Allies in June 1944, the Koch band continued its activities in Milan.[22]

The Muti, Carità, and Koch bands were three of the most vicious Fascist squads. There were scores of others, involving thousands of men and boys. It is probably impossible to exaggerate their atrocities. They tortured and murdered their victims, Jews and non-Jews alike. They extorted vast fortunes from the desperate families of their prisoners, often killing those same prisoners in the end. They raided homes, offices, convents, and synagogues without cause or authorization, carrying off everything of value.

In the power vacuum that existed during the first three or four months of the occupation, the semi-autonomous bands were virtually uncontrollable. Many were linked to individual high-ranking Fascist politicians. The Muti Legion, for example, was allegedly tied to Roberto Farinacci and financed by his personal coterie of industrialists.[23] The Carità and Koch bands were directly subsidized by Minister of the Interior Guido Buffarini Guidi; Koch's men even operated their own prison.[24] No Italian authorities directly controlled them. In fact, the bands survived by cultivating personal relationships with German SS units in their area. They did everything possible to please the Nazis, including, above all, persecuting Jews. To the eternal disgrace of the nation, October and November 1943 were months in which Italians, on their own initiative, seized Jewish co-nationals and turned them over to the foreign occupiers of their own country.

By December, the situation had changed in two important respects. First, as will be seen shortly, the Republic of Salò at the end of November defined a policy of arrest and internment of Jews, but not release to the Germans. Italians persecuting Jews were now acting within the law, not merely on their own initiative. Second, as the Republic of Salò established its own military and police forces, it attempted to incorporate the semi-autonomous bands. If the bands' formal status sometimes changed, however, their deadly activities continued unabated.

When the arrest and internment of Jews became government policy after December 1, 1943, the legally constituted military and police units of the Republic of Salò responded with varying degrees of zeal. The regular police were perhaps the least enthusiastic about their new assignment. Occasionally, a fanatic provincial prefect (or *capo di provincia*, as he was called during the Salò period) or local police chief (*questore*) demanded an active role from a particular police department. More often, though, police gave the arrest of Jews a low priority or ignored it altogether.

Much more dangerous was the Guardia Nazionale Repubblicana (GNR). Organized as a "political army" under Lieutenant General Renato Ricci in November 1943, the GNR merged the former Fascist Volunteer Militia (MVSN), the remnants of the *carabinieri* (80,000 at the time of the armistice), and the Italian African Police (PAI). Financed largely by the German SS, the GNR was formally under the jurisdiction of the Ministry of the Interior. It could not conscript recruits independently, but it was assigned at least 25,000 draftees in October 1943. On paper, the GNR numbered about 140,000 in early 1944, a figure reduced by death and, especially, desertion to about 72,000 in April 1945.[25]

Among other roles, the GNR was an internal political police force, with political investigative powers denied the regular police. While most arrests of Jews before December 1943 can be attributed either to the Nazis or the semi-autonomous bands, many after that date were performed by the GNR. Like the police, however, the GNR was inconsistent. *Carabinieri* elements often revealed a particular distaste for Jewish persecution. The *carabinieri*, considered politically unreliable, were finally separated from the GNR in September 1944, but thousands had already been shipped to Germany to man anti-aircraft posts and guard Luftwaffe bases. Thousands more had deserted.

Like the *carabinieri*, draftees assigned to the GNR also tended to be notably lacking in zeal. Despite ruthless conscription methods, including the arrests of parents of draft dodgers and the recall of family ration cards, only about 48 percent of those called in October 1943 actually appeared. Even these often reported singing "Bandiera rossa," a left-wing hymn, and booing Fascist songs. Desertion rates were high.[26]

Despite unreliable units, however, the deadly nature of the GNR should not be underestimated. Former militiamen, in particular, were often fanatic Fascists. The semi-autonomous squads absorbed into the GNR also contributed to its reputation for ruthlessness and brutality. The 72,000 members remaining in April 1945 were vicious, dedicated men with nothing left to lose and nowhere else to go. As such, they were a force greatly to be feared.

Other military organizations under the Republic of Salò included, of course, a conventional, supposedly apolitical army, headed by Defense Minister Marshal Rodolfo Graziani. Some 640,000 soldiers and officers from the pre-armistice army were in German concentration camps struggling against starvation and disease. Graziani's new army of four divisions consisted primarily of about 44,000 reluctant conscripts. These were supplemented with about 13,000 former soldiers imprisoned in Germany, who "volunteered" in order to escape the appalling conditions.[27] Trained in Germany, Graziani's divisions entered Italy around the middle of 1944. Most Italian civilians greeted them with hostility. They engaged in less regular combat and more anti-partisan action than they wanted, and their morale plummeted. But they do not figure in the story of Jewish persecution.

Also active against partisans was the Decima Mas (X Mas) naval unit of Prince Junio Valerio Borghese. Before the armistice, the X Mas had been responsible for developing and utilizing special naval weapons, such as manned torpedos and small boats loaded with dynamite. The unit had operated effectively against the British in the Mediterranean. On September 8, Prince Borghese was ordered to destroy his war matériel and proceed to Malta. He disobeyed, remained at La Spezia, and despite the fact that he was a staunch monarchist, made deals with the Germans and the Republic of Salò.

During the occupation period, the X Mas attracted about ten thousand volunteers, of whom five thousand were retained and five thousand were transferred to the San Marco Division of the regular army. Nominally a division, the X Mas in fact consisted of several autonomous battalions. Its activities gradually shifted from sea to land, and it ultimately focused on brutal expeditions against partisans in Piedmont, Lombardy, and Friuli-Venezia Giulia. Among many atrocities, men from the X Mas killed eleven hostages from a single village on one occasion, and six on another. Like the army, however, the X Mas generally did not engage in searches for Jews. [28]

Far more threatening to Jews but appearing rather late in the story, the Brigate Nere were not created until June 1944. As GNR morale sank after the fall of Rome and the obvious discontent of the *carabinieri*, Alessandro Pavolini, secretary of the Fascist party, persuaded Mussolini to legalize his dream. The Fascist party itself was armed and mobilized. All male party members between the ages of eighteen and sixty and not in military service were required to join the Brigate Nere. Every *federale*, secretary of a provincial Fascist party federation, became the chief of a brigade.

In statistical terms, the Brigate Nere were not successful.

The Fascist party itself claimed 250,000 members in November 1943 and 487,000 in March 1944. The Brigate Nere never exceeded 30,000, according to Marshal Graziani—admittedly a hostile witness, as he hated Pavolini. A German report placed Brigate Nere strength at 22,000 in April 1945.[29]

Volunteers for the Brigate Nere tended to be deserters or criminals escaping the law, totally destitute and demoralized men attracted by the salaries and housing, old men with long Fascist affiliations, and boys of thirteen or fourteen. Indeed, photographs of Pavolini inspecting his troops are striking for the number of children in uniform. But despite their weaknesses, the Brigate Nere were greatly feared by Jews and anti-Fascists alike. With little military discipline they became virtual bandits, robbing, raping, and murdering civilians at will. Jews who fell into their clutches could expect no mercy.

The final Italian force to be feared was the Italian SS, which numbered twenty thousand men during the occupation. These men represented a last stage of national degradation, for they swore allegiance to a foreign ruler, Adolf Hitler. Most of them came from the ranks of the Camicie Nere, the "black shirt" Fascist militia that had fought beside the regular Italian army in Africa, the Balkans, and Greece. Many units had gone over en masse to the Germans at the time of the armistice, out of personal conviction and disgust with their own government. Others had joined up to avoid concentration camps or, in some cases, to get out of them. Once enrolled in the SS, a man could not change his mind. Each soldier had a personal dossier on file in Berlin, with the name and address of his family in Italy. The penalty for desertion was never in doubt.

Some Italian SS battalions were organized as combat units of the Waffen SS, while others served as police units. Some police units were sent to foreign countries—Russia, Hungary, even Holland—but most, along with all the combat battalions, were used to fight partisans in Italy. Only two Italian Waffen

The Italians and The Holocaust

SS battalions ever saw action at the front, briefly, at Anzio and Nettuno in April 1944.

Most Italians, Fascist and non-Fascist alike, regarded the Italian SS as traitors. The SS often responded by treating local Salò bureaucrats with hearty contempt. Their record for sadistic brutality equals that of the SS in all countries. Their victims were partisans, uninvolved civilian hostages, and Jews. [30]

Not all of this, of course, was yet clear in September 1943, when Jews in Italy were making the decisions upon which their lives would depend. Most did not know that the Nazis were collecting lists. Few believed that the new Italian government of Salò would totally abandon them and order their arrest by the end of November. Only a handful had heard of the massacres on Lago Maggiore, the arrests at Merano, the roundup of foreigners from France. Those incidents had occurred far away, near the frontiers. But gradually, events came closer.

On September 28, Italian Jews in Cuneo were arrested during a house-to-house roundup conducted, not by Germans, but by Fascist militia and *carabinieri*. [31] Also on September 28, German soldiers destroyed a synagogue in Vercelli, between Milan and Turin, in the heart of northern Italy. Vercelli's Jews numbered 325 in 1938. At about the same time, Nazis arrested several Jews in Novara, a community near Vercelli with 170 Jews. Many other Jews escaped when sympathetic friends sent warnings. [32]

By October, the Holocaust in Italy was in full swing. A deportation train left Trieste on Yom Kippur, Saturday, October 9, carrying at least one hundred Jews. None returned. [33] A single raid in Fiume in October netted about a hundred unfortunates, mostly Croatian, Russian, Polish, and Bulgarian Jews. [34] A similar raid in Ancona scheduled for October 9 failed to produce results when a Catholic priest, Don Bernardino, warned Rabbi Elio Toaff. The rabbi in turn advised his congregation to stay away from Yom Kippur services at the synagogue that day. A simultaneous raid on Ancona's old ghetto found no one at home. [35]

Ancona was indeed fortunate. Despite the fact that in size, its Jewish community of 1,031 ranked tenth in the nation according to the 1938 census, only ten Jews from the city were deported during the Holocaust, and one of these returned. [36] The abortive October roundup clearly prompted everyone to go into hiding, and to remain there until liberation.

Only the Jews of Ancona had much to be grateful for that October. The situation in Milan and Turin was more typical. In Milan, just after curfew on the evening of October 16, about two hundred Jews were arrested in their homes by well-organized German SS troops carrying lists. [37] The great roundup in Rome had occurred that same day. As in Rome, the Milanese raid constituted the final warning, and those who survived it immediately left their homes.

Many Milanese Jews continued to work, shop, and gather at Jewish institutions, however, leaving themselves open to Nazi deception and betrayal by informers. About fifteen people were caught at the synagogue on November 8, when Gestapo agents disguised as refugees gained entrance to the building. [38] Students taking final exams at Milan's Jewish School were more fortunate. They held exams the first day with a guard and had an escape route planned. The second day, they moved into the home of a sympathetic non-Jewish government school examiner. [39]

A total of 846 Jews were deported from Milan during the Holocaust, of a community of 7,482 Italian and foreign Jews in 1942. [40] Many of these victims were caught by the Koch band, which invaded churches, convents, and hospitals. Also, except for the two hundred arrested in the initial roundup on October 16, most Jews were caught after being betrayed by informers. Informers were usually motivated by

rewards ranging from 1,000 to as much as 9,000 lire per arrested Jew—a significant amount in 1943, when the average
industrial worker earned about 29 lire a day.[41] Others acted
from Fascist conviction, anti-Semitic prejudice, or personal
revenge.

Carlo Modigliani, a survivor, describes the constant fear and
uncertainty of daily life for Milanese Jews. Although he had
moved away, he had to return to Milan regularly to collect his
food-ration coupons. During the German occupation, he was
terrified of being recognized. One day he met a former acquaintance who knew he was Jewish. The man scolded him
angrily for being there, adding that he could turn him in. "We
poor Jews," Modigliani commented, "were totally at the mercy
of everyone."[42]

Clearly, for anyone who had a choice, it was perilous to
remain in one's own city. Even in remote villages, however, the
danger of detection remained. In his little village of a thousand
people many miles from Milan, Modigliani met a man who had
once lived in his former apartment building. Much worse, the
man was a captain in the Fascist militia. The captain invited
Modigliani to his home for an evening of conversation and
music. Modigliani, not knowing how much the man knew but
fearing that a polite refusal might arouse suspicion, went in an
agony of fear. The evening proved pleasant and uneventful. Six
months after the war, Modigliani met the captain, himself now
awaiting trial for Fascist activities, in the street. The man
admitted, "I was fully aware of the delicate position in which
you found yourself."[43]

In Turin, a city with 4,060 Jews in 1938, the Holocaust did
not begin with a huge October roundup. Italian Fascists in
effect served notice of pending trouble early that month when
they broke into the Jewish Community library, seized most of
the books, and burned them in a great bonfire in the Piazza
Carlina. Most Turinese Jews seem to have gone into hiding

soon after that incident, much sooner than Jews elsewhere. The first arrests occurred on October 16, the day of the Rome and Milan roundups, but only two elderly women were found at home. As in Milan, the October exams were held secretly, with some teachers acting as guards. Oral exams were held in parks, or while walking through the streets.

Eleven Turinese Jews were arrested in a single day, October 27, all as the result of informers. Some were lured into shops where SS agents awaited them. Others were caught at their work places. One family was caught when they returned to Turin to shop. These victims were all exercising certain precautions, but they showed too much trust in former acquaintances. Most Italians rewarded that trust, but every exception meant certain death. 44

Florence, home of Dante and cradle of Italian culture, had a Jewish population of 2,326 in 1938. As in Milan and Turin, most Florentine Jews were well-educated, industrious, and middle-class. Their chief rabbi after 1943 was a man of exceptional courage, talent, and dedication. The story of Rabbi Nathan Cassuto is inextricably linked to the story of the people he served. 45

Nathan Cassuto was born in Florence in 1909. After receiving his university degree in medicine and surgery in 1933, he served for a time as an army doctor. He then embarked upon what promised to be a brilliant medical career, combining active practice, research, and teaching. He published several important articles. In 1938, he won a scholarship to study at the prestigious Rockefeller Institute in New York City. His future seemed assured.

However, 1938 was the year of the racial laws. Nathan Cassuto's medical career ended almost before it had begun. The Fascist government denied him a passport to travel to New York to accept the scholarship that might have saved his life.

He could not teach. He could not even practice medicine outside the Jewish community.

Cassuto's father was a biblical scholar, and the son shared his father's interests. Well before 1938, Nathan had attended a rabbinical college and taken a second degree. This was an unusual step for a medical doctor and assimilated Jew in tolerant Italy, but it held him in good stead. When the racial laws abruptly terminated his medical career, Nathan Cassuto accepted a position as vice-rabbi in Milan.

In the fateful year 1943, Cassuto was appointed chief rabbi of Florence. He must have considered refusing the appointment; he surely understood the terrible responsibility and danger it entailed. But he accepted. He moved back to his native city with his young family—his wife Anna Di Gioacchino, whom he had married in 1934, and their children.

After the September 8 armistice, Rabbi Cassuto began to urge Florentine Jews to disperse and hide. The contrast between his behavior and that of Rome's Community leaders, apart from the chief rabbi, is striking. Cassuto's sister would later testify at the Eichmann trial, "My brother went from house to house to warn them to hide themselves in convents or in little villages, under false names." [46] Hundreds followed his advice. Meanwhile, former Florentine *squadristi* and other thugs and criminals organized the deadly Carità band.

Thanks in part to Rabbi Cassuto, the Carità band found few Florentine Jews in their homes. Arrests proceeded so slowly that Nazis and Fascists were forced to try new tactics. On Saturday, November 6, German SS troops surrounded the synagogue of Florence and arrested the few they found inside. [47] Three days later, these victims joined the second deportation train to leave Italian soil. This train carried at least four hundred Jews from Florence, Siena, and Bologna to Auschwitz. Only eighty-five are even known by name. Conditions during the journey were similar to those experienced by Roman Jewish deportees three weeks earlier. Thirteen men and ninety-four women passed the selection and escaped immediate gassing. None is known to have returned. [48]

November 27 was a night of terror in Florence, with at least three brutal raids. In the largest attack, Nazis and Fascists tipped off by a young Italian informer invaded the Convent of the Franciscan Sisters of Mary in the Piazza del Carmine. About thirty Jewish women and children, most of them from foreign countries and other Italian cities, were hiding there. [49] Among them was Vanda Abenaim Pacifici, wife of the chief rabbi of Genoa, who had carefully hidden her there, returned to his dangerous work in Genoa, and been arrested even before her. [50] There also were the aunt and the twenty-year-old cousin of Memo Bemporad, a wealthy Tuscan industrialist, and the seven-year-old, curly-blond-haired son of another cousin. [51] All were deported.

Apparently only two women escaped arrest that night during the Carmine raid. One, Bemporad's eighty-four-year-old grandmother, escaped when she showed a young Fascist militiaman the military medals won by her son, who died in combat in World War I. The Fascist hid her in a corner and told her not to move, but she was not able to help her other family members. [52] In a less elevating case, a second woman, a twenty-one-year-old French refugee, escaped when she "gave herself," a report says, to a Fascist militiaman, who then allowed her to flee through a window. [53]

Also on November 27, another Nazi and Fascist group armed with grenades and machine guns attacked a Catholic recreation center, capturing over twenty foreign Jewish men. Meanwhile, others raided the Convent of the Sisters of Saint Joseph, where several Jewish women had found shelter. Some of these women managed to survive the raid by dressing as nuns. [54]

The people captured on November 27 were taken to Verona

to await deportation. They did not wait long. A train, the fourth organized on Italian soil (the third had left Borgo San Dalmazzo on November 21, with Jews who had fled from France), left Milan on December 6. It stopped briefly in Verona to pick up, among others, the Jews recently caught in Florence. That fourth train carried at least six hundred people. Sixty-one men and thirty-five women passed the selection at Auschwitz. Three men returned.[55]

Rabbi Nathan Cassuto escaped on November 27, only to be arrested the following evening. He might have escaped altogether if he had chosen to remain in hiding. Instead, he attended a final secret meeting of a committee he had set up to provide fugitives with hiding places, money, food, and false documents. An affluent Polish refugee serving on the committee employed an Italian private secretary and translator named Marco Ischia. Ischia informed the SS of the meeting place, and everyone present was caught.

The next day, Ischia set still another trap. Nathan's wife Anna, hiding with her parents and children in the Convento della Calza, received word that she could learn about her husband's fate if she went to the Piazza della Signoria. Accompanied by her brother-in-law Saul Campagnano and the distinguished Jewish leader Raffaele Cantoni, she did so. The Nazis were waiting.

Under daily interrogation for two months, Anna denied that she was Nathan's wife. She did not want to complicate matters for her husband, and she was afraid she might reveal the hiding places of her children and parents under torture. On the eve of Nathan's departure from Florence, she finally admitted her identity in the hope that she might follow him. They were sent together to San Vittore Prison in Milan, and on January 30, 1944, they were deported on the same train to Auschwitz. Altogether, this fifth deportation train carried at least 700 people, of whom 180 were from Tuscany. Of the total of 700,

97 men and 31 women passed the selection; 13 men and 8 women returned.

Anna Cassuto was, miraculously, one of those survivors. She worked at the Birkenau labor camp until October 1944, and in a munitions factory from October to February 1945. She then moved to several other camps, contracted typhoid fever, and ended her odyssey in a quarantine center in Theresienstadt. The Allies liberated her on May 9, 1945, before the Nazis could complete their final extermination plans.

Anna last saw her husband on the arrival platform at Auschwitz. He, too, passed the selection and entered the men's section of the labor camp. Like Anna, he worked in several different places, apparently serving as a doctor for a time. At one point during his ordeal, he received a brief message from his wife, learning that she was still alive. In January 1945, as the Russians approached Auschwitz, Nathan Cassuto was among a group of tattered and famished prisoners who marched seventy kilometers in the snow to another camp. He was subsequently murdered by the Nazis at Gross Rosen in mid-February, to prevent his liberation by the Russians. He was thirty-four years old. [56] A prisoner who had known Rabbi Cassuto reminisced after the war, "I knew Nathan at the camp of Monowitz-Auschwitz where I had the honor of winning his affection and his friendship. Thanks to him, I passed hours of serenity at his side, oases of peace in the midst of Hell." [57]

Anna's parents and sons survived the war. The boys' survival followed a common pattern among fugitive Italian Jews. When refuge in the convent became too dangerous, they were placed with separate non-Jewish families. Daniel lived with Mario and Lina Santerini; David, with Ezio and Anna Calzi. The boys lived as an intimate part of these new families, with the constant danger of discovery and possible death for all. [58] A neighbor, shopkeeper, servant, teacher, anyone who knew that an outsider had joined a family group could have betrayed them.

The Italians and The Holocaust

The story of the Cassuto family—a tale of suffering, tragedy, and partial survival—should rightfully have ended in 1945. But for them, the horror was not yet over. With her children and parents, Anna moved to Israel after the war. She found work at the Hadassah Hospital in Jerusalem. On April 13, 1948, during the Arab-Israeli War, she was riding to work in an armed convoy of buses through Arab-held territory when the Arabs attacked. Anna Di Gioacchino Cassuto, survivor of Auschwitz, was murdered along with seventy others. Three years after her liberation, she became an innocent civilian victim in yet another war. She was only thirty-seven. [59]

While terror reigned in Rome, Milan, Turin, and Florence that October, the 2,263 Jews of Genoa (in 1938) remained unmolested. Because the German occupiers of the city had been deliberately lenient, most civilians felt confident about their future. About 5:00 on Tuesday afternoon, November 2, the two small children of Bino Polacco were playing in the peaceful little square in front of the synagogue where their father worked as a janitor. Suddenly, two German SS men appeared and seized the children, threatening to kill them if their father did not produce the Community lists. He promptly did so. Then the Nazis forced him to telephone everyone on the lists, summoning them to a meeting at the synagogue the next morning. Again he obliged. [60]

Most Genovese Jews had already left home to escape the air raids. Others survived the ensuing roundup because a Genovese Jew named Massimo Teglio learned of the seizure of the lists and telephoned warnings. Still others, walking to Polacco's morning meeting, escaped at the last minute when Romana Rossi in Serotti, a non-Jewish woman who lived near the synagogue, warned them from her window. Unfortunately, she also warned an Italian woman serving as a Nazi interpreter. She was arrested and imprisoned, to be released only after the Esso

Standard Oil Company where her husband was an executive intervened on her behalf.[61]

About twenty Jews were arrested at the synagogue the morning of November 3, including the janitor Bino Polacco, his wife Linda, and their two children, ages six and four.[62] During the days that followed, others were caught throughout the city. Two of these must have been the parents of Pino Levi Cavaglione, arrested on November 11. The lovely fishing villages of the Italian Riviera were not exempt either. At least three Jews were caught in Ventimiglia, five in Bordighera, ten in San Remo, and several in Chiavari. In contrast to Genoa, most of the arrests in the coastal villages were carried out by Italian Fascists.[63]

Riccardo Pacifici, chief rabbi of Genoa, had long understood the danger that threatened his people. Before the armistice, he had worked long and hard as a Delasem delegate, publicizing the plight of interned foreign Jews, collecting money and clothing for them, and even visiting the internment camp at distant Ferramonti on three occasions. After the armistice, he prudently placed his wife and children in two Florentine convents (his wife was seized from one on November 27), but he himself refused to leave Genoa. Instead, he accepted an offer from Cardinal Pietro Boetto, archbishop of Genoa, and moved into a Church-owned apartment not far from the synagogue.[64]

Rabbi Pacifici declined the summons to the meeting at the synagogue on November 3, but he agreed to meet janitor Bino Polacco at the Galleria Mazzini that same day. This, too, was a trap.[65] Nazis seized Pacifici and began beating him even before he arrived at Marassi Prison. Romana Rossi in Serotti saw him there with a swollen eye and already covered with blood.[66]

On the morning of December 1, about a hundred Jews from Genoa and surrounding Ligurian villages were loaded into the boxcars of a train that pulled up directly in front of the prison. They spent a few days at San Vittore Prison in Milan. On December 6, they boarded the deportation train that carried at least six hundred Jews to Auschwitz. Three returned. [67] Rabbi Pacifici died in a gas chamber at Auschwitz immediately upon arrival, on December 12. He was thirty-nine years old.

A simple marble plaque stands today in front of the synagogue in Genoa, in the quiet square where Bino Polacco's children played on the afternoon of November 2. The plaque honors Rabbi Pacifici who, like Rabbi Cassuto of Florence, could have escaped but chose instead to die with his people. On April 11, 1980, vandals defaced the plaque. It now bears a large indelible black swastika.

During the months of October and November 1943, roundups and raids such as those in Rome, Trieste, Milan, Turin, Florence, and Genoa were repeated on a smaller scale in many other Italian cities and towns. Sometimes arrests were accompanied by violence and even murder. On November 15 in Ferrara, for example, Fascist fanatics shot eleven hostages, including four Jews, beneath the walls of the Este Castle. They claimed that the act was a reprisal for the assassination of the local Fascist party secretary the day before. The assassination victim, a Fascist moderate, had in fact been killed by radical fanatics like themselves, and they knew it. [68] Their brand of fascism—cynical, blood-thirsty, and corrupt—had gained supremacy with the advent of the Republic of Salò.

Surprisingly enough, Jews in some towns continued to live peacefully throughout October and November. In Asti, for example, with a tiny Jewish community of 150 in 1938, Jews were apparently not troubled until December. Even in Venice, with a much larger community of 2,189, the worst did not occur until December. Sometimes Jews were ignored because they were just too few in number. More often, local Fascist officials were not personally committed to Jewish persecution, and the Nazis were preoccupied with other matters. In every case, however, the lull was only temporary.

By early December, then, four deportation trains had departed from Italian soil. One carried the 330 foreign Jews from France; the other three carried over two thousand people, most of them Italian citizens, to Auschwitz. Several additional trains had left from Trieste, officially no longer on Italian soil.

All this occurred in the total absence of any new Italian government policy toward Jews. Officially, the pre-armistice racial laws remained in effect. Officially, Jews were citizens, entitled to protection under the laws of their land. Unofficially, they were the helpless victims of the German occupying forces, and their own government's acquiescence. Furthermore, Italian Fascists, sometimes government employees but more often fanatic civilians or paramilitary volunteers, hastened to curry favor with their foreign controllers. Informers betrayed their neighbors, *squadristi* seized Jews and delivered them to the German SS, and Italian journalists seemed to compete in the virulence of their anti-Semitic diatribes. It was a time of shame.

But the worst was yet to come.

8

Policy and Prisons

ARTICLE SEVEN of the Carta di Verona, the political manifesto of the new Italian Social Republic, declared, "All those belonging to the Jewish race are foreigners. During this war they belong to an enemy nationality." Fascist party delegates convened at Verona on November 14, 1943, to approve the manifesto. Article seven passed without opposition, amid spontaneous expressions of enthusiasm from the floor.[1]

Apologists suggest that the Fascist delegates were not interested in the Jewish question—that article seven simply passed by default. While the vocal support from the floor hardly indicated indifference, it is probably true that most delegates cared little about either the political manifesto or the new government programs. Most cared only about revenge and personal vindication. They had lost face in July when Mussolini had fallen, and now their enemies would pay. Their need for scapegoats was so vast and irrational that they included all Jews in the category of anti-Fascist enemy. For Jews, it was the end of the line.

Although Jews became enemy aliens on November 14, official Italian policy toward them remained unclear until the end of the month. On the evening of November 30, the infamous police order number five was broadcast over the radio. At 9:00 A.M. on December 1, Minister of the Interior Guido Buffarini Guidi sent the order to his prefects. They in turn passed it on to their police chiefs, and it became official. Police order number five declared that all Jews residing in Italy, even if granted certain specific exemptions under earlier racial laws, were to be arrested and interned in concentration camps within the country. Their property and possessions were to be confiscated, with the proceeds directed to help Italians rendered indigent by enemy air raids. Individuals born of mixed marriages but officially declared Aryan under the racial laws were to be placed under special police vigilance. Ten days later, the order was amended slightly. Jews who were gravely ill, over the age of seventy, or members of mixed families including Jewish spouses, were not to be arrested.[2]

Police order number five dramatically altered the scene. No longer were Italians who arrested Jews regarded as German agents or free-lancers operating from self-interest. Now all Italian law-enforcement agents were obligated to arrest Jews. It was their professional duty, whether they liked it or not.

Apologists for moderates in the Republic of Salò present two conflicting justifications for the police order. First, they maintain that it was useful to appease the Nazis, but was never intended to be carried out. Thus, they argue, Minister Buffarini Guidi announced the order on the radio the night before he sent it to his police, giving Jews time to flee. Then, they continue, he modified his order on December 10, exempting precisely those who were unable to flee—the sick and the aged.

This justification may contain a grain of truth, for it is certainly the only rational explanation for Buffarini Guidi's behavior. The police order did serve to alert Jews that their last thread of hope was gone—that they could expect nothing from their own government. Carlo Modigliani, for example, describes his shock and complete dismay when he heard the news, and the extra precautionary steps he then took. [3] But like Modigliani, most Jews were already hiding by December 1. It is somewhat specious to argue that a measure that further endangered Jews in fact helped them by forcing them to take even greater precautions. Furthermore, the argument that police order number five was never intended to be carried out is negated by the obvious fact that it *was* carried out, with vigor.

A second (and conflicting) justification for the police order suggests that Fascist moderates decreed the arrest and internment of Jews in order to save them from deportation by the Germans. [4] It must be noted that the order never mentioned deportation, and there is no evidence that it was intended. Jews were to be held in concentration camps in Italy. Apologists point out that from early December 1943 to mid-February 1944, most arrested Jews were in fact interned in Italy and not released to the Nazis. Most Italian police agents probably believed internment to be the ultimate objective, as officially it was. The commander of the central Italian concentration camp at Fossoli, for example, told Jews interned there on several occasions that if he ever had to hand them over to the Nazis, he would dismantle the camp. When the time came, of course, he delivered them for deportation. [5] He had little choice, short of suicidal resistance.

This second justification for Salò policy toward Jews is equally unconvincing. Despite the fact that most Jews arrested in December, January, and February were interned in Italy, some continued to be delivered to the Nazis. A fifth deportation train left Milan on January 30, 1944, in the middle of the period under discussion. It carried at least 700 people to Auschwitz, with no serious opposition from the Italian government.

At least 180 of the 700 deportees came from as far south as Tuscany. Many Tuscans had been captured during raids at Gabbro and Guasticce on December 20; others had been taken from an Italian internment camp at Bagni di Lucca on January 25.[6] Police order number five had not saved them from deportation.

Above all, however, the justification for the order fails to convince because it is contrary to everything known about the Republic of Salò. The new government was powerless to resist any German demand, and Mussolini knew it. He could not end the imprisonment in Germany of 640,000 officers and men from his former army. How could he possibly have expected to resist a Nazi demand for the deportation of Italy's Jews, once they were conveniently interned? The answer is that he and his advisors did not care. Mussolini needed a Jewish policy, and internment was a logical outgrowth of the declaration of Jews as enemy aliens. He did not necessarily want the Jews to be deported and murdered, but he did not worry about how he would resist future Nazi demands for them. The Jews were few in number, and Mussolini had other problems.

The Germans immediately saw the potential for exploiting the police order. After the first easy roundups, Jews became harder to find. The SS was hard pressed to release the man-power necessary to ferret individuals out of private hiding places. Now Italians, on their own initiative, were proposing to do the dirty work. It was a convenient solution.

Three days after the announcement of the police order, Adolf Eichmann's leading Jew-hunters Theodor Dannecker and Friedrich Bosshammer met in Berlin with Eberhard von Thadden of the German Foreign Ministry to discuss how best to exploit the situation. Bosshammer offered the opinion that the German SS should immediately press the Italian police for the deportation of all interned Jews. Von Thadden was more restrained. Why, he argued, should we frighten the Italians?

The Italians and The Holocaust

Let them make their arrests in good faith. We can always act later. His view prevailed at the meeting, but its actual application was erratic.[7]

From early December 1943 to mid-February 1944, the Holocaust in Italy was conducted primarily by Italians according to Italian rules. From the very beginning, however, the Nazis supervised and tried to interfere. German SS police appointed as liaisons to local police headquarters often insisted that Italian exemptions for aged, ill, or converted Jews be ignored. Sometimes the Italians yielded to German wishes; sometimes they did not. National police chief Tullio Tamburini certainly yielded, however, when he instructed all *capi delle province* on January 22 to work out "suitable arrangements with the local German authorities" and if necessary, to arrest and intern "all Jews even if hitherto exempt or privileged."[8] A more cynical disregard for the policy of his own government can scarcely be imagined.

On the other hand, during the same period Minister of the Interior Buffarini Guidi occasionally tried to reaffirm Italian policy. On January 20, he ordered his bureaucrats to take steps to convince German authorities that interned Jews must remain on Italian soil.[9] The efficacy of this measure is revealed by the fact that a deportation train left Milan ten days later. Many of its seven hundred passengers were sick, over seventy, converts, or members of mixed families who should not even have been arrested. Others were not immune from arrest under Italian law, but none of the seven hundred should have been deported. Deportation not only contravened Italian policy, but was also contrary to the German objectives agreed upon at the meeting of von Thadden, Dannecker, and Bosshammer in Berlin on December 4. Clearly, the SS in Italy was acting as a free agent.

Bosshammer replaced SS Captain Dannecker as Eichmann's chief of the anti-Jewish campaign in Italy at the end of January.

He arrived in Verona in time to inspect the deportation train that had left Milan on January 30. As he was even less disposed than his predecessor to respect the laws of the Republic of Salò, Nazi interference grew. Jews were seized from Italian internment camps and not heard from again. Jewish spouses in mixed marriages were arrested, and all official Italian inquiries about them were ignored. Raids on the hospitals and old-age homes sheltering the technically exempt sick and elderly intensified. Police order number five seemed a dead letter.

On March 7, Buffarini Guidi again protested, reminding Germans of the Italian exemption policy. [10] The Nazis ignored him. In April, Bosshammer informed his agents, who in turn informed Italian police, that the SS wanted all Jews regardless of age and health, and that German, not Italian, definitions of who was Jewish were to apply. [11] Italian Aryanization decrees were set aside.

Under Bosshammer's leadership, on February 8, the German SS police took over Fossoli, the principal Italian internment camp near Modena. Before the takeover, no deportation trains had left directly from the camps where, under Italian law, Jews were to be interned. Now, deportations from the camp began immediately. Italian police throughout central Italy were ordered to send their Jewish prisoners to Fossoli. On February 19, 1944, a train carried 141 Libyan Jews of British nationality to Bergen Belsen. Because the Nazis did not gas British Jews, they survived. [12] On February 22, however, another train left Fossoli. This train, the seventh from Italian soil, carried 650 people to Auschwitz. Of these, 97 men and 29 women survived the selection; 15 men and 8 women returned after the war. [13]

Eight more trains carried Jews from Italian soil before the war ended. Four of them left from Fossoli. A train to Auschwitz on April 5, 1944, carried 835 people, most of them from Fossoli but some picked up at Mantua and Verona; 47 returned. Another on May 16 carried from 575 to 672 prisoners; 57 returned. Still another on June 26 collected 517 Jews from Fossoli and picked up more than 400 others at Verona. Of the 517 from Fossoli, 32 returned. [14]

Finally, toward the end of July 1944, Fossoli prepared to close down. The Allies were approaching Pisa and Florence, partisans were operating dangerously close to the camp, and German troops were in retreat. Fossoli's last Jewish prisoners, those who had hitherto enjoyed privileged status, were prepared for deportation. The group included Jewish spouses in mixed marriages, the children of such marriages, and remnants of the Jews who had helped run the camp. The bridges over the Po had been destroyed by July, and there was no train service between Modena and Verona. The last prisoners rode in trucks as far as the river, crossing it in boats on a beautiful clear night, under a full moon. In the confusion, several escaped. At Verona, deportees from Fossoli joined Jews from other Italian prisons. The deportation train left Verona on August 2.

The Nazis carefully applied their classification system to the very end. Jews on the August 2 train were divided into special categories, and their destinations differed. The train divided at Innsbruck. About three hundred, including the Jewish spouses from mixed marriages, went on to Auschwitz. Twenty-eight returned. Fifty-nine women found to be the offspring of mixed marriages were sent instead to Ravensbruck, where sixteen survived. Twenty-eight men, also born of mixed marriages, went to Buchenwald, where fourteen survived. Another thirty-eight to forty, of undetermined backgrounds, went to Bergen Belsen, and nearly all returned. [15]

To this sorry chronology, it should be added that Interior Minister Guido Buffarini Guidi visited Fossoli at some point between June 22 and July 3, 1944, accompanied by a group of Italian police. [16] At least three, possibly four, trains had carried

Italian Jews from Fossoli to Auschwitz by that time. Italian laws decreeing internment, but not deportation, remained on the books. Buffarini Guidi, in visiting Fossoli, gave deportation his tacit approval.

Because several trains carried prisoners from different places, it is not possible to state precisely how many Jews were deported from Fossoli itself. There must have been at least 2,600. At least another 1,400 Jews were deported from other camps and prisons under Italian jurisdiction after the issuance of police order number five. The vast majority of these victims had been arrested by Italians, under Italian law. It is true that Italians did not control events in their own country during the German occupation. But Italians made laws abetting the Holocaust. Italian militiamen, police, and *carabinieri* made arrests, helped load the deportation trains, and occasionally accompanied them as far as Auschwitz itself. They cannot escape responsibility.

The difficult question of what people knew of the ultimate fate of Jewish deportees again arises here. Whether the Jews themselves understood or even suspected that extermination awaited them at Auschwitz remains unclear. Wachsberger did not know for several days that his wife and child had been gassed even though he was present in the same huge camp. The strong Roman Jews who passed the selection but then chose to ride with the old, the mothers, and the children, did not know they were riding to their deaths. What then did civil servants in far-away Italy know when they legislated and carried out arrests and internments, and when they permitted deportations? What did informers know? What, for that matter, did those who sheltered Jews at risk to their own lives know about the Holocaust?

In most cases, people probably suspected but were not sure. They were not sure in part because they did not want to know. It was easier, much easier, not to know. They were also unsure

The Italians and The Holocaust

because the truth was not believable. There was no real proof of the gas chambers. There were so many rumors, and so many thousands of people were being deported. Italian soldiers, British prisoners-of-war, anti-Fascists, partisans—all were being deported every day. The camps were terrible, and many died. That was credible. But deliberate mass extermination was not.

Should they have believed? Perhaps. Allied and neutral radios were broadcasting accurate information about the death camps by the end of 1943. The Nazis were deporting children, desperately sick people, complete invalids, and the feeble aged. No one could believe they were destined for work camps. *Carabinieri* and militiamen accompanied trains to the gates of Auschwitz, smelled the burning bodies, and undoubtedly talked to Nazi guards and Jewish prison workers.[17] They saw thousands of Jewish prisoners, emaciated but still alive. They probably did not ask too many questions. Besides, even if they were sure, who would believe them?

The question of knowledge is important. There is a difference between sending a person to prison, where he will work, suffer, and perhaps die, and actually murdering him. Lack of certainty about the death camps, however, does not absolve guilt. Italians may not have been certain, but particularly at the higher levels of bureaucracy, they did not know because they did not want to know. The guilt of even the best of the law makers and enforcers of the Italian Social Republic lies not only in the fact that they arrested and interned individuals whose only offense was a result of birth, but also in that they abandoned interest in their very survival.[18]

Not all Salò officials acted for reasons of expediency, careerism, or indifference. A few acted with real conviction. The most notorious of Italy's anti-Semites was Giovanni Preziosi, already seen in chapter 3 as the defrocked priest and Fascist fanatic who translated and circulated the "Protocols of the Elders of

Zion" in 1921 and proclaimed his virulent hatred in *La Vita Italiana* throughout the 1920s. Until 1943, he remained an ominous figure lurking in the shadows. Mussolini disliked him. His brief and noisy career under the Republic of Salò was a result of machinations performed not in Italy, but in Germany.

By sheer chance, Preziosi arrived in Nazi Germany on July 26, 1943, the day Mussolini fell from power. Because he could not go home again, Preziosi spent the next several months trying to make a name for himself in Germany as an anti-Semite. His chief contact and protector in the Third Reich was Alfred Rosenberg, the Nazi party ideologist and Minister of the Occupied Eastern Territories who was tried and hung at Nuremberg after the war. Hitler received Preziosi at his eastern command headquarters at Rastenburg, East Prussia. Preziosi told the Führer at that meeting that Mussolini had fallen because he had never resolved the problem of the Jews and the Freemasons.

Preziosi repeated these charges in a series of six articles in *Volkischer Beobachter*, the official Nazi party newspaper, and in a number of Italian-language radio broadcasts from Munich. He asserted that Jewish influence in Italy had been enormous since the *Risorgimento*, that Fascist moderates had personal connections with Jews, and that Mussolini had been remiss in not solving the problem.

On January 31, 1944, Preziosi sent Mussolini a twelve-page memorandum in which he declared, among other things, that "the first task [of the RSI] is not to create a national constitution of the State, but to eliminate the Jews." In his list of victims he included "half-breeds, spouses of Jews and all who have a drop of Jewish blood," as well as converts, Aryanized Jews, and Freemasons. He sent a copy of the memorandum to Hitler. [19]

In part to bring him back to Italy and under some control, Mussolini appointed Preziosi Inspector-General for Race on

The Italians and The Holocaust

March 15, 1944. On April 18, the Council of Ministers ratified the appointment. For the next year, Preziosi worked on various meaningless projects. He attempted without success to enact a new racial code modeled on the German Nuremberg laws. He struggled to establish some real authority in the face of the obstruction of ministers not unnaturally displeased by his earlier charges against them. He continued to accuse other government officials of peculation and ideological softness. He even proposed a "racial super-police," as he called it, modeled on the Gestapo, for the single purpose of hunting down Jews and confiscating their goods. He operated, for the most part, in a vacuum. [20]

Preziosi represents the most virulent, obsessive, and rare variety of Italian anti-Semite. He nevertheless cannot be remembered for any significant contribution to policy making, despite occasional allegations to the contrary. He would make a handy scapegoat for apologists of both the Fascist moderates and the Nazi occupiers, but the chronology does not fit. [21] The Republic of Salò had defined its internment policy for Jews and turned its back on subsequent deportations long before Preziosi was ratified as Inspector-General for Race in April 1944. The Nazis had taken over Fossoli, intensified deportations, and begun to comb hospitals, old-age homes, and mental institutions without Preziosi's encouragement. Giovanni Preziosi was like a man gone mad, raving but ignored. His more moderate colleagues were far more lethal. [22]

Primo Levi, a young chemist and future distinguished author, was captured by the Fascist militia on December 13, 1943. A member of Giustizia e Libertà, Italy's major non-Marxist anti-Fascist organization, Levi had left his home city of Turin to join the partisans in the mountains. When captured, he revealed his own ignorance of the Holocaust by informing the Fascists that he was Jewish. He thought that would explain his presence in a remote mountain area. Better, he thought, to be interned as a Jew than executed as a partisan. Levi was unaware that not all partisans were executed, while nearly all Jews were gassed. He arrived at Fossoli at the end of January 1944. [23]

Fossoli, as Primo Levi knew it, was a large rectangular camp, measuring two kilometers by one. It was located near Carpi, a town eighteen miles north of Modena. The Carpi train station, just a brief truck ride away, was on the line that led directly north to Verona and then to the Brenner Pass. Other major lines from central Italy fed into that northern line. For Nazi purposes, the location was ideal.

Before the September 1943 armistice, Fossoli had held British prisoners-of-war. By the time Buffarini Guidi ordered the arrest and internment of Italian Jews, the British had long departed. The barracks, electric and barbed wire, observation towers, and flood lights at Fossoli remained in place. Ten barracks were set aside for Jews. The other twenty held political prisoners and common criminals.

Jewish prisoners at Fossoli, strictly separated from other inmates, were forced to wear a yellow rectangle on their shirts. Conditions, difficult for all, were worse for them. Barracks designed to house from eighty to a hundred prisoners often held twice that number. Food rations barely sustained life. Survivors often recall famished Jewish children who risked life and limb to enter the non-Jewish section of the camp to beg for bread. [24] Before German SS police took over in February 1944, however, prisoners were usually not beaten or tortured, and daily labor was not excessive. Prisoners could occasionally send letters and receive packages. For many, conditions at Fossoli were superior to those in the prisons and camps from which they had come.

Where had they come from? Arrested Jews were usually held locally until there were enough of them to warrant transfer to Fossoli. In larger cities, they were held in local prisons—places like Regina Coeli in Rome, San Vittore in Milan, Marassi in Genoa, Murate for men and Santa Verdiana for women in Florence. In smaller cities and towns, accommodations were improvised. Italian authorities often requisitioned public institutions—a school, an old-age home, a seminary, or a synagogue. Jews could be held there for days, weeks, or even months, often without heat, beds, or sanitary facilities.

Prisons and detention centers were under Italian jurisdiction. German SS police established liaison offices at most major prisons, and as time went on, they interfered more and more. They were particularly interested in Jewish prisoners. At Regina Coeli and elsewhere, they eventually claimed supreme authority in the wings reserved for Jews. [25] But Italians were responsible for the physical conditions, which were often abominable. At San Vittore in Milan, it was so cold during the winter of 1943–44 that water on the floor froze and remained as sheets of ice two inches thick. [26] Food, clothing, and blanket allotments barely kept people alive, and could be denied as punishment. Not surprisingly, Enea Fergnani, a non-Jewish lawyer imprisoned at San Vittore, recalls two suicides in December alone. Two desperate Jewish men hurled themselves from a third-floor interior balcony. In the months that followed, there were others. [27]

Italian prison officials and Fascists from outside conducted interrogation and torture sessions as regularly as did the Nazis. Of the treatment he received at the time of his arrest in Rome, the Jewish tenor Emilio Jani recalls, "Unfortunately I must admit that . . . the Germans behaved better than the Fascists. . . ." [28] Fergnani remembers special humiliations for the Jews at San Vittore, as when they were forced to lick large segments of the filthy floor. He also relates that Jews were denied the daily hour of courtyard exercise enjoyed by other prisoners. They could not purchase extra food, receive letters, or secure medical care. [29] And like other prisoners, they were at the mercy of spies and informers who infiltrated the cells. At Marassi in Genoa, an eighteen-year-old girl planted among the prisoners reported an anti-Fascist priest. His sole offense was bringing three hundred lire and a packet of biscuits to the Jewish mother of one of his former students. The priest, too, soon found himself in prison. [30]

In smaller detention centers outside the largest cities, conditions varied widely. At Mantua, Jews were held in a former Jewish rest home. They were arrested, guarded, and supplied entirely by Italian regular police. Food was scarce and discipline harsh, but life was tolerable. Sixty-three Jews, most of them arrested immediately after police order number five in December 1943, remained in Mantua for four months. On April 4, 1944, four Italian police selected forty-two for deportation. They joined a convoy that had already left Fossoli. An air-raid siren was sounded as they left their prison and joined the train, so no one would see. Only one returned from Auschwitz after the war. [31]

In Borgo San Dalmazzo, Italian Jews were held in the same military barracks used earlier to house the refugees from southern France. It was staffed by *carabinieri*, under local police supervision. The detainees suffered from scarcity, neglect, and indifference, but not brutality. On February 16, while local residents slept, about twenty-six departed for Fossoli on the 5:39 A.M. train. [32]

In Asti, where local Jews were held in a requisitioned seminary from December 1943 to May 1944, conditions of internment must have been quite tolerable. According to Augusto Segre, who tried to warn friends of their danger before he fled the city in September, Italian police began to arrest Jews in Asti immediately after they received police order number five. Jews held in the seminary were allowed out during the day, so long as they returned each evening. Not only did no one try to escape, but some Jews actually turned themselves in. Deprived of all means of making a living, they chose to live under arrest, with the consequent free room and board.[33]

Segre's story seems unbelievable. Had the Jews of Asti not heard about the Roman roundup, the Florentine raids, the arrests in nearby Turin and Genoa, the numerous trains that had already carried hundreds of their brethren to the "labor camps"? Did they act as they did because they believed the Italian police who assured them that internment in Italy did not mean deportation? Even allowing for the fact that the brightest and the strongest from their midst had already fled, the behavior of those remaining behind remains a mystery. About thirty-eight Jews from Asti were eventually deported. Three returned after the war.

At Fossoli itself, conditions deteriorated after the German SS police arrived in early February. The Italian camp commander and vice-commander remained as figureheads, but SS Sergeant Major Hans Haage, a fanatic Nazi, assumed supreme authority. Primo Levi was there at the time. He recalls that the SS, in an effort to ease tensions and reassure the inmates, publicly rebuked Italian administrators on February 20 for deficiencies in the camp and spoke of opening an infirmary. Then on February 21, they abruptly announced a deportation for the next day. They read 650 names. For anyone failing to report, ten others would be shot.

The women on the list spent the day trying to keep busy, wrapping bundles, washing clothes, bathing the children. The men who could not pretend to be busy talked quietly among themselves. They had no more illusions. Primo Levi, whose name was on the list, remembers, "We had spoken to Polish and Croat refugees and we knew what departure meant."[34] The train left for Auschwitz on schedule. Levi was among the twenty-three who returned.

For those remaining at Fossoli, assassination and torture now began. Pacifico Di Castro, whose wife and seven children had been caught in the Rome roundup and deported in October, was murdered by a prison guard because he felt ill and did not report for work. SS Sergeant Major Haage shot a Jewish prisoner one morning for target practice, without a trace of emotion. An elderly deaf man was shot in the base of the head because he did not answer "present" during roll call. [35] These cases were reported by survivors. There were undoubtedly others, witnessed by prisoners who did not survive.

Non-Jewish political prisoners also suffered at Fossoli, particularly after the German SS takeover. Enea Fergnani remembers Poldo Gasparotto, a respected young Milanese partisan affiliated with Giustizia e Libertà who was taken from his barracks and murdered on the night of June 22, 1944. A deportation convoy had left Fossoli the day before, carrying political prisoners to Mauthausen. Gasparotto had apparently been trying to coordinate an escape. [36]

Three weeks later, on July 11, the German SS read a list of seventy non-Jewish political prisoners who were to prepare themselves for deportation at dawn. The next day at the appointed time, the men entered the truck that was to carry them to the station. The truck stopped in a field where eight Jewish prisoners had been forced to dig a huge pit. In groups of twenty, the political prisoners were made to kneel beside the pit. There, they were mowed down by machine guns. Two managed to escape; the other sixty-eight died. Later it was learned that the murders had occurred in reprisal for a partisan attack in Genoa in which seven German soldiers had been killed. [37]

As the executions of Gasparotto and the seventy other political prisoners at Fossoli suggest, non-Jewish anti-Fascists and even apolitical civilians suffered terribly during the German occupa-

The Italians and The Holocaust

tion of Italy. Including the soldiers interned after the armistice, hundreds of thousands of Italians were deported. They were never gassed, however, and most eventually returned. But over 10,000 Italians, including at least 170 priests, were killed in reprisal murders.[38] In the village of Marzabotto alone, at least 1,830 civilians, including the priest and many women and children, were massacred for allegedly harboring partisans.[39] Thousands of other people died in air raids. In comparison to these raw figures (but not, of course, in comparison to percentages of population), the number of Jews who perished in the Holocaust in Italy is small. Yet the Holocaust remains unique and must be remembered apart from other tragedies. It cannot be regarded as another of the vicissitudes of an excessively brutal war.

Anti-Fascists who died at the hands of the SS and the Fascists were, for the most part, adult men and women who had made a conscious choice. Occasionally they may have simply chosen among a number of undesirable alternatives: military conscription, forced labor service, a German concentration camp, or life with the anti-Fascist partisans. Still, they had chosen, and their sacrifice was ennobled by that choice. Holocaust victims had not chosen.

Civilian victims of urban air raids or village reprisal murders, of course, were not involved by choice. They differed from Holocaust victims, however, in that their selection was pure chance. They did not die because of a vaguely defined condition of race or religion. They died simply because they happened to be in the wrong place at the wrong time. A tragedy, surely, but different in kind from the Holocaust.

The Jewish victims of the Holocaust were denied both the dignity of choice and the hope of random selection. Some Italian Jews, of course, died as partisans; others died in air raids and reprisal killings. They were not Holocaust victims. The men, women, and children who perished in the Holocaust died because an inexorable power had decreed that human beings with certain qualifications should, without exception, without choice, without random selection, be destroyed. It was a terrifying, inhuman concept beyond reason, argument, or persuasion. It was beyond comprehension and beyond imagination. It was the central horror of our time.

On July 21, 1944, Enea Fergnani was transported from Fossoli to Gries, a concentration camp in the suburbs of Bolzano, no longer technically on Italian soil. Ten days later, Fossoli was emptied and closed because of the approach of the Allies. Henceforth, Gries became the official holding camp for prisoners, Jews and non-Jews alike, awaiting deportation. Gries had a capacity of about three thousand prisoners, although it was often crowded to four thousand or more. Usually about 5 percent of the prisoners were Jewish and, as at Fossoli, they were housed separately. The yellow star here replaced Fossoli's yellow rectangle.

Descriptions of daily conditions at Gries vary. A Jewish survivor, Corrado Saralvo, found conditions at Gries somewhat preferable to those in San Vittore Prison.[40] The non-Jewish Fergnani found life more difficult than at Fossoli. Rations were scarce and bad, the work more arduous and dangerous, and the German and Ukrainian guards ferocious and unpredictable.[41]

Cases of torture and assassination clearly exceeded those at Fossoli. As many as three hundred prisoners seem to have been murdered at Gries, and many of these were Jewish. One survivor remembers the particular bestiality of an SS woman, Elsa Lächert, who came to Gries from a death camp in Poland. In one case, Lächert confined a forty-year-old Jewish woman to a cell and ordered guards to throw pails of icy water on her three times a day. When the woman still clung to life after three days, Lächert herself strangled her. She then forced the dead woman's seventy-five-year-old mother into the same cell and left her there to die of starvation.[42]

At least two convoys carried Jews from Gries to Nazi death camps. On October 24, 1944, a train left for Auschwitz carrying 300 prisoners, of whom at least 150 were Jewish. All the non-Jews were admitted to the camp, but only about 46 Jews passed the selection and escaped the gas chambers. Of these 46, 11 men and 4 women returned after the war. A second train carried 150 prisoners from Gries to Flossenburg and Ravensbruck on December 14. At least 80 of the 150 were Jewish. All were admitted to the camps. Of the 80, 2 men and 2 women returned.[43]

Corrado Saralvo's account of his deportation train from Gries to Auschwitz, probably on October 24, is strikingly similar to accounts a full year earlier. Little, it seems, had changed, and deportees were still unaware of pending extermination. Like others before him, Saralvo writes of two prisoners who might have escaped through a boxcar window, but who were convinced by others fearing reprisals to remain on the train. Of the sick, the weak, and the very young selected for the gas chambers upon arrival, he writes, "None of them seemed to have an intuition of the fate which awaited them and even we only learned of it later."[44]

The most terrible prison camp on what before September 1943, had been Italian soil existed in Trieste. After the Germans occupied and annexed Trieste, Pola, Fiume, Gorizia, and Udine to the Third Reich, they decided that the new region should have a concentration camp complete with a crematorium. They selected La Risiera, an old rice-refining factory in the San Sabba section of the city. They imported SS agent Erwin Lambert, an expert in crematoria who had perfected his skills at Treblinka and Sobibor, to supervise the conversion. For local Jews and non-Jews alike, La Risiera, or

San Sabba as it was often called, became the principal symbol of Nazi repression and terror.

Management of La Risiera was entrusted to the Einsatzkommando Reinhardt, one of the most ruthless special units of the SS. Men from the Einsatzkommando had actively participated in roundups of Polish Jews in Lvov, Cracow, Tarnow, Lublin, and Warsaw. They were responsible for thousands of street murders, tortures, and public humiliations. They had conducted millions to death camps at Belzec, Sobibor, Treblinka, and Auschwitz. Their commander in Trieste, SS General Odilo Lotario Globocnik, a personal friend of Adolf Eichmann, had directed the roundups in Lublin. Among their 120 members at Trieste were Franz Stangl, former commander at Sobibor and Treblinka; Dietrich Allers, director of the German euthanasia campaign in 1939; Christian Wirth, former director of extermination units at Belzec, Sobibor, and Treblinka; and Georg Michalezyk, trained at Belzec, Sobibor, and Majdanek. These men were experienced, determined, and ruthless.[45]

Einsatzkommando Reinhardt lived up to its reputation. Tens of thousands of prisoners, Jews and non-Jews, Italians and Yugoslavs, passed through La Risiera. Survivors remember the clanking of cell doors opening and closing in the night, prisoners screaming as they marched through the corridors, executions in the courtyard accompanied by blaring music to cover the sound. They remember fierce dogs and ferocious Ukrainian guards. The crematorium, with a capacity of from fifty to seventy corpses a day, functioned regularly. Sacks of human ashes were dumped into the harbor.[46] One survivor retains an even more terrifying image. An SS man passed his cell, leading a curly-haired toddler by the hand. The child, Jewish, tripped and fell. The man kicked him in the head with the full force of his heavy boot. The child's head literally exploded.[47]

Estimates of deaths at La Risiera range from 3,000 to 4,500.[48] The victims were usually partisans. Probably only about 50 were Jews. For Jewish prisoners, death was more certain, but it came elsewhere. Jews from Trieste, Udine, and Gorizia, and from cities as far west as Venice and Padua, as well as hundreds from Yugoslavia to the east, were gathered at La Risiera to await the deportation trains. At least twenty-two trains left Trieste for Auschwitz in a period of thirteen months, between early October 1943 and November 1, 1944. The number of deportees is not known. [49]

Among many poignant messages on the walls of cells at La Risiera, one especially conveys the monstrous tragedy that destroyed whole families. It reads:

> Arrested September 21, 1944—Venice
> Husband Aldo Sereni born December 19, 1894—Deported October 12
> Wife Giannina Bordignon Sereni May 24, 1896
> Children: Ugo Sereni   January 6, 1925
>   Paolo Sereni   May 24, 1927
>   Elena Sereni   March 30, 1930
>
> May God protect my family—the Mother

Mrs. Sereni later added to the inscription:

> Ugo, Paolo and Elena Sereni departed for Germany January 11, 1945—the Mother
>
> January 6, 1945   birthday of Ugo—the Mother

And then, still later:

> May God bless my children and my husband. I am desolate—Giannina Sereni Bordignon [50]

Words fail before such an inscription. And yet the Serenis had more reason for hope than most captured Jewish families.

Giannina Sereni was not Jewish, but her husband was. Because of her Aryan status, her husband and children should not even have been arrested under the terms of police order number five. Once arrested, there was little hope for her husband, as she must have known when she recorded his early departure. Her children, however, were of mixed blood, and half-Jews, at least from Fossoli, did not usually go to Auschwitz. Paolo Sereni in fact returned from Ravensbruck after the war. By that time, his mother had been murdered at La Risiera.[51]

Before the war, the Sereni family had operated a small shop near the Piazza San Marco. Thousands of tourists had visited each year. Thousands would return after the war. Undamaged, the Piazza San Marco would remain as a monument to human creativity, industry, and love of life. Yet unnoticed by the tourists, whole families had disappeared without a trace—a testimony of human hatred, cruelty, and lust for destruction.

9

The Italian Phase

A FEW DAYS after police order number five authorized their action on December 1, an Italian team of police, *carabinieri,* and Fascist agents launched a midnight raid on the Casa Israelitica di Riposo, a Jewish nursing home in the former ghetto in Venice. They arrested all the patients, including those too old or sick to move. At the same time, with air raid sirens wailing to divert attention and mask the screams of the victims, Italian police pounded on the doors of Jewish homes throughout the city. They arrested everyone they found.

The terrified prisoners were taken to the Collegio Marco Foscarini. The school had been transformed into a primitive detention center lacking all facilities. Even the old and the sick slept on benches or on the floor. No one was fed. Neighbors heard children crying from hunger, and threw food in through the windows. The Jews remained at the school for ten days.

On December 15, the prisoners were moved to the Casa di Ricovero, a Jewish recuperation center. The sick and those over seventy were freed in accordance with Minister of the Interior

Guido Buffarini Guidi's directives of December 10. It was a fleeting reprieve. Most were quickly rearrested by German SS police and deported directly to Auschwitz. The young and the strong remained for a time at the recuperation center, where conditions were terrible. The Fascists had looted the building on the night of the original raid, so there were no supplies. There were not enough beds and practically no food. Some non-Jewish Venetians tried to smuggle supplies in to the starving group. One of them, a mason named Giovanni Pianon, invented various jobs in order to secure a pass to the building. He carried messages and supplies in and out for months. [1]

On the last day of 1943, ninety-three Jews left the group at the recuperation center and set out for Fossoli. Escorted by Italian police and *carabinieri*, they rode in two third-class train cars. At first, they wrote to relieved relatives and friends in Venice that they were well. Then there was silence. They, too, ended their days at Auschwitz. [2]

The province of Venice had a Jewish population of 2,189 in 1938, according to the census of that year. During the Holocaust, 212 Jews were deported. Fifteen returned. [3] Ninety-three were deported as a result of a single raid conducted entirely by Italians.

With police order number five, the Italian phase of the Holocaust began. Government policy was defined and clear. Security forces were committed to the arrest and internment of Jews, and internment camps, with the exception of Gries, were functioning at full capacity. Most Jews, now warned, were in hiding, but in December the manhunt began in earnest.

Statistics tell the tale. Before police order number five, four deportation trains had carried about 2,385 Jews to Auschwitz. That figure includes the train of December 6, which presumably contained prisoners arrested before the police order. After the order went into effect, trains carried at least 4,210 Jews to

The Italians and The Holocaust

Auschwitz alone. That figure includes the 150 deported from Gries to Auschwitz, but it does not include the hundreds of Jews deported by way of German-annexed Trieste. Nor does it include the 1,805 men, women, and children deported by the German SS from the former Italian colonies of Rhodes and Cos. They began their terrible journey on July 23, 1944, and arrived at Auschwitz a full twenty-five days later. Of the 1,805, 555 passed the selection, and 183 returned. [4]

The 2,385 deportees before early December 1943 had been arrested mostly by the German SS or by autonomous Fascist squads hoping to curry Nazi favor. In Rome alone, Nazis deported over 1,000 Jews as a result of the October 16 roundup. The 4,210 deported after police order number five were arrested mostly by Italian police, *carabinieri*, or militiamen acting under government orders. In Rome, Italian security forces, for the most part, arrested at least 835 Jews before the liberation of the city in June, despite the fact that they were in hiding and were much more difficult to find. [5] The vast majority of Italians may have abhorred these arrests and assisted their Jewish neighbors, but obviously, many did not.

In Rome, Jewish arrest statistics can be broken down by the month. After the October 16 roundup, only 3 more Jews were arrested that month. For the next three months, arrests continued at a low rate: 28 in November, 31 in December, and 29 in January. They soared dramatically during the next three months, to 141 in February, 163 in March, and 201 in April. There were, finally, 98 in the month before Rome's liberation. [6]

The chronology shows that in Rome, at least, Italian security forces reacted slowly to police order number five. There is even a suggestion of deliberate stalling. On December 10, national police chief Tullio Tamburini telegraphed to police headquarters throughout the country the instructions of Interior Minister Buffarini Guidi, issued the same day, that Jews over seventy, sick, or in mixed families were not to be arrested. He acted promptly, but that same message was not passed from Rome's central police headquarters to the local precincts until December 20. The rest of the month passed with the exchange of orders, counterorders, and requests for clarification of orders. Meanwhile, the police, uncertain whom to seize and whom to spare, made few arrests.[7]

The sudden increase in February coincides precisely with the arrival at German SS security police headquarters in Verona of Eichmann's new representative in Italy, Friedrich Bosshammer. While Bosshammer's predecessor, Theodor Dannecker, had operated with a small mobile unit almost independently of security police channels, and had shifted his activities from city to city, Bosshammer integrated his operation with the German security police bureaucracy to which it formally belonged. Bosshammer exercised his power to demand full cooperation in Jewish matters from all German and Italian security police. He insisted on being informed of all arrests of Jews. He took over Fossoli and, when the Jewish section there became too full, ordered deportations. He effectively coordinated the anti-Jewish campaign in Italy which, until February, had remained disjointed.[8] Pressure for arrests mounted. In response, Roman police chief Pietro Caruso, also newly installed in February, instructed his agents to "proceed urgently with the arrest of pure Italian and foreign Jews." Contrary to his own government's policy of exemptions for the sick, aged, and mixed families, he added that "all family components must be detained."[9]

Roman Jews were caught in several different ways. First, individual informers, usually attracted by rewards of 5,000 lire for Jewish males and about half that amount for women and children, deliberately tracked down former friends and neighbors and turned them in. Informers came from every walk of life. They included housewives, former servants, shopkeepers, former business competitors, dedicated Fascist activists, and children. One non-Jewish wife turned in her Jewish husband, and then despaired when her son was arrested too.[10] One Roman informer, among the most notorious and successful, was an eighteen-year-old Jewish girl. Celeste Di Porto, so beautiful that her family called her Stella (Star), had a new nickname by the end of the occupation. Known as the Black Panther, she was directly responsible for the arrests of fifty Jews, even though she herself had lost several relatives during the October roundup.[11]

Twenty-six of the Black Panther's fifty victims were among the 335 men and boys murdered by the German SS at the Ardeatine Caves on March 24, 1944. The Ardeatine Caves massacre occurred as a reprisal for thirty-three German SS police—ironically, new recruits from the South Tyrol, formerly part of Italy but annexed to the Third Reich in 1943—killed during a partisan attack in Rome's Via Rasella on March 23. Ten Italians in prison for political offenses were to be killed for each SS man who died. The Nazis threw in a few more for good measure. To fill the quota, they also included most Jewish males in Roman prisons at the time, although they were not accused of political crimes. The 335 men and boys, tied together, were driven to the network of manmade caves that comprised part of the Christian catacombs along the Appian Way. There they were forced to wait for hours while those ahead of them entered the caves in groups of three. Inside, they had to kneel on the growing pile of corpses, to await the shot in the back of the head that would kill them. At the end of the day, the caves were sealed.[12]

Most non-Jewish victims of the Ardeatine Caves massacre were dedicated anti-Fascists, adults, and individuals apart from their families. Most Jewish victims, about 77 of the total of 335, were nonpolitical, of varying ages, and in family groups.[13] The youngest victim at the caves, Michele Di

Veroli, was Jewish. He had celebrated his fifteenth birthday the previous month. Michele died with his father, Attilio Di Veroli. At least six other Jewish victims were members of a single family. They included Franco Di Consiglio, just seventeen, and Mosè Di Consiglio, the oldest Ardeatine Caves martyr, age seventy-four. Mosè was born the year the Roman ghetto was abolished. In addition to the Di Veroli and Di Consiglio families, there were several other Jewish groups of fathers, sons, and brothers. [14] Also killed in the caves was Aldo Finzi, Jewish convert, Undersecretary of the Interior in the 1920s, and member of the first Fascist Grand Council. There was no discrimination in the caves.

Lazzaro Anticoli, a twenty-six-year-old Roman Jewish peddler and prizefighter, had been arrested the very morning of the massacre. Before marching out of his cell to his death, he managed to scribble a brief note. "If I never see my family again, it is the fault of that sellout Celeste Di Porto. Avenge me." After the war, it was learned that Lazzaro Anticoli's name had been added to the list of Ardeatine Caves victims at the last minute and another name had been removed. The man thus saved was Celeste Di Porto's brother. [15]

Other Roman Jews were caught by one of at least six little bands of Italian civilians organized in the city especially for that purpose. The groups' objective was to collect reward money and any personal possessions they could seize. Group members carried special permits authorizing them to make arrests. Because they knew the local scene and were dedicated to a single purpose, they operated with deadly effectiveness. [16]

Equally feared was the infamous Koch band, which hunted and tortured Jews and anti-Fascists as brutally as did the Gestapo in Via Tasso. [17] More officially, the GNR and, especially, its Italian African Police contingent joined the hunt with varying degrees of enthusiasm. Finally in February, after Pietro

Caruso became the new Roman police chief, the regular police also began a determined effort to arrest Jews. At this point, as seen, arrests soared.

Jews were caught in every conceivable hiding place: in the homes of friends, in cellars and attics, in abandoned buildings, in shops and warehouses. Many were caught when Fascists and Nazis raided the churches and convents where they were hiding. At least eleven Jews and many anti-Fascists were caught when Fascist and some German SS contingents launched coordinated raids on several Vatican properties on December 22. At least six other Jews, including two Swiss citizens, were seized by Caruso's police and Koch's band during a raid on the Basilica of Saint Paul Outside the Walls on February 3. [18] Because attacks on Vatican properties were a violation of extraterritorial rights, German army elements, fearing a papal rebuke, tried to keep German SS participation to a minimum. The SS, willing to let Italian Fascists perform the dirty work, usually complied. Fascist radicals were in turn delighted to be used.

Perhaps the saddest Jewish victims in Rome were the poor, disoriented individuals caught still living in the old ghetto. They had lost families and friends in the October roundup. Despite repeated warnings that the enemy would return, they could not abandon what remained of their lives. They were picked up in the ghetto's main square, in the streets, in their own apartments. They had, it seems, nothing more to live for. [19]

Luciano Morpurgo recounts the day during the German occupation, while he was living in Rome with false papers, when he somehow found himself guiding a German medical officer and a Lutheran minister on a scenic tour of the city. They passed by the old ghetto, and the two Germans expressed their surprise. They did not know that Jews had ever lived in the city. Morpurgo told them they were no longer there. Hitler had taken them all away. The Germans said nothing. [20]

Of a Jewish community of about 12,000 in 1938, at least 1,700 Jews were deported from Rome during the brief nine months of the occupation. Over 250 of these were children. About 105 men and women returned after the war. None of the children survived. [21]

In most cities in northern and central Italy, the Holocaust followed a pattern similar to that in Rome. Nearly everywhere, victims numbered from 15 to 20 percent of prewar Jewish populations. Nearly everywhere, informers and semi-autonomous bands were active. Trieste even shared with Rome the dubious distinction of producing a Jewish informer. Known as Graziadio Mauro Grini, the Trieste informer was the son of a Jewish tailor and a blind mother, both imprisoned, along with his brother, at La Risiera. Grini occasionally explained his actions as necessary to save his family, but survivors have claimed that he earned up to 7,000 lire per victim. He operated over a large area, with offices as far away as Milan, and he was often seen walking in Milan's fashionable Galleria with two German soldiers as escorts. He is reported to have betrayed over three hundred former acquaintances in Trieste, a hundred in Venice, and nearly as many again in Milan and Padua. Those numbers seem almost impossible, but Grini's name appears again and again in survivors' testimony. [22]

Without the help of informers, it was increasingly difficult to find Jews well hidden by sympathetic neighbors. Some were caught by chance when defects in their false documents were detected during routine checks. Others were netted in labor roundups or searches for partisans or draftdodgers. Still others were recognized by chance. One of these was Mario Finzi, recognized by a former acquaintance during a routine document check in his native Bologna. Most of Celeste Di Porto's victims were also caught by chance, when she recognized them in the streets of Rome. She greeted them heartily, and they were immediately picked up by three or four men following behind her. [23]

Most healthy and capable Jews, however, were caught not by chance, but through some combination of subterfuge, torture, and blackmail. The possibilities were endless. Police, necessarily Italians, posed as Jewish welfare agents and announced distributions of food for the indigent. They infiltrated Jewish services and meetings. When they caught one Jew in an apartment, they waited there for days to arrest all others who knocked on the door. When they arrested one family member, they interrogated and tortured him or her to learn the location of family and friends. To the torture they added the promise, never kept, to spare a loved one, or a threat, often fulfilled, to kill a child. Their tactics were effective.

Michela Fernanda Momigliano, who hid in Milan during the occupation, relates a trick the Italian police used to try to catch her. A sympathetic woman who had rented Michela's apartment sent her a message through a trusted intermediary. A man had called at the apartment, claiming to have a letter from a deported relative. Michela went to the woman's shop, and learned the man's address. She considered going for the letter, but decided it might be a trap. Just as she told the woman of her fears, a man entered the shop asking for her. Michela pretended to be a customer. The woman said Michela had not yet contacted her. The man left and someone followed him—to police headquarters. [24]

As time passed, the Nazis, impatient with slow tactics and anxious to fill quotas, began to turn to easier game. With limited help from Fascists and Italian police, they began to seize the old and infirm from hospitals, old-age homes, and mental institutions. In so doing, they not only ignored Italian government orders to spare the sick and the aged, but they abandoned all pretense that "resettlement" involved work camps. Those who saw invalids packed into boxcars could have no more illusions.

Some of the worst hospital incidents occurred in Turin, Trieste, Florence, and Venice. On March 7, 1944, a Jewish hospice in Turin was raided. The sick and aged patients were held in a local prison for a month until they were shipped to Fossoli and then to Auschwitz. On March 28, three hundred patients from two hospitals and a psychiatric institute in Trieste were deported. Sixty-two were so old and sick that they died during the journey to Auschwitz. Several others never even reached the train. Judged non-transportable, they were taken to La Risiera and murdered.[25]

In Florence on the morning of April 6, the SS raided a Jewish hospice on the banks of the Arno and seized twenty-one aged men and women. Their victims waited two months in a Florentine prison until they were sent to Fossoli and Auschwitz. In August, the SS turned their attention to Venice. On the seventh, guided by the notorious Grini, they seized thirteen elderly Jews from a nursing home outside the city. On the seventeenth, again with Grini, they arrested twenty-two others who had been detained at the recuperation center in Venice since the December raids. Among the prisoners was Adolfo Ottolenghi, chief rabbi of Venice. The victims were held a few days and then sent to Trieste, where all news of them ceased forever. A final hospital raid began in Venice on October 6. For five days, the SS, aided again by the informer Grini and by Italian Brigate Nere and *carabinieri*, combed hospitals and mental institutions for Jewish patients. They made twenty-one arrests. Their oldest victim was eighty-three.[26]

To the tragic toll of deportation and reprisal victims must be added the nearly two hundred Jews who were simply murdered on the spot. In Gubbio, about forty kilometers northeast of

The Italians and The Holocaust

Perugia, for example, on March 27, 1944, a German SS patrol guided by a Fascist GNR militiaman shot three young Jewish men who had been hiding in the countryside. This small incident was recorded.[27] Others may never be known.

Many brutal murders occurred as the Allies approached, when deportation was no longer feasible and panic-stricken Nazi and Fascist fanatics decided to take matters into their own hands. One such case occurred in Pisa, with the Allies only a few days away. On August 1, 1944, a German SS unit pounded on the door of Commendator Giuseppe Pardo Roques, a gentle and dignified former president of the local Jewish Community and former vice-mayor of the city. Inexplicably, the seventy-year-old gentleman had lived at home undisturbed during the entire occupation. By August, he was sheltering six other elderly Jewish friends. Five Catholics also lived in his house, including his maid, the widow of his driver, her sister, and two friends whose home had been destroyed in an air raid.

One Catholic man was out when the Nazis arrived, but a Catholic neighbor, Dante Ristori, was at the house getting water from the well in Pardo Roques's garden. The Nazis locked everyone in the kitchen pantry and loaded everything of value into their waiting truck. After two hours, neighbors heard Pardo Roques scream, "I have given you everything! Leave me my life!" Then they heard two shots, followed by three grenade explosions from the pantry. Seven Jews and five Catholics, friends in life, died together in the house in Pisa that day.[28]

Equally terrible is the story of Roberto Einstein, native of Munich and cousin of the world-famous Albert Einstein. Roberto had studied in Italy before World War I, married an Italian Jewish student named Nina Agar Mazzetti, and remained in Florence to work as an engineer. In 1944, he was living secretly in the country outside Florence with his wife and two daughters, ages twenty-seven and eighteen.

On the evening of August 2, 1944, a unit of German SS arrived at the house. Somehow Roberto managed to escape. The Nazis took his wife and daughters outside and forced his wife to call for him for an hour. Two acquaintances held Roberto and covered his mouth, preventing him from going to them. The Nazis returned to the house with their captives. Shots rang out, the house went up in flames, and the Nazis eventually left. Roberto and his acquaintances recovered the charred bodies. The daughters had been raped. Florence was liberated about a week later. Roberto lived on, tormented and disoriented, for a year. On the anniversary of the murders, he killed himself with cyanide at the grave site of his loved ones. [29]

About a month after the brutal incidents in Pisa and outside Florence, the Allies approached Forli. There on September 5, the SS seized ten foreign Jews from local prisons, took them to an air field, and shot them in the back of the head. Twelve days later, they repeated the atrocity, killing seven other foreign Jews. Then on the twenty-eighth, two Jews from Ferrara were hanged. [30]

The German occupation of Italy that had begun with the murders of Jews at Lago Maggiore ended with a similar tragedy. This time, however, after twenty bitter months of degradation and horror, the perpetrators were not Germans, but Italians. On April 25, 1945, as they were running for the frontier, a group of Fascist militiamen paused in Cuneo to seize six foreign Jews from prison. These prisoners were refugees from France who had crossed the Alps into Italy at the time of the armistice. They had regarded the Italians as benefactors —a people worthy of their trust. For the most part, Italians had lived up to that image. Now, just hours before the liberation, Italian militiamen—products of twenty-three years of Fascist dictatorship—betrayed them. The six Jews—two from Vienna, two from Warsaw, one from Paris, and one from Luxembourg —were murdered, and their bodies were thrown under a bridge.[31]

And so the nightmare ended. As Jews came out of hiding and returned to looted homes and apartments, the full impact of the Holocaust in Italy became apparent. Considering the brevity of the occupation, the highly assimilated and thus easily disguised nature of Italian Jews, and the anti-Fascist, anti-racist inclinations of most Italians, the losses were high. Approximately 37,100 Italian and 8,100 foreign Jews were present in Italy in September 1943. Of these, at least 4,439 Italian and 1,915 foreign Jews were deported. Another 210 Jewish deportees were of undetermined citizenship, and still another 237, deported from Trieste, have not yet been classified as native or foreign. Altogether, then, at least 6,801 Jews were deported— about 15 percent of the population.[32] Another 292, at least, were murdered.[33]

Regional breakdowns of deportation statistics tend to vary, in part because of uncertainty about the real residences of victims. One source, however, cites Rome at the top of the list with 1,727 deportees; Milan second with 896; and Trieste third with 620. Other cities with over 200 deportees include Turin and its environs (407), Florence with Siena (263), Fiume (258), Genoa with La Spezia (244), and Venice (212).[34]

The Holocaust in Italy had not been a mere sideshow. Every Jewish community, every Jewish person, was affected and scarred. Survivors understood they were alive because non-Jewish Italians had helped. The dead left their own testimony in the letters from prison, the notes thrown from trains, the entry books at Auschwitz, the scratches in stone. Their government had abandoned them. Their countrymen had hunted them. Their neighbors had betrayed them. The Holocaust had not been a purely German affair.

10

Survival in Italy

A S SOON as he learned of the armistice, Augusto Segre knew he would have to hide. It was a Friday, and his mother was preparing the Sabbath meal at their home in Asti. "You know, Mamma, don't worry, but I am afraid tonight we will not dine at home." With his mother, his aunt, and his brother's family, he walked, without luggage, to the train station. He had no plans, no idea what train to take.

The Germans had already arrived, and the station was chaotic. Italian soldiers, abandoning weapons and uniforms, were struggling to get onto the trains. German soldiers were pursuing them. Young Segre thought of the comfort of home, and of the meal he was missing. He wondered if he had made the right choice. Would he and his family have been safer if they had remained at home?

At the station Segre met a family friend—a young Aryan woman, as he described her in the terminology of the day. When she asked where he was going, he admitted he did not know. She took him and his family to her parents' home, a

journey requiring a three-hour train ride and a long walk. They
arrived about midnight. They were safe there for a time, but
in a few days they had to move again. [1]

Every head of a Jewish household, whether man or woman,
parent or grown child, had to make crucial decisions based on
little information during the occupation. The decisions were
agonizing, for life itself depended on them. When and where
should a family move? How long should they stay in one place?
How should they travel? Would young children and very old
relatives be safer with the family, or should they be separated
and left with non-Jewish friends? Should the family socialize
and try to simulate normal lives? Should they, to avoid suspicion, send their children to school? Should they go to mass?
What about the sick? How could they receive medical care?
Even the deceased were a problem. How could they be buried?

Some people simply would not flee. In the hour or two
before he left, Segre tried to warn other Jews in Asti. Many
resented his advice. One man loudly and publicly insulted him
as a traitor and a coward. [2] Leaving home meant acknowledg-
ing a terrible danger, and many, particularly in the beginning,
were reluctant to do that. Many paid with their lives.

Jews who were poor, elderly, sick, or handicapped often
believed they had no choice but to remain where they were.
Most did not survive. One woman who did wrote after the war
that she and her sister had remained in their second-floor
apartment in Trieste because they could not afford to move.
When the Nazis came, they hid with non-Jewish friends on the
fourth floor. The Nazis seized a Jewish woman from the third
floor who had no legs and had not been out in twenty years.
They threw her into their truck. [3]

Many old people could not bear to tear themselves from
their roots and admit in the process that their government had
forsaken them. As Wanda Padovano of Florence wrote of her

reluctant parents, "How could they, accustomed all their lives to being respected by Jews and non-Jews, think that a blast of madness could invade and so upset the minds of the Italians?" She herself, like Segre, had no illusions. She had visited Palestine several times and talked with German Jews there. She forced her parents to move, she admits, "with much energy and a little violence." She saved their lives.[4]

Many other people, initially reluctant to flee, at least prepared hiding places and awaited events. This policy often worked. Vittorio Luzzati, for example, stayed at home in Savona, near Genoa, until someone at police headquarters warned him that it was time to leave. Then he fled to a predetermined spot in the Valle d'Aosta.[5] Many Jews received such warnings, often from police or Fascist sources. However, many did not. A decision to postpone hiding was particularly hazardous in major cities such as Rome, Turin, Milan, and Trieste, where the Holocaust began just a month after the German occupation, with massive, carefully planned roundups.

Having decided to hide, a household head then had to plan where to go. Many urban residents, somehow vainly hoping the Fascists and Nazis would only search cities, moved to their country homes or to the homes of rural relatives. Jews from Genoa often moved to apartments along the coast. People from Turin, Florence, and Milan moved into hill towns. But Jewish homes in rural areas were equally well-known to the police. When the hunt extended out from the cities, they too became targets.

Many urban Jews were able to hide in rural pensions, rented rooms, or country homes belonging to friendly non-Jews. These fugitives fared better than those in Jewish homes, but it soon became painfully apparent that life in rural areas was hazardous for everyone. Remote areas were often the most dangerous of all. Vittorio Luzzati found himself with his wife and son in Brusson, near St. Vincent in the wild and rugged Valle d'Aosta. Twice a friendly priest warned them to hide while Fascist militiamen searched the village. Finally, they fled to an even more remote village, accessible only by mule path. After a climb of several hours through the snow at night, they arrived at a hamlet at an altitude of 1,800 meters. Only Monte Rosa and the Matterhorn, two of the highest peaks in Europe, stood between them and Switzerland. With infinite relief, they rented a room. Almost immediately, they were asked to leave. Fascist militiamen were approaching, and the populace was terrified. [6]

The problem, of course, was that in late 1943 and 1944 rural Italy was literally crawling with men wanted by the Nazi and Fascist police. About eighty thousand Allied prisoners-of-war in Italy at the time of the armistice had escaped and were wandering about trying to cross into Allied-occupied territory. [7] To these were added thousands of former Italian soldiers, now unwilling to fight for the Republic of Salò and technically deserters. Eventually other men and boys headed for the hills by the thousands to escape conscription for military and labor service. Many became partisans, attacking German and Italian military installations and personnel behind the lines.

The Jews were only a tiny fraction of these desperate fugitives. Occasionally, strong partisan contingents protected them. More often, however, a partisan presence further endangered them by attracting Nazi and Fascist search teams to remote areas that they might otherwise have ignored. Terrified local residents, aware of ferocious reprisals in villages harboring fugitives, became reluctant to help anyone. Countless families like the Luzzatis were turned away. Others were arrested by chance during searches for partisans, escaped prisoners, and draft evaders.

On the other hand, police preoccupied with other game occasionally overlooked Jews who fell into their hands. Alfredo

Saltiel was caught but released by Germans looking for British prisoners. [8] Luzzati had an equally close call. He and his family, having decided to abandon the Valle d'Aosta for an urban refuge, were on a train for Milan when it was searched. Seated apart so that "a possible bad fate for one would not drag the others along with it," they remained in speechless terror as a group of militiamen, some with fixed bayonets, entered their car. Luzzati remembers, "the visit fortunately was very brief, and since it was directed . . . to a search for rebels and not for Jews, it was extremely superficial for us three who had no exterior sign of belonging to the *maquis.*" [9]

Rural hiding places were also hazardous because of the intensely personal nature of daily life. Unlike city residents accustomed to strangers, country folk knew everything about everyone. Villages were full of the bored, the elderly, the unoccupied, the young—all deeply curious about newcomers. No Jew could dream of hiding in a village without perfect documents and an excellent excuse for being there. He also, of course, needed to speak perfect Italian. Only a very brave or very desperate foreign Jew would attempt to survive the intense scrutiny of a rural refuge.

A situation impossible in normal times, however, was somewhat eased by thousands of non-Jewish "legal" refugees in rural areas attempting to escape the war. Many had left cities in terror of Allied air raids. Others had fled north to escape the battle zone, only to find that they could not return when their native villages fell to the Allies. These thousands of legal refugees provided a cover for Jews and partisans alike. Indeed, as Luciano Morpurgo commented, so many false documents named southern cities as the bearers' place of origin that it became dangerous for anyone to be from Naples or Bari! [10]

Jews attempting to pass as legitimate refugees in small towns faced hundreds of daily problems. Most did not dare send their children to school for fear they would betray their families, but then they had to invent excuses for their absence. Many prudently attended mass every Sunday. Men and boys had to avoid medical examinations. Everyone had to mix with villagers occasionally to avoid suspicion, yet not all people were capable of maintaining the disguise. Every family contained a senile old person, an especially talkative child, or even an innocent, unaware adult who had great difficulty pretending. Everyone lived in fear that a phrase, a gesture, a look would give them all away.

Many fugitives ran short of money and had to work, but work put them into contact with more people and created more tension. Carlo Modigliani supported his mother and himself by teaching at a technical school in Varese. He realized that he should also join his colleagues in the cafés after work, to avoid suspicion. During work, he had to endure racist speeches from visiting Fascist officials. At the cafés, he had to listen while local Fascist bullies denounced the Jews. On the street, he occasionally met other Milanese refugees who recognized him. He writes of a constant nagging fear that never diminished. [11]

Because of the danger of searches and the lack of privacy in villages, many Jews chose the anonymity of a large city. Some simply moved in with a friend for the duration of the war. If the friend had children or talkative relatives or servants, however, this option was dangerous anywhere. A better solution, and the hardest to find and afford, was to rent a private apartment in a distant neighborhood. Carlo Milano, for example, lived for six months with his wife and two daughters in a Roman boarding house. Later he rented an apartment. A friendly Roman policeman supplied him with a card identifying him as a Neapolitan war refugee and with a residence permit and ration book. His life during the occupation was relatively tranquil.

Although Carlo Milano was safer from police searches and public scrutiny in the city than in a village, he ran a constant

risk of being recognized and betrayed. The owner of the boarding house where he stayed knew all about him and could have
turned him in at any time. His bankers knew him and illegally
cashed his monthly World War I pension checks for him. He
had been a prominent official in the Jewish Community before
the occupation, with many friends and acquaintances. He must
have met people who knew him almost daily.[12] Carlo Milano
would have been safer in a city where he was totally unknown.
The same factors that made hiding in Rome dangerous for
him, however, also made it possible. A fugitive needed contacts
to secure documents, money, and living quarters. A stranger
had no contacts.

Fugitives who hid in cities where they were unknown tended
to be foreigners who would have been strangers anywhere.
These refugees had enormous problems. They had no money
or documents, and often did not even speak Italian. They were
entirely dependent upon clandestine aid networks. Delasem,
the Jewish support organization expressly designed to help
foreign refugees before the occupation, had gone underground
after the armistice. Most of its members had themselves gone
into hiding or been arrested. By the end of 1943, Delasem's
functions were being performed in large part by courageous
and dedicated non-Jews, usually priests.

And so the story of survival shifts from the problem of where
to hide to the question of whom to trust. Almost no one could
survive without help. Clearly in the forefront of those offering
help were a large number of men and women of the Roman
Catholic church.

There were many reasons why priests, monks, and nuns
could be helpful. First of all, fugitives tended to gravitate to
them more readily than to anyone else. Men and women of the
Church could usually be trusted, not necessarily to give help,
but at least not to turn in a petitioner. Second, those willing

to help had access to particular resources. Large convents and monasteries had extra rooms and could feed extra mouths without strain. Foreign men and women could disguise themselves as monks or nuns, and their lack of facility in Italian would arouse few questions. There had always been significant numbers of foreigners connected to the Church living in Italy.

In addition, Italian priests with broad local contacts, special knowledge of who was trustworthy, and access to their own institutional bureaucracy could more easily find people to assist their rescue efforts. In so doing, they naturally became the centers of informal little networks. All fugitives, including those disguised as monks and nuns, needed false documents; parish priests usually knew reliable local printers and municipal workers who could supply them. Many fugitives needed hiding places; priests like Monsignor Vincenzo Barale, secretary to the archbishop of Turin, contacted parish priests in his diocese and asked them to take a few. Fugitives in hiding needed money; urban coordinators gave funds to priests traveling to rural regions on Church business. Fugitives attempting to reach Switzerland needed resting places along the way; urban priests referred them to rural colleagues.

Contact with people in need and access to special resources partially explain the extraordinary assistance rendered by men and women of the Church, but not entirely. All rescuers still needed exceptional courage, stamina, and dedication. Churchmen and women could entertain no illusions about the treatment they would receive if captured. While Nazis and Fascists occasionally treated a prisoner-priest with respect or even released him from prison upon the appeal of his bishop, these were exceptions to the rule. [13] More often, priests suspected of hiding Jews and partisans were treated with even greater brutality and contempt than other prisoners. At least 170 priests were murdered in reprisal killings during the occupation for helping anti-Fascists and Jews. Several were beaten or otherwise tortured to death, shot in the back, hung, or had their throats cut by Germans and Italians alike. Hundreds were deported. [14]

Some churchmen and women may have hoped initially that they would remain immune from suspicion and arrest. Others may have been willing to take excessive risks because they had no dependent families: no wives and children. But clearly the priests, monks, and nuns who risked and occasionally lost their lives to help Jews, independently and without encouragement from the Vatican, demonstrated great courage and compassion. Theirs was an altruism that laypeople may often expect as a matter of course from the religious, but that can never be taken for granted. In Italy, most men and women of the Church were a credit to their calling.

Father Maria Benedetto, a French Capuchin monk in Rome, demonstrated perhaps more than anyone else the courage, ingenuity, and resources a clever priest could marshal to help Jews. Father Benedetto was long acquainted with Jewish problems. Before the war, he was a professor of theology and Hebrew at the Capuchin seminary in Marseilles, where he was known as Father Marie Benoît. During the Vichy period, he transformed his monastery into a rescue center, helping hundreds of Jewish and anti-Nazi refugees hide or escape the country. After the German occupation of most of southern France, he moved to Italian-occupied Nice and continued his activities. He met Angelo Donati and worked with him to convince Guido Lospinoso to resist Nazi demands. He introduced Donati to Vatican officials during the desperate negotiations to evacuate refugees from southern France in August 1943. [15] In Rome after the armistice, Father Benedetto met Settimio Sorani and other Jewish Delasem leaders. When Sorani and the others had to go underground, they entrusted Rome's Delasem section to him.

During the nine months of the German occupation of

The Italians and The Holocaust

Rome, Delasem operated out of Father Benedetto's Capuchin monastery in the Via Sicilia. Delasem archives were hidden there, meetings occurred regularly, and refugees were processed and directed to hiding places throughout the city. Father Benedetto and his assistants, usually other priests, rented rooms in hotels and small boarding houses and provided their fugitives with documents. Most dangerous of all, they visited them often to bring food, clothing, money, and moral support. In a city crawling with SS troops and Fascist spies, no one was safe. Couriers in every conceivable disguise dodged pursuers and had many narrow escapes.

After liberation, Father Benedetto stated that in September 1943 his network had supported just over one hundred foreign Jews. By June 1944, the number had grown to 4,000. Of these, 1,500 were foreigners and 2,500 were Italians. The rescue operation cost about twenty-five million lire. Much of the money came from Delasem's Roman funds, but Father Benedetto often had to persuade suppliers to accept credit, guaranteed by deposits of the American Joint Distribution Committee in London. [16] Father Benedetto received no money from the Vatican.

In Italy's northern cities, the German occupation lasted twice as long as in Rome, doubling, in a sense, the hazards of rescue work. Many northern cities nevertheless had their own version of Father Benedetto. In Genoa, Don Francesco Repetto, priest and secretary to the archbishop, Cardinal Pietro Boetto, was particularly outstanding. Don Repetto and Cardinal Boetto both worked with Delasem before the occupation. As seen, Cardinal Boetto also sheltered Genoa's Chief Rabbi Pacifici for a time. By the end of 1943, Don Repetto was the acknowledged head of Genoa's clandestine Jewish support network. Like Father Benedetto, he recruited scores of men and women to help him. His people carried messages from the archbishop to priests throughout Liguria and Piedmont, asking them to lend a hand. They provided fugitives with shelter, food, documents, and money, helping hundreds to reach Switzerland.

On July 3, 1944, Don Repetto narrowly escaped arrest by the SS. He was forced to hide for the remainder of the war, and Don Carlo Salvi, also of Genoa, continued his work. Don Salvi extended his services throughout northern Italy, traveling as far as the Veneto to help refugees. [17]

In Turin, Monsignor Vincenzo Barale directed rescue operations. Because of his location, Monsignor Barale worked especially with Jewish refugees from France. He called upon rural priests to help, and they readily responded. He regularly supplied fugitives with food and money. His activities continued until August 1944, when a Jewish man he had helped was caught and, stricken with terror, gave his name. Monsignor Barale was arrested and imprisoned in Turin, but he was not deported. He died in 1979. [18]

In Florence as early as September 1943, Chief Rabbi Nathan Cassuto, Raffaele Cantoni, and other Jews on a special committee to aid refugees decided to call on Cardinal Elia Dalla Costa for assistance. The cardinal agreed to help, and referred them to the Dominican Father Cipriano Ricotti at the Convent of San Marco and the parish priest Don Leti Casini at Varlungo. The cardinal also supplied Fathers Ricotti and Casini with letters in his name, asking all religious institutions to open their doors to Jewish fugitives. At least twenty-one did so, and at least 220 Jews, but perhaps double that figure, were sheltered. [19]

The recollections of Vittorio Luzzati, the Jewish lawyer from Savona introduced earlier in this chapter, describe a Milanese support network. In Brusson in the Valle d'Aosta where he first fled, Luzzati met Don Carlo Ferrero, a young priest residing in the village temporarily for health reasons. As so often happened, Luzzati confided in the priest and received indispensable aid from him several times. When Luzzati decided that the countryside was too dangerous, he asked his new friend for an urban contact. The priest recommended Cardinal Ildefonso Schuster, archbishop of Milan. "At my astonishment that I—a Jew—could present myself to the cardinal, Don Carlo continued to repeat with firmness and conviction: Go to Schuster!"

At the archbishop's palace, Luzzati met the cardinal's secretary, who referred him to Don Paolo Liggeri. Don Liggeri directed a clandestine network that covered all of Lombardy and led, in many cases, to Switzerland. He gave Luzzati and his wife and son shelter, food, and time to collect clothing and money. After about two months in Milan, the Luzzati family found its way into Switzerland. [20]

On March 24, 1944, about a month after Luzzati had left, German SS and Fascist GNR agents raided Don Liggeri's Istituto La Casa. They found eleven Jews hiding there. Don Liggeri was arrested and deported to Mauthausen. He suffered a year of starvation and hard labor there and at Dachau. He survived to return to Italy after the war. [21]

Many priests were not so fortunate. In Tuscany, Father Aldo Mei, a twenty-two-year-old priest in his first parish, was shot beneath the old city walls of Lucca on August 4, 1944. Caught two days before, he had admitted hiding at least one Jew and some partisans. [22] In Turin, a thirty-nine-year-old Dominican monk named Giuseppe Girotti sheltered many Jews until he was betrayed by a spy on August 29, 1944. Father Girotti was deported to Dachau, where he was murdered by lethal injection on the eve of liberation. [23]

Father Mei in Tuscany and Father Girotti in Turin offered help independently of any clandestine network. Indeed, one reference to Girotti sheds light on the nature of the networks themselves. Monsignor Barale who directed the Turin network knew Girotti well, but never knew he was helping Jews. Even

Girotti's own superior at his monastery did not know. As Monsignor Barale says, it was safer that way. [24] In all probability, then, the word "network" should be used with caution, and the word "organization" is not applicable. Don Repetto, Monsignor Barale, Don Liggeri, and even Father Benedetto may not have known all the details of the fugitives, hiding places, and couriers in their networks. It was safer that way.

Jewish survivors have reported many individual incidents of help from men and women of the Church. Usually, fugitives knew little about a network or a referral system. They knew who directly touched their lives, however, and their stories are impressive. Only a sample can be presented here.

Bernardo Weisz tells of Don Egidio Bertollo, priest of a parish near Padua. Don Bertollo warned Weisz of approaching danger and hid him in his church for eight days. Then the priest took Weisz and two members of his family, with their household goods, on a wagon trip to his home village of Onara, thirty kilometers from Padua. He found them a place to stay free of charge for twenty-three months. [25]

Another survivor tells of Reverend Professor Frigo, from a seminary in Vicenza. Reverend Frigo supplied false documents to Jewish fugitives until he was arrested, imprisoned, and beaten. He somehow managed to eat several photographs that were to have been used on documents. He revealed nothing. [26]

In a quieter but equally moving story, Enrichetta Levi tells of a Roman convent of sisters who had always lived in total seclusion. Nonetheless, in 1943 they took in her father and her husband. Sister Maria Rita, who had lived there apart from the world for forty years, succeeded in getting them documents as non-Jewish refugees. Despite her long seclusion, she somehow knew exactly what to do. [27]

Frida Morpurgo Colbi, who fled from Rome to her family's country house in nearby Velletri in September 1943, learned that her city apartment had been searched during the October 16 roundup. She then found refuge in a convent. Only the Mother Superior and her assistant knew she was Jewish. To maintain her disguise as a non-Jewish refugee, Frida was allowed to attend mass regularly, even though she had specifically informed the Mother Superior that she would never convert. [28]

During the winter of 1943–44, Davide Nissim and his wife found shelter with Don Giuseppe Péaquin, parish priest of a little village in the Valle d'Aosta. At the same time, Don Péaquin was also housing a family of Yugoslavian Jews, none of whom spoke Italian. His was one of those villages where everyone knew what everyone else was doing. Many of Don Péaquin's parishioners complained to him of the danger he was bringing to the entire population. His bishop also expressed strong disapproval. Don Péaquin ignored parishioners and bishop alike. After three months, he accompanied the Nissims to Milan, where he introduced them to Don Paolo Liggeri. Through Don Liggeri's network, they reached Switzerland. Don Péaquin, on the other hand, continued to help others and eventually had to seek refuge with the partisans. [29]

Monsignor Italo Ciulli of Gambassi, near Florence, hid at least five Jews, including two children, in an old-age home under his jurisdiction. He did not reveal their religion, but someone in the village guessed it. His refugees survived, but only after the war did they learn how difficult it had been to prevent that one villager from informing. [30]

Angiolo Orvieto and his wife, on the other hand, found shelter in a Capuchin home for the elderly poor near Borgo San Lorenzo, north of Florence. Orvieto recalls that all one hundred patients there knew they were Jewish. In eleven months, no one reported them. [31]

At least three hundred Jews, none of them local residents,

were saved through spectacular priestly initiative in Assisi. With help and encouragement from Assisi's Bishop Giuseppe Nicolini, Father Rufino Niccacci, head of the seminary of Saint Damiano, found shelter for terrified families fleeing raids and roundups in Florence and elsewhere. Among other accomplishments, Father Niccacci convinced the Poor Clares, a mendicant order of nuns who ran a guest house at the Monastery of San Quirico, to admit a group of Jews to their cloisters, where no man had entered since the founding seven hundred years before. He recruited Luigi Brizi, a local printer, to fabricate documents in his shop at night. He accompanied Jewish fugitives by train to Florence, where they were met and taken on to Genoa and, ultimately, to safety. He guided another group south to Pescocostanzo in the Abruzzi, where a local priest and a team of smugglers escorted them into Allied territory. Like so many other priests, Father Niccacci was eventually arrested. He was taken to a prison in Perugia, where he could hear the sound of executions echoing from the courtyard. Somehow, he survived. [32]

In Perugia, too, at least one hundred Jews found shelter. Their special benefactor was sixty-year-old Don Federico Vincenti, of the Church of San Andrea. Father Vincenti enjoyed the support of his superior, Archbishop of Perugia Mario Vianello. He also received help from Father Niccacci from nearby Assisi, and, especially, from Luigi Brizi's printing press. [33]

Well to the north of Assisi and Perugia, and scarcely twenty kilometers from the soon-to-be notorious Fossoli, the ninety-two Jewish orphans at Villa Emma also sought hiding places after the Germans occupied Italy. Most of them entered the local seminary in the nearby village of Nonantola. Nazis and Fascists knew they were hiding somewhere, and churchmen in the region became prime suspects. Soldiers and police combed their institutions. Monsignor Pelati, rector of the seminary, assured interrogators that no foreign youths lived under his roof. All the extra beds, he explained, were for seminarians on vacation.

Two teachers at this seminary, Don Arrigo Beccari and Don Ennio Tardini, were particularly active in rescue operations. They accompanied many young orphans, some disguised as priests, on a flight into Switzerland. To others, they distributed Delasem supplies of food, medicine, and clothing that had been stored at Villa Emma. Don Beccari sheltered other Jews and partisans in his parish church at Rubbiara. Don Tardini lodged some refugees with his parents and others with his sister. Both men were eventually arrested and imprisoned by Italian Fascists. [34]

It cannot, of course, be assumed that all Italian churchmen and women were sympathetic to Jews. In one distasteful case, Don Morigi, chaplain of the Muti Legion, used four or five kilograms of silver seized from a Milanese Jew to embellish his church. [35] Such cases, however, were unusual.

Less rare, however, were churchmen, and particularly bishops and archbishops, with strongly pro-Fascist sympathies. Archbishop Boccoleri of Modena is an example. Like so many of his colleagues in the upper end of the Church hierarchy, Archbishop Boccoleri saw fascism as the last bulwark against communism, and feared its demise. Accordingly, he sent letters to at least two of his priests, threatening them with suspension if they did not cease their associations with partisans. They ignored him, and one, Don Elio Monari, subsequently died in an SS prison. Archbishop Boccoleri also assisted at several lavish funerals for Fascists killed in action, but never visited villages in his diocese where SS massacres had occurred. [36]

Although the archbishop of Modena favored fascism, he did not endorse the Holocaust, but neither did he object to it in word or deed. He was not alone. Nevertheless, for every Archbishop Boccoleri there was a priest or monk with Fascist associations who did oppose the Holocaust. There was, for example, Father Umberto Loiacono of Florence, chaplain to the 92nd Fascist Militia Legion, who quietly sheltered Jewish refugees on the side. [37] From his association with the militia, Father Loiacono's politics may be presumed. The politics of the other churchmen and women rescuers cited here are unknown, and unimportant. What is important is that they viewed the Holocaust as above and beyond politics. They understood their duty as children of God, as Italians, and as human beings, and they had the courage of their convictions.

Like men and women of the Church, certain other professionals had a career-related capacity to assist fugitives. Doctors could declare them ill and find places in institutions under false names. Municipal bureaucrats could scramble or destroy prewar files and records of the Jewish Community; others with access to official forms and stamps could produce false documents. Local politicians could use their authority to shelter and supply refugees. *Carabinieri* and police agents could warn targets of pending arrests. In every category, countless Italian men and women took advantage of their special opportunities.

In the medical field, Doctor Brenno Babudieri, professor of pathology at the University of Rome, hid Bruno Maestro in the room where he kept experimental typhoid cultures under refrigeration. On the door he placed a sign in German and Italian, "Entrance prohibited: serious danger of mortal infection." [38] Doctor Luigi Parravicini of the Lombard nobility hid many Jews in his hospital at Niguarda, near Milan. When he himself had to go into hiding, he transferred some Jews to different hospitals and put others in his family home. [39] Doctor Domenico Coggiola of the Mauriziano Hospital in Turin created a special infectious ward. He kept many Jews there, hiding their identity. [40]

Doctors protecting patients known to be Jews could not

simply put them into hospitals; they had to make and keep them sick. At Regina Coeli Prison in Rome, doctors often gave Jews and partisans special injections to create high temperatures. [41] In Venice, doctors removed a perfectly healthy appendix from Letizia Morpurgo in Fano, and then managed to prevent her incision from healing. Letizia's husband was in the same hospital with a simulated heart condition and a temperature kept high through injections. One assistant doctor, Letizia remembers, was so zealous in his desire to help that he marked her husband's chart with a high temperature for a week in advance. [42]

Such policies were not without risk for doctors and patients alike. Prisons and hospitals were full of spies, some even posing as doctors. Induced illness over a long period could be damaging. Letizia's husband lost sixty-six pounds, and his doctor warned him that he might permanently ruin his health. Finally, there was always the possibility that the SS would seize a patient regardless of his health. In that case, his lowered resistance would further jeopardize survival. While many sick people were deported, however, many others were not. As Letizia's husband remembers, some SS officers had an incomprehensible desire to maintain the charade of deportation to labor camps, and avoided the public ejection of hospital patients incapable of work. [43]

Among bureaucrats, the name of Giovanni Palatucci, a commissioner in the office for foreigners at police headquarters in Fiume, stands out. When the Germans first occupied Italy, Palatucci secretly had all files and lists of Jews at police headquarters destroyed. He ordered the municipal records office not to release information about Jews without first advising him. Thus he was able to learn of pending searches and raids and warn many victims. During the first year of the occupation,

Palatucci also helped Jews sail secretly from Fiume to Bari, behind Allied lines. He even sheltered them while they waited for a boat. He was arrested in September 1944, and deported to Dachau. He died there on February 10, 1945, ten weeks before liberation. He was forty years old. [44]

Like Palatucci, Angelo De Fiore was a commissioner in the office for foreigners at police headquarters in Rome. Making the best of his opportunities, he hid files, scrambled names, and saved hundreds of lives. [45] Similarly, Giacomo Bassi, communal secretary of a little village near Milan, took a desperate Jewish family of five under his protection. He obtained blank identity forms and stamps from his own office, registering the family as Sicilian refugees. He provided ration books, and found two school rooms where they could live. He watched over them and warned them of raids until liberation. Giacomo Bassi thus saved two teenagers, a child of five, and their parents. [46]

Isacco Milesi, Fascist mayor of Roncabello, north of Bergamo, took nine foreign Jews under his protection. A family with two sons and a daughter, two elderly Yugoslavian sisters, and an elderly Viennese couple had been interned at Ferramonti in 1940, and then sent as enforced residents to villages in the province of Bergamo. When the Germans occupied Italy, they all had to hide. Recognizing their danger, Milesi, himself the father of seven children, supplied the nine strangers with a house, documents, and ration cards. He then reported to the provincial prefect that there were no Jews in his village. Meanwhile, the entire village knew the truth. The local priest constantly beseeched his parishioners to guard the secret, and the local teacher did the same at the school. The communal secretary and the village barber, arrested and tortured to make them reveal the presence of any Jews, remained silent. The foreigners survived. [47] Well to the east of Bergamo, in the province of Treviso, Count Annibale Brandolini d'Adda, also a Fascist mayor, acted similarly. Many foreign Jews had been interned in his village. Foreseeing the danger after September 8, he furnished many with documents and helped them hide. [48]

Even a single spontaneous bureaucratic gesture could help save a life. Ernesto Muraca, a southern Italian policeman working in Florence in 1944, happened to be present when an elderly Jewish couple applied for a notarized document proving their status as non-Jewish refugees from the south. When asked his origins, the nervous old man became confused and began to stammer the truth. Muraca coolly intervened. He assured the questioner that he had known the old man for years when he, Muraca, had been a policeman in Naples. The fighting and bombing in that region had been terrible, and clearly the old man was not in his right mind. In fact, Muraca had never seen him, and the old man had never been in Naples in his life. But he obtained his identification documents. [49]

Many survivors also remember *carabinieri* who helped them. Bruno Mattei from Fiume hid for ten months with his wife and daughter in the home of Ostillo Barbieri, a local resident in a town south of Parma. About thirty Yugoslavian Jews were also hiding in the region. Giacomo Avenia, commander of the local *carabinieri* station, not only knew all their hiding places, but continually sent warnings when raids and searches were being planned.

One day, however, the *carabiniere*'s warning of a raid came too late. Mattei and his family were caught, and the SS questioned their host Barbieri and the *carabiniere* Avenia. "Is this man a Jew?" the Germans wanted to know. Barbieri and Avenia assured them that he was not. The SS accepted the answer but added, "If we should learn that these are Jews, they will be put against the wall and shot and you two as well." After that narrow escape, the Mattei family remained in the town for a time. The family had no ration books, but the townspeople supplied them with food. Mattei relates that everyone there knew about them, yet no one ever informed.

After a second raid, however, Mattei moved his family to the home of a parish priest in a more remote mountain village. When the SS searched there as well, they had another close call, but they survived. Both Barbieri and Avenia were eventually deported for other reasons, but they did not betray their trust. They returned after the war. According to Mattei, the SS caught only two of the thirty or more Jews known by so many to be hiding in the general area. One of these was an elderly woman; the other was a young man who had joined the partisans. [50]

Like Mattei, Abramo Recanati hid with his wife and two daughters in the home of a friend, with the full knowledge of the local marshal of *carabinieri*. Unlike Mattei, Recanati's family was betrayed by an informer, and the three women were caught and deported to Auschwitz on August 1, 1944. Defying all statistical probability, the two girls returned to Italy in July 1945. Recanati writes, "Of my wife Rachele, unfortunately, there was no more news. She was added to the long list of innocent victims slain by Teutonic ferocity." [51]

Many Jewish survivors also remember the *carabiniere* Vittorio Borri, stationed at Fossoli. Borri seems to have been responsible, among other things, for the flow of letters and packages in and out of the concentration camp. Ignoring regulations, he constantly permitted extra food, clothing, and money to slip by him and reach the prisoners. On one occasion, he was caught passing extra bread into a cattle car filled with Jewish children bound for Auschwitz. He was nearly arrested. One survivor of Fossoli recalls that Borri told him he wanted to resign. He could not stand working in such a tragic place. The prisoner convinced him to remain, to continue the little help he was able to give. [52]

The Italians and The Holocaust

Carabinieri often did not like their jobs. Giuseppe Funaro was among the seventeen Jewish orphans, all under the age of sixteen, who were housed in a villa in a village near Livorno. In April 1944, Germans occupied the villa and ordered two *carabinieri* to escort the children by train to Fossoli. The local Fascist party secretary, owner of the villa, tried to intervene to save the children, but he failed. With visible disgust, the *carabinieri* obeyed orders. On the way to Fossoli, the train was derailed in an air raid. The *carabinieri* kept their young charges safe during the attack, treating them with kindness. They found a priest and other residents in a nearby village who housed and fed the children for a time. Then they led them back to Livorno, as slowly as possible. In the confusion of the moment, the orphans were forgotten, and all of them survived.[53]

Augusto Segre and his family were also saved by a friendly *carabiniere*. In the autumn of 1943, Segre worked in the office of a winery in Castagnole, in the province of Asti. Everyone there knew he was Jewish. On December 1, 1943, the day the Republic of Salò decreed that all Jews were to be arrested, the local *carabinieri* commander visited the winery and spoke with Segre's sympathetic employer. Then, without greeting Segre whom he knew well, he left abruptly. The employer immediately passed along the message. "He is a fine man; he came here to tell me, 'My heart bleeds to have to arrest an honest person, but tomorrow morning at 8:00 I have to arrest the lawyer and his family.' " Segre fled at once.[54]

Like everyone else, the *carabinieri* were not always sympathetic. Five days after Segre's *carabiniere* obstructed the new government policy, others in Todi arrested Giuseppe Levy and his mother and brother. The Levy family spent the rest of the war in the Todi jail, while a local noblewoman and the bishop successfully impeded their transfer to Fossoli.[55] According to Alfredo Saltiel, *carabinieri* in Tuscany were often zealous in rounding up Jews in hiding. [56] But in a brief survey of survivor references to *carabinieri,* favorable accounts strongly outnumber the unfavorable. Help was particularly impressive because the *carabinieri* were already under official suspicion for lack of zeal. Fascist fanatics distrusted them, apparently with good reason, and watched their performance closely. It could not have been easy for them to have been as helpful as they were.

If survivor accounts of sympathetic *carabinieri* are plentiful, however, stories of helpful Fascist militiamen are rare. Giancarlo Sacerdoti, however, remembers one. His aged grandmother, too old and fragile to survive the hardship of flight, remained behind in a little village and passed her days playing poker with the local commander of the Fascist militia. She always let him win. The commander, addressing her as Signora Levi, told her that when the order came for her deportation, he would give her plenty of time to hide. "Then you will come back," he explained, "to play poker, because you are the best and the nicest player in Republican Italy." [57]

Gastone Orefice also tells of a sympathetic Fascist militiaman. During the occupation, Orefice and his brother and cousin hid for a time in a religious institution in Florence. When raids made it dangerous to stay on, they left to seek a new refuge. They were caught in an identity check in a train station. They had false papers, but they were all young men who, if they had not been Jewish, would have been in uniform. Also, he says, "it was very obvious that we were frightened." As a group of German SS and three or four Fascists looked on, one Fascist studied them carefully. Orefice is convinced that he knew the truth. He told the Nazis they were all right, saving their lives. [58]

While, as seen, many Fascists in uniform behaved with a brutality that rivaled the Nazis, some, like Orefice's man, subverted their orders. One wonders how many of the latter were in a position similar to that of twenty-year-old Redentore

The Italians and The Holocaust

Ordan from the province of Venice. Ordan, a student at the Magistrate School at Padua, had been forced into the Salò army one day with his entire class. He never tried to desert. He knew that his family was hiding a Jewish fugitive. His desertion would have provoked a search of his home and caused the discovery and deportation of his family's guest. [59]

Help for Jews in Italy came from individuals in every walk of life. Odoardo Focherini, for example, was an active Catholic layman and administrator of a conservative Catholic newspaper called *L'Avvenire d'Italia*. Focherini, age thirty-six during the occupation, was a devoted family man with seven children. He lived in Carpi, the village near Fossoli where Jews were loaded onto the trains headed for Auschwitz.

Focherini's concern for the Jews began well before the armistice, when he learned about Nazi anti-Semitism from a group of refugees from Warsaw. He helped that group and several others before the occupation. When the Holocaust extended into his own country, Focherini turned his attention to Italian Jews. As one friend remembers, "The persecuted became his persecutors and waited long hours for him at his place of work, at his home, at the newspaper office." He helped them find hiding places in the local religious institutions he knew so well. He referred them to priests like Don Dante Sala, who escorted 105 Jews to Switzerland before his own arrest in early December 1943. [60] Focherini was caught on March 11, 1944, at the hospital bedside of a Jew he had helped leave Fossoli for feigned medical reasons. He was not even allowed to see his family again. Taken first to San Giovanni in Monte Prison in Bologna and then to Fossoli, he was finally deported to Flossenburg. He died there later that year, on Christmas Eve. [61]

There were thousands of other courageous non-Jews who risked everything to help their Jewish compatriots. Some paid with their lives, and with the lives of their loved ones. Pio

Troiani from Borbona di Rieti was shot with his son and brother for harboring a variety of fugitives: Jews, British prisoners-of-war, and former Italian soldiers. [62] Torquato Fraccon, an active Catholic layman from Vicenza, was deported with his eighteen-year-old son for helping Jews. Neither man returned. One person Fraccon saved became a professor at the University of Padua, and wrote a moving letter ten years later recalling his courage and sacrifice. [63]

Giuseppe Sala, president of the Society of Saint Vincent de Paul, did not die for the help he gave Jews, but he did suffer torture and deprivation for two months at San Vittore Prison in Milan. Both before and after his arrest, he helped hundreds, finding hiding places and delivering food, money, and clothing through a clandestine aid network. [64] Similarly, Gennaro Campolmi, foreman at a major Florentine shoe factory owned by the Jewish Passigli family, suffered arrest and torture but did not reveal the hiding place of Mrs. Passigli and her three children. Mrs. Passigli's husband, father-in-law, and brother-in-law had already been arrested, and they died in a Nazi concentration camp. After his own release from prison, Gennaro Campolmi, like Giuseppe Sala, continued to help other Jews. [65]

An unnamed male survivor writes of Giovanni and Lina Carli, from a small town near Venice. Giovanni was an invalid from World War I; Lina was an elementary school teacher. Despite the fact that they had five small children and were in desperate financial straits, they took three Jewish fugitives into their home and coped with searches by the Brigate Nere on several occasions. [66]

Another survivor, Leopoldo Kostoris, writes of an elderly postman who saved his life by intercepting a letter from an informer to the German command. The letter, denouncing Kostoris as a Jew and giving his false name and hiding place, never reached its destination. [67] Still another survivor owed her life and that of her two daughters to Camillo Stagni, her lawyer. The three women happened to be in Stagni's office when a bomb was thrown from the building. Six or seven German and Italian police began to comb the premises. When they reached Stagni's office, the lawyer assured them that he was alone. The women were in another room, and he knew he might be searched. He was not, and the women survived.[68]

Some of the most moving stories involve the contributions of Italian peasants, men and women at the very bottom of the economic scale. Federico Sartori, for example, with a tiny house in the country near Padua barely big enough for his family of five, took in a Jewish family of thirteen that had knocked in vain on other doors.[69] Ida Granzotto Battistella, a peasant widow with five children, also sheltered a Jewish family at her farmhouse in the province of Treviso during the entire German occupation. The fugitives did not have false identity cards, and the region was constantly searched for partisans. Mrs. Battistella trained her children, between the ages of five and eighteen, to watch for Nazi-Fascist troops and warn her when they were about.[70]

Sisto and Alberta Gianaroli were peasants who lived with their seven children, between the ages of two months and sixteen years, in a farmhouse near Polinago, in the province of Modena. From March 1944 to April 1945, they sheltered Amerigo Ottolenghi, an engineer, and his family in an old mill. At first, Ottolenghi paid them a modest rent, but eventually he ran out of money and could pay nothing. Friendly peasants from the area brought him food and clothing. During the winter of 1944–45, the farm and mill were only a few kilometers from the famous Gothic Line, the German line of defense across the Apennines. Ottolenghi recalls living between a hill occupied by partisans and a plain held by Nazis and Fascists. Survival was precarious for everyone. On several occasions, Ottolenghi and his family escaped Fascist searches by living for days at a time in a hole dug into the bank of a river. Sisto Gianaroli kept them alive by bringing them food at night and hot milk at dawn. Miraculously, they all survived.[71]

The postwar testimony of Italian Jews reveals many varieties in the pattern of survival. Many sophisticated, highly educated survivors write of the simple people who helped them—peasants, maids, janitors who hid them in attics or cellars, or saved their possessions. Other survivors, simple people themselves, apologize for their inability to express their thoughts, and then write movingly of help from a lawyer, doctor, bishop, or bureaucrat. Survivors lived in cities and villages, in convents and isolated farmhouses. A few lived without much trouble in a single spot; most moved from place to place, with a number of benefactors. As will be seen, five or six thousand crossed into Switzerland or into the Allied-occupied zone.

Despite the varieties of experience, certain constants emerge. Early recognition of danger was important. In Rome, over half the deportees were caught in the first massive roundup, and the proportion was also high in other large cities where roundups occurred. Financial resources were also extremely useful, for they allowed people to rent rooms away from home and buy food, false documents, and, occasionally, a passage to Switzerland. Good health and relative youth were almost prerequisites—the sick and the elderly could not move from place to place, obtain adequate health care, or even maintain disguises with facility. Friends and contacts from better days were also of great help.

Some people survived without early recognition of danger. With luck and the beneficence of strangers, some survived without money, health, youth, or previous contacts. But no one survived without courage, determination, flexibility, and ingenuity. Courage enabled people to flee on a moment's notice, climb mountain trails at night in the snow, live for weeks in

The Italians and The Holocaust

a hole in the ground in winter, make agonizing decisions. Determination gave them the strength to make sacrifices—to place a child or aged parent with a friendly Christian family; to leave a loved one behind if he lacked the strength to make the trip across the frontier; to fight for life when part of the family was already dead. Flexibility helped them live without a permanent refuge, moving from house to house often without even knowing the names of those to whom they were entrusting their lives. And ingenuity provided ideas—where to go, whom to trust, what disguise to use, what answers to give to the suspicious.

There were, of course, no guarantees, for above all the other qualities, survivors needed almost incredible good luck. No matter how perfect their plan, they had to avoid constant searches, escape the curiosity of neighbors, evade the occasional spy or informer. They lived from day to day, with a tension that was almost unbearable. But with luck, they survived.

11

Switzerland

AFTER evading police for many months, Vittorio Luzzati decided to leave his refuge with Don Liggeri in Milan and try to reach Switzerland. It was the most difficult decision of his life. He seemed safe in Milan, and the trip to Switzerland was extremely dangerous. He would risk not only his own life, but that of his wife and son. He decided nevertheless to try, and he made it. A month later, Don Liggeri's institute was raided, and all Jews there were arrested. Luzzati's decision had saved his life. [1]

In December 1943, Chief Rabbi Adolfo Ottolenghi of Venice also decided to join a group headed for Switzerland. His entire group was arrested in Como, and all were ultimately deported to Auschwitz. Ottolenghi's decision cost him his life. [2] Letizia Morpurgo in Fano and her husband had been invited to join the same group, but they thought it was dangerously large and conspicuous. They decided to take their chances in Italy. They survived. [3]

During the twenty months of German occupation, hundreds

of thousands of people, Italians and foreigners, Jews and non-Jews, faced the same life-or-death decision as Luzzati, Ottolenghi, and Morpurgo in Fano. Should they abandon their hiding places and try to leave the country? Thousands decided to leave. Some, mainly British prisoners-of-war, crossed the front lines and reached Allied-occupied territory. Others, particularly those living near Italy's eastern coast, fled south in Adriatic fishing boats. For most Jews, however, concentrated as they tended to be in northern Italy and encumbered by children and elderly people, the southern options scarcely existed. They, along with many non-Jews, looked north to Switzerland.

Approximately 38,000 Italians and 6,000 foreigners entered Switzerland between September 1943 and April 1945. Of these 44,000, between 5,000 and 6,000 were Jews.[4] Perhaps 85 percent of all refugees entered through the Swiss canton of Ticino, passing near Lakes Maggiore, Lugano, and Como, north of Milan. Others crossed the mountains from the Valle d'Aosta, Domodossola, or, more frequently, the Valtellina. The Valtellina route led north along the eastern side of Lake Como, east to Sondrio, and into Switzerland from the Italian town of Tirano. Alternatively, refugees could continue north from Lake Como to Chiavenna and enter Switzerland from Castasegna, not far from St. Moritz.

All routes were hazardous in the extreme. Towns and villages near the frontier were crawling with German and Fascist soldiers. Trains leading north from cities such as Brescia, Bergamo, Turin, Novara, and especially Milan were regularly searched. Every passenger needed sound documents and a convincing explanation for his or her trip. Inns and hotels along the way were filled with spies and informers.

Carlo Modigliani, living and working with false documents in a village near Varese, north of Milan, found himself in the center of an emigration route into the Swiss Ticino. He remembers a particular *trattoria* near a little railroad station, where Jews frequently stopped to spend the night. The proprietress regularly denounced them to the police. She was killed by enraged Italians in the first days after the war, and her daughter barely escaped the same fate.[5]

Refugees lucky enough to reach the frontier usually found a barrier of electric and barbed wire, guarded by Nazi and Fascist soldiers with police dogs. Many survivors write of waiting for hours in an icy woods or thicket while roving patrols passed by. Several flights ended abruptly when a child inadvertently touched an electric wire and set off an alarm. A few refugees recall being caught by a sympathetic Italian or even a German soldier (Fascists occasionally complained that German frontier guards were over-aged reservists lacking in zeal) and being merely turned back into Italy.[6] Most of those caught were not so fortunate. Their numbers will never be known.

Refugees healthy and hearty enough to climb to a more remote section of the frontier could sometimes avoid the wire, the guards, and the dogs. Vittorio Luzzati and his wife and son walked from Lanzo d'Intelvi westward toward Lake Lugano. They crossed the border at an altitude of one thousand meters above the lake. Their guide told them when they were in Switzerland, for they had no way of knowing. Apart from reaching Lanzo d'Intelvi in the first place (Luzzati does not tell us how he managed it), their biggest problem was not crossing the frontier but hiking down to Lake Lugano without a trail after their guide departed.[7]

Escape into Switzerland, then, generally involved two problems: approaching the frontier and crossing it. Some refugees solved the first problem unassisted. They tended to be people with friends, relatives, or contacts in villas near the frontier,

The Italians and The Holocaust

impeccable documents, and a perfect command of Italian. They were also necessarily traveling in small family groups that did not attract attention.

More often, however, refugees approached the frontier with the help of a complex network of courageous benefactors. Their odyssey usually began in a convent or church in a large city, where a man like Don Repetto in Genoa or Don Liggeri in Milan organized their escape route. They moved north slowly on local trains, often traveling early in the morning or late at night and making many stops. Sometimes they rode in wagons; sometimes they walked. They stayed in convents, private homes, barns, and huts. Local residents brought them food. Refugees often waited days for their next move. Sometimes a hostile villager tipped off the police, a resting place was raided, and a trip ended in tragedy before the refugees even approached the frontier. More often, however, the travelers reached the end of the Italian line—a fishing village like Cannero, Cannobio, Laveno, or Luino on Lago Maggiore where they could meet a boat; an isolated hamlet in the Valtellina or a village north of Varese or outside Como, like Chiasso or Cernobbio, from which they might hike across the frontier.

The second step—the actual crossing of the frontier—involved a different set of problems, for no refugee could proceed without an experienced guide. Guides knew the remote trails, the holes in the wire, the routines of the border guards, the schedules of boat patrols, and the soldiers who might look the other way, with or without payment. No one from another region could know those things. Don Repetto and Don Liggeri and the scores of devoted men and women who helped them could do no more at this point than try to recommend guides who could be trusted.

The frontier guides who escorted Jews tended to be professionals, in the business for money. Politely referred to as *passatori*, they were more often called *contrabbandieri*, or smugglers. They knew the border well because they made their livelihood from crossing it illegally. Not all guides were *contrabbandieri*, certainly, but most of those who worked from conviction were committed to the Resistance and otherwise occupied. While they would probably not have refused an appeal from a Jewish civilian met by chance near the frontier, they preferred not to be burdened by groups of women, children, and elderly people. They were mainly concerned with guiding other partisans, political refugees, and, to retain Allied favor and support, British prisoners-of-war.

Other factors may also have influenced the tendency of Jewish refugees to gravitate toward professional guides. Guides interested in earning money and influenced by their own stereotyped image of Jews as bankers, businessmen, and men of means often sought out Jewish refugees and their benefactors. Jews themselves, usually inexperienced in illegal activities such as clandestine border crossings, tended to put their faith in professionals, men with whom they could make a concrete deal. As one man wrote to his parents of the guide he had decided to retain, "He is certainly a serious person and he is in this business 'officially,' one might say; in other words, he is not concerned with us merely by chance."[8] The all-too-human tendency to believe that the more one pays, the more one obtains, also came into play. Desperate men and women ready to pay anything for their lives and those of their children were easy victims.

Prices were indeed high. Most guides charged from 5,000 to 9,000 lire for every man, woman, and child; the average daily wage of an industrial worker in 1944 was 45.25 lire.[9] Many Jews, often without income since the 1938 racial laws, could not afford the trip. Non-Jewish benefactors who devoted their limited resources to feeding and housing Jews hiding in Italy could not meet the costs of a guide to Switzerland. The best a network organizer like Don Repetto or Don Liggeri could do was establish regular relationships with individual guides, produce significant numbers of paying refugees, and then negotiate the inclusion of two or three non-paying travelers in any given group.

Guides who could be trusted were a valuable commodity. Benefactors with regular rescue networks were most able to produce them, for guides whose results could be monitored and who wanted more work were less likely to exploit their clients. Free-lance guides had clients entirely at their mercy, and the possibilities for exploitation were endless. Some guides took the money and promptly abandoned their charges. Others delivered them to the border guards, doubtless for another fee. Still others stopped near the frontier and demanded more money. Others, or perhaps the same ones, presented themselves to their clients' families or friends back in Italy, extorting still more cash from other helpless victims.

The luckiest refugees, and the wisest, were those who secured guides with some kind of personal recommendation. Vittorio Luzzati traveled to a villa at Lanzo d'Intelvi that belonged to a friend of his brother-in-law. There his host introduced him to two local *contrabbandieri* whom he presumably knew personally. [10] Another survivor writes of Doctor Lodovico Targetti and his wife Silvia, who had a villa at Cernobbio on Lake Como, near the frontier. The Targettis took in over fifty Jews and helped them find local guides. [11]

Still another man remembers Ulisse Getulli, who had a house at Codegliano, near Varese. Getulli himself seems to have guided one couple, trying three times to follow a goat path across the border. Twice they hid in the forests and turned back to avoid patrols, but on their third attempt, they made it. They arrived in Switzerland on December 4, 1943, only to have the Swiss border guards refuse entry to the woman in their party. [12]

For in addition to approaching and crossing the frontier,

refugees from Italy faced still a third problem. Once across the border, they had to present themselves to Swiss guards to obtain permits to remain in the country. Depending upon Swiss policy at the moment, refugees could be accepted or rejected. If they were rejected, they were usually given two choices. They could go back the way they had come, thus avoiding the guards on the Italian side and probable arrest. If they refused that option, they were marched back across at official entry points, into the waiting arms of Nazi and Fascist soldiers.

Excluding brief periods when the frontier seems to have been totally closed, Swiss policy toward the admission of Jewish refugees from Italy can be divided into three phases. Before December 1, 1943—that is, before the political manifesto of the Salò government declared all Italian Jews to be enemy aliens and police order number five demanded their arrest and internment—the official Swiss position was that Jews in Italy were not in danger. Consequently, during most of October and November, Swiss border guards were instructed to turn back all civilians except political refugees, men and women over age sixty-five and their spouses, pregnant women, the sick, boys under sixteen and girls under eighteen, the parents of children under six, and individuals related to Swiss citizens. In actual practice, exceptions were also made for civilians with known political, economic, and scientific achievements.

After December 1, Swiss policy softened. Swiss border guards were unofficially advised to disregard the official guidelines for the admission of Jewish refugees. Rejections thus dropped significantly, but the Swiss retained their guidelines in case of future need. The guidelines themselves changed only in July 1944, when the category of political refugee was significantly broadened. Guards were ordered to admit "foreigners truly menaced . . . for political or other reasons, and who, to avoid the menace, have nothing except the possibility of refuge in Switzerland." "Other reasons," of course, meant reasons of race and religion. [13]

There is no way of knowing how many Jews were sent back to Italy. How many heartbreaking cases were there like that of Israel Contente, rejected in September 1943, with his wife and three children, ages eighteen, seventeen, and five, at a time when the frontier was apparently closed completely? [14] How many individuals were there like the friend Carlo Modigliani saw one morning near Varese—a woman exhausted, dirty, and broken, after a night spent crossing the border and a rejection at the end of the line? [15] Fortunately, most rejected refugees returned the way they had come and avoided arrest, but return to Fascist Italy meant that their lives were still in jeopardy.

Despite official policy, the actual behavior of guards on both sides of the frontier varied considerably. Cesare Vivante, for example, crossed the border at sunset on foot from Viggiù, northwest of Como. Swiss border guards informed him and his group of Venetian Jews that if they did not return immediately the way they had come, they would deliver them directly to the Germans at Chiasso in the morning. The Swiss escorted them back, but on the way, one guard took pity on them. They should return at midnight, he told them quietly, for he would be alone at the frontier post then. They did so and were admitted. [16]

Dr. Rino Verona experienced similar vicissitudes. He was not only refused entry to Switzerland in December 1943, but the Swiss guards who rejected him also insisted that he return to Italy through the regular entry point. The Italian guard there apologetically explained that if Verona returned that way, he would have to report him. Could he return to Italy the way he had left? Poor Dr. Verona apparently shuffled back and forth for some time, until he finally found a Swiss guard who let him leave by the unofficial route. In the process, Italian guards fed and housed him for two nights! [17]

While survivors often describe how they crossed the frontier, they rarely mention who helped them reach it in the first place. Accounts of the trip north tend to be vague and incomplete. Probably they knew very little even at the time. Rescuers undoubtedly provided few details about names and rest-stop locations, and revealed nothing about a covert network. The caution is understandable, but one would like to know more today. A few stories must suffice.

Florentine survivors remember Gina Silvestri, a courageous non-Jew who often accompanied small groups of refugees on the train to Milan. From Milan, she somehow took them to Laveno, on the eastern side of Lago Maggiore. From a point north of Laveno, she found fishing boats to take them to the Swiss shore. Silvestri must have had help, but survivors mention only her. [18]

Like Silvestri, Don Dante Sala, priest of a village parish north of Modena, lived far from the Swiss frontier. He is nevertheless believed to have accompanied 105 people toward the border between September and his arrest in early December 1943. He usually moved with groups of from seven to ten people, and never with more than twelve. He must have made the trip nearly every week!

Don Sala's groups apparently traveled by train from Modena to Milan. From Milan they sometimes moved north to Malnate and Varese, where two other priests offered shelter, and then on to Luino on Lago Maggiore. Alternatively, they went to Como and then Cernobbio. At Luino or Cernobbio they were entrusted to professional guides. Don Sala's guides apparently charged only 3,000 lire per person, and even took some free. When the priest was arrested at the North Station in

The Italians and The Holocaust

Como, there was some thought that he had been betrayed by rival *contrabbandieri.* Don Sala was subject to a brutal interrogation and imprisoned in Como for two months. During that time, he lost thirty-three pounds. He was fortunate that his superiors were able to have his trial transferred from a military to a civil court, and he was ultimately released for lack of proof.[19]

Ada De Micheli Tommasi, a teacher from Milan, organized a rest center at Sormano, seven kilometers from Canzo. Don Carlo Banfi, the Sormano parish priest, worked with her. Jewish refugees paused at Sormano and found food and shelter. Ada often accompanied them for portions of their journey.

Ada De Micheli Tommasi was eventually arrested. Police officers in Como threatened to shoot her and her husband if they did not talk. They did not, but were released anyway. Meanwhile, Don Carlo Banfi accompanied a group of about eighteen refugees to Switzerland. When he crossed the border, the archbishop of Lugano advised him that it was too dangerous to return.[20]

Lina Leoni Crippa was a fifty-one-year-old teacher, also from Milan. She helped hundreds of Jews pass into Switzerland, often putting them in touch with guides. She was arrested and spent five months at San Vittore Prison. Deported to Ravensbruck and Mauthausen, she returned to Italy with her health destroyed.[21]

Madre Donata, at the Istituto Palazzolo in Milan, sheltered hundreds of Jews who were awaiting documents and a passage to Switzerland. The old and the sick sometimes remained with her when their families went on. When one group of refugees caught in Como gave her name, she was arrested. Seventeen Jews were staying at her institute at the time. By the time the police returned for them, they had escaped.[22]

Madre Donata often referred the strongest Jewish fugitives

to Adele Cappelli Vegni, who lived in Milan. Cappelli Vegni had organized a shelter in a convent at Torno, above Lake Como, for those who hoped to emigrate to Switzerland. She helped refugees reach the convent, where they waited for the guides. [23]

Among those Cappelli Vegni saved was forty-one-year-old Renata Lombroso. One day in December 1943, Renata returned home from work just as Nazis were arresting her mother. The concierge locked her in a room to prevent her from joining the old woman. She saw her mother pass by between two guards, with her head held high. Unable to return to her apartment and without clothes or money, Renata wandered about Milan in desperation. She was about to turn herself in when she met Madre Donata and Adele Cappelli Vegni. Of the latter, she later wrote, "The meeting with this woman was among the most beautiful of my life, she immediately showed me a great trust, she made me sleep in her own bed, and the next day she directed me to a little convent in Torno on Lake Como." After many more adventures, Renata reached Switzerland. Her mother did not survive. Of her, Renata wrote, "Blessed mother, you who loved everyone and hated no one paid for me who profoundly hated our enemies." [24]

Little is known of the men and women who staffed the shelters on the route to Switzerland, of the peasants who brought in extra food, of the guides themselves, or of residents near the border who watched the proceedings in terror, knowing their villages could be searched and destroyed at any time, yet who did not betray the refugees. Their stories have largely disappeared with the passage of time. The story of one villager, however, remains bright and clear—representative of other humble men and women in rural areas of northern Italy who could not stand by as desperate human beings struggled to cross a frontier and leave a country that they loved, but that no longer protected them.

Twenty-four-year-old Lorenzo Spada ran the butcher shop in Demonte, near Cuneo. He was also an active and enthusiastic partisan. Ermanno Tedeschi, a Jewish engineer from Ferrara, had hidden with his family for a few months in Liguria, further south, but when his refuge there became too dangerous, he found himself in Demonte. He met young Spada by chance.

Lorenzo Spada hid and fed the Tedeschi family of five as long as he could, but Demonte, in the center of a partisan zone, was a constant SS and Fascist target. On the night of February 8, 1944, Spada personally led his new acquaintances through the mountains toward Switzerland. He delivered them safely to a guide and gave them money from his own small supply with which to pay him. The guide took them across the border, and the Tedeschi family survived.

Lorenzo Spada, on the other hand, was eventually caught in a hospital where he was recovering from a wound inflicted during a partisan action. He was tortured by the Brigate Nere and hung in the square of his own village on August 21, 1944. He died not because of the help he gave to Jews, but because he was a partisan. He is honored for both.[25]

12

The Best of Their Generation: Italian Jews and Anti-fascism

ALDO, Carlo, and Nello Rosselli were born around the turn of the century into an affluent Tuscan family renowned for its patriotic and Republican associations. An earlier generation of Rossellis had known and aided the patriot Giuseppe Mazzini in London in the 1840s. Sara Levi Nathan, whose mother was a Rosselli, had corresponded with the great man for years and entertained him in her home. Pellegrino Rosselli owned the house in Pisa where Mazzini died on March 10, 1872. He donated the house to the nation.

Sara Nathan's son Ernesto, a Republican like his forefathers, became the first Jewish mayor of Rome in 1907. He left an unblemished record of integrity, political courage, and dedicated public service. Sara's daughter Enrichetta married Sabatino Rosselli and became the grandmother of Aldo, Carlo, and Nello.

The boys' mother, Amelia Pincherle, from Venice, was also from an illustrious and patriotic Jewish family. An ancestor had been a minister in Daniele Manin's Republican cabinet in 1848. Amelia wrote of her parents' generation, "It belonged to that period which still remained aware of the benefits of the liberation from the ghettos." [1] Of herself she wrote:

> [We were] Jews . . . but above all Italians. I, too, then, born and raised in that profoundly Italian and Liberal atmosphere, preserved from my religion only its purest essence, in my heart. Religious elements of a solely moral character; and that was the only religious teaching I gave my children. [2]

Since the boys' father died in 1911, when they were still young, they were especially influenced by their mother and their uncle Gabriele Pincherle, a Liberal senator in Rome. Amelia and Gabriele ardently supported Italy's intervention in World War I to help defeat the reactionary Hapsburgs and to obtain Trent and Trieste for Italy. Aldo, born in 1895, was called for service in that war. A medical student at the time, he could easily have joined a safe Red Cross unit. Instead, declaring that he and his family had wanted the war, he insisted on the infantry. He was killed in combat in 1916. [3]

Carlo, born in 1899, served in the army from 1917 until the armistice (Nello, born in 1900, was too young for the war). After his demobilization, Carlo studied economics and politics at the University of Florence. Influenced by two prominent professors, Gaetano Salvemini and Piero Calamandrei, he became associated with the *circolo di cultura*, a well-known group of anti-Fascist intellectuals. He joined the Socialist party in 1924, after Fascist thugs murdered the Socialist anti-Fascist deputy Giacomo Matteotti. In 1925 he helped produce eight issues of the famous anti-Fascist periodical *Non Mollare!* (Do Not Weaken). In 1926, after narrowly escaping a police roundup, he moved to Milan and published a weekly anti-Fascist review, *Quarto Stato* (Fourth Estate). Contributors to both publications included the best of Italy's non-Marxist, anti-Fascist intellectual community.

Late in 1926, young Carlo Rosselli was involved in an adventure worthy of a Hollywood film. Filippo Turati, former member of Parliament and highly esteemed elder statesman in the moderate wing of the Socialist party, was clearly in danger. When his lifelong companion Anna Kuliscioff died the previous year, Fascist thugs threatened violence at her funeral. Since then, they had continued to harass Turati. The old man was too weak and ill to survive a beating. Because he was unable to obtain a passport, his friends persuaded him to emigrate secretly.

Turati's apartment in Milan was under constant police surveillance. Nevertheless, Rosselli arranged for him to escape one night by climbing into an adjoining apartment through a hole in the wall and exiting through a back door. Rosselli escorted him first to friendly homes near Milan, where he waited with the hope of getting to Switzerland. When that proved impossible, Turati hid in Ivrea with Camillo Olivetti, founder of the Olivetti Typewriter Company, and then in Turin with Professor Giuseppe Levi, father of Mario (who would be involved in 1934 in the Ponte Tresa affair described in chapter 3) and Natalia (who later became Natalia Ginzburg).

One icy night in December 1926, Adriano Olivetti, son of Camillo, met Turati in Turin and drove him down twisting mountain roads, avoiding a number of road blocks, to Savona on the Ligurian coast. There he waited five days for a motor launch, in the company of Carlo Rosselli, Ferruccio Parri (first prime minister of Italy after the war), and Sandro Pertini (born in 1896, a young lawyer from Savona in 1926, and much later, president of Italy from 1978 to 1985). Finally, in a winter storm, with waves breaking over the boat, no stars in the sky, and a faulty compass, they struggled toward freedom. After twelve harrowing hours, they found themselves in Corsica. [4]

From Corsica the boat carried Turati and Pertini to Nice and safety. Rosselli and Parri returned to Italy, where they were arrested and tried with great publicity. Before a regular court at the famous "trial of the professors" in Savona, they were permitted to argue in their own defense that they had merely broken passport regulations to save an old man from violence. In so doing, they were able to denounce the brutality of the Fascist regime. In his summation, Rosselli revealed the strong sense of social duty he inherited from his family: "A Rosselli secretly hosted at Pisa the dying Mazzini, an exile in his own land. It was logical that another Rosselli, later, would make an effort to save from the Fascist fury one of the most noble and unselfish spirits of his country." [5] Rosselli and Parri received light official sentences, although Rosselli was later "unofficially" sentenced to a five-year confinement on the island of Lipari.

The disproportionate number of Jews involved in the Turati rescue is one of many remarkable aspects of the case. Adriano Olivetti's father Camillo, an anti-Fascist and an old friend of Turati, was Jewish; his mother Luisa Revel was Protestant. Carlo Rosselli was Jewish, as was Professor Levi. In a country where only one-tenth of 1 percent of the population was Jewish, the preponderance is surprising.

It cannot be inferred, of course, that most Italian Jews were anti-Fascists. As has been seen, Jews, like all other Italians and in roughly similar proportions, were divided in their politics. Many fine men and women, the best of their generation, were dedicated anti-Fascists almost from the beginning. Others, strongly nationalistic and terrified of bolshevism, saw fascism as the guarantor of law, order, and national glory. Many supported Mussolini right up to the time of the racial laws. The majority, as in the non-Jewish population, remained indifferent to politics, wishing only to be left alone.

Some analysts of the Italian Jewish Resistance like to find a "natural Jewish vocation" for anti-fascism—an affinity rooted in a deep commitment to nineteenth-century liberalism, freedom, political equality, and social justice. The triumph of those principles after 1848, they argue, resulted in Jewish emancipation, and Jews in the 1920s and 1930s remained dedicated to their preservation. Jews instinctively understood that they could not thrive in a society that denied basic legal rights to any minority, be it Socialist, Communist, Freemason, Protestant, or Jewish.[6]

The thesis does not apply to the majority of Italian Jews, any more than to the majority of Italian non-Jews, who were, after all, also beneficiaries of the principles of 1848. It does seem to apply to many individual Jewish anti-Fascists, however. Men as diverse in their politics as Carlo and Nello Rosselli, Eugenio Chiesa, Claudio Treves, Giuseppe Emanuele Modigliani, Emilio Sereni, and Umberto Terracini articulated similar values and understood that the denial of equal protection before the law was unacceptable. Their anti-fascism had not emerged from their emotions, from some private fear or vendetta, or from careerism and political maneuvering. It was firmly grounded in an intellectual and cultural tradition.

There was nothing necessarily Jewish about that tradition, of course, and non-Jewish anti-Fascist intellectuals shared it fully. Many Italian Jews who, in the 1920s, were unconcerned about fascism and quite willing to cooperate with Mussolini for the advancement of personal interests, in fact often complained that anti-Fascist Jewish émigrés were scarcely Jews at all. Most had drifted far away from their religious roots, and some barely thought of themselves as Jews. What could possibly be Jewish about their anti-fascism?

The Italians and The Holocaust

Nello Rosselli addressed the question indirectly at a Zionist conference at Livorno on November 2, 3, and 4, 1924. "I am a Jew," he declared, "who does not go to temple on Saturday, who does not know Hebrew, who does not observe any religious practice." How, then, was he Jewish at all?

> I call myself a Jew . . . because . . . the monotheistic conscience is indestructible in me, . . . because every even disguised form of idolatry repels me, . . . because I regard with Jewish severity the duties of our lives on earth, and with Jewish serenity the mystery of beyond the tomb—because I love all men as in Israel it was commanded . . . and I have therefore that social conception which it seems to me descends from our best traditions.[7]

Rosselli explained not only why he was a Jew, but why he was an anti-Fascist. His anti-fascism was not political, but was rooted in his disgust for "state-worship" and "Duce-worship," his respect for humanity, and his severe sense of social responsibility. Many Jewish anti-Fascist intellectuals would have expressed their commitment similarly. Umberto Terracini, Communist, went to a Jewish elementary school, learned Hebrew, and was observant until he was about thirteen.[8] Emilio Sereni, Communist, grew up in a family that observed the Jewish holidays, and his brother Enzo was a fervent Zionist.[9] Giuseppe Emanuele Modigliani, Socialist, referred constantly to his Jewish roots.[10] Eugenio Chiesa, Republican, spoke proudly of his Jewish father and the formative influence of Judaism.[11] Others were even farther removed from Judaism, perhaps remembering only an observant grandmother or great-grandmother. Nevertheless, nearly all would have said that their adult sense of social justice and responsibility had originated in their childhood training, and that this training had been rooted in a Jewish tradition.

While Italian Jews may not have been disproportionately involved in the pre-1943 anti-Fascist movement, they do seem to have been overrepresented in leadership roles. Carlo Rosselli was the undisputed founder and leader of Giustizia e Libertà. Treves and Modigliani formed, with the non-Jewish Turati, the triumvirate that led the moderate wing of the Socialist party. Sereni and Terracini were among the six or seven most important figures in the Italian Communist party. And among less politicized anti-Fascist spokesmen, there was an inordinate number of Jews.

All these men made immense personal sacrifices. Many in the prime of life spent dozens of dreary years in prison or confinement. Others, unable to work or even live in Italy, were forced to emigrate. When they left, Fascists confiscated all their personal assets. In foreign countries, they lived lonely, often impoverished lives, unable to find meaningful work, shadowed by foreign police and Italian Fascist agents, in constant danger of arrest or assassination. Carlo Rosselli gave up a substantial fortune at home to live a tragically short and uncomfortable life in France. Emilio Sereni gave up a similarly prosperous existence in Rome to live in France as a factory worker and, later, a small farmer. They and others like them made their choices in the 1920s, when Mussolini was still popular in Italy. There was little reason to think that much would change during their lifetimes.

When change finally came, conditions for anti-Fascists became worse. Many émigrés who were not yet elderly or dead returned to Italy during the Badoglio period, and many other anti-Fascists were released from prison. After the German occupation and the restoration of Mussolini, these were joined by thousands of other patriots, determined to destroy the Nazis and Fascists who were keeping Italy in the war. The period of armed resistance began. Resistants now had no refuge, no home, no income, no way to feed their families. Arrest meant torture, deportation, and death.

Many new Resistants, such as, among the Jews, Emanuele

The Italians and The Holocaust

Artom, Primo Levi, and Enzo Sereni, to name just three of the best-known cases, were only mildly political. Many had kept their distaste for Mussolini in abeyance until 1943. Others had seemed to support the regime, holding positions in the army, the universities, or private business. After 1943, previously uncommitted individuals joined the Resistance for a variety of reasons. Jews often joined to escape deportation, to avenge a deported family, or simply to hold life and limb together. Non-Jews joined to escape military service or labor conscription, to seek revenge for some private wrong, for adventure, or merely to eat. Motives differed, but in every case the struggle became a desperate matter of life and death.

While the Jewish community was perhaps not disproportionately active in the pre-1943 anti-Fascist movement, statistics suggest that it was overrepresented in the armed resistance. The highest estimate of general Italian participants is 230,000, or .5 percent of a national population of 45,000,000. The lowest estimate of Jewish participation is 1,000, or about 2 percent of a total wartime population of 45,200.[12] The situation is not surprising, for after 1943, no Jew could have any illusions about fascism, while non-Jews might still cling to antiquated notions of Italian grandeur and anti-bolshevism. Nevertheless, studies of Jewish Resistants unearth case after case of individuals who did not have to get involved. Many escorted their families safely to Switzerland or to Allied territory, only to volunteer to return to the war zone. Italian Jews may have had particularly good reasons to be anti-Fascists, but their reasons for wishing to stay alive were as compelling as anyone else's. They showed courage and commitment, both as Jews and as Italians.

Carlo Rosselli did not complete his five-year sentence on Lipari. In July 1929, after the failure of an earlier attempt, a forty-foot motor boat flying a British flag and registered in the name of a Mr. Cave, father of Rosselli's British wife Marion, picked up him, Emilio Lussu, and Francesco Fausto Nitti, as they waited in the water off a Lipari beach. The boat's driver was Italo Oxilia, the same man who had carried Turati through the winter storm to Corsica. After an eighteen-hour ride this time, the boat arrived in Tunisia, where Rosselli caught a mailboat to Marseille. [13] He established himself in Paris.

Late in 1929 in Paris, Carlo Rosselli founded his famous Giustizia e Libertà, intended as a coordinating body for all non-Communist opponents of fascism. With no comprehensive political platform, Giustizia e Libertà was a movement rather than a party. *Giellisti,* as they were called from the Italian pronunciation of the letters *g* and *l,* agreed on only one principle—they were all fervent Republicans. King Victor Emmanuel III had allowed Mussolini to seize power and had irrevocably compromised the monarchy. The monarchy, like fascism, must go.

The *giellisti* were democratic Republicans, committed to social justice, civil liberties, and international peace. Most were mildly Socialist, urging the socialization of public utilities and some heavy industry, agrarian reform, cooperatives, and progressive taxation. They believed that fascism could be combatted through bold and dramatic individual action. From bases in foreign countries, they sponsored several spectacular flights over Italian cities, where pilots, alone in antiquated little planes, dropped tons of anti-Fascist literature into public squares from low levels. Within Italy, they distributed anti-Fascist flyers and pamphlets, mailed journals, and put up posters. Giustizia e Libertà organizations in one Italian city were regularly broken up by police, only to appear somewhere else. [14]

As seen in chapter 3, anti-Fascist Jews seem to have had a particular affinity for Giustizia e Libertà. Sion Segre Amar, himself a *giellista* arrested at Ponte Tresa in 1934, explains:

> This is why many Jews felt inclined toward G.L.: they felt Fascism
> as an obstacle to their own ideologies and in G.L. [they found] a
> force (even though very modest) for struggle against that obstacle,
> but without mental constrictions or excessively rigid programs. [15]

Most *giellisti*, Jewish and non-Jewish alike, seem to have been
highly educated, high-minded, middle-class intellectuals or
professional men, uncommitted to a particular political party.
Giustizia e Libertà suited them perfectly. From there, most
went on to the Action party, organized in 1941 as an heir to
Rosselli's movement.

Many Jewish *giellisti* have already appeared in this book.
Mario Levi and Sion Segre Amar were seen in connection with
the Ponte Tresa incident in 1934. Leone Ginzburg, brilliant
Russian immigrant, nationalized Italian, scholar and journalist,
and husband of Natalia Ginzburg, has also been seen, both in
connection with the Ponte Tresa affair and as a member of the
armed resistance who died under torture in Rome's Regina
Coeli prison. Before Ponte Tresa, Levi, Segre Amar, and especially Ginzburg were active participants in a secret Giustizia e
Libertà group in Turin.

Carlo Levi, a medical doctor, artist, and novelist best known
abroad for his moving book *Christ Stopped at Eboli*, was a close
friend of Carlo and Nello Rosselli and another early leader of
Giustizia e Libertà. Arrested with Segre Amar and Ginzburg
in 1934, he was soon released, but in 1935 he was arrested again
and sent to confinement in Lucania, in southern Italy. *Christ
Stopped at Eboli*, written later while he was hiding from the
Nazis, describes his experiences in confinement and the
ignorant and impoverished peasants he would not otherwise
have known.

Like Leone Ginzburg, Carlo Levi went from Giustizia e
Libertà to the armed resistance after 1943. He was active
primarily in Tuscany, serving on the Tuscan Committee of

National Liberation, editing an anti-Fascist journal, and participating in street fighting in Florence in the summer of 1944. He survived to become a senator from Lucania in 1963. When he died in 1975 at the age of seventy-three, he was president of a federation of Italian emigrants, serving the needs of the people he had come to know when Mussolini sent him into confinement. [16]

The story of Vittorio Foà belongs more to the period of the armed resistance, but he too began activities in the ranks of Giustizia e Libertà. He was a member of the Turin group with Ginzburg, Segre Amar, and Mario Levi. After they were arrested, he directed the group for a time. His arrest in 1935 virtually ended Giustizia e Libertà activities in Italy. Foà was sentenced by the Special Tribunal to fifteen years in prison. Released by Badoglio in August 1943, he joined the Action party and became active in national Resistance coordinating committees. He survived the war to become a well-known parliamentary deputy and labor leader. [17]

Max Ascoli, one of the best-known Italian anti-Fascist émigrés in the United States in the 1930s, was not formally a *gielliste,* but he was a close friend and confidante of Carlo Rosselli. Born in Ferrara in 1898, Ascoli's career was just beginning when Mussolini took power. The young university graduate was a relentless anti-Fascist, publishing numerous articles in journals like *Non Mollare!* and *Quarto Stato.* He was a scholar and teacher of law and legal philosophy, but his politics prevented him from securing a much-desired university professorship. In 1931 he gladly accepted a scholarship from the Rockefeller Foundation for study in the United States, and never again lived in Italy. In 1933, he became a professor of political philosophy on the graduate faculty at the New School for Social Research in New York City. He was appointed dean of faculty in 1939.

As the danger of war mounted in Europe, Ascoli worked

hard to make Americans understand the nature of German national socialism and Italian fascism. He made countless speeches and published numerous anti-Fascist articles in *The Nation* and other periodicals. He also maintained close contacts with other exiles from Europe. Throughout the war years, he continued these activities. He returned to Italy briefly when the war was over, but after fourteen years, his real home was in New York. Max Ascoli remained in the United States, launching a new magazine, *The Reporter,* in 1949. [18]

Other close friends of the Rosselli brothers were the previously mentioned father and son from Ivrea, Camillo and Adriano Olivetti. Camillo, named in honor of Camillo Cavour, founded the Olivetti Typewriter Company in 1909. He was a courageous anti-Fascist from the very beginning. Until 1925, he wrote numerous newspaper articles demanding economic reforms and calling upon Italian industrialists to defend civil liberties and exercise social responsibility. He unequivocably condemned industrialists who helped finance fascism. In 1926, he supported his son's efforts to help his old friend Turati emigrate from Italy.

During the 1930s, Camillo gradually withdrew from company involvement, and Adriano replaced him. The anti-Fascist sentiments and activities of both men continued. In 1934, the Olivetti Company, which employed numerous Jewish engineers and managers, was dangerously implicated in the Ponte Tresa affair. Several employees, including Gino Levi, Mario's brother, were arrested.

The Olivetti Typewriter Company, following the example of its founder and his son, remained an anti-Fascist center throughout the 1930s—and throughout the war. In 1941 and 1942, it was among the chief financial backers of the Action party, heir of Giustizia e Libertà. In July 1943, Adriano Olivetti was arrested for conspiring to end the war and locked into

Regina Coeli. He was released just hours before the Germans took over.

When the Germans occupied Italy, Camillo and his wife Luisa went into hiding. Some of their six grown children were in the United States, but others, like Adriano, also had to hide. Camillo died of illness in December 1943, at the age of seventy-five, while hiding with a peasant family. None of his family could attend his burial, but hundreds of non-Jewish workers, in tribute to his humane factory management policies, risked Nazi wrath to stand in the rain in the little Jewish cemetery in Biella to pay their last respects.

Luisa died about a year later. Forty-three-year-old Adriano managed to get from Rome to Switzerland early in 1944. He worked there with other anti-Fascist exiles to hasten the end of the war. Meanwhile, trusted non-Jews, along with one or two courageous Jews with false documents, managed the company with its several thousand employees. The factory in Ivrea became an important partisan coordinating center. Twenty-four Olivetti employees died in the struggle for liberation. [19]

Carlo Rosselli was distinguished for his organization and for the friends and followers, Jews and non-Jews, he attracted. By the mid-1930s, however, both his organization and his life were drawing to a close. Many adherents, insisting that Giustizia e Libertà should be more Socialist and less reformist and intellectual, withdrew support. Many others were sent to prison or confinement in Italy. Still others would be killed in the Spanish Civil War, fighting in Rosselli's Italian Column—the first unit of Italian anti-Fascists to reach Spain. In August 1936 Rosselli himself was badly wounded in Spain at Monte Pelato, near Huesca, and sent back to France to recover from phlebitis. In France he did not rest, but continued to urge men to volunteer for the fight against fascism in Spain. "Today in Spain, tomorrow in Italy," he proclaimed. Fascism, he believed, would always lead to war, and could only be stopped by force. Hundreds, from all over the world, responded to his appeal. It was his finest hour.

On June 6, 1937, Nello Rosselli traveled to France to visit his older brother. Nello had been arrested after Carlo's escape from Lipari in 1929, and served six months of a five-year sentence. He was released when fellow historians publicly protested that he was not involved in Carlo's escape and should be permitted to resume his professional work. He was in fact a highly esteemed historian, with several well-known works on the *Risorgimento* and the working-class movement to his credit. [20] In 1936, he was invited to give a lecture series in the United States, where he could have settled with his family. He declined, saying that his place was in Italy to help his friends in the anti-Fascist struggle.

On June 9, 1937, Carlo and Nello left their hotel at Bagnoles-de-l'Orne in Normandy for an afternoon drive. They stopped to assist with a car that seemed to have mechanical difficulties. Cagoulards, French Fascist thugs, leaped upon them and, after a fierce fight, butchered them. Their bodies lay near the road for two days.

An investigation ultimately revealed that an Italian military information unit had hired the Cagoulard murderers for the price of one hundred guns. The clear implication was that Galeazzo Ciano, then Italian foreign minister, had grown concerned about Rosselli's Spanish Civil War activities and decided that he must be stopped. But Carlo and Nello Rosselli could not be stopped so easily. As news of their murders flashed around the world, more than 200,000 people accompanied their hearse to Père Lachaise cemetery in Paris. Fascist brutality was exposed again, and the uncommitted paused to consider Carlo's words. Fascism meant war and violence, and must not be tolerated. [21]

After the death of her sons, Amelia Rosselli left Italy with her daughters-in-law and her grandchildren. She returned in 1946, to live out her days quietly in her family home in Florence, where she died in 1955. She had had three sons. All had died before her, for their country. If they had lived, their country would ultimately have abandoned them because they were Jews.

While Jews were disproportionately represented among Rosselli's *giellisti*, they were also numerous in the democratic, reformist wing of the Socialist party. Within the triumvirate that led that wing for years—Filippo Turati, Claudio Treves, and Giuseppe Emanuele Modigliani—two, Treves and Modigliani, were Jewish. All three were parliamentary deputies with national reputations before Mussolini's rise to power. All three went into exile in France.

Claudio Treves achieved recognition, if not always acclaim, for his courageous parliamentary speeches before and during World War I. At first he urged neutrality in a conflict that did not concern Italy. After Italian intervention in May 1915, he advocated a negotiated peace. A phrase in a speech in July 1917, declaring as a goal, "Next winter no longer in the trenches," electrified the nation and earned him enthusiastic praise from supporters and vile denunciations from opponents. The latter did not refrain from anti-Semitic insults as well.

After the war, Treves made his distaste for fascism as obvious as his distaste for war. When Mussolini took power in 1922, his life became increasingly endangered. He fled to Paris in 1926, leaving his wife and two young sons behind in difficult financial straits. In Paris, he became editor of *La Libertà,* the weekly publication of the Concentrazione Antifascista, a coalition of Italian Republican and Socialist parties and trade unions. He died suddenly in 1933, a year after Turati, and was buried at Père Lachaise. After the war, his and Turati's remains were moved to an honorary site in Milan's Cimitero Monumentale. [22]

Giuseppe Emanuele Modigliani demonstrated the courage of his convictions most vividly in a single act. In November 1922, newly appointed Prime Minister Mussolini introduced himself to the Chamber of Deputies with the declaration that he could have turned that "deaf and gray hall into a bivouac for Blackshirts." Modigliani, alone among the deputies present, stood up and cried, "Long Live Parliament!" [23]

Modigliani had a reputation among his friends for referring constantly to his Jewish origins, to the occasional recorded annoyance of Jews (Rosselli) and non-Jews (Turati) alike. [24] Like Turati and Treves, he was obliged to emigrate to Paris in 1926, leaving his mother and sister in Italy (his brother, the painter Amedeo Modigliani, had died in Paris in 1920). In exile, Giuseppe edited *Rinascita socialista,* an anti-Fascist review. He also drafted, in 1927, the original charter of the Concentrazione Antifascista. He remained active throughout the 1930s, constantly reiterating his suspicion of Stalinists and Italian Communists during the Popular Front era. When the Germans occupied France in 1940, Modigliani, now elderly, escaped with his wife to Geneva, where he continued to write Socialist articles. In October 1944, he returned to Italy with Ignazio Silone to support the Resistance. [25]

While Jews were not numerous within the Italian Communist party in the 1920s, they did provide two well-known leaders—Umberto Terracini and Emilio Sereni. Terracini was born in 1895 into a strictly observant family. He attended a Jewish elementary school in Turin, where he learned to speak and read Hebrew. Like nearly all Jews of his generation, however, he attended a state high school, and he gradually put aside the rituals of orthodoxy. Presumably he was no longer a strict believer when he joined the Socialist Youth Federation in 1911, at the age of sixteen.

After serving in World War I, Terracini studied law at the University of Turin, where he became a close friend of Antonio Gramsci and Palmiro Togliatti. With them, he became a founder of the Italian Communist party in 1921. Under fascism, Terracini spent thirteen years in prison and in confinement at Ponza and Ventotene. He was released belatedly during Badoglio's interregnum—the original amnesty of Mussolini's political prisoners had excluded Communists. Late in August 1943, in precarious health, Terracini decided to recuperate at his brother's house on Lago d'Orta, just a few kilometers west of Lago Maggiore and Meina. A few days later, the Germans occupied Italy.

Late one night soon after the occupation, the local Fascist secretary pounded on the Terracinis' door. The Germans had arrived, he warned, and had demanded lists of resident Jews. Within fifteen minutes, the brothers were ready to leave. The Fascist took them by boat to his own house on the lake, and hid them there for forty-eight hours. During that period, as seen in chapter 1, the Jews of Meina were massacred. Finally their protector arranged for a guide to escort them over the mountains to Switzerland. A Fascist official had saved the life of a Communist whom Mussolini had imprisoned for thirteen years.

Terracini returned to Italy in 1944 to join the armed resistance in the Val d'Ossola, a strategically vital valley that led from Lago Maggiore toward the Simplon Pass. Partisans had liberated the area between September 8 and 10, 1944, and set up a popular republic. Terracini became a secretary general of the new government, which controlled a region of thirty-two towns, including Domodossola, and 85,000 people. When the area was reconquered after five weeks by German troops, Brigate Nere, and militiamen of the GNR, Terracini escaped again to Switzerland. He remained there until just before liberation. In 1946, he became president of the Constituent Assembly, which drafted Italy's Republican constitution. He was a member of the Communist party directorate, and he became a senator in 1948. In 1964, he was his party's unsuccessful candidate for president of Italy. [26]

Emilio Sereni was born in 1907 into a prosperous old Roman family. His uncle, Angelo Sereni, a lawyer, served as president of the Jewish Community of Rome for over thirty years. His father Samuele was a physician to the king's court, with offices in the Quirinal Palace. He acquired the position through his personal acquaintance with the Queen Mother.

Emilio's parents were not strictly observant, but they kept the high holidays and raised their four children with a respect for Jewish traditions. For a period in the early 1920s, two of the children, Emilio and his older brother Enzo, became more observant than their parents. The brothers learned Hebrew and became Zionists, a decidedly unfashionable step among affluent Roman Jews at the time. [27] Emilio even pursued an agricultural course of study at the university, to further his Zionist aims. Unlike Enzo, however, who emigrated to Palestine in 1927, Emilio finally abandoned Zionism. After completing his university studies and military service, he joined the anti-Fascist Communist underground. He was arrested in 1930 and sentenced by the Special Tribunal to twenty years in prison. He had a wife and newborn child.

In 1935, Sereni was granted amnesty, and he and his family escaped to Paris. He taught himself a new trade and worked in a machine shop until the Germans occupied northern France. He then escaped to the unoccupied zone, where he supported himself and his family for more than two years by farming. He continued his political work, organizing Italian Communists in France and trying to retain contact with anti-

Fascists within Italy. In June 1943, he was arrested by Vichy police in Italian-occupied France and handed over to the Italians. He was sentenced to twenty years in prison and transferred to Italy. He arrived about the time Mussolini fell.

Under Badoglio, Sereni was granted amnesty a second time. The Germans promptly rearrested him, holding him in an SS prison wing in Turin for many months. Because the SS failed to discover he was Jewish, he escaped execution. He lived to serve as Communist delegate to the national Resistance coordinating committee for northern Italy, directing the final partisan insurrections before liberation, negotiating Mussolini's surrender, and, failing in that, approving his summary execution. After the war, he served as a deputy in the Constituent Assembly and as a minister for postwar assistance in the government of Alcide De Gasperi. He later became minister for public works. A member of the Communist party central committee, Sereni became a senator in 1948, and a deputy twenty years later. [28]

Illustrative of the quieter breed of anti-Fascists are those who rejected the loyalty oath imposed upon all university professors in 1931. The oath itself was relatively harmless. Professors had to swear to be loyal to the king, his royal successors, and the Fascist regime. They had to promise to teach with the purpose of forming citizens who would be industrious, honest, and devoted to the nation and the Fascist regime, and swear that they belonged to no organizations that were incompatible with that duty. About 1,200 professors signed. Twelve professors did not sign. They immediately lost their jobs. Of the twelve, three were Jewish. They were Giorgio Levi della Vida, professor of comparative Semitic languages at the University of Rome; Vito Volterra, professor of mathematics at the University of Rome and later at the University of Pennsylvania; and Giorgio Errera, professor of chemistry at the University of Pavia. [29]

The Italians and The Holocaust

Of the 1,200 professors who signed the oath, many were Jewish. Seven years later, the Fascist regime to which they pledged their loyalty forced them all to resign. But in 1931, most Jews, like most non-Jews, ignored politics and tried simply to continue their normal lives.

The three Jewish professors who did not sign, like the many Jews in the early anti-Fascist movement, did not act in their capacity as Jews. Fascism was not yet anti-Semitic. It posed no personal threat to them. They resisted as democrats, as humanists, as Italians.

Gino Donati, a Jew from Modena, was a career army officer serving in Africa in 1938. As such, he was undoubtedly nationalistic and supportive of Italy's expansionist goals. One memorable day, Donati received notice of a promotion. In the same mail, he found a letter advising him of his release from military service. The racial laws had taken effect.

Donati returned to his Jewish roots. He became a Zionist working to prepare young Jews for emigration to Israel. After the armistice, he escaped to Switzerland, but he returned almost immediately to join the armed resistance. He was among the first to die in combat. [30]

Vittorio Fiz was an accountant in a bank in Vercelli. He had no sense of being a Jew until he lost his job as a result of the racial laws. At that point, he became actively anti-Fascist. In 1944, he joined the armed resistance. He saw much action, but survived to see liberation. [31]

Donati and Fiz illustrate a later type of anti-Fascist, Jewish and non-Jewish alike. They were not intellectuals or political people; they did not oppose fascism because it offended an abstract sense of justice. They became opponents of the regime because fascism directly affected their personal lives. For Jews, the turning point came with the racial laws. Young men denied university educations and professional careers could not remain indifferent. For non-Jews, the change came somewhat later, with Mussolini's disgrace, the obvious military debacle, the German occupation, and the onset of military and labor conscription. Thousands eventually escaped into the hills and joined the original anti-Fascists to form the armed resistance.

Between one and three thousand Italian partisans were Jewish. While they came from a variety of backgrounds, most, like Italian Jews in general, were from the middle class. Most seem not to have paid much heed to their Judaism. Pino Levi Cavaglione, Communist, scarcely mentions it in his memoirs. [32] A few, however, like Emanuele Artom, found themselves delving deeply into the meaning of this heritage that was causing so much pain. [33] All fought in non-Jewish units, among men who had never known Jews and were quite uninterested in racial and religious issues. Jewish partisans themselves often developed friendships with other Jews; men as different as Pino Levi Cavaglione and Emanuele Artom both write of Jewish comrades. But all fought primarily as Italians, beside other Italians and against other Italians.

Many Jewish partisans, including Emanuele Artom, Pino Levi Cavaglione, and Primo Levi, have been seen in previous chapters. All, like all non-Jews, deserve to be remembered. Only a few can be selected here, with apologies to the tens of hundreds who are omitted.

Eugenio Calò was born in Tuscany in 1906, into a family of modest means. In 1938 he and his wife Carolina settled in Arezzo, where Eugenio established a small machine shop. He barely managed, with hard work, to support his family. When the Germans occupied Italy, he moved his pregnant wife and three small children to an isolated country house where he hoped they would be safe. He joined the Resistance, visiting his family only occasionally.

On the last day of December 1943, Italian Fascists, hoping

to capture Eugenio, raided the Calò family hiding place. Eugenio was at home, but managed to escape through a window. His wife was seized and imprisoned with the children, aged eighteen months, five, and six. She was interrogated for four months in the hope that she would help police capture her husband. She revealed nothing, and was transferred to Fossoli with the children.

On May 16, 1944, Eugenio Calò's family was among the several hundred Jewish prisoners packed into boxcars bound for Auschwitz. Carolina went into labor that night, and her fourth child, a boy, was born in the sealed car. They arrived at Auschwitz on May 23, and the mother and four children went directly to the gas chambers.

Eugenio continued to organize and lead partisan units in Tuscany until July 1944. On July 2, he and his group and about twenty captured Germans managed to cross Allied lines. He then volunteered to return to occupied territory, to reestablish communications with a partisan unit in Val di Chiana. Returning from this mission on July 12, he was captured near Arezzo, along with about forty-seven other partisans and civilians. The partisans were tortured brutally, but they revealed nothing.

On July 14, the Germans forced Calò and his men to dig a great pit. They then buried their prisoners up to their necks, beside large sticks of dynamite. Still no one talked. The Germans ignited the dynamite.

After the war, Eugenio Calò was posthumously awarded the gold medal for military valor. [34]

Mario Jacchia was born in Bologna in 1896. His father, a Jewish lawyer from Trieste, was an ardent Italian patriot and irredentist, agitating for Italian measures to "redeem" Trieste from the Hapsburgs. When Italy intervened in World War I, Mario volunteered for military service. He became an officer in an Alpine regiment, was gravely wounded, and returned to the front after refusing disability leave. He won two silver medals, one bronze, and a cross of war for military valor.

After the war, Mario completed his university studies and became a lawyer. As a war veteran, nationalist, and anti-Socialist, he flirted briefly with fascism and joined the local Bolognese Fascist party group. When he resigned after Socialist deputy Giacomo Matteotti's murder in 1924, resentful Fascist thugs sacked his law office and beat him so badly he had to recover in the hospital. Despite continual harassment, he went on to practice law in Bologna for over twenty years.

In 1943, Mario Jacchia joined the armed resistance and quickly became a leading organizer and commander in Emilia. At 2:30 in the afternoon of August 3, 1944, the house in Parma where he was meeting with other partisan leaders was betrayed by a spy and surrounded by Fascist militiamen. When a partisan guard sounded the alarm, Mario ordered the others to escape. He remained to burn compromising documents and was caught. He was interrogated and tortured, first by Fascists and then by Nazis, for nearly a month. At the end of August, he was executed.

According to a friend who knew him for many years, Mario Jacchia had no sons to fight for freedom in Italy. He armed his daughter Valeria and sent her off to fight in the battle of Monte Fiorino. She continued the tradition of her forefathers. Her great-great-grandfather had died in 1848, fighting for the Roman Republic. [35]

Mario Jacchia was also awarded a posthumous gold medal for military valor.

Sergio Forti was born in Trieste in 1920. Because he had already enrolled at a university, he was allowed to complete his studies in naval engineering despite the racial laws. Also despite the laws, he was working in a shipyard in Viareggio when the Germans occupied Italy. He managed to keep plans, designs,

The Italians and The Holocaust

instruments, motors, and even arms out of German hands. Probably denounced by an informer, his house was searched in October 1943, and he barely escaped with his family to Norcia, about forty-five kilometers northeast of Spoleto.

Memo Bemporad, a wealthy Jewish Tuscan textile manufacturer, also took refuge with his family in Norcia for a short time after October 1943. At the small inn where he stayed, there was just one other family: twenty-three-year-old Sergio Forti, his father, mother, brother, and sister. "Very reserved and distinguished people," Bemporad recalls, "tall, thin, formal, they resembled the Finzi Continis as De Sica represented them in his film. We thought they were Jewish but not wishing to embarrass them nor to reveal in turn that we were, we exchanged only a few courteous and vaguely friendly words." [36]

In Norcia, Sergio joined a partisan unit that was particularly active in assisting escaped Allied prisoners-of-war. On June 14, 1944, a German patrol surprised him, another partisan, and two British soldiers as they were attempting to blow up a bridge. The two British soldiers escaped. Sergio then convinced the Germans to hold him as a hostage and allow the other partisan to leave, to bring in the British. As prearranged, the three did not return. Forti was brutally tortured and murdered the same day.

Sergio Forti was among the first gold medal winners of the Resistance. His medal was awarded in February 1945, even before liberation. [37]

Rita Rosani, also born in Trieste in 1920, was a teacher at the Jewish School in her home city until 1943. When the Germans occupied Italy, she secured a hiding place for her parents, Czechoslovakian Jews named Rosenthal who had lived in Italy for years. She immediately joined the armed resistance. She fought in several actions in the area of Verona.

The Best of Their Generation

On September 17, 1944, two partisans who had been captured and tortured were forced to lead a unit of about five
hundred German and Fascist soldiers to their hiding place.
Rita's band of about fifteen partisans was attacked and tried
briefly to resist. During their retreat, Rita was wounded and
fell. According to her commanding officer, an Italian Fascist
soldier found her and finished her with a shot in the head.

A plaque at the synagogue of Verona now honors Rita
Rosani, as does another at the Jewish School in Trieste where
she taught. She was the only known woman partisan in Italy
to die in combat. She was awarded a gold medal, posthumously. [38]

Franco Cesana was born on September 20, 1931. The racial
laws caught him at age seven, in elementary school in Bologna.
He had to leave for the Jewish School, in makeshift quarters
in the synagogue. A schoolmate there remembers him as "dear
and good, honest in his ideals. He was a Zionist and religious.
He was very young, a baby, and he would become a hero." [39]

When his father died in 1939, Franco moved to Turin and
entered a rabbinical school. He studied there and in Rome
until 1943. When the Germans occupied Italy, Franco's family
went into hiding in the Apennines near Bologna. There they
moved from hut to hut, always in danger of betrayal and death.
His older brother, Lelio, joined the partisans. Despite his
mother's wishes, Franco ultimately followed.

One day in September 1944, Franco ventured out on a
scouting mission with his brother. He was caught by German
rifle fire. His brother heard his last words, the most famous
Hebrew prayer "Shema' Israel, A-donai E-lohenu, A-donai
Echad." "Hear, O Israel, the Lord our God, the Lord is One."
His comrades retrieved his body and returned it to his mother
on September 20, 1944, his thirteenth birthday. Franco
Cesana was eventually buried in the Jewish cemetery in

Bologna. His tombstone reminds the world that he was "the youngest partisan in Italy." [40]

Besides Calò, Jacchia, Forti, and Rosani, at least two other Jewish Resistance fighters won posthumous gold medals for military valor. Eugenio Curiel, born in Trieste in 1912, was a brilliant assistant professor of physics at the University of Padua until he lost his position as a result of the racial laws. An anti-Fascist at a young age, he was a clandestine Communist organizer among university students and industrial workers throughout the 1930s. He was arrested in 1939 and confined at Ventotene until August 1943. He immediately resumed his anti-Fascist activities, becoming a highly effective partisan organizer and editor of Resistance publications.

On February 24, 1945, only two months before liberation, Curiel was recognized on a street in Milan by a squad of Brigate Nere. They shot and wounded him. When he tried to flee, they caught and beat him to death, leaving his mangled body where he fell. An old woman who witnessed the murder left flowers beside him. [41]

Like Curiel, Eugenio Colorni, born in Milan in 1909, was an anti-Fascist while still very young. A university graduate in philosophy, he hoped to secure a professorial appointment, but his politics made it impossible. He taught at a secondary school and joined Giustizia e Libertà first and the Socialist party later. Also like Curiel, he was arrested and confined at Ventotene from 1939 to 1943.

During the occupation, Colorni was an active Resistance organizer. He helped reestablish the Socialist Youth Federation and edited the clandestine newspaper *Avanti!* In May 1944, just a few days before the liberation of Rome, he was caught on a tram by Fascists from the Koch band who had been following him for some time. They shot him as he tried to flee, and he died two days later. As an early acquaintance later remembered, he knew nothing of guns. [42]

Nearly all Jewish partisans suffered an additional burden of fear for the safety of their families. Many had no news from their families at all. Others, like Eugenio Calò, were aware of family tragedies. While Giorgio Diena and his younger brother Paolo were fighting with the Resistance, they learned that their father had been arrested and deported. Like Calò's family, Professor Diena did not return. Paolo also died, killed in action in the autumn of 1944. [43]

The mother, father, and sister of Giorgio Latis were arrested in September 1943, when they tried to escape to Switzerland. They were deported and never heard from again. Giorgio joined the Resistance and was killed in Turin on April 27, 1945. He was one of the last partisans to die. [44]

Osvaldo Tesoro, industrialist from Naples, suffered the same agony of dread, with a different outcome. He was in Naples and his wife and children were in Florence at the time of the occupation. After participating in the famous Four Days of Naples, Osvaldo concentrated on a search for his family. When he finally managed to reach Florence in early August 1944, a month before its liberation, he learned that his loved ones had been deported. He rejoined the Resistance in a rage, fighting ferociously in the battle for Florence. He subsequently learned that his family had merely gone into hiding. He found his wife, feverish but alive, with the two older children in the cellar where they had lived for three months. His baby girl, whom he had never seen, was dead from malnutrition and disease. [45]

A privileged few enjoyed the knowledge that their families were safe abroad. In a sense, however, these partisans were the most impressive of all, for they too could have chosen exile.

They could have escaped the conflict, rationalizing that their families needed them.

Gianfranco Sarfatti was sixteen years old when the racial laws forced him to leave school. He continued his studies privately and became involved with the anti-Fascist movement. In February 1944, he found a guide to escort his parents and himself to Switzerland. When they were secure, he quietly returned to Italy and joined a partisan brigade fighting in the Valle d'Aosta.

In a letter in August 1944, Gianfranco Sarfatti told his parents why he returned to Italy to join the armed resistance. He wrote:

> Reflect that while it seems that all the world is collapsing and that the ruins must cover everything, your children, by different means, it is true, are looking toward the future and toward reconstruction, devoting all their forces to it.
>
> You are suffering; but millions of parents have been and still are in anxiety; and this must no longer be.
>
> And as I have recognized your sorrow in the sorrow of all suffering fathers and mothers, you must recognize your children in all the babies and in all the young people who have been born in this tormented world. [46]

On February 21, 1945, a spy revealed the position of Sarfatti's unit to German and Fascist soldiers. Gianfranco and several others fell in an ambush and died in the snow, not far from the frontier where they could have been safe.

Enzo Sereni, older brother of Emilio, left his comfortable family home in Rome in 1927 at the age of twenty-two and emigrated to Palestine. His young wife, Ada Ascarelli, accompanied him. Their baby daughter stayed with his parents until they were settled. Together, Enzo and Ada helped found the Kibbutz Givat Brenner, near what was then the southern edge of the area of Jewish settlement. With two thousand members today, Givat Brenner, near Rehovot, is one of the largest kibbutzim in Israel. [47]

For over a decade, Enzo and Ada labored to carve a new community out of the wilderness. A son and a second daughter were born to them. The kibbutz slowly began to prosper. The Serenis were fully involved in a life far from hate-torn Europe. They could easily have chosen to remain there. The hardest part of their lives should have been behind them.

Despite his great distance from Europe, Enzo Sereni clearly understood the Nazi menace. He had made several trips to Germany in the early 1930s to address Zionist groups, and he had seen the danger himself. Also, by 1934, Givat Brenner numbered 160 German Jews among its 300 members. [48] The refugees brought tales of persecution with them. When war finally broke out in Europe, Enzo knew immediately that he could not sit back and watch. Despite the pacifist ideals that had guided his life—he had refused to carry a rifle on guard duty at the kibbutz—he joined the British Intelligence Service in 1940. He performed several missions in Egypt and Iraq.

In the spring of 1944, Enzo finally succeeded in persuading the British to send him into occupied Italy. His mission was to reach Florence, contact partisan units there, gather maps and military information, and assist escaped British prisoners-of-war. In his own mind, he added the mission of contacting and aiding Italian Jewish fugitives. At the age of thirty-nine, he embarked upon a four-day parachuting course. It consisted of six daylight jumps.

Toward midnight on May 15, 1944, Enzo Sereni and a companion, similarly trained only in daylight jumps, parachuted into Tuscany. Because of strong winds, the two men landed far from their intended spot and dangerously close to a German construction unit. Enzo was captured immediately, in the uniform of a British captain in a Palestinian unit. After four days of interrogation and torture at Verona, he was sent to Gries. On October 8, he was shipped by cattle car to Dachau. He was registered as a British Jew, born in Palestine.

For over a month, Enzo Sereni worked at a hard labor site near Dachau. He served as an interpreter for Italian prisoners, endeared himself to them all, and became their spokesman. On the night of November 17, 1944, he was called away from the barracks and returned to Dachau. Someone had apparently learned that he was neither British nor Palestinian, but Italian. It is not known how he died. [49]

Enzo Sereni, one of the few Italian Zionists in the Resistance —for the simple reason that there were few Zionists in Italy —privately added the goal of helping Jews to his list of official objectives. He was an exception. Most Italian Jewish partisans did little to help their coreligionists directly. They knew about the deportations, of course, although they were as uncertain as everyone else about the fate of Jewish deportees. But Jewish civilians in hiding were comparatively few in number and dispersed throughout the country. Most Jewish partisans, like their non-Jewish comrades, did not know where they were or how to help them. Unlike the case in France—where there were far more Jews, partisans and fugitives alike—there seems to have been, in Italy, no exclusively Jewish underground operation organized to conduct Jews into exile in neutral countries. [50] Jewish and non-Jewish partisans shared the belief that the best way to help all persecuted peoples was to defeat the Germans as soon as possible.

Jewish partisans fought in totally integrated units. Again in part because Jews were proportionately few in Italy and in part because they were so totally assimilated, there were no wholly Jewish Resistance units as in other countries. Italian Jews fought as Italians, for their country, for their principles, and for all persecuted peoples. They would not have liked to be singled out from their comrades as somehow different. Reflecting this view forty years later, the organized Jewish communities in Italian cities today, not wishing to make distinctions among heroes, do not keep complete lists of members who were Resistants.[51]

Yet identification of Jewish anti-Fascists serves one useful purpose, for it forever lays to rest the argument that Jews did not fight back against their oppressors. Indeed, in Italy, Jews fought back in higher proportions than non-Jews. Similarly, Jewish civilians did not contribute to their own destruction. They did not submit passively. They rarely reported voluntarily for internment, and they did not allow their own agencies to organize them for deportation.[52] In a country where Jews were assimilated, not highly visible, and linked to the community at large by ties of friendship and mutual tolerance, they behaved under stress exactly like everyone else. And the best of the young adult generation suffered and often sacrificed their lives —not just for Jews, not just for Italians, but for all people.

13

Conclusion

APPROXIMATELY 85 percent of Italy's Jews survived the Holocaust. That statistic puts Italy, with Denmark, at the top of the list of occupied nations for its percentage of Jewish survivors. Yet Italy had certain disadvantages in her effort to save Jews. In contrast to their attitudes toward the Danes, Norwegians, and Dutch, the Nazis regarded Italians as racially inferior. The poor Italian military performance before the armistice, Badoglio's betrayal of the Axis alliance, and the subsequent strength of the Italian anti-Fascist Resistance transformed Nazi contempt for their ally into profound distrust and hatred. Germans established Mussolini's puppet regime at Salò and paid lip service to the fiction of a German-Italian alliance, only to ignore totally their ally's expressed wish to keep Italian Jews confined in Italy. They treated satellite regimes in Bulgaria and Hungary with greater respect. [1]

Why, then, did so many Italian Jews survive? The fact that the Holocaust began late in Italy was helpful. By September

1943, most Italians had heard about the deportation of Jews, although they did not believe rumors of extermination. Italian Jews may at first have thought that they, loyal, prosperous, and assimilated citizens in a state allied to Germany and home to the Vatican, would be exempt, but when the first roundups confirmed what they knew of other countries' experiences, they hid. Also by September 1943, after German routs in Russia, North Africa, and Sicily, Hitler's total defeat seemed probable. Italian Jews could hope that they would not have to hide for long. Their hope gave them the courage to try.

While liberation did not come as quickly as many expected, the danger period was shorter for Jews in Italy than for those in most other occupied countries. Rome and Florence were liberated in the summer of 1944, after less than a year of occupation; northern Italy, with Genoa, Turin, Milan, Venice, and Trieste, suffered for another eight months. Jews in hiding were caught every week, and sometimes every day, during that twenty-month period. Clearly, more would have been found if the period had been longer.

Most of Poland, on the other hand, was occupied for more than five years. The Netherlands, Belgium, and northern France were occupied for well over four years. The organized murder of Jews in Poland began in December 1941.[2] Deportations from Belgium and northern France began early in 1942, and from the Netherlands, in July of the same year. It is a wonder that any Jews could endure the physical and emotional strains of hiding for so long. In Italy, with such a comparatively late and short danger period, one occasionally wonders why so many Jews were caught, rather than so few.

A late and short danger period, however, while helpful, was not always a decisive factor in survival. The Germans did not occupy Hungary until March 1944. Mass deportations of Hungarian Jews did not begin until April 27, six months later than in Italy. By that time, Nazi plans for the Jews were clearly known, Hitler's imminent defeat was obvious, and Jews hoping to hide could not have thought it would be necessary for long. Yet the Hungarian countryside east of the Danube was efficiently cleared of Jews by the end of June. With full Hungarian cooperation, more than 380,000 Hungarian Jews were deported in two months. [3]

Probably more important to survival than the late, short danger period were the specific general characteristics of Italian Jews. First, they were few in number—one-tenth of 1 percent of the population (similarly, Danish Jews represented only two-tenths of 1 percent). Sympathetic Christians could handle their needs for shelter, food, and documents. Second, most had some financial resources. Generally middle-class to begin with, they had not been impoverished by years of ghettoization. Money facilitated survival.

Most important, however, Italian Jews' physical appearance, clothes, language, friendships and contacts with non-Jews, and general assimilation in their communities usually enabled them to pass. Memo Bemporad tells of the meal he shared with German officers; Luciano Morpurgo recalls the Germans he guided around Rome. [4] Germans, unfamiliar with foreign customs and nuances of language, could often be fooled. Natives posed a graver problem. Yet the families of Giancarlo Sacerdoti and Memo Bemporad lived with several different non-Jews for months without their hosts ever learning they were Jewish. [5] Italian Jews with good false papers could clear any Fascist document check unless they panicked or were personally recognized. The same was usually true of native Jews in France, Denmark, Belgium, the Netherlands, and even Germany. The physical ability to pass sometimes gave them the courage to try. [6]

In contrast, in Eastern Europe and, especially, in Poland, many Jews looked and dressed distinctively, spoke the language of their country with an accent, lived apart from Christians, and knew little of their customs and religion.[7] They had few friends or contacts outside their communities. For these Jews, the possibility of passing did not exist. They could only survive by disappearing, remaining out of sight for months or years, totally dependent on the patience and good will of non-Jews. Jews and their helpers both faced greater risks of detection in these cases, and many on both sides tended not to try at all.[8]

Another less tangible characteristic of Italian Jews, perhaps more typical of them than of their Dutch, Belgian, Danish, or even French counterparts, may have contributed to their survival. Italian Jews seem to have shared with their Catholic compatriots an amiable inclination to ignore the law. The tendency was apparent at the very onset of the racial laws. Despite the prohibition, Memo Bemporad reserved rooms at a beach hotel for his family's summer vacation. More important, to avoid confiscation of his substantial businesses and properties, he took complicated steps to transfer them to Catholic friends who could be trusted to return them when the crisis had passed.[9] He and Carlo Modigliani kept their Aryan maids.[10] The lawyer Enzo Levi continued to serve non-Jewish clients, either secretly or through private arrangements with non-Jewish lawyer friends.[11] These men and others like them were ignoring unjust regulations, it is true, but they were still breaking the law and risking punishment. Jews in other Western European countries may also have overlooked anti-Semitic laws and regulations, but the Italians seem to have acted with a natural spontaneity and self-assurance uniquely their own.

During the occupation, this amiable inclination hardened into an iron determination to evade the law. It seems never to have occurred to most Italian Jews to obey their government's orders to report for internment, as did many Dutch, German, Hungarian, and Czech Jews.[12] Italian Jews became as talented at securing false documents as their non-Jewish friends were at producing them. They became as adept at fooling the authorities as their non-Jewish compatriots, who were busy evading military and labor conscription, saving automobiles, foodstuffs, and livestock from requisition, and supplying the black market.

Like their Christian compatriots, Italian Jews were supremely individualistic. The Nazis never organized an Italian *Judenrat*, a Jewish agency to provide social services and, ultimately, to transmit German orders. Most Italian Jews survived the Holocaust with no formal organizational help or hindrance. Indigenous aid organizations of Jews and non-Jews working together usually (except in Rome, where there were so many native Jews in hiding) limited their operations to foreign refugees and to Jews hoping to escape to Switzerland. Most Italian Jews in hiding lived by their own wits and resources, found their own rescuers, and dealt with individuals rather than organizations.

The peculiar combination in Italy of a later and short danger period, the low percentage of Jews, the ability of Jews to pass, and the imaginative daring of Jews as individuals was not enough to insure an 85 percent survival rate. The hunted could never have survived without help. All Jewish survivors owed their lives to their own initiative, to luck, and to the help of one or several non-Jews. And so the focus shifts from victims to rescuers.

Every country produced rescuers. Even Poland produced courageous rescuers, despite the great visibility of Jews, the generally anti-Semitic Catholic population, and the ferocious Nazi reprisals against despised Slavs who defied them. [13] Germany produced rescuers, despite the intense vigilance of the Gestapo. [14] France produced far more rescuers than is generally recognized, despite her somewhat exaggerated reputation for anti-Semitism. [15] Belgium produced whole networks of rescuers, which took full responsibility for hiding and supplying

Jewish children.[16] But Catholic Italy shares with Protestant Denmark the distinction of saving the highest percentages of Jewish lives. Why, in Italy, was this so?

To some extent, the same factors that encouraged Jews to hide encouraged non-Jews to hide them. Because the danger period began after the Allied invasion of Italy, many rescuers must have believed that their efforts would not be needed for long. Because the number of Jews was proportionately low, rescuers were not overwhelmed by a sense of futility, or frightened that they would be swamped by requests for help. And because Italian Jews could pass so easily, their rescuers were less endangered. But these are rational answers, based on an assumption that rescuers coolly analyzed risk factors before acting. That was decidedly not the case. A commitment to rescue Jews was usually an emotional decision—spontaneous, uncalculated, and irrational. What caused or encouraged it?

First, by September 1943, most Italians were disgusted with the war, the Fascists, and their German allies. The war had brought the death of their young men, the destruction of their cities, the loss of their African colonies, hunger and disruption at home, and finally, the German occupation of most of their country and the annexation of Trent and Trieste. The Fascists had begun and lost the war. And the Germans, after abandoning Italian soldiers to their fate in Russia and Sicily, had prevented Italy from giving up an obviously lost cause. Public anger was demonstrated by the thousands of Italians who joined the anti-Fascist Resistance, the miniscule numbers of former soldiers who volunteered to fight for the Republic of Salò, and the huge numbers of draft evaders and deserters after September 1943. Most Italians were fed up, and in their disgust, many helped anyone victimized by the war.

But this, too, is only a partial answer. Poles also hated the Germans and organized a significant Resistance movement, but some Polish partisans actually murdered Jewish partisans.

The Italians and The Holocaust

After the war, Catholic Poles murdered Jewish survivors, and even other Poles discovered to have sheltered Jews. [17] Hungarians in the summer of 1944 also resented German occupation and their continued forced involvement in a war that the regent, Admiral Nicholas Horthy, far more than Mussolini, had tried to avoid. [18] They, too, knew the war was lost. But they did not convert their hatred for the war into a rescue of their Jews.

Clearly, the immediate factors favorable to Jewish rescue during the Holocaust must be placed in the context of the customs and traditions of individual countries. The most pertinent tradition, of course, is the existence or absence of anti-Semitism. For many reasons, modern Italy lacked an anti-Semitic tradition. Italy had been united by anticlerical Liberals, at the expense of reactionary, clerical, and potentially anti-Semitic factions. To be powerful, important, or merely relevant in Italy, one had to be modern, Liberal in the nineteenth-century sense of the word, nonclerical, tolerant, and by extension, oblivious to religious differences. Those who were not did not count. [19]

While these attitudes prevailed among the urban upper and middle classes, they did not necessarily affect workers and peasants. Indeed, one might examine the lower classes for clericalism and anti-Semitism, in reaction, as happened elsewhere, to the liberalism of their political, economic, and social superiors. But in Italy, one would search in vain. The chief explanation here may involve the fact that there were in Italy so few Jews. There were few Jewish industrialists, landlords, or shopkeepers to employ, compete with, or, in workers' eyes, exploit Christians. And those who were Jewish did not appear to be. Their employees and competitors may not even have known. [20] Most Italians outside major urban areas probably knew no Jews at all.

The high degree of assimilation of Italian Jews may also have worked against the growth of anti-Semitism in all classes. People resent most deeply those who differ from themselves—those who visibly reject their food, dress, language, schools, and customs, as if to say that their ways are superior. As seen, Italian Jews differed from their compatriots only in their religion, and that difference they honored quietly, without ostentation, and often irregularly. Italian Catholics, equally unostentatious and irregular in their observance of religion, were not deeply concerned about individuals, Jews and atheists alike, who did not share their beliefs.

Again, this explanation has its limits. Dreyfus, not visibly different from his colleagues, was resented and victimized. German and Austrian Jews, highly assimilated, were resented, victimized, and ultimately murdered. But they confronted other factors nonexistent in Italy. Dreyfus was especially persecuted by an aristocratic, clerical class that in Italy had been dispossessed during the *Risorgimento*. German and Austrian Jews were more numerous, and therefore more frequent competitors. And eventually, of course, their image in society was affected by the masses of unassimilated *Ostjuden* fleeing west.

The lack of a national anti-Semitic tradition is not in itself enough to explain Jewish rescue efforts. The Netherlands, Belgium, and even Germany had substantial non-Jewish populations free from anti-Semitism—though to much less a degree than Italy. Yet Jews fared badly in all three countries. The lack of an anti-Semitic tradition certainly helped rescue efforts, however, in many ways. Most obviously, there were more individuals free from anti-Jewish prejudices ready to consider helping.[21] Equally important, rescuers were less afraid that their friends and neighbors would disapprove of, and even betray, them. Potential informers, also, may have hesitated, unwilling to incur the censure and even the retribution of their more benevolent compatriots. The lack of an anti-Semitic tradition, finally, deprived the Nazis and their local cronies of a base upon which to build their hysterical propaganda image of the Jew as villain, enemy, traitor, capitalist exploiter, Communist exploiter, and creator of all ills.

The combination of immediate and long-term factors favorable to Jewish rescue may be enough to explain the high survival rate in Italy, without indulging in broad concepts of national character. Such concepts can be easily exaggerated, and readers who object to Jewish stereotypes will do well to object equally to Italian ones. Such generalizations also may contribute little. They are nonetheless tempting, despite their limitations.

Already touched upon is the latitude with which many Italians interpret their religion—a latitude that perhaps disposes them to be tolerant of dissenters. Also mentioned is the amiable Italian inclination to ignore the rules. Perhaps "ignore" is too strong a word; perhaps "bend" or "interpret" are better ones; perhaps the inclination is no stronger among Italians than among other peoples. Nevertheless, Italians did bend the rules, and saved lives. Italian nuns bent the rules of their orders, and allowed outsiders, even men, into their secluded cloisters. Italian priests ignored the laws of their land and, occasionally, the instructions of their superiors. Bankers sometimes did not report Jewish bank accounts; innkeepers did not report unusual guests; landlords did not report unusual tenants; villagers did not report newcomers. It is not accurate to say that they minded their own business. That is not an Italian trait, nor probably is it a trait of any other people. Rather, they did not report what they knew to the authorities. The traditional peasant contempt for the authorities prevailed.

Contempt for the authorities translates easily into a suspicion of propaganda and rhetoric of any kind. That trait, too, Italians demonstrated during the occupation. In the face of an obviously contrasting reality, no one could tell them that the war was not lost, that fascism meant glory, or that Jews were their enemy. Supreme individualists, skeptics, and realists, they thought for themselves, and they knew better.

When commenting on informers, Carlo Brizzolari makes a tantalizing reference to another character trait—"the age-old national vice of the Italians: that of doing evil to one's neighbors while giving aid to strangers."[22] It is difficult for an outsider to comment on such a generalization. Certainly informers who "did evil to their neighbors" were the exception rather than the rule, but certainly the Italians aided strangers. Like many descriptions of national traits, this one provokes reflection but remains elusive.

Can generalizations of national character help explain the Jewish experience during the Holocaust in other countries? Can the Dutch and German tradition of respect and obedience to authority, for example, help explain low survival rates? It is possible, but again, such explanations are limited. The Danes, too, have a tradition of respect for authority, yet Danes, like Italians, rescued their Jews. Why? Unlike Italians, the Danes did not defy authority to save Jews. Unlike the Republic of Salò, their authority—their king and their political leaders— never sanctioned anti-Semitism. Encouragement for the rescue movement, which consisted primarily of a dramatic, rapid exodus to Sweden in October 1943, came from above. The Danes, rarely anti-Semitic but almost always anti-German, courageously followed their leaders' example.[23]

In many cases after the war, non-Jewish Italians who had saved Jews, when asked about their motivations, were annoyed and even angered by the very question. "How can you ask me such a question?" one man inquired. "Do you mean to say that you do not understand why a devout Catholic like myself had to behave as I did in order to save human beings whose lives were in danger?"[24]

Countless other rescuers, when honored for their deeds after the war, repeated the simple phrase, "I did my duty," or "I did what needed to be done." Most did not regard their own deeds as exceptional, assuring others that "anyone in my place would have done the same." [25] Indeed, according to the explanations of Italian rescuers offered so far, that belief would seem reasonable. Most Italians disliked the war, fascism, and the Germans. Most Italians were not anti-Semitic. Most Italians were individualists, distrustful of authority, inclined not to take rules and rhetoric too seriously. Yet most Italians did not aid Jews. They remained terrified of punishment, preoccupied with their own struggle for survival, and indifferent or unaware of the suffering of others. What is lacking in our explanation of rescue activities?

In the last analysis, we must acknowledge that the non-Jewish men and women who rescued Jews during the Holocaust were exceptional people, different from the average. They differed in their altruism—their unnatural, irrational readiness to show compassion toward other human beings and to sacrifice their own interests to assist them. Altruism implies the possibility of real sacrifice, including, in this case, the loss of life. Altruism negates the possibility of rewards other than emotional satisfaction. Altruism involves aid to strangers, not family or close friends. Altruism would seem to be unnatural, against all instincts for survival, the exception rather than the rule. [26]

Rescuers of Jews in all countries exhibited unusual altruism. In Italy, only altruism can explain Pio Troiani and Torquato Fraccon, who allowed their sons to become involved in rescue work, with the result that the sons were executed with the fathers. Only altruism explains Sisto and Alberta Gianaroli, who risked the lives of their seven children, the youngest two months old, by sheltering Jews. [27] Political, religious, and cultural factors facilitated their decisions, but only altruism can explain why they acted when others did not. In all cases, it would have been so much easier to do nothing.

Does the high number of rescuers in Italy imply that Italians generally are more compassionate and altruistic than other people? Certainly the answer is negative. On the contrary, despite their international reputation as a warm and immensely humane people, Italians are not known for the civic virtues or dedication to charity sometimes associated with altruism. The point is that altruism was an essential factor, but still one of many, in Jewish rescue work.

Without denigrating the exceptional courage and compassion involved, it should be stated that it was slightly easier to help Jews in Italy than, for example, in Poland. Italian rescuers did not face the prospect of immediate execution for themselves and their entire families with quite the same certainty as Polish rescuers. [28] Nor did Italian rescuers have to risk the disapproval of an entire anti-Semitic society, often even including their priests. [29] On the other hand, Italian rescuers lacked the certainty of Polish rescuers that the Jews they sheltered would otherwise be murdered. With only rumors of the death camps and no direct experience of the execution of entire Jewish families at the instant of discovery, they made supreme sacrifices to save victims from "labor camps," not gas chambers. As one historian has written of another case, "The danger involved in this activity [helping Jews] seemed greater than what was expected to happen." [30] Nor did Italians share the certainty of Polish rescuers that the Jews had nowhere else to go. In Italy, it was easier to justify a refusal to help with the thought that they would find someone else.

The focus on Jewish survivors and courageous rescuers distracts attention from one equally critical phenomenon. If the war was so unpopular and the society so free from anti-Semitism and so skeptical of rhetoric, how can we explain the thousands of Italian men who volunteered for groups like the Muti Legion or the Carità and Koch bands? These men raided churches and convents even against German instructions, and tortured and murdered their countrymen without mercy. They arrested Jews on their own initiative, long before Mussolini called for Jewish internment. How do we explain the 10,000 volunteers for the Decima Mas, the 72,000 soldiers still in the GNR in April 1945, the 22,000 in the Brigate Nere, or the 20,000 in the Italian SS?[31] These men butchered partisans and village hostages indiscriminately. They spared only the Jews whom, after torture and interrogation, they turned over to the Nazis.

How do we explain the effusively anti-Semitic Italian press (there was no other in occupied Italy), the informers, the prison guards whose cruelty to political prisoners was exceeded only by their cruelty to Jews? Or the politicians who decreed that Jews should be interned, even while they knew internment would insure deportation? Or the police, *carabinieri*, and militiamen who carried out the decree, obeying orders in a most "un-Italian" fashion? Or the guards who worked at the camps and escorted the trains?

It is easy to say that these people were a minority. They were that, but they were not few in number. It is easy, too, to say that they were murderers, thieves, ex-convicts. Many, particularly among the semi-autonomous bands, the Italian SS, and the Brigate Nere, were exactly that. But most were not such dregs of society, but rational men and women who had made conscious choices. Among these were the careerists and opportunists—"moderate" politicians, bureaucrats, and members of the press, carrying out orders without reflection, never initiating persecution but indifferent to its existence. Among them also were the informers who worked for a reward and would do so anywhere. These people would serve any regime and expect to survive it. They usually did.

In a final category were the believers—those not skeptical of propaganda like most of their compatriots. Among these were the little people, like the authors of anonymous letters denouncing Jews for no reward. Among them also were the Fascist collaborators, men so compromised by past actions that there was no going back. They had believed the Duce's rhetoric about Italian glory at the expense of other nations, authoritarian order at the expense of all dissenters, anti-communism at the expense of left-wing democrats. They had followed him, only to find themselves serving a lost cause and despised by their countrymen. With each disillusionment, they became more embittered, desperate, and violent.

These were the men who, when one of them was murdered by a partisan in Alessandria, near Turin, gratuitously sacked and destroyed the synagogue—as if the Jews had caused their troubles. These were the men who, while fleeing the country just before liberation, pulled six Jews from the local jail in Cuneo and executed them.[32] They left behind a legacy of death, destruction, and prejudice. The legacy of those who rescued Jews cannot quite obliterate it.

The Jews in Italy before the Holocaust strongly resembled most American, Canadian, and Western European Jews today. Mildly observant and respectful of their heritage, they were nevertheless fully integrated, represented in all political parties and factions, and thoroughly steeped in the customs and culture of their day. Proportionately few in number, they were concentrated in the largest urban centers and almost unknown in rural areas. They lived, finally, in a society with little prejudice and no formal barriers to their achievement.

And yet the Holocaust occurred in Italy. Its roots lay in the racial laws imposed upon a reluctant populace by their Fascist dictator. It peaked only during the German occupation—a time that brought the worst elements of the society to the

surface and intimidated all others. It was opposed by courageous individuals who saved thousands. But still the Holocaust
occurred, endorsed by the government and the press, enforced
by thousands of Italian fanatics, and sustained by a terrorized,
preoccupied, or just indifferent majority. The Holocaust in
Italy was a twisted legacy—a blend of courage and cowardice,
nobility and degradation, self-sacrifice and opportunism. In
contrast to other countries, perhaps, the worthy behavior out-
weighed the unworthy, but the horror was nonetheless real.

Could such a horror happen again? Our tendency is to say,
most assuredly, no. Yet Italians before 1938 would have said
no, with even more assurance. We should perhaps reflect carefully on their experience, for like them, we take pride in our
tolerance of minorities. Prejudice is decidedly unfashionable.
Many of our minorities may be less assimilated, more alien, and
far poorer than Italian Jews before 1938, but we believe that
they enjoy every opportunity. We have our anti-Semites and
our racists, but we tend to regard them as a lunatic fringe.

We might ponder the history of the Holocaust in Italy, and
ask again how it began. Did it begin with the Nazi occupation
of Italy in 1943, or the racial laws in 1938? Or did it begin with
the dictatorship itself, with the denial of equality before the
law to the first dissenter? Did the Holocaust begin when the
first black-shirted thug truncheoned his victim or administered
the castor oil?

We might also examine again how most Italians behaved
from the onset of fascism. Did Italians act with compassion
and humanity to the persecuted of every political and religious
persuasion? Did they do as much as they could? Or should
they, and the Jews as well, have recognized the danger sooner,
with the first denial of liberty and free speech?

We might also ask ourselves whether we, as creatures without prejudice, would act as well as most Italians did under
similar pressures. Would we risk our lives for persecuted

minorities? Would we be more sensitive to the first assaults upon our liberties, when the only ones really hurt in the beginning are Communists, Socialists, democratic anti-Fascists, and trade unionists? And finally, we might be more aware than we are of the horrors that a racist lunatic fringe can commit, even in the best of societies.

NOTES

Numbers in brackets refer to the original complete citation of a particular reference within each chapter.

CDEC is an abbreviation of the Centro di Documentazione Ebraica Contemporanea, which is located in Milan.

The abbreviations "f." and "s.f." refer to the folders and subdivisions of folders (*fascicoli* and *sottofascicoli* in Italian) in which documents are filed at the CDEC.

Dedication

The account of Emilia Levi and her parents is from Primo Levi, *If This Is a Man*, trans. Stuart Woolf (London: Bodley Head, 1960), 12. In a new edition (New York: Summit Books, 1986), the title has been changed to *Survival in Auschwitz*.

Prologue

1. For more on Sara and Ernesto Nathan, see chapter 12.

2. This story was told to the author by Giorgina Nathan Burdett, the daughter of Giuseppe, on June 4, 1985, in Rome.

3. See chapter 9.

4. Jewish deportees from the Italian peninsula, clearly named and verified, included 4,439 Italian citizens, 1,915 foreigners, 210 people of unknown origin, and 237 recently ascertained deportees from Trieste whose origins have not been stated. In addition, the 1,805 Jews deported from the Italian colonies of Rhodes and Cos were also Italian citizens (since the Treaty of Lausanne in 1924). For the statistics of Italian, foreign, and unknown-origin Jews, see CDEC, Milan, *Ebrei in Italia: Deportazione, resistenza* (Florence: Tipografia Giuntina, 1975), 9. For the newly ascertained deportees from Trieste, see Liliana Picciotto Fargion, "La deportazione degli ebrei dall'Italia: Indagine statistica," unpublished but intended for publication by the Institut für Zeitgeschichte in Munich, in a statistical study, country by country, of victims of the Holocaust. I am extremely grateful to Picciotto Fargion, director of research at the

CDEC, for making the results of her most recent research available to me. On Rhodes and Cos, see also Hizkia M. Franco, *Les Martyrs juifs de Rhodes et de Cos* (Elisabeth-ville, Katanga: Imprimeries et Papeteries Belgo-Congolaises 'Imbelco,' 1952). Franco's deportation figures (1,673 from Rhodes and 94 from Cos) are slightly lower than those of the CDEC. I have chosen those of the CDEC because they are more recent. For details on the deportations from Italy, see chapters 8 and 9.

5. Percentage figures are elusive, primarily because of uncertainty about the exact number of Jews actually in Italy at the time of the occupation. The most recent estimate is from Picciotto Fargion [4]. The number 45,200 breaks down into 37,100 Italian Jews, 7,000 foreigners, and about 1,100 refugees from southern France who entered Italy after the armistice (see chapter 5).

1 / The Holocaust Comes to Italy

1. Liliana Picciotto Fargion, "La deportazione degli ebrei dell'Italia: Indagine statistica," unpublished but intended for publication by the Institut für Zeitgeschichte in Munich, in a statistical study, country by country, of victims of the Holocaust. For more on the foreign Jews in Italy, see Klaus Voigt, "Notizie statistiche sugli immigrati e profughi ebrei in Italia (1938–1945)," *Israel: "Un decennio" 1974–1984: Saggi sull'ebraismo italiano* (Rome: Carucci, 1984), 407–20.

2. These figures do not include Jews in the Italian colonies. Over 24,000 Jews lived in Libya, 4,372 in the Dodecanese Islands, 193 in Eritrea, 11 in Somalia, and an estimated 40,000 in Ethiopia. Census figures are cited at length in Renzo De Felice, *Storia degli ebrei italiani sotto il fascismo* (1961; Turin: Giulio Einaudi, 1972), 5–14.

3. For further details and documentation on the racial laws and forced labor, see chapters 3 and 4.

4. De Felice [2], 361, cites an emigration figure of 5,966 by October 1941, from a government study on file at the Central Archives in Rome; after that date, very few more could leave. The estimate of converts is from Salvatore Jona, "Contributo allo studio degli ebrei in Italia durante il fascismo," *Gli ebrei in Italia durante il fascismo: Quaderni del Centro di Documentazione Ebraica Contemporanea*, II, March 1962, 20. As will be seen in discussion of the racial laws in chapter 3, the government did not recognize all post–1938 converts as automatic non-Jews.

5. Roberto Battaglia, *Storia della Resistenza italiana (8 settembre 1943–25 aprile 1945)* (Turin: Giulio Einaudi, 1953), 89.

6. Charles F. Delzell, *Mussolini's Enemies: The Italian Anti-Fascist Resistance* (Princeton: Princeton University Press, 1961), 278.

7. Ibid., 277.

8. Michael R. Marrus and Robert O. Paxton, *Vichy France and the Jews* (New York: Basic Books, 1981), 260. On internment camps in the unoccupied zone, see pp. 165–76; on Laval's agreement to German demands for foreign Jews from the unoc-cupied zone, see pp. 228–34.

9. Claude Levy and Paul Tillard, *La Grande Rafle du Vel d'Hiv (16 juillet 1942)* (Paris: R. Laffont, 1967).

10. Marrus and Paxton [8], 261 and 263.

11. CDEC, Milan, *Ebrei in Italia: Deportazione, resistenza* (Florence: Tipografia Giuntina, 1975), page insert, "Deportazione degli ebrei dall'Italia."

12. For details on the Jewish refugees from France in Italy, see chapter 5.

13. Giuseppe Mayda, *Ebrei sotto Salò: La persecuzione antisemita 1943–1945* (Milan: Giangiacomo Feltrinelli, 1978), 79–90; *Ebrei in Italia* [11], 31.

Notes

14. CDEC, Milan, f. Fatti di Meina. See also Mayda [13], 83–86. Most of the bodies in fact rose to the surface the next morning, and were taken to the center of the lake and thrown in again. After this, only one was ever recovered for a proper burial. See *Ebrei in Italia* [11], 31.

15. Mayda [13], 89.

2 / Italy's Jews

1. Cecil Roth, *The History of the Jews of Italy* (Philadelphia: Jewish Publication Society of America, 1946), 23. The best general history of Jews in Italy from ancient times to the present is Attilio Milano, *Storia degli ebrei in Italia* (Turin: Giulio Einaudi, 1963).

2. See descriptions in Milano [1], 459–646; Roth [1], 329–94; and Attilio Milano, *Il ghetto di Roma: Illustrazioni storiche* (Rome: Staderini, 1964).

3. The boy, Edgardo Mortara, eventually took Holy Orders and became a distinguished Catholic missionary. See Roth [1], 471–72.

4. Ibid., 462.

5. Ibid., 476.

6. Ibid., 480.

7. For details, see H. Stuart Hughes, *Prisoners of Hope: The Silver Age of the Italian Jews, 1924–1974* (Cambridge, Mass.: Harvard University Press, 20–21).

8. Roth [1], 479. It is interesting to note that in the United States, despite a considerably larger Jewish population, there were only sixteen Jewish senators between 1789 and 1980. Of these, only six served before World War II. Also, only ten Jews were cabinet members between 1789 and 1980. Of the ten, only two (Oscar S. Straus, in 1908, and Henry Morgenthau, Jr., from 1933 to 1945) served before the war.

9. Gina Formiggini, *Stella d'Italia Stella di David: Gli ebrei dal Risorgimento alla Resistenza* (Milan: U. Mursia, 1970), 45; and (no author cited) *Gli israeliti italiani nella guerra 1915–1918* (Turin: F. Servi, 1921).

10. Roth [1], 480. Yale College, it might be noted, had no full professor who was Jewish until 1946. See Dan A. Oren, *Joining the Club: A History of Jews and Yale* (New Haven, Conn.: Yale University Press, 1985), 261.

11. Enzo Levi, *Memorie di una vita (1889–1947)* (Modena: S.T.E.M. Mucchi, 1972).

12. Emanuele Artom, *Diari: gennaio 1940–febbraio 1944* (Milan: Centro di Documentazione Ebraica Contemporanea, 1966), 28–31.

13. Sion Segre Amar, "Sui 'fatti' di Torino del 1934 Sion Segre Amar ci ha scritto. . . . ," *Gli ebrei in Italia durante il fascismo: Quaderni del Centro di Documentazione Ebraica Contemporanea*, II, March 1962, 131.

14. Carlo Modigliani, *Una croce e una stella: Dal mio diario* (Milan: Gastaldi, 1959), 14.

15. Salvatore Jona, "Contributo allo studio degli ebrei in Italia durante il fascismo," *Gli ebrei in Italia durante il fascismo* [13], 8.

16. Interview with Ora Kohn, quoted in *Voices from the Holocaust*, ed. Sylvia Rothchild (New York: New American Library, 1982), 54–55.

17. Interview with Gastone Orefice, quoted in *Voices from the Holocaust* [16], 58.

18. Jona [15], 20.

19. Ora Kohn [16], 56.

20. CDEC, Milan, 5-H-b: *Vicissitudini dei singoli—particolare*, f. L, s.f. Relazione

Notes

di Renata Lombroso di Milano, personal testimony of Lombroso, Milan, August 30, 1973.

21. Augusto Segre, *Memorie di vita ebraica: Casale Monferrato-Roma-Gerusalemme 1918–1960* (Rome: Bonacci, 1979), 24.

22. Renzo De Felice, *Storia degli ebrei italiani sotto il fascismo* (1961; Turin: Giulio Einaudi, 1972), 73–75.

23. Segre [21], 64.

24. Gastone Orefice [17], 210.

25. De Felice [22], 75.

3 / The Racial Laws

1. Barbara Allason, *Memorie di un'antifascista* (Florence: Stabilimenti Grafici Vallecchi, n.d. but shortly after 1945), 157–58; Natalia Ginzburg, *Family Sayings*, revised trans. by D. M. Low (1967; Manchester: Carcanet Press, 1984), 83. Originally published as *Lessico famigliare* (Turin: Giulio Einaudi, 1963). Natalia Ginzburg, born Natalia Levi, was Mario Levi's sister.

2. Sion Segre Amar, "Sui 'fatti' di Torino del 1934 Sion Segre Amar ci ha scritto. . . . ," *Gli ebrei in Italia durante il fascismo: Quaderni del Centro di Documentazione Ebraica Contemporanea*, II, March 1962, 125. For more on Giustizia e Libertà, see chapter 12.

3. *Corriere della Sera*, March 31, 1934, anno XII, 1, for example, described the Ponte Tresa affair and listed the names of the seventeen held for trial, in an article entitled "Ebrei antifascisti al soldo dei fuorusciti," or "Anti-Fascist Jews in the Pay of Anti-Fascist Italians in Exile."

4. Segre Amar [2], 126. Zionism was never strong among Italian Jews before World War II. Only about 2,000 Italians officially supported Zionist congresses in the 1920s, and only about 150 emigrated to Israel between 1926 and 1938. See Umberto Nahon, "La polemica antisionista del 'Popolo di Roma' nel 1928," in Daniel Carpi, Attilio Milano, Umberto Nahon, eds., *Scritti in memoria di Enzo Sereni: Saggi sull'e-braismo romano* (Milan: Editrice Fondazione Sally Mayer, 1970), 248.

5. Cited in Renzo De Felice, *Storia degli ebrei italiani sotto il fascismo* (1961; Turin: Giulio Einaudi, 1972), 147–48.

6. Ibid., 138–39.

7. Nahon [4].

8. Emil Ludwig, *Talks with Mussolini*, trans. Eden and Cedar Paul (1932; Boston: Little, Brown, 1933), 70–71.

9. For more on Preziosi's ideas and role in the 1920s and 1930s, see Renzo De Felice, "Giovanni Preziosi e le origini del fascismo (1917–1931)," *Rivista storica del Socialismo*, fascicolo 17, September–December 1962, anno V, 493–555; Maria Teresa Pichetto, *Alle radici dell'odio: Preziosi e Benigni antisemiti* (Milan: Franco Angeli, 1983); De Felice [5], 45–54; and Giuseppe Mayda, *Ebrei sotto Salò: La persecuzione antisemita 1943–1945* (Milan: Giangiacomo Feltrinelli, 1978), 182. Interestingly enough, the young Preziosi (he was born in 1881) worked among Italian immigrants in the United States from 1905 to 1912, before he became a nationalist. He worked in Philadelphia, in Cleveland with the Italian-American journal *La Voce del popolo italiano*, and in Chicago in 1908 with Francesca Saverio Cabrini, the future saint.

10. Augusto Segre, *Memorie di vita ebraica: Casale Monferrato-Roma-Gerusalemme 1918–1960* (Rome: Bonacci, 1979), 59–65.

11. De Felice [5], 168–75.

12. For detailed analysis of the link between Mussolini's foreign policy priorities

Notes

and the anti-Semitic press, see especially Anselmo Calò, "Stampa e propaganda an-tisemita del regime fascista prima delle leggi razziali (1936–1938)," *Israel: "Un de-cennio" 1974–1984: Saggi sull'ebraismo italiano* (Rome: Carucci, 1984), 115–63. On anti-Semitic graffiti in Ferrara, see De Felice [5], 168–75.

13. See Meir Michaelis's thorough study of this question in his *Mussolini and the Jews: German-Italian Relations and the Jewish Question in Italy, 1922–1945* (Oxford: Clarendon Press, 1978), 107–91. Luigi Preti, *Impero fascista ed ebrei* (Milan: U. Mursia, 1968), 157 and De Felice [5], 191 agree that the Germans exercised no direct pressure.

14. On right-wing Catholic anti-Semitism, see Preti [13], 124, and De Felice [5], 314–17. Both authors make it clear, however, that the Catholic mainstream, including Pope Pius XI (who died in 1939 and was succeeded by Pope Pius XII), opposed racial, if not religious, anti-Semitism. See Preti, 124–25, and De Felice, 285–91.

15. For the text of laws regulating relations between Italian citizens and native Africans in the Italian colonies, including a penalty of from one to five years for sexual relations between whites and blacks, see "Esempi di legislazione razziale fascista," *Gli ebrei in Italia durante il fascismo* [2], II, 155–60.

16. To indicate the intensity of the anti-Jewish press campaign even in the most prestigious Italian newspapers, Preti [13], 121–22, lists twelve articles on the subject in *Corriere della Sera* in July and August 1938, and six in *La Stampa*.

17. For the text of the manifesto, see De Felice, [5], 541–42.

18. The ten "experts" are listed, with their professional positions, in Salvatore Jona, "Contributo allo studio degli ebrei in Italia durante il fascismo," *Gli ebrei in Italia durante il fascismo* [2] II, 7–31, 19.

19. For the text of the November 17 laws, see De Felice [5], 562–66.

20. Ibid., 569. If the reader is confused, pity the poor bureaucrats!

21. Ibid.

22. Memo Bemporad, *La Macine: Storia di una famiglia israelita negli ultimi 60 anni di vita italiana* (Rome: Carucci, 1984), 51–52. Enzo Levi, *Memorie di una vita (1889–1947)* (Modena: S.T.E.M. Mucchi, 1972), 90, also confirms that no one with a hint of anti-fascism could secure an exemption, regardless of his military record.

23. Eucardio Momigliano, *Storia tragica e grottesca del razzismo fascista* (Verona: Arnoldo Mondadori, 1946), 101–7, discusses the corruption involved in the securing of exemptions, or, as he calls it, "the sale of racial indulgences."

24. Bemporad [22], 54.

25. Momigliano [23], 102.

26. De Felice [5], 361.

27. Ibid., 339; Jona [18], 20. Apparently some applicants for Aryanization, includ-ing Finance Minister Guido Jung and Militia General Maurizio Rava, claimed eligibil-ity on the grounds that their mothers had had sexual relations with Aryans. See Guido Lodovico Luzzatto, "La partecipazione all'fascismo in Italia e all'estero dal 1918 al 1938," *Gli ebrei in Italia durante il fascismo* [2], II, 42.

28. Momigliano [23], 112–15.

29. In fact, the Italian definition of a Jew did not differ greatly from the German definition. The chief difference was that while in Italy a baptized half-Jew was declared a full Aryan, in Germany a half-Jew not adhering to the Jewish religion (the baptism rule did not apply) and not married to a Jew was declared a non-Aryan *Mischling* of the first degree. A *Mischling* was subjected to some restrictions, but not deported. Also, an individual with only one Jewish grandparent was, in Germany, a *Mischling* of the second degree, and restricted but not deported. In Italy, that same individual was clearly Aryan. For detailed explanation of the German definition of a Jew, see Raul Hilberg, *The Destruction of the European Jews* (1961; New York: New Viewpoints,

1973), 43–53 and 268–77. A revised and definitive edition of Hillberg's book was published, under the same title, by Holmes & Meier in New York in 1985.

30. De Felice [5], 361. By 1940, the number of foreign Jews who had been granted the right to remain in Italy had increased to 2,950. See Klaus Voigt, "Notizie statistiche sugli immigrati e profughi ebrei in Italia (1938–1945)," *Israel* [12], 407–20.

31. De Felice [5], 362. After the racial laws decreed that foreign Jews must leave Italy, Jewish refugees obviously could not obtain the Italian residence and work permits that had been so readily available previously. From late 1938 to August 1939, most refugees entered Italy with simple tourist visas. When these, too, were denied them, they entered with transit visas, issued even though their means of leaving the country were not guaranteed. See Voigt [30], 407–20.

32. De Felice [5], 328.

33. Ibid., 361; Jona [18], 20. Among the many talented Italian Jewish emigrants was the young Franco Modigliani, who received a doctorate in law at the University of Rome in 1939. He later became an American citizen and a professor at MIT. In 1985 he won the Nobel Prize in Economic Science.

34. Gina Formiggini, *Stella d'Italia Stella di David: Gli ebrei dal Risorgimento alla Resistenza* (Milan: U. Mursia, 1970), 193–98.

35. Fabio Della Seta, *L'incendio del Tevere* (Trapani: Editore Celebes, 1969), 16. Sylvia Lombroso, *No Time for Silence*, trans. Adrienne W. Foulke (New York: Roy, 1946), 26–27 and 93, also mentions three suicides.

36. Formiggini [34], 59–60.

37. H. Stuart Hughes, *Prisoners of Hope: The Silver Age of the Italian Jews, 1924–1974* (Cambridge, Mass.: Harvard University Press, 1983), 119. For more on Bassani, see 114–49.

38. Carlo Modigliani, *Una croce e una stella: Dal mio diario* (Milan: Gastaldi, 1959), 40–42.

39. Enzo Levi [22], 108. On his children's education, 86–87.

40. Della Seta [35], 15.

41. See also Giancarlo Sacerdoti's description of his teachers at the Bologna Jewish School in *Ricordi di un ebreo bolognese: Illusioni e delusioni 1929–1945* (Rome: Bonacci, 1983), 76–85.

42. Della Seta [35], 40–41. See also a personal account by Giorgio J. Piperno, "Fermenti di vita giovanile ebraica a Roma durante il periodo delle leggi razziali e dopo la liberazione della città," 293–313, in *Scritti in memoria di Enzo Sereni* [4].

43. Giorgio Bassani, *The Garden of the Finzi-Continis*, trans. Isabel Quigly (London: Faber and Faber, 1965). Originally published as *Il giardino dei Finzi-Contini* (Turin: Giulio Einaudi, 1962).

44. Modigliani [38], 83–85.

45. Interview with Gastone Orefice, quoted in *Voices from the Holocaust*, ed. Sylvia Rothchild, (New York: New American Library, 1982), 210–11.

46. Enzo Levi [22], 99.

47. Emanuele Artom, *Diari: gennaio 1940–febbraio 1944* (Milan: Centro di Documentazione Ebraica Contemporanea, 1966), introd. by Eloisa Ravenna and Paola De Benedetti, 8.

48. From an interview with this author, New York, May 1983.

49. Momigliano [23], 92–93.

50. Erbsen interview [48].

51. Enzo Levi [22], 76–77.

52. Modigliani [38], 64.

53. U. Alfassio Grimaldi and G. Bozzetti, *Farinacci il più fascista* (Milan: Bompiani, 1972), 240. For appraisals of Farinacci's anti-Semitism, see Harry Fornari,

Notes

Mussolini's Gadfly: Roberto Farinacci (Nashville: Vanderbilt University Press, 1971), 177–89, and Michaelis [13], 418–19.

54. Sacerdoti [41], 66.
55. Bemporad [22], 52–53.
56. De Felice [5], 278.
57. Momigliano [23], 135.
58. Bemporad [22], 54–55.
59. Gemma Volli, "Trieste 1938–1945," *Gli ebrei in Italia durante il fascismo* [2], III, November 1963, 38–50.
60. De Felice [5], 285–91.
61. Ibid., 283–85.
62. Segre [10], 130–31.

4 / The War Years: June 1940–September 1943

1. Renzo De Felice, *Storia degli ebrei italiani sotto il fascismo* (1961; Turin: Giulio Einaudi, 1972), 364.
2. Israele Kalk, "I campi di concentramento italiani per ebrei profughi: Ferramonti Tarsia (Calabria)," *Gli ebrei in Italia durante il fascismo: Quaderni della Federazione Giovanile Ebraica d'Italia*, Turin, April 25, 1961, 63–71. Israele Kalk had immigrated to Italy and become a citizen before 1919. His status was therefore not subject to revocation under the racial laws. He visited Ferramonti several times, in an effort to organize aid to inmates there.
3. CDEC, Milan, 5-H-b: *Vicissitudini dei singoli—particolare*, f. P, s.f. Rabbino Pacifici Riccardo, declaration of Mrs. Orvieto about her brother Rabbi Pacifici, Rome, September 1960, 2. Rabbi Pacifici of Genoa, later deported and gassed at Auschwitz, visited Ferramonti twice in 1942 and once in July 1943, to bring aid and religious comfort to prisoners there. For more on Pacifici, see chapter 7.
4. Ibid., 3. For a somewhat less favorable description, see Francesco Folino, *Ferramonti: Un lager di Mussolini: Gli internati durante la guerra* (Cosenza: Edizioni Brenner, 1985). Folino stresses the continued low quality and scarcity of food, the poor medical care, and the occasionally corrupt prison officials. His text includes long quotations from prisoners' correspondence and official documents.
5. De Felice [1], 364.
6. Carlo Levi, *Christ Stopped at Eboli*, trans. Frances Frenaye (New York: Farrar, Straus, 1947). Originally published as *Cristo si è fermato a Eboli* (Turin: Giulio Einaudi, 1945). For more on Carlo Levi, see chapter 12.
7. "Eyewitness Testimony 34. Survival in Italy," *Jewish Responses to Nazi Persecution: Collective and Individual Behavior in Extremes*, ed. Isaiah Trunk (New York: Stein and Day, 1979), 211–16.
8. Natalia Ginzburg, *Family Sayings*, revised trans. by D. M. Low (1967; Manchester: Carcanet Press, 1984), 135–38. Originally published as *Lessico famigliare* (Turin: Giulio Einaudi, 1963).
9. For more on Natalia and Leone Ginzburg, see N. Ginzburg [8], 79, 106–7, and 132–44; Barbara Allason, *Memorie di un'antifascista* (Florence: Stabilimenti Grafici Vallecchi, n.d. but shortly after 1945), 133–37; H. Stuart Hughes, *Prisoners of Hope: The Silver Age of the Italian Jews, 1924–1974* (Cambridge, Mass.: Harvard University Press, 1983), 95–113; and Gina Formiggini, *Stella d'Italia Stella di David: Gli ebrei dal Risorgimento alla Resistenza* (Milan: U. Mursia, 1970), 349–55.
10. See chapter 3. Klaus Voigt estimates that by April 1943, 6,000 of the 7,000 foreign Jews in Italy were in internment camps or enforced residence, and only about

1,000 were still undetained. See his chapter, "Notizie statistiche sugli immigrati e profughi ebrei in Italia (1938–1945)," in *Israel: "Un decennio" 1974–1984: Saggi sull'ebraismo italiano* (Rome: Carucci, 1984), 407–20.

11. Augusto Segre, *Memorie di vita ebraica: Casale Monferrato-Roma-Gerusalemme 1918–1960* (Rome: Bonacci, 1979), 280.

12. Primo Levi, *The Reawakening: A Liberated Prisoner's Long March Home Through East Europe*, trans. Stuart Woolf (Boston: Little, Brown, 1965), 30–31. A new edition was published by Summit Books of New York in 1986. Originally published as *La Tregua* (Turin: Giulio Einaudi, 1963).

13. Zeitschel to the Commandant of Security Police and the S.D. in France, May 24, 1943, in Leon Poliakov and Jacques Sabille, *Jews under the Italian Occupation* (Paris: Centre de Documentation Juive Contemporaine, 1954), doc. 19, 89–90; photographic reproduction of German original, 191–92.

14. See chapter 5.

15. Michael R. Marrus and Robert O. Paxton, *Vichy France and the Jews* (New York: Basic Books, 1981), 228–34 and 260.

16. De Felice [1], 363.

17. Ibid.

18. On Jews and anti-Semitism in Trieste, see Silva Bon Gherardi, *La persecuzione antiebraica a Trieste (1938–1945)* (Udine: Del Bianco, 1972); Gemma Volli, "Trieste 1938–1945," *Gli ebrei in Italia durante il fascismo: Quaderni del Centro di Documentazione Ebraica Contemporanea*, III, November 1963, 38–50; and Hughes [9], 30–33.

19. De Felice [1], 391–92. See also CDEC, Milan, 5-h-b [3], f. R, s.f. Ravenna Gianni di Ferrara. Ravenna remembers that when Fascists sacked two synagogues, authorities did nothing and newspapers simply reported a lively Fascist demonstration in the old ghetto.

20. Emanuele Artom, *Diari: gennaio 1940–febbraio 1944* (Milan: Centro di Documentazione Ebraica Contemporanea, 1966), 31–34.

21. Ibid., 33–34.

22. Segre [11], 268.

23. De Felice [1], 389–92.

24. Segre [11], 268–69.

25. CDEC, Milan, 5-H-b [3], f. P, s.f. Umberto Pugliese.

26. Segre [11], 197–99.

27. Artom [20], 44–47.

28. Ibid., 47.

29. CDEC, Milan, 5-H-b [3], f. M, s.f. Morpurgo Marcello di Gorizia.

30. Ibid., f. R, s.f. Ravenna Gianni di Ferrara.

31. De Felice [1], 366.

32. Segre [11], 258.

33. Carlo Modigliani, *Una croce e una stella: Dal mio diario* (Milan: Gastaldi, 1959), 46–48.

34. Segre [11], 361–65.

35. Ibid., 230–49.

36. De Felice [1], 413–19. The best general studies of Italian Jewish assistance agencies are Massimo Leone, *Le organizzazioni di soccorso ebraiche in età fascista* (Rome: Carucci, 1983) and Settimio Sorani, *L'assistenza ai profughi ebrei in Italia (1933–1947): Contributo alla storia della "Delasem"* (Rome: Carucci, 1983). Sorani was a director of the Rome office of Delasem from 1939 to the end of the war.

37. For accounts of two Delasem volunteers, see Segre [11], 249–56, and Pacifici [3].

Notes

38. On Mario Finzi, see Formiggini [9], 346–49; Giancarlo Sacerdoti, *Ricordi di un ebreo bolognese: Illusioni e delusioni 1929–1945* (Rome: Bonacci, 1983), 83–84 and 167; Gemma Volli, "Gli ebrei nella lotta antifascista," *Emilia*, anno VII, n. 8–9, August–September 1955, 226–30; and (no author cited but preface by Fabio Fano) *Mario Finzi: Lettere a un amico, brani musicali, ricordi e testimonianze* (Bologna: Edizioni Alfa, 1967), a general tribute, including long extracts from his letters and musical compositions.

39. Ilva Vaccari, *Villa Emma: Un episodio agli albori della Resistenza modenese nel quadro delle persecuzioni razziali* (Modena: Istituto Storico della Resistenza, 1960).

40. For more on the priests who helped the orphans at Villa Emma, and on penalties for rescuers generally, see chapter 10. Italian Fascists in fact arrested two priests from the seminary at Nonantola, but, lacking evidence, did not deport them.

41. Fabio Della Seta, *L'incendio del Tevere* (Trapani: Editore Celebes, 1969), 164.

42. Luciano Morpurgo, *Caccia all'uomo!* (Rome: Casa Editrice Dalmatia S.A., 1946), 85.

43. Ibid., 87.

44. De Felice [1], 428–30.

45. Giuseppe Mayda, *Ebrei sotto Salò: La persecuzione antisemita 1943–1945* (Milan: Giangiacomo Feltrinelli, 1978), 55.

46. Hizkia M. Franco, *Les Martyrs juifs de Rhodes et de Cos* (Elisabethville, Katanga: Imprimeries et Papeteries Belgo-Congolaises 'Imbelco,' 1952), 108, estimates that 1,673 of the 1,727 Jews living on Rhodes in July 1944, were deported, and 94 of the 100 on Cos. Liliana Picciotto Fargion, "La deportazione degli ebrei dall'Italia: Indagine statistica," (unpublished but intended for publication by the Institut für Zeitgeschichte in Munich), in a statistical study, country by country, of victims of the Holocaust, believes the total number of deportees to have been slightly higher at 1,805. In Corfu, occupied by Italy during World War II, approximately 1,795 of the 2,000 Jews present were deported. For Corfu, see Raul Hilberg, *The Destruction of the European Jews* (1961; New York: New Viewpoints, 1973), 451–53. A revised and definitive edition of Hilberg's book was published, under the same title, by Holmes & Meier in New York in 1985.

47. For more on Badoglio's policy toward Jews in the occupied territories, see chapter 5.

48. Artom [20], 62–63.

49. Ibid., 70–71.

50. Roberto Battaglia, *Storia della Resistenza italiana (8 settembre 1943–25 aprile 1945)* (Turin: Giulio Einaudi, 1953), 89.

5 / Italians and Jews in the Occupied Territories

1. Primo Levi, *The Reawakening: A Liberated Prisoner's Long March Home Through East Europe,* trans. Stuart Woolf (Boston: Little, Brown, 1965), 30–31. A new edition was published by Summit Books of New York in 1986. Originally published as *La Tregua* (Turin: Giulio Einaudi, 1963).

2. Daniel Carpi, "The Rescue of Jews in the Italian Zone of Occupied Croatia," *Rescue Attempts during the Holocaust: Proceedings of the Second Yad Vashem International Historical Conference, Jerusalem, April 8–11, 1974,* ed. Yisrael Gutman and Efraim Zuroff (Jerusalem: "Ahva" Cooperative Press, 1977), 465–525; and Jacques Sabille, "Attitude of the Italians to the Persecuted Jews in Croatia" in Leon Poliakov

and Jacques Sabille, *Jews under the Italian Occupation* (Paris: Centre de Documentation Juive Contemporaine, 1954), 131–50.

3. CDEC, Milan, 5-H-b: *Vicissitudini dei singoli—particolare,* f. H, s.f. Julia Hirschl, letter from Hirschl, November 3, 1980.

4. Carpi [2], 488.

5. Ibid., 496.

6. Ibid., 502–3.

7. Hirschl [3]. Mrs. Hirschl estimates the number of Jews caught on Arbe at 400, rather than the 204 cited earlier.

8. Levi [1], 43.

9. Jacques Sabille, "Attitude of the Italians to the Jews in Occupied Greece" in Poliakov and Sabille [2], 153–60; and Raul Hilberg, *The Destruction of the European Jews* (1961; New York: New Viewpoints, 1973), 442.

10. Sabille [9], 157.

11. Ibid.

12. Hilberg [9], 451–53; and Nora Levin, *The Holocaust: The Destruction of European Jewry 1933–1945* (1968; New York: Schocken Books, 1973), 523.

13. Jean-Louis Panicacci, "Les Juifs et la question juive dans les Alpes-Maritimes de 1939 à 1945," *Recherches régionales Côte d'Azur et contrées limitrophes: Bulletin trimestriel,* ed Archives départementales des Alpes-Maritimes, n.d. but after 1983, 239–330; and Michael R. Marrus and Robert O. Paxton, *Vichy France and the Jews* (New York: Basic Books, 1981), 165–76, 228–34, and 260–65.

14. Italian Foreign Ministry order, telegram 34/R 12825, December 29, 1942, cited in English translation in Leon Poliakov, "The Jews under the Italian Occupation in France," in Poliakov and Sabille [2], 23. A photographic reproduction of the Italian original is printed on p. 183.

15. Ibid., 25.

16. "Present State of the Jewish Question in France," report by SS Obersturmführer Röthke, Paris, July 21, 1943, printed in English translation in Poliakov and Sabille [14], doc. 25, 104–6.

17. Testimony of Alfred Feldman, September 6, 1976, in Alberto Cavaglion, *Nella notte straniera: Gli ebrei di S. Martin Vésubie e il campo di Borgo S. Dalmazzo, 8 settembre–21 novembre 1943* (Cuneo: Edizioni L'Arciere, 1981), 44.

18. Memoirs of Bronka Halpern, quoted in Cavaglion [17], 43.

19. Poliakov [14], doc. 8, 68–70.

20. Ibid., doc. 9, 73.

21. Ibid., doc. 10, 74.

22. Ibid., doc. 12, 76.

23. Ibid., doc. 13, 77–78; photographic reproduction of German original, 189–90.

24. Ibid., doc. 18, 84–85.

25. Ibid., doc. 22, 97–98.

26. Ibid., report of SS Sturmbannführer Mühler, Security Police, Marseille, July 10, 1943, doc. 24, 101–3; photographic reproduction of German original, 195–96.

27. Renzo De Felice, *Storia degli ebrei italiani sotto il fascismo* (1961; Turin: Giulio Einaudi, 1972), 432. See also "General Considerations on the Jewish Question in Southern France," doc. 21, Poliakov [14], 93–96; and report of Mario Brocchi, official of Servizio Informazioni Esercito (Army Information Service) stationed in Nice during the Italian occupation, written in January 1945, after the occupation but before the end of the war, quoted in full in Renzo De Felice, "Un nuovo documento sulla condizione degli ebrei nella zona d'occupazione italiana in Francia durante la seconda guerra mondiale," *Israel: "Un decennio" 1974–1984: Saggi sull'ebraismo italiano* (Rome: Carucci, 1984), 179–84.

Notes

28. Poliakov [14], 39–42; De Felice, *Storia degli ebrei* [27], 432–33; Cavaglion [17], 27–32. Donati was introduced to the Vatican by an exceptional French Capuchin monk named Father Marie Benoît, who had already worked with him and with Lospinoso in France to help Jews. Father Benoît moved permanently to Rome after the Germans occupied the Italian zone of southern France. There under the name of Father Maria Benedetto, he continued his Jewish rescue operations on a much larger scale. For more on Father Benedetto, see chapters 6 and 10.

29. Poliakov [14], 40–44; Panicacci [13], 271–79; and Serge Klarsfeld, *Vichy-Auschwitz: Le Rôle de Vichy dans la solution finale de la question juive en France–1942*, II (Paris: Librarie Arthème Fayard, 1983), 117–26. According to Panicacci, Appendix XVIII, p. 329, 1,820 Jews, including 494 (27.1 percent) individuals born in France, were deported from the Côte d'Azur as a result of the autumn 1943 roundups. Klarsfeld agrees, but points out that since at least 25,000 Jews were hiding in the area between Cannes and Menton, including Nice, the number of deportees actually represents a failure from the Nazi perspective. He attributes the failure to the few SS men available for the operation and to the growing sympathy of French civilians for persecuted Jews. Serge Klarsfeld himself was an eight-year-old refugee living with his family in a hotel in Nice at the time of the roundups. His father hid the family but allowed himself to be arrested, to protect their hiding place. The elder Mr. Klarsfeld did not survive.

30. Cavaglion [17], 38–41.

31. Ibid., 59–69; Giuseppe Mayda, *Ebrei sotto Salò: La persecuzione antisemita 1943–1945* (Milan: Giangiacomo Feltrinelli, 1978), 71–73.

32. Memoirs of Bronka Halpern, quoted in Cavaglion [17], 71.

33. Feldman testimony in Cavaglion [17], 56.

34. The poster is reproduced in the photo section of this book.

35. Cavaglion [17], 80.

36. Testimony of Gerbino, a resident in Entraque, quoted in Mayda [31], 74.

37. Cavaglion [17], 98–103; CDEC, Milan, *Ebrei in Italia: Deportazione, resistenza* (Florence: Tipografia Giuntina, 1975), 14; and Liliana Picciotto Fargion, "La deportazione degli ebrei dall'Italia: Indagine statistica," (unpublished but intended for publication by the Institut für Zeitgeschichte in Munich), in a statistical study, country by country, of victims of the Holocaust.

38. Testimony collected and recorded by Mayda [31], 76.

39. Cavaglion [17], 108–9, 115. For more on Don Repetto, see chapter 10.

40. From an account by Father Benedetto, who first received the funds in Rome (see chapter 10), cited in Cavaglion [17], 121. See also Carlo Brizzolari, *Gli ebrei nella storia di Genova* (Genoa: Sabatelli, 1971), 303.

41. Testimony of Don Brondello quoted in Cavaglion [17], 125.

42. CDEC, Milan, 9/2: *Medaglia d'oro: Riconoscimento ai benemeriti*, f. Benemeriti (medaglia d'oro), s.f. Tiburzio Giuseppe.

43. Testimony of Luciano Elmo, May 17, 1974, quoted in Cavaglion [17], 125–26.

44. Letters quoted in Cavaglion [17], 128–29.

45. Cavaglion [17], 135; *Ebrei in Italia* [37], 33. See also chapter 9.

46. General Giuseppe Pièche, a commander of *carabinieri* in northern Croatia and Slovenia credited with massive efforts to persuade Italian authorities to protect Jews, informed the Foreign Ministry in Rome in November 1942 that deported Jews were being gassed in the boxcars. His message was passed on to Mussolini on November 4, 1942. See a copy of an Italian Foreign Ministry memorandum relaying Pièche's message to Mussolini, stamped "Seen by Duce," reproduced as doc. 9 in Carpi [2], 520. General Pièche was honored by the Italian Jewish Community in 1955 for his

rescue work. See CDEC, Milan, 9/2 [42], f. Benemeriti (medaglia d'oro), s.f. Pièche gen. Giuseppe.

47. Carpi [2], 473.

48. Italian Consul General M. Calisse, quoted by French Prefect Ribière, January 14, 1943, doc. 2, Poliakov [14], 55.

6 / Rome, 1943: The October Roundup

1. Michael Tagliacozzo, "La persecuzione degli ebrei a Roma," *L'occupazione tedesca e gli ebrei di Roma: Documenti e fatti,* ed. Liliana Picciotto Fargion (Rome: Carucci, 1979), 149–71, 158. Tagliacozzo was in Rome on October 16, 1943.

2. Ibid. See also report of Ugo Foà, president of the Jewish Community of Rome, November 15, 1943, printed in Luciano Morpurgo, *Caccia all'uomo!* (Rome: Casa Editrice Dalmatia S.A., 1946), 126; and Silvio Bertoldi, *I tedeschi in Italia* (Milan: Rizzoli, 1964), 128. Twenty-one years after the roundup, Bertoldi interviewed Settimio Calò, who told him, "I lived because I always hoped to have one back, just one, maybe Samuele, who was only four months old. . . . The day the war ended, I went as far as the Brenner, looking for them. Nothing. No one came back. . . . Only I remained alive, and I would like to be dead. I wake up at night, and I sleep little. I drink a glass of wine every night. . . . I drink to erase the nightmare." Calò's brother's wife and four children were also deported, and his wife's brother was killed in the Ardeatine Caves massacre.

3. Tagliacozzo in *L'occupazione tedesca* [1], 157–58.

4. Testimony quoted by Tagliacozzo in *L'occupazione tedesca* [1], 156–57.

5. Arminio Wachsberger, "Testimonianza di un deportato da Roma," *L'occupazione tedesca* [1], 176.

6. Testimony of Sbaffi, quoted by Michael Tagliacozzo, "La Comunità di Roma sotto l'incubo della svastica: La grande razzia del 16 ottobre 1943," *Gli ebrei in Italia durante il fascismo: Quaderni del Centro di Documentazione Ebraica Contemporanea,* III, November 1963, 8–37. This article covers the same material as the article by the same author in *L'occupazione tedesca* [1], but it is far more comprehensive.

7. Piero Modigliani, *I nazisti a Roma: Dal diario di un ebreo* (Rome: Città Nuova Editrice, 1984), 21–23.

8. Robert Katz, *Black Sabbath: A Journey Through a Crime Against Humanity* (Toronto: Macmillan, 1969), 190; Wachsberger report [5], 176–79. Wachsberger remembers that Admiral Capon produced a personal letter from Mussolini, thinking that it might help him.

9. Foà report [2], 126–27.

10. Ibid., 126.

11. Ibid., 127.

12. Official report to Berlin by SS Lieutenant Colonel Herbert Kappler, chief of German security police in Rome, October 17, 1943, quoted in *L'occupazione tedesca* [1], 19.

13. Wachsberger report [5], 175.

14. Pope Pius XII succeeded Pius XI in March 1939. On Pius XII's policy of avoiding any indication of partiality between belligerents and his behind-the-scenes efforts to urge all belligerents to refrain from brutality to civilians, without condemning any, see Carlo Falconi, *The Silence of Pius XII,* trans. Bernard Wall (Boston: Little, Brown, 1970); Renzo De Felice, *Storia degli ebrei italiani sotto il fascismo* (1961; Turin: Giulio Einaudi, 1972), 463–64; Saul Friedländer, *Pius XII and the Third Reich: A Documentation,* trans. Charles Fullman (New York: Knopf, 1966); and Alberto

Notes

Giovannetti, *Il Vaticano e la guerra* (1939–1940) (Città del Vaticano: Libreria Editrice Vaticana, 1960) and *Roma città aperta* (Milan: Editrice Ancora, 1962).

15. Fabio Della Seta, *L'incendio del Tevere* (Trapani: Editore Celebes, 1969), 129. For other Vatican efforts to help Jewish scholars, see Meir Michaelis, *Mussolini and the Jews: German-Italian Relations and the Jewish Question in Italy, 1922–1945* (Oxford: Clarendon Press, 1978), 289.

16. On Almansi, see De Felice [14], 76, 413–15, and 455–57; and Robert Katz [8], 39–41; on Foà, see Katz, 16–18.

17. Sorani to Katz [8], 31.

18. The most articulate apologist for Almansi is his son, Renato J. Almansi, in "Mio padre, Dante Almansi," *La Rassegna Mensile di Israel*, xlii, May–June 1976, 251–52. Part of the son's defense is printed in Michaelis [15], 360–61. Other defenders, including De Felice [14], 414–15, and Augusto Segre, *Memorie di vita ebraica: Casale Monferrato-Roma-Gerusalemme 1918–1960* (Rome: Bonacci, 1979), 235–36, stress Almansi's effective leadership of the Union of Italian Jewish Communities from 1939 to 1943 and his successful promotion of Delasem. A leading critic of Almansi and Foà is Chief Rabbi Israel Zolli, who claimed after the liberation of Rome that he had desperately tried to convince them in September 1943 to close the synagogue and the Jewish Community offices and advise Roman Jews to hide. According to Zolli, Almansi and Foà both told him they had private assurances from high places and ignored his warnings. They in turn later denied that Zolli had ever warned them. See Zolli's memoirs, published under the name Eugenio Zolli, *Before the Dawn: Autobiographical Reflections* (New York: Sheed and Ward, 1954), 138–63. See also Katz [8], 199–306, who revived the controversy in 1969 by unequivocally endorsing Zolli and condemning Foà and Almansi. For more on Zolli, see this chapter, footnote 34.

19. CDEC, Milan, 5-H-b: *Vicissitudini dei singoli—particolare*, f. A, s.f. Ascarelli Castelnuovo Silvana di Roma.

20. Morpurgo [2], 87–106.

21. Modigliani [7], 17–18.

22. Wachsberger report [5], 176.

23. Tagliacozzo in *L'occupazione tedesca* [1], 152.

24. Foà report [2], 114.

25. Ibid., 115. For descriptions of the gold incident, see Giacomo Debenedetti, *16 ottobre 1943* (Rome: O.E.T., 1945), 16–26; Tagliacozzo in *L'occupazione tedesca* [1], 153; Tagliacozzo in *Gli ebrei in Italia durante il fascismo* [6], 8–15; Katz [8], 62–102; and Giuseppe Mayda, *Ebrei sotto Salò: La persecuzione antisemita 1943–1945* (Milan: Giangiacomo Feltrinelli, 1978), 96–99.

26. Debenedetti [25], 20. This short firsthand account of the October round-up by a well-known Roman Jewish scholar and critic appeared shortly after the liberation of the city. It remains one of the best sources of information about the tragedy.

27. Kappler deposition, June 27, 1961, quoted in Tagliacozzo, *Gli ebrei in Italia durante il fascismo* [6], 12. In 1948, an Italian military tribunal sentenced Kappler to life imprisonment for his role in the Ardeatine Caves massacre, but agreed that he had concocted the gold extortion plan simply to lull the Roman Jews into a false sense of security in order to extract information from them. The court added fifteen years to his life sentence for planning the extortion scheme without authorization. See Katz [8], 309. On August 15, 1977, Kappler, still a prisoner, escaped from a Roman military hospital where he was being treated for stomach cancer. He died in his home in Soltau, West Germany on February 9, 1978, age seventy-six.

28. This is Tagliacozzo's opinion, stated in his article in *L'occupazione tedesca* [1], 153–54. For details on how Himmler's order for the deportation of Jews had become

known to German military and diplomatic personnel, see Tagliacozzo in *Gli ebrei in Italia durante il fascismo* [6], 10–15, and Katz [8], 53–58.

29. Katz [8], 102. The RSHA (the agency that fused the security police of the state and the Nazi party), one of twelve head offices of Heinrich Himmler's SS, had been charged with executing the Final Solution in July 1941. Within the RSHA, Adolf Eichmann's section IV-B-4 had the job. Section IV, the Gestapo, was one of seven RSHA divisions. Gestapo unit B (there were five others) was concerned with subversive elements affiliated with sects. Section IV (Gestapo)-B (sects)-4 was concerned with Jews. Eichmann's unit consisted of about twenty men. In individual countries, Eichmann operated through special Jewish "experts." In Italy, these were, first, Theodor Dannecker, who directed the Rome roundup, and, after February 1944, Friedrich Robert Bosshammer. Theoretically, Eichmann's representatives coordinated other SS personnel in matters concerning Jews. By far the most important of these were the SS security police who committed the atrocities in northern Italy in the autumn of 1943, conducted several major roundups, and served as German liaisons to local Italian prisons, police headquarters, and other government agencies. For details, see especially Liliana Picciotto Fargion, "Polizia tedesca ed ebrei nell'Italia occupata," *Rivista di Storia Contemporanea*, n. 3, 1984, 456–73.

30. Foà report [2], 115.

31. Katz [8], 87, from his interview with Renzo Levi. Zolli [18], 160–61, says that he too went to the Vatican and received a promise for a loan. He advised Foà, but Foà, he says, later denied it.

32. Foà report [2], 119.

33. See remarks of Giuseppe Dosi of the Italian police, quoted in Tagliacozzo, *Gli ebrei in Italia durante il fascismo* [6], 20.

34. See Zolli's account in *Before the Dawn* [18], 138–63. See also Katz [8], 19–24 and 43. Zolli and his family survived the Nazi occupation of Rome by hiding with Catholic families and, according to some, in the Vatican itself. After Rome's liberation, Jewish Community leaders charged him with abandoning his post and his people, and relieved him as chief rabbi. The Allies reinstated him, but bitter recriminations from both sides further divided the Community. In a sensational move in February 1945, Zolli effectively resolved the feud by converting to Catholicism, taking the name Eugenio after Pope Pius XII, formerly Cardinal Eugenio Pacelli. Zolli claimed to have had mystical visions of Jesus for a long time. Others attributed his conversion to his gratitude to Catholics who had sheltered him and other Jews and to his own weak and unstable character. For Zolli's version, see *Before the Dawn*. For condemnation of Zolli, see Louis I. Newman, *A "Chief Rabbi" of Rome Becomes a Catholic: A Study in Fright and Spite* (New York: Renascence Press, 1945).

35. Katz [8], 145.

36. These statistics were supplied by Father Benedetto in his report on Delasem activities, written on July 20, 1944; cited in full in De Felice [14], 615–16.

37. Father Benedetto, under the name Father Marie Benoît, has been seen in chapter 5, footnote 28. For more on his rescue activities, see chapter 10. Father Benedetto stresses in his report that Sorani, except for a fifteen-day period when he was under arrest, always remained at the head of the Delasem committee. See report in De Felice [14], 615–16.

38. *L'occupazione tedesca* [1], 39. The author adds on p. 11, however, that because of their unofficial status in Rome and their lack of family and friends, more refugees may have been deported but not recorded even among the total of 1,800 deportees from Rome.

39. Foà report [2], 122. For more on the looting of the libraries, see Debenedetti [25], 28–32.

Notes

40.   The number 365 is from the Kappler report [12]. Gestapo under Kappler's command were not directly involved in the roundup, for their chief had claimed that they would be occupied elsewhere that day. The roundup was instead directed by SS Captain Theodor Dannecker (see footnote 29). A rabid anti-Semite from Munich, Dannecker had directed anti-Jewish actions in France, including the Vélodrome d'Hiver roundup in Paris in July 1942. He brought to Italy forty-four officers and men from a Waffen SS Death's Head formation, part of an *Einsatzgruppe* experienced in massacring Jews in Russia. In Rome, he completed his force with three German SS police units. See Tagliacozzo, *Gli ebrei in Italia durante il fascismo* [6], 19. Despite West German government claims that Dannecker committed suicide in his prison cell in 1945, many authorities believe that he escaped and disappeared. See Raul Hilberg, *The Destruction of the European Jews* (1961; New York: New Viewpoints, 1973), 705.

41.   Wachsberger report [5], 176–78.

42.   Ibid., 177–78.

43.   Kappler report [12], 19. Kappler claimed that 1,259 people were arrested and 1,007 remained after non-Jews were released. That places the number freed at 252. In fact, however, more than 1,007 Jews were deported on October 18. CDEC, Milan, *Ebrei in Italia: Deportazione, resistenza* (Florence: Tipografia Giuntina, 1975), 13, places the number of deportees at about 1,035; *L'occupazione tedesca* [1], 42, claims at least 1,030. In all probability, the additional deportees were Jews arrested before or after the main roundup.

44.   *L'occupazione tedesca* [1], 113. The family names of many Italian Jews are place names, such as Ravenna, Pisa, Pavia, Milano, Romano, Terracina, D'Ancona, Modena, Pugliese, Voghera, Sinigaglia, and Fiorentino.

45.   Wachsberger report [5], 178. Wachsberger made a point of remembering her, saying "I want to record the courage of an Italian woman, nurse for a young epileptic Jewish boy. . . ."

46.   Ibid.

47.   Ibid., 177.

48.   Ibid., 177, and Katz [8], 219.

49.   Katz [8], 223–24. Debenedetti [25], 78, writes of two deliveries that night.

50.   Wachsberger report [5], 179; Katz [8], 209–10, 251–55, from interviews with survivors.

51.   Unless otherwise indicated, description of the terrible journey to Auschwitz and the events that occurred there is from Katz [8], 229–89, who gathered testimony from survivors.

52.   Wachsberger report [5], 179.

53.   Ibid.

54.   Katz [8], 250, from his own interview with Wachsberger. In his report [5], 179, Wachsberger does not mention the Fascist with the gun, but says simply "the Fascist guard insisted."

55.   Katz [8], 252–53. Wachsberger tells us that the Jews asked him to explain to the Nazi guards that they had been part of the convoy. "If only I had known that they were carrying us all to be butchered . . . ," he laments. See Wachsberger report [5], 179.

56.   Katz [8], 268, from his interview with Wachsberger.

57.   Wachsberger report [5], 179. Dr. Josef Mengele is most notorious for the "medical" experiments he performed on inmates at Auschwitz, including children. He disappeared after the war, allegedly with U.S. complicity. In June 1985, Brazilian police exhumed the remains of a man believed to have died in a drowning accident in São Paulo in 1979. The body was identified as Mengele, who had apparently lived in Brazil since about 1961.

58.   The numbers 450 (who passed the initial selection) and 250 (who then chose to join the others on the truck) are from Wachsberger's interview with Katz [8], 271. In Wachsberger's report [5], 179, he estimates that 300 passed the selection and 150 of these chose to ride. That estimate is not possible, however, for the Auschwitz log indicates that 149 men and 47 women were admitted to the camp. That entry is printed in *L'occupazione tedesca* [1], 163–64. Except for the statistical discrepancy, Wachsberger's two accounts of what happened on the platform at Auschwitz are the same.

59.   *L'occupazione tedesca* [1], 163–64.

60.   Wachsberger report [5], 186.

61.   Ibid., 179–80.

62.   Katz [8], 293; Tagliacozzo in *L'occupazione tedesca* [1], 164.

63.   Katz [8], 293–94.

64.   Ibid., 341. Like most Holocaust statistics, the number of survivors from the first Roman deportation train varies slightly. Katz claims that fourteen men and one woman survived; the statistics of eleven survivors from the coal mines and three from the Warsaw group are his. Tagliacozzo, in *L'occupazione tedesca* [1], 164, claims that seventeen men and one woman returned. *Ebrei in Italia* [43], 13, claims fifteen men and one woman.

65.   Katz [8], 269.

66.   The article is cited in Morpurgo [2], 109–10. Leone Ginzburg was a director of the newspaper in Rome. He was caught in November 1943. For more on Ginzburg, see chapter 4.

67.   See text of telegram printed in Tagliacozzo, *Gli ebrei in Italia durante il fascismo* [6], 15–16. See also Möllhausen's memoirs, *La carta perdente: Memorie diplomatiche (25 luglio 1943–2 maggio 1945)* (Rome: Sestante, 1948).

68.   Text printed in Tagliacozzo, *Gli ebrei in Italia durante il fascismo* [6], 16–17.

69.   Katz [8], 134–39, from a personal interview with Möllhausen; and Michaelis [15], 364. Silvio Bertoldi [2], 35–37, interviewed Weizsäcker's secretary Albert von Kessel after the war, and stated that it was not clear whether Weizsäcker actually informed the Pope. Ernst von Weizsäcker, in his book *Memoirs*, trans. John Andrews (Chicago: Henry Regnery Company, 1951), never mentions the October 16 roundup. Weizsäcker was tried after the war for activities as state secretary under Foreign Minister Joachim von Ribbentrop from April 1938 to April 1943, before he became the German ambassador to the Vatican. He was sentenced to seven years for, among other things, not having hindered the deportation of French Jews. He actually served two and a half years. See Bertoldi, 36 and 275. In his *Memoirs*, Weizsäcker claims that he always disliked Hitler and remained in office first to help avert war and later to help bring about peace. His son Richard von Weizsäcker, an officer on the eastern front in World War II, was elected president of the Federal Republic of Germany (West Germany) in July 1984, by a specially constituted federal assembly consisting of members of the Bundestag and an equal number of electors chosen by popular representative bodies of the Länder.

70.   Friedländer [14], 117–25, prints texts of various messages informing the Vatican of the fate of deported Jews. See also Walter Laqueur, *The Terrible Secret: Suppression of the Truth about Hitler's 'Final Solution'* (Boston: Little, Brown, 1980), 54–58, and Falconi [14], 46–65.

71.   Laqueur [70], 50; and Friedländer, 125–26.

72.   Friedländer [14], 125–29. Descriptions of Gerstein by three Protestant ministers who knew him well, including Pastor Martin Niemöller, are quoted at length in Rolf Hochhuth, "Sidelights on History," an essay published at the end of his play *The Deputy*, trans. Richard and Clara Winston (New York: Grove Press, 1964). One

Notes

churchwarden wrote, p. 291, "A personality like Kurt Gerstein's is necessarily a twilight figure. Or rather, viewed by the standards of the average man, he must seem absolutely incredible. The uncanny mastery with which he camouflaged his inward Christian being by an outward demeanor of the perfect SS man, with the sole aim of giving succor to others, made a mockery of all ordinary standards." Gerstein allegedly committed suicide in a French prison after the liberation of France, although Hochhuth, p. 294, claims that he may have been killed by the French Resistance or by hardcore SS prisoners.

73. Laqueur [70], 54–58. Laqueur points out, p. 56, that "the Vatican . . . had direct or indirect channels of communication with every European country but Russia," and he concludes that "the Vatican was either the first, or among the first, to learn about the fate of the deported Jews."

74. Letter printed in Katz [8], 202, and Tagliacozzo, *Gli ebrei in Italia durante il fascismo* [6], 30. For background of the letter, see Katz, 198–203, and Michaelis [15], 366.

75. Report printed in Tagliacozzo, *Gli ebrei in Italia durante il fascismo* [6], 30.

76. Michaelis [15], 369.

77. Ibid., 370; Tagliacozzo, *Gli ebrei in Italia durante il* fascismo [6], 31.

78. Michaelis [15], 370–71; Tagliacozzo, *Gli ebrei in Italia durante il fascismo* [6], 31–32.

79. According to Michaelis [15], 364, the Pope did take some private initiative to help Jews, personally ordering that extraterritorial Vatican sanctuaries in Rome be opened to them. In addition, at least one scholar believes that the Pope may have asked some bishops outside Rome to help Jews. See Mae Briskin, "Rescue Italian Style," *The B'nai B'rith International Jewish Monthly*, 100, no. 9 (May 1986): 20–25. Of course, any direct personal order would have had to be kept very quiet to protect those who were actually sheltered. Nevertheless, references to such an order are rare and evidence for it is slight.

80. Ibid., 365. Michaelis cites a personal memorandum from Michael Tagliacozzo, dated June 16, 1975, as his source. Different estimates exist. A Vatican spokesman after the war implied that about three thousand Jews were sheltered in Vatican City alone, while another researcher placed the number at a few dozen. Hilberg [40], 429. See also Giovannetti, *Roma città aperta* [14], 179.

81. Guenther Lewy, *The Catholic Church and Nazi Germany* (New York: McGraw-Hill, 1964), 303–4; and Falconi [14], 92.

82. Kappler report [12], 19. I have used Michaelis's translation, in Michaelis [15], 367–68.

83. For testimony of one saved by such a call, see Tagliacozzo, *Gli ebrei in Italia durante il fascismo* [6], 24–25. As seen, Piero Modigliani [7] was also saved by a telephone call.

84. Morpurgo [2], 181.

85. Ibid., 276. As will be seen in chapter 8, the same police order number five that on December 1, 1943 called for the arrest and internment of all Jews in Italy also demanded the total confiscation of their property and possessions, to benefit air raid victims. A legislative decree on January 4, 1944, stated that Jews had no right to possessions or assets of any kind. All assets were to be confiscated and transferred to a special *Ente di Gestione e Liquidazione Immobiliare* (EGELI), created at the time of the racial laws to receive property declared excessive then. In fact, the seizure of Jewish assets had begun well before these regulations, and many confiscations never reached EGELI. Many possessions, especially portable jewelry, were held in police and prefect offices, allegedly to keep them from the Nazis. Other assets went to finance local charities or political organizations. Some were seized by the Germans. Some

Notes

inevitably lined private pockets. For details, see Adolfo Scalpelli, "L'Ente di Gestione e Liquidazione Immobiliare: Note sulle conseguenze economiche della persecuzione razziale," *Gli ebrei in Italia durante il fascismo: Quaderni del Centro di Documentazione Ebraica Contemporanea,* II, March 1962, 92–112; and Mayda [25], 220–34.

86. *L'occupazione tedesca* [1], 41.

87. CDEC, Milan, 5-H-b [19], f. V, s.f. Veneziano Benedetto di Roma, copy of letter, November 7, 1943. For another anonymous informer's letter denouncing a Jew, see the photo section of this book.

88. *L'occupazione tedesca* [1], 38 and 42. Tagliacozzo, *Gli ebrei in Italia durante il fascismo* [6], 37, places the number at over two thousand.

89. Katz [8], Appendix I, 331–40, lists all who were deported after the October 16 roundup.

90. Services in the main synagogue follow the ancient Roman rite; the Sephardic rite is performed in a room downstairs. There are five other small synagogues in Rome, two with a Roman rite and three with a Sephardic.

7 / Autumn 1943: The Nightmare Begins

1. CDEC, Milan, 9/1: *Riconoscimento benemeriti nell'opera di soccorso,* f. Venezia; also Giuseppe Mayda, *Ebrei sotto Salò: La persecuzione antisemita 1943–1945* (Milan: Giangiacomo Feltrinelli, 1978), 69–70.

2. Bernard Berenson, *Rumor and Reflection: 1941–1944* (London: Constable, 1952), 127–35.

3. Letizia Morpurgo in Fano, *Diario: Ricordi di prigionia* (Trieste: Tipo-Litografia Leghissa, n.d. but after 1966).

4. Pino Levi Cavaglione, *Guerriglia nei Castelli Romani* (Rome: Giulio Einaudi, 1945).

5. For Ovazza's personal opinions, see issues of *La nostra bandiera,* 1934–1938, and also his *Il problema ebraico: Risposta a Paolo Orano* (Rome: Casa Editrice Pinciana, 1938), written in response to Paolo Orano's virulently anti-Zionist and anti-Semitic *Gli ebrei in Italia* (Rome: Casa Editrice Pinciana, 1937). On Ovazza and *La nostra bandiera* generally, see Renzo De Felice, *Storia degli ebrei italiani sotto il fascismo* (1961; Turin: Giulio Einaudi, 1972), 150–59, and Guido Valabrega, "Prime notizie su 'La nostra bandiera' (1934–1938)," *Gli ebrei in Italia durante il fascismo: Quaderni della Federazione Giovanile Ebraica d'Italia,* Turin, April 25, 1961, 21–33.

6. Mayda [1], 90–95.

7. Carlo Modigliani, *Una croce e una stella: Dal mio diario* (Milan: Gastaldi, 1959), 50–64.

8. Giancarlo Sacerdoti, *Ricordi di un ebreo bolognese: Illusioni e delusioni 1929–1945* (Rome: Bonacci, 1983), 108–12.

9. De Felice [5], 453. There were 2,332 Jews in the province of Livorno in 1938.

10. CDEC, Milan, 5-H-b: *Vicissitudini dei singoli—particolare,* f. A, s.f. Ascarelli Castelnuovo Silvana di Roma.

11. Sylvia Lombroso, *No Time for Silence,* trans. Adrienne W. Foulke (New York: Roy, 1945), 76.

12. Luciano Morpurgo, *Caccia all'uomo!* (Rome: Casa Editrice Dalmatia S.A., 1946), 87–106.

13. Lombroso [11], 95.

14. See prologue, footnote 5.

15. Mayda [1], 64.

16. Ibid., 77.

Notes

17. "Eyewitness Testimony 34. Survival in Italy," *Jewish Responses to Nazi Persecution: Collective and Individual Behavior in Extremes*, ed. Isaiah Trunk (New York: Stein and Day, 1979), 211–16. For Mrs. K. L.'s experiences in internment, see chapter 4.

18. For the sources of the statistics cited here, see prologue, notes 4 and 5.

19. On Ancona, see Mayda [1], 67.

20. The Italian Social Republic acquired the Salò label because the official news agency Stefani was also located in the town, and news dispatches bore the name. 'On the Republic of Salò, see especially Giorgio Bocca, *La Repubblica di Mussolini* (Rome and Bari: Laterza, 1977); Silvio Bertoldi, *Salò: Vita e morte della Repubblica Sociale Italiana* (Milan: Rizzoli, 1976); F. W. D. Deakin, *The Last Days of Mussolini* (Harmondsworth, England: Penguin Books, 1966), a revised edition of parts 2 and 3 of *The Brutal Friendship* (London: Weidenfeld & Nicolson, 1962); and Charles F. Delzell, *Mussolini's Enemies: The Italian Anti-Fascist Resistance* (Princeton: Princeton University Press, 1961), 261–71.

21. Bocca [20], 192–95. The Muti Legion was named for the Fascist martyr Ettore Muti, killed on August 24, 1943, during the Badoglio period, in a scuffle with *carabinieri*. See Bocca, 6–8. Francesco Colombo was shot during liberation. Bertoldi [20], 212.

22. On the Carità and Koch bands, see Bocca [20], 192–95; and Aldo Lualdi, *La Banda Koch: Un aguzzino al servizio del regime* (Milan: Valentino Bompiani, 1972). Mario Carità was killed in Alto Adige in May 1945 while resisting the Allied soldiers who had come to arrest him. Pietro Koch, thirty-seven years old when the war ended, was tried in Rome in a single day and executed the following day, June 5, 1945. See Bertoldi [20], 214 and 221–22; and Lualdi, 138–42.

23. Bocca [20], 191–92.

24. Ibid., 192; and Lualdi [22], 170.

25. Giampaolo Pansa, *L'esercito di Salò: La storia segreta dell'ultima battaglia di Mussolini* (Verona: Arnaldo Mondadori, 1970), 22–27, 131. The GNR lost its autonomy by legislative decree in August 1944 and was incorporated into the regular army at that time.

26. Ibid., 37–68.

27. Pansa [25], 201–28; Bocca [20], 55–73, 151–53, 273–77.

28. Ricciotti Lazzero, *La Decima Mas: La compagnia di ventura del "principe nero"* (Milan: Rizzoli, 1984); Bertoldi [20], 127–42; and Bocca [20], 278–83. For the unit's pre-armistice activities, see Junio Valerio Borghese, *Decima flottiglia mas: Dalle origini all'armistizio* (Milan: Garzanti, 1950), or in trans. by James Cleugh, *Sea Devils* (London: A. Melrose, 1952). In 1949, an Italian court convicted Borghese of collaboration with the Germans and sentenced him to twelve years in prison. An amnesty reduced the sentence to four years, but he actually served only a few days. He became a director of the neo-Fascist party, the Italian Social Movement (Movimento Sociale Italiano, or MSI), which is very much alive today. Delzell [20], 267.

29. Pansa [25], 164 and 189; and Bertoldi [20], 227–39. See also Ricciotti Lazzero, *Le Brigate Nere: Il partito armato della Repubblica di Mussolini* (Milan: Rizzoli, 1983) and Arrigo Petacco, *Pavolini: L'ultima raffica di Salò* (Milan: Arnaldo Mondadori, 1982).

30. Ricciotti Lazzero, *Le SS Italiane: Storia dei 20,000 che giurarono fedeltà a Hitler* (Milan: Rizzoli, 1982).

31. The 1938 census registered 182 Jews in Cuneo. See De Felice [5], 10.

32. Mayda [1], 68–69.

33. Ibid., 139; and CDEC, Milan, *Ebrei in Italia: Deportazione, resistenza* (Florence: Tipografia Giuntina, 1975), 29. The province of Trieste's Jewish population of

Notes

6,085 in 1938 was drastically reduced by external and internal migration to about 2,300 in September 1943. Ultimately, at least 620 Jews from Trieste were deported. De Felice [5], 10 and 453; Mayda [1], 139; and Silva Bon Gherardi, *La persecuzione antiebraica a Trieste (1938–1945)* (Udine: Del Bianco, 1972), 238.

34. Mayda [1], 140. Mayda estimates Fiume's Jewish population at about 1,500 in September 1943. Ultimately, 258 Jews were deported from here, of whom 22 returned. De Felice [5], 453. It is not clear how many of the 258 were refugees.

35. Mayda [1], 67–68.

36. De Felice [5], 10 and 453.

37. Mayda [1], 144–45. For a vivid description of the roundup, see Giancarlo Ottani, *Un popolo piange: La tragedia degli ebrei italiani* (Milan: Spartaco Giovene, 1945).

38. Mayda [1], 144–45.

39. Modigliani [7], 83–85.

40. Mayda [1], 145. The 1938 census recorded 10,219 Jews in Milan Province. See De Felice [5], 10. De Felice, 453, records 896 Milanese Jewish deportees, with 50 returning. His and Mayda's differing figures point up the difficulty of determining the exact origins of many deportees.

41. See list of average daily industrial wages in Maurice F. Neufeld, *Italy: School for Awakening Countries—The Italian Labor Movement in Its Political, Social, and Economic Setting from 1800 to 1960* (Ithaca, New York: Cornell University Press, 1961), 540.

42. Modigliani [7], 118.

43. Ibid., 119–21.

44. Mayda [1], 132–35.

45. CDEC, Milan, 5-H-b [10], f. C, s.f. Nathan Cassuto. See also *Ebrei in Italia* [33], 37–40.

46. Mayda [1], 136.

47. Mayda [1], 135. One wonders why anyone was there at all. According to Paola Pandolfi, *Ebrei a Firenze nel 1943: Persecuzione e deportazione* (Florence: Università di Firenze, Facoltà di Magistero, 1980), 46–47, Vice Rabbi Fernando Belgrado, who survived the Holocaust, has stated that Chief Rabbi Cassuto had permanently closed the synagogue after Yom Kippur, October 9.

48. *Ebrei in Italia* [33], 13–14.

49. CDEC, Milan, 5-H-b [10], f. R, s.f. Ravenna Falco Gabriella di Ferrara, testimony of a survivor caught at the convent.

50. Ibid., f. A, s.f. Abenaim Pacifici Vanda di Firenze. Mrs. Pacifici did not survive. Rabbi Pacifici's story is told later in this chapter.

51. Memo Bemporad, *La Macine: Storia di una famiglia israelita negli ultimi 60 anni di vita italiana* (Rome: Carucci, 1984), 135–37.

52. Ibid.

53. Mayda [1], 135–36, from testimony he collected.

54. Mayda [1], 136.

55. *Ebrei in Italia* [33], 14–15.

56. Ibid., 15–18 and 37–38; Pandolfi [47], 58–63; and Mayda [1], 136–37.

57. *Ebrei in Italia* [33], 38.

58. CDEC, Milan, 9/1 [1], f. Firenze, letter from Emma Di Gioacchino, mother of Anna Cassuto, February 20, 1955. According to Mrs. Di Gioacchino, another Cassuto child, a girl born just two months before her parents' arrests, died alone in a hospital. Mario Santerini took great risks by attending her interment to learn her burial place.

59. *Ebrei in Italia* [33], 39–40; and Mayda [1], 147.

Notes

60. From an account by Massimo Teglio, quoted at length in Carlo Brizzolari, *Gli ebrei nella storia di Genova* (Genova: Sabatelli, 1971), 306, and an account by Salvatore Jona, "La persecuzione degli ebrei a Genova," *Genova*, April 1965, quoted in Mayda [1], 142.

61. CDEC, Milan, 9/1 [1], f. Genova, s.f. Romana Rossi in Serotti.

62. Mayda [1], 142.

63. Ibid., 142–44.

64. CDEC, Milan, 5-H-b [10], f. P, s.f. Rabbino Pacifici Riccardo, declaration of Mrs. Orvieto about her brother Rabbi Pacifici, Rome, September 1960; and Brizzolari [60], 307–8.

65. Brizzolari [60], 307–8, from testimony of Father Francesco Repetto, the secretary to Cardinal Boetto. There is some diverse testimony here, for Signora Orvieto [64] stated that her brother was caught when he obeyed Polacco's original telephone summons to come to the synagogue.

66. Jona's account [60], cited in Mayda [1], 142.

67. *Ebrei in Italia* [33], 15.

68. Mayda [1], 114–18.

8 / Policy and Prisons

1. Giorgio Bocca, *La Repubblica di Mussolini* (Rome and Bari: Laterza, 1977), 88–96; Giuseppe Mayda, *Ebrei sotto Salò: La persecuzione antisemita 1943–1945* (Milan: Giangiacomo Feltrinelli, 1978), 111–13; Renzo De Felice, *Storia degli ebrei italiani sotto il fascismo* (1961; Turin: Giulio Einaudi, 1972), 434–35.

2. Mayda [1], 126–28.

3. Carlo Modigliani, *Una croce e una stella: Dal mio diario* (Milan: Gastaldi, 1959), 85–93.

4. Glauco Buffarini Guidi, son of the minister, makes this justification in his *La vera verità: I documenti dell'archivio segreto del ministro degli interni Guido Buffarini Guidi dal 1938 al 1945* (Milan: Sugar, 1970), 48–50. De Felice [1], 434, concludes that "the intention of Mussolini and the 'moderates' was without doubt to concentrate all Jews until the end of the war . . . and to postpone a solution of the question until the end of the war."

5. De Felice [1], 438.

6. CDEC, Milan, *Ebrei in Italia: Deportazione, resistenza* (Florence: Tipografia Giuntina, 1975), 15–18.

7. Meir Michaelis, *Mussolini and the Jews: German-Italian Relations and the Jewish Question in Italy, 1922–1945* (Oxford: Clarendon Press, 1978), 378–79. For the bureaucratic roles of Eichmann, Dannecker, and Bosshammer, see chapter 6, footnote 29.

8. Michaelis [7], 380–81.

9. Buffarini Guidi [4], 48–50; and De Felice [1], 438.

10. Michaelis [7], 382–83.

11. Ibid.

12. *Ebrei in Italia* [6], 18.

13. Ibid., 18–19.

14. Ibid., 19–22. The May 16 train divided at Innsbruck and carried another 163 Jews who were from neutral or enemy nations, and thus not subjects for elimination, to Bergen Belsen. Of these, 158, including a child born in the camp, survived.

15. Ibid., 24–26. One of the Jewish spouses from a mixed marriage sent to Auschwitz was Ruth Weidenreich Piccagli, who survived. She describes her terrible

experience in *Nei lager c'ero anch'io*, ed. Vincenzo Pappalettera (Milan: U. Mursia, 1973), 20–23, 70–74, 131–37, and 139–42. Her husband was a non-Jew, and her father, a Jewish refugee doctor from Germany. It is interesting to note that the Germans did not deport their own Jews in mixed marriages or the children of such marriages (unless those children adhered to the Jewish religion or married full Jews; see chapter three, footnote 29). Nazi policy toward spouses of Germans and toward German half-Jews was tempered by their respect for the German partner or parent. There was no guarantee of a similar respect for Jews whose spouse or parent was Italian.

16. Enea Fergnani, *Un uomo e tre numeri* (Milan: Speroni Editore, 1945), 138–39; Paolo Liggeri, *Triangolo rosso: Dalle carceri di S. Vittore ai campi di concentramento e di eliminazione di Fossoli, Bolzano, Mauthausen, Gusen, Dachau, marzo 1944–maggio 1945* (Milan: La Casa, 1946), 50–53. Both men were political prisoners at Fossoli and witnessed the visit.

17. CDEC, Milan, 5-H-b: *Vicissitudini dei singoli—particolare*, f. L, s.f. Levi Enrica di Trieste, testimony of Signora Enrica Levi, states that her mother in Trieste received from her father a note that he had thrown from his train onto the snow outside Auschwitz and that an Italian *carabinieri* who had accompanied the train delivered; f. I, s.f. Italia Raffaele di Trieste, testimony of Gisella Italia, who received a similar note from her husband at Auschwitz, delivered by two Italian militiamen, one of whom, she said, had a deported Jewish wife and had volunteered to accompany a deportation train in the hope of finding her; f. P, s.f. Pace Renato di Roma, testimony of Pace, who sent a note to his family from Mauthausen by means of an Italian guard who accompanied the train.

18. The behavior of Italian officials during the occupation is in stark contrast to that of Danish officials under similar conditions. After about 477 Danish Jews were deported to Theresienstadt in October 1943, Danish officials maintained a constant barrage of inquiries as to their welfare. All but 40 or 50 of those Jews survived; none were gassed. The situation was not the same in Italy, for Italian Jewish deportees, far more numerous, went directly to Auschwitz, an extermination center rather than a transit camp. Once there, they could not have been saved. The point here, however, is that Italian government officials, knowing no more and no less than the Danes, did not follow up on the fate of their deported countrymen, as the Danes did. For more on Denmark, see the conclusion at the end of this book.

19. De Felice [1], doc. 35, 594–601, prints the text of Preziosi's memorandum.

20. Mayda [1], 176–83; and Silvio Bertoldi, *Salò: Vita e morte della Repubblica Sociale Italiana* (Milan: Rizzoli, 1976), 331–37.

21. For example, the account given by Glauco Buffarini Guidi, son of the "moderate" Minister of the Interior, makes it sound as if most Jews remained in Italian internment camps until Mussolini was compelled *(costretto)* to appoint Preziosi. The claim is absurd, for, as seen, 650 Italian Jews left Fossoli on February 22. Another 835 left on April 5, thirteen days before Preziosi's appointment was ratified. See Buffarini Guidi [4], 50.

22. On April 26, 1945, Giovanni Preziosi and his wife threw themselves from the fifth-floor window of a large house on the Corso Venezia in Milan. Preziosi apparently feared the vengeance of Jews. He left a note for his son, declaring that he would one day be proud of him. Mayda [1], 250–51.

23. Primo Levi, *If This Is a Man*, trans. Stuart Woolf (London: Bodley Head, 1960), 4. In a new edition (New York: Summit Books, 1986), published with Levi's *The Reawakening*, the title has been changed to *Survival in Auschwitz*. The book was originally published as *Se questo è un uomo* (Turin: Francesco De Silva, 1947). Subsequent Italian editions are published by Einaudi.

24. Testimony of Dante Bizzarri, a political prisoner, quoted by Mayda [1], 188–

Notes

89. See also Fergnani [16], 138; and Emilio Jani, *Mi ha salvato la voce: Auschwitz 180046* (Milan: Ceschina, 1960), 63–72.

25. Amedeo Strazzera-Perniciani, *Umanità ed eroismo nella vita segreta di Regina Coeli: Roma 1943–1944* (1946; Rome: Tipo-Litografia V. Ferri, 1959). Strazzera-Perniciani, member of a Catholic lay order devoted to assisting prisoners, worked at Regina Coeli during the occupation.

26. CDEC, Milan, 5-H-b [17], f. M., s.f. Montefiore Evelina—Montefiore Ginesi Bianca, Milano, testimony of Signora Bianca in Ginesi and Signorina Evelina Montefiore, her sister, Milan, November 22, 1966.

27. Fergnani [16], 19–97, esp. 36, 40, and 44. For more on conditions at San Vittore, see Giancarlo Ottani, *Un popolo piange: La tragedia degli ebrei italiani* (Milan: Spartaco Giovene, 1945), 37–46 and 98–102; and Liggeri [16], 3–108. Liggeri was a Catholic priest, arrested in Milan in March 1944, for helping Jews. For more on Liggeri, see chapter 10. Conditions in Fascist prisons had been wretched long before the German occupation. For one personal account of the filth, rats, overcrowding, solitary confinement, and brutality of guards in Fascist prisons long before the war, see Francesco Fausto Nitti, *Escape: The Personal Narrative of a Political Prisoner Who Was Rescued from Lipari, the Fascist "Devil's Island"* (New York and London: G. P. Putnam's Sons, 1930).

28. Jani [24], 32.

29. Fergnani [16], 19–97; and Montefiore [26].

30. Carlo Brizzolari, *Gli ebrei nella storia di Genova* (Genoa: Sabatelli, 1971), 327.

31. Mayda [1], 209–11. De Felice [1], 10 and 453, lists Mantua as a province with 589 Jews in 1938, 39 deportees, and 1 return.

32. Mayda [1], 211–12.

33. Augusto Segre, *Memorie di vita ebraica: Casale Monferrato-Roma-Gerusalemme 1918–1960* (Rome: Bonacci, 1979), 304–5.

34. Levi [23], 5.

35. Mayda [1], 185–86. See also Liliana Picciotto Fargion, *L'occupazione tedesca e gli ebrei di Roma: Documenti e fatti* (Rome: Carucci, 1979), 32. Picciotto Fargion writes that Pacifico Di Castro had five children, and that he was killed because he did not understand an order shouted at him in German.

36. Fergnani [16], 133–35.

37. Ibid., 142–56. For more on conditions at Fossoli in June and July 1944, see Liggeri [16], 111–82.

38. Ilva Vaccari, *Il tempo di decidere: Documenti e testimonianze sui rapporti tra il clero e la Resistenza* (Modena: S.T.E.M. Mucchi, 1968), 14.

39. Charles F. Delzell, *Mussolini's Enemies: The Italian Anti-Fascist Resistance* (Princeton: Princeton University Press, 1961), 429. SS Major Walter Reder, an Austrian, was sentenced to life imprisonment in Italy in 1951 for this and several other crimes. In a gesture of good will toward Austria, the Italian government released him, a sick man, in January 1985. He was, at that time, the last Nazi war criminal held in Italy.

40. Corrado Saralvo, *Più morti più spazio* (Milan: Baldini & Castoldi, 1969).

41. Fergnani [16], 159–71. Liggeri [16], 185–99, and Ottani [27], 109–31, also emphasize the unpredictable cruelty of the guards at Gries.

42. Ottani [27], 114–17.

43. *Ebrei in Italia* [6], 27. By December 1944, convoys no longer went to Auschwitz. The camp, threatened by the approaching Russians, was in the process of evacuating its prisoners. Auschwitz was liberated on January 27, 1945.

44. Saralvo [40], 10–19.

45. Silva Bon Gherardi, *La persecuzione antiebraica a Trieste (1938–1945)*

(Udine: Del Bianco, 1972), 213–16. Globocnik's father was a Slav and his mother a Hungarian. His family settled in Klagenfurt, Austria, in 1923. He is believed to have killed himself with poison in Austria in May 1945.

46. CDEC, Milan, 5-H-b [17], f. K, s.f. Kabiglio Alberto, personal testimony. Kabiglio arrived at La Risiera on March 4, 1944, with about one hundred people from Arbe. He says more arrived a few days later. These must have been the 204 Jews left behind on Arbe (see chapter 5). See also Carlo Schiffrer, "La Risiera," *Trieste: Rivista politica della regione*, anno VII, n. 44, July–August 1961, 21–24; and Bruno Piazza, *Perché gli altri dimenticano* (Milan: Giangiacomo Feltrinelli, 1956), 9–17.

47. Schiffrer [46], 21–24.

48. Bon Gherardi [45], 220; and Mayda [1], 138–39.

49. By 1975, the CDEC had ascertained the names of 837 Jewish deportees on the 22 trains from Trieste, of whom 760 did not return. See *Ebrei in Italia* [6], 29–30 and inserted page, "Deportazione degli ebrei dall'Italia." Subsequent CDEC research has brought the number to 1,074 deportees, of whom 999 did not return. See Liliana Picciotto Fargion, "La deportazione degli ebrei dall'Italia: Indagine statistica," (unpublished but intended for publication by the Institut für Zeitgeschichte in Munich, in a statistical study, country by country, of victims of the Holocaust).

50. Schiffrer [46], 21–24.

51. Letizia Morpurgo in Fano, *Diario: Ricordi di prigionia* (Trieste: Tipo-Lito-grafia Leghissa, n.d. but after 1966), 73.

9 / The Italian Phase

1. CDEC, Milan, 9/1: *Riconoscimento benemeriti nell'opera di soccorso*, f. Venezia.

2. Giuseppe Mayda, *Ebrei sotto Salò: La persecuzione antisemita 1943–1945* (Milan: Giangiacomo Feltrinelli, 1978), 129–30.

3. Renzo De Felice, *Storia degli ebrei italiani sotto il fascismo* (1961; Turin: Giulio Einaudi, 1972), 10 and 212.

4. CDEC, Milan, *Ebrei in Italia: Deportazione, resistenza* (Florence: Tipografia Giuntina, 1975), 13–30; Liliana Picciotto Fargion, "La deportazione degli ebrei dall'Italia: Indagine statistica," unpublished but intended for publication by the Institut für Zeitgeschichte in Munich, in a statistical study, country by country, of victims of the Holocaust; and Hizkia M. Franco, *Les Martyrs juifs de Rhodes et de Cos* (Elisabeth-ville, Katanga: Imprimeries et Papeteries Belgo-Congolaises 'Imbelco,' 1952). As explained in footnote 4 of the prologue and footnote 46 of chapter 4, Franco's estimates of deportees are slightly lower than those of Picciotto Fargion and the CDEC. I might add that the number of deportees on each train will not add up to the total number of deportees from Italy. The figures for each train are taken (by the CDEC) from what is known of it from camp records and other sources; the total number of deportees includes only named and solidly verified individuals. In a few cases, only some of the Jews known to be on a particular train can be identified and thus included in national totals.

5. Liliana Picciotto Fargion, *L'occupazione tedesca e gli ebrei di Roma: Documenti e fatti* (Rome: Carucci, 1979), 41. Not all arrested Jews were deported. Picciotto Fargion, p. 42, finds that after October 16, 709 more Roman Jews were deported. About 77 others were killed at the Ardeatine Caves massacre (see footnote 13).

6. Ibid., 41. An additional 141 Jews were arrested at unknown dates.

7. Ibid., 32.

8. For explanation of the formal bureaucratic status of Bosshammer's office, see

Notes

chapter 6, footnote 29. See also Liliana Picciotto Fargion, "Polizia tedesca ed ebrei nell'Italia occupata," *Rivista di Storia Contemporanea,* n. 3, 1984, 456–73; and same author, "La deportazione degli ebrei dall'Italia: Indagine statistica" [4]. Bosshammer was not arrested in West Germany until 1968. He was tried by a court in West Berlin in 1971 for complicity in the deportations of 75,000 Jews from Rumania, 51,000 from Bulgaria, 17,500 from Czechoslovakia, and 3,496 from Italy, as well as in the killing of 832 Jews from Czechoslovakia. He was sentenced to life imprisonment but released after a few months because he was dying of cancer. He died in Berlin in December 1972, age sixty-four. See Mayda [2], 180.

9. *L'occupazione tedesca* [5], 29.

10. Carlo Brizzolari, *Gli ebrei nella storia di Genova* (Genova: Sabatelli, 1971), 321–22.

11. Silvio Bertoldi, *I tedeschi in Italia* (Milan: Rizzoli, 1964), 120–21; and Robert Katz, *Black Sabbath: A Journey Through a Crime Against Humanity* (Toronto: Macmillan, 1969), 296–97.

12. Attilio Ascarelli, *Le Fosse Ardeatine* (Bologna: Editrice Nanni Canesi, 1965); Robert Katz, *Death in Rome* (New York: Macmillan, 1967); and Michael Tagliacozzo, "La persecuzione degli ebrei a Roma," *L'occupazione tedesca* [5], 149–71.

13. *L'occupazione tedesca* [5], 111–13, lists 77 names. *Ebrei in Italia:* [4], 32, states that there were 78 Jewish victims; Ascarelli [12], 168, and Tagliacozzo [12], 167, state 75.

14. Tagliacozzo [12], 167. Tagliacozzo says that seven members of the Di Consiglio family died, while the list in *L'occupazione tedesca* [5], 111–13, shows six with that name.

15. Bertoldi [11], 120–21. Bertoldi interviewed Lazzaro Anticoli's daughter after the war. He states that Celeste Di Porto's father, profoundly shamed by his daughter's deeds, turned himself in to the Germans and died in a concentration camp. Her brother joined the Foreign Legion. She herself repented after the war and converted to Catholicism. Tried and sentenced to twelve years in prison, she served only seven.

16. Luciano Morpurgo, *Caccia all'uomo!* (Rome: Casa Editrice Dalmatia S.A., 1946), 142–349.

17. Giorgio Bocca, *La Repubblica di Mussolini* (Rome and Bari: Laterza, 1977), 195–97.

18. Amedeo Strazzera-Perniciani, *Umanità ed eroismo nella vita segreta di Regina Coeli: Roma 1943–1944* (1946; Rome: Tipo-Litografia V. Ferri, 1959), 111–13; Meir Michaelis, *Mussolini and the Jews: German-Italian Relations and the Jewish Question in Italy, 1922–1945* (Oxford: Clarendon Press, 1978), 390. The forty-four-year-old Caruso, a veteran of the 1922 march on Rome, was caught and tried in Rome after the liberation of the city. He was executed in September 1944.

19. Diary of Rosina Sorani, sister of Settimio Sorani, entry for February 2, 1944, quoted in Katz, *Black Sabbath* [11], 296.

20. Morpurgo [16], 189.

21. De Felice [3], 453, says 1,727 were deported and 105 returned. *L'occupazione tedesca* [5], 42, says 1,739 were deported and 114 returned. Tagliacozzo [12], 170, believes that 2,091 were deported. Statistics vary for several reasons. Women were occasionally listed by both maiden and married names; some statistics include Romans arrested elsewhere; many deportees are not known by name or place of origin.

22. For survivor testimony on Grini, see CDEC, Milan, 5-H-b: *Vicissitudini dei singoli—particolare,* f. B, s.f. Bisson Isacco di Trieste; f. B, s.f. Breiner Erich di Abbazia—Breiner Ruth Rosenwasser di Abbazia; f. F, s.f. Testimonianza di Lidia Frankel in Grini (no relation); f. K, s.f. Kabiglio Alberto; f. P, s.f. Pollak Giulio di Trieste; and f. M, s.f. Montefiore Evelina—Montefiori Ginesi Bianca, Milano (the

reference to Grini is Grun). Survivor accounts differ as to whether Grini's father and brother helped Jewish prisoners or collaborated with the Nazis, but they all agree on Grini's role. Grini disappeared after the war. He is believed to have been killed by the Germans themselves as they prepared to abandon La Risiera. One survivor (s.f. Breiner) claimed to have seen his blood-stained shirt. For more on Grini, see Silva Bon Gherardi, *La persecuzione antiebraica a Trieste (1938–1945)* (Udine: Del Bianco, 1972), 217.

23. For more on Finzi, see chapter 4. On Celeste Di Porto's methods, see Dan Kurzman, *The Race for Rome* (Garden City, New York: Doubleday, 1975), 151–52.

24. CDEC, Milan, 5-H-b [22], f. M, s.f. Momigliano Michela Fernanda.

25. Mayda [2], 203–8.

26. Ibid., 205–6, 215, and 243–45.

27. *Ebrei in Italia* [4], 32.

28. Silvano Arieti, *The Parnas* (New York: Basic Books, 1979).

29. Mayda [2], 242–43.

30. *Ebrei in Italia* [4], 33.

31. Alberto Cavaglion, *Nella notte straniera: Gli ebrei di S. Martin Vésubie e il campo di Borgo S. Dalmazzo, 8 settembre–21 novembre 1943* (Cuneo: Edizioni L'Arciere, 1981), 135; and *Ebrei in Italia* [4], 33. See also chapter 5.

32. See prologue, footnotes 4 and 5.

33. *Ebrei in Italia* [4], 10.

34. De Felice [3], 453.

10 / Survival in Italy

1. Augusto Segre, *Memorie di vita ebraica: Casale Monferrato-Roma-Gerusalemma 1918–1960* (Rome: Bonacci, 1979), 299–307.

2. Ibid., 304.

3. CDEC, Milan, 9/1: *Riconoscimento benemeriti nell'opera di soccorso*, f. Trieste, survivor letter.

4. CDEC, Milan, 5-H-b: *Vicissitudini dei singoli—particolare*, f. P, s.f. Padovano Wanda nata a Bologna, "Testimonianza di Wanda Padovano."

5. CDEC, Milan, 5-H-b [4], f. L, s.f. Vittorio Luzzati, Savona, "L'odissea di un Ebreo," personal testimony of Luzzati.

6. Ibid.

7. Winston S. Churchill, *Closing the Ring* (Boston: Houghton Mifflin, 1951), 187–88. Churchill adds that Italian partisans and civilians guided at least ten thousand escaped Allied prisoners-of-war to safety behind their lines.

8. CDEC, Milan, 9/1 [3], f. Firenze, "Stralcio dal memoriale inviato il 25 Agosto 1944 alla communità israelitica di Firenze," personal testimony of Alfredo Alberto Saltiel.

9. Luzzati [5].

10. Luciano Morpurgo, *Caccia all'uomo!* (Rome: Casa Editrice Dalmatia S.A., 1946), 285.

11. Carlo Modigliani, *Una croce e una stella: Dal mio diario* (Milan: Gastaldi, 1959).

12. CDEC, Milan, 5-H-b [4], f. M, s.f. Milano Carlo di Roma, personal testimony of Milano.

13. Cardinal Ildefonso Schuster of Milan, for example, appealed to the Germans for better treatment of imprisoned priests and was successful in some cases. See A.

Notes

Cauvin and G. Grasso, *Nacht und Nebel (notte e nebbia)* (Turin: Casa Editrice Marietti, n.d. but after 1980), 25.

14. Ilva Vaccari, *Il tempo di decidere: Documenti e testimonianze sui rapporti tra il clero e la Resistenza* (Modena: S.T.E.M. Mucchi, 1968), 14 and 446–63.

15. See chapter 5.

16. CDEC, Milan, 9/3: *Riconoscimenti ai benemeriti nell'opera di soccorso*, f. Benedetto; Renzo De Felice, *Storia degli ebrei italiani sotto il fascismo* (1961; Turin: Giulio Einaudi, 1972), Father Benedetto's report on the activities of Delasem, July 20, 1944, reprinted in full, 615–16; Fernande Leboucher, *Incredible Mission*, trans. J. F. Bernard (Garden City, New York: Doubleday, 1969); and Alberto Cavaglion, *Nella notte straniera: Gli ebrei di S. Martin Vésubie e il campo di Borgo S. Dalmazzo, 8 settembre–21 novembre 1943* (Cuneo: Edizioni L'Arciere, 1981), 27–28 and 121.

17. CDEC, Milan, 9/2: *Medaglie d'oro: Riconoscimento ai benemeriti*, f. Benemeriti (medaglie d'oro), s.f. Repetto don Francesco and s.f. Salvi don Carlo; Cavaglion [16], 115–17 and 120–23; and Carlo Brizzolari, *Gli ebrei nella storia di Genova* (Genoa: Sabatelli, 1971), 303–11 and 321–28. For Don Repetto's help to Jewish refugees from southern France, see chapter 5.

18. CDEC, Milan, 9/2 [17], f. Benemeriti (medaglie d'oro), sf. Don Vincenzo Barale. See also Cauvin and Grasso [13], 20, for testimony of an assistant parish priest called upon by Don Barale to aid about sixty foreign Jewish refugees. He received money from Don Barale every ten days for that purpose.

19. Paola Pandolfi, *Ebrei a Firenze nel 1943: Persecuzione e deportazione* (Florence: Università di Firenze, Facoltà di Magistero, 1980), 36–40. Chief Rabbi Cassuto and his committee to aid foreigners are discussed in chapter 7 of this book.

20. Luzzati [5].

21. CDEC, Milan, 9/1 [3], f. Milano, survivor letter, May 26, 1955. See also Luzzati [5]. For Don Liggeri's personal account of his imprisonment, see his *Triangolo rosso: Dalle carceri di S. Vittore ai campi di concentramento e di eliminazione di Fossoli, Bolzano, Mauthausen, Gusen, Dachau, marzo 1944–maggio 1945* (Milan: La Casa, 1946).

22. Vaccari [14], 453. See also "Sui margini del breviario scrisse l'addio alla vita," *Corriere della Sera*, April 31, 1949.

23. Cauvin and Grasso [13], 9–90.

24. Ibid., 21.

25. CDEC, Milan, 9/2 [17], f. Benemeriti (medaglie d'oro), s.f. Cellurale Dott. Olindo—Vicenza, letter from Bernardo Weisz.

26. CDEC, Milan, 9/1 [3], f. Milano, survivor statement.

27. CDEC, Milan, 5-H-b [4], f. L, s.f. Enrichetta Levi, personal testimony of Levi.

28. CDEC, Milan, 5-H-b [4] f. M, s.f. Morpurgo Colbi Frida di Sinigallia (Pr. di Ancona), personal testimony of Morpurgo.

29. CDEC, Milan, 9/1 [3], f. Biella, statement of Davide Nissim, December 13, 1954.

30. CDEC, Milan, 9/1 [3], f. Firenze, survivor letter, April 18, 1955.

31. CDEC, Milan, 9/1 [3], Firenze, letter from Angiolo Orvieto, February 14, 1955.

32. Alexander Ramati, *The Assisi Underground: The Priests Who Rescued Jews* (New York: Stein and Day, 1978). Ramati interviewed Father Niccacci.

33. Ibid.

34. Vaccari [14], 84–85. For more on the Villa Emma orphans, see chapter 4.

35. Ibid., 87.

36. Ibid., 173–212.

37. CDEC, Milan, 9/1 [3], f. Firenze, survivor statement.

38.   CDEC, Milan, 9/1 [3], f. Trieste, letter from Bruno Maestro, December 5, 1954.

39.   CDEC, Milan, 9/1 [3], f. Milano, survivor statement.

40.   CDEC, Milan, 9/2 [17], f. Benemeriti (medaglie d'oro), s.f. Sen. Dott. Domenico Coggiola.

41.   Amedeo Strazzera-Perniciani, *Umanità ed eroismo nella vita segreta di Regina Coeli: Roma (1943–1944)* (1946; Rome: Tipo-Litografia V. Ferri, 1959), 183–87.

42.   Letizia Morpurgo in Fano, *Diario: Ricordi di prigionia* (Trieste: Tipo-Litografia Leghissa, n.d. but after 1966), 30–57.

43.   Ibid., 41.

44.   CDEC, Milan, 9/2 [17], f. Benemeriti (medaglie d'oro), s.f. Palatucci Giovanni—Fiume.

45.   Ibid., s.f. De Fiore Dott. Angelo—Forlì.

46.   CDEC, Milan, 9/1 [3], f. Milano, letter from Israel Contente, May 3, 1955.

47.   CDEC, Milan, 9/1 [3], f. Milano, survivor statement, May 26, 1955.

48.   CDEC, Milan, 9/1 [3], f. Venezia, survivor statement.

49.   Maestro [38].

50.   CDEC, Milan, 9/1 [3], f. Milano, letter from Bruno Mattei, May 24, 1955.

51.   CDEC, Milan, 9/1 [3], f. Milano, letter from Abramo Recanati, June 25, 1955.

52.   CDEC, Milan, 9/1 [3], f. Milano, survivor letters, 1945. See also Emilio Jani, *Mi ha salvato la voce: Auschwitz 180046* (Milan: Ceschina, 1960), 66.

53.   Giuseppe Funaro, "Vicende dell'orfanotrofio israelitico di Livorno dopo l'otto settembre 1943," *Gli ebrei in Italia durante il fascismo: Quaderni della Federazione Giovanile Ebraica d'Italia*, Turin, April 25, 1961, 72–77. Funaro was one of the orphans saved.

54.   Segre [1], 316.

55.   CDEC, Milan, 9/1 [3], f. Milano, letter from Giuseppe Levy, May 29, 1955.

56.   Saltiel [8].

57.   Giancarlo Sacerdoti, *Ricordi di un ebreo bolognese: Illusioni e delusioni 1929–1945* (Rome: Bonacci, 1983), 168.

58.   Interview with Gastone Orefice, quoted in *Voices from the Holocaust*, ed. Sylvia Rothchild (New York: New American Library, 1982), 211.

59.   CDEC, Milan, 9/1 [3], f. Trieste, letter from Bruno Montanari, December 15, 1954.

60.   See chapter 11.

61.   CDEC, Milan, 9/2 [17], f. Benemeriti (medaglie d'oro), s.f. Focherini Odoardo—Carpi. See also Vaccari [14], 93–99.

62.   CDEC, Milan, 9/2 [17], f. Benemeriti (medaglie d'oro), s.f. Troiani Pio.

63.   CDEC, Milan, 9/2 [17], f. Benemeriti (medaglie d'oro), s.f. Fraccon Torquato—Vicenza.

64.   CDEC, Milan, 9/2 [17], f. Benemeriti (medaglie d'oro), s.f. Avv. Giuseppe Sala.

65.   CDEC, Milan, 9/2 [17], f. Benemeriti (medaglie d'oro), s.f. Campolmi Gennaro—Firenze. See also Memo Bemporad, *La Macine: Storia di una famiglia israelita negli ultima 60 anni di vita italiana* (Rome: Carucci, 1984), 146–47.

66.   CDEC, Milan, 9/1 [3], f. Venezia, survivor statement, doc. 280.

67.   CDEC, Milan, 9/1 [3], f. Trieste, letter from Leopoldo Kostoris, December 4, 1954.

68.   CDEC, Milan, 9/1 [3], f. Firenze, survivor statement.

69.   CDEC, Milan, 9/1 [3], f. Venezia, survivor statement, doc. 232.

Notes

70. CDEC, Milan, 9/2 [17], f. Benemeriti (medaglie d'oro), s.f. Granzotto Ved[va] Battistella Ida—Motta di Livenza, survivor letter, December 2, 1954.

71. CDEC, Milan, 9/1 [3], f. Milano, letter from Ing. Amerigo Ottolenghi, June 6, 1955.

11 / Switzerland

1. CDEC, Milan, 5-H-b: *Vicissitudini dei singoli—particolare*, f. L, s.f. Vittorio Luzzati, Savona, "L'odissea di un Ebreo," personal testimony of Luzzati.

2. Letizia Morpurgo in Fano, *Diario: Ricordi di prigionia* (Trieste: Tipo-Litografia Leghissa, n.d. but after 1966), 72.

3. Ibid.

4. Michele Sarfatti, "Dopo l'8 settembre: Gli ebrei e la rete confinaria italo-svizzera," *La Rassegna Mensile di Israel*, special issue edited by the CDEC, XLVI, n. 1-2-3, January–June 1981, 151–54.

5. Carlo Modigliani, *Una croce e una stella: Dal mio diario* (Milan: Gastaldi Editore, 1959), 62.

6. See, for example, a report from a member of the Guardia Nazionale Repubblicana, quoted at length in Sarfatti [4], 162.

7. Luzzati [1].

8. Letter from Gianfranco Sarfatti, February 6, 1944, quoted in Sarfatti [4], 159.

9. See list of average daily industrial wages in Maurice F. Neufeld, *Italy: School for Awakening Countries—The Italian Labor Movement in Its Political, Social, and Economic Setting from 1800 to 1960* (Ithaca, New York: Cornell University Press, 1961), 540.

10. Luzzati [1].

11. CDEC, Milan, 9/1: *Riconoscimento benemeriti nell'opera di soccorso*, f. Milano, survivor testimony.

12. CDEC, Milan, 9/1 [11], f. Verona, survivor testimony.

13. Sarfatti [4], 169–73.

14. CDEC, Milan, 9/1 [11], f. Milano, letter from Israel Contente, May 3, 1955.

15. Modigliani [5], 99.

16. Testimony of Cesare Vivante cited in Sarfatti [4], 172.

17. CDEC, Milan, 5-H-b [1], f. V, s.f. Dr. Rino Verona, Milano, personal testimony of Dr. Verona.

18. CDEC, Milan, 9/1 [11], f. Firenze, letter from Giorgio Forti, February 20, 1955.

19. Ilva Vaccari, *Il tempo di decidere: Documenti e testimonianze sui rapporti tra il clero e la Resistenza* (Modena: S.T.E.M. Mucchi, 1968), 93–99.

20. CDEC, Milan, 9/2: *Medaglie d'oro: Riconoscimento ai benemeriti*, f. Benemeriti (medaglie d'oro), s.f. De Micheli Tommasi Dottoressa Ada—Milano; and busta 9/1 [11], f. Milano, letter from Vittorio di M. Hassan, April 18, 1955.

21. CDEC, Milan, 9/2 [20], f. Benemeriti (medaglie d'oro), s.f. Prof. Lina Leoni Crippa.

22. Claudio Sartori, *La mamma di San Vittore: Memorie di Madre Enrichetta Maria Alfieri* (Brescia: La Scuola, 1952). For testimony of one she helped save, see CDEC, Milan, 5-H-b [1], f. L, s.f. Relazione di Renata Lombroso di Milano, personal testimony of Lombroso, Milan, August 30, 1973.

23. CDEC, Milan, 9/1 [11], f. Milano, survivor testimony.

24. Lombroso [22].

25. CDEC, Milan, 9/2 [20], f. Benemeriti (medaglie d'oro), s.f. Spada Lorenzo.

Notes

12 / The Best of Their Generation: Italian Jews and Anti-fascism

1. *Memoriale* of Amelia Rosselli, quoted in Nicola Tranfaglia, *Carlo Rosselli dall'interventismo a "Giustizia e Libertà"* (Bari: Laterza, 1968), 13. For more on the Rossellis, see Aldo Garosci, *Vita di Carlo Rosselli,* 2 vols. (Florence: Vallecchi, 1973), and Gaetano Salvemini, *Carlo and Nello Rosselli, a Memoir* (London: For Intellectual Liberty, 1937).

2. *Memoriale* in Tranfaglia [1], 13.

3. Salvemini, *Carlo and Nello Rosselli* [1], 7.

4. Aldo Chiarle, *La "fuga" di Filippo Turati e il processo di Savona* (n.p.: Edizioni Giors, n.d. but after the war). Also, Ferruccio Parri described the escape in *L'Umanità,* October 9, 1948, quoted in Bruno Caizzi, *Camillo e Adriano Olivetti* (Turin: Unione Tipografica-Editrice Torinese, 1962), 138–40. Natalia Ginzburg remembered Turati's visit to her parents' apartment in Turin in her *Family Sayings,* revised trans. by D. M. Low (1967; Manchester: Carcanet Press, 1984), 68–70; originally published as *Lessico famigliare* (Turin: Giulio Einaudi, 1963). She was ten years old at the time. See also Aldo Garosci, *Storia dei fuorusciti* (Bari: Laterza, 1953), 30; Tranfaglia [1], 343–49; and Turati's account quoted in Gina Formiggini, *Stella d'Italia Stella di David: Gli ebrei dal Risorgimento alla Resistenza* (Milan: U. Mursia, 1970), 270.

5. Quoted in Formiggini [4], 271. On the trial, see Chiarle [4], 25–121; and Tranfaglia [1], 349–57.

6. For examples of this view, see two articles in *Gli ebrei in Italia durante il fascismo: Quaderni del Centro di Documentazione Ebraica Contemporanea:* Raffaele Jona, "Antifascismo: Vocazione dell'ebraismo?," III, November, 1963, 146–52, and Guido Lodovico Luzzatto, "La participazione all'antifascismo in Italia e all'estero dal 1918 al 1938," II, March 1962, 32–44. For a more balanced view in the same periodical, see Meir Michaelis, "Appunti bibliografici sulla persecuzione antisemita," II, 45–54. Speaking of the period before the racial laws, Michaelis says, p. 47, "no expert could agree with the affirmation that the majority of Italian Jews [were] anti-Fascist."

7. Quoted in Renzo De Felice, *Storia degli ebrei italiani sotto il fascismo* (1961; Turin: Giulio Einaudi, 1972), 89–90.

8. From an interview with Terracini, printed at length in Formiggini [4], 414.

9. For Emilio and Enzo's family, see Ruth Bondy, *The Emissary: A Life of Enzo Sereni,* trans. from Hebrew by Shlomo Katz (Boston: Little, Brown, 1977), 3–11.

10. Recorded by Guido Ludovico Luzzatto [6], 38. Luzzatto knew Modigliani personally.

11. Ibid., 39. Luzzatto also knew Chiesa.

12. Liliana Picciotto Fargion, "Sul contributo di ebrei alla Resistenza italiana," *La Rassegna Mensile di Israel,* vol. XLVI, n. 3–4 (terza serie), March–April 1980, 134; Salvatore Jona, "Contributo allo studio degli ebrei in Italia durante il fascismo," *Gli ebrei in Italia durante il fascismo* [6], II, 23. Charles F. Delzell, *Mussolini's Enemies: The Italian Anti-Fascist Resistance* (Princeton: Princeton University Press, 1961), 548, estimates total Italian Resistance fighters at 200,000. CDEC, *Ebrei in Italia: Deportazione, resistenza* (Florence: Tipografia Giuntina, 1975), 45, estimates Italian Jewish Resistance fighters at 3,000, or 6.6 percent of the Jewish population.

13. For a description of the escape by one participant, see Francesco Fausto Nitti, *Escape: The Personal Narrative of a Political Prisoner Who Was Rescued from Lipari, the Fascist "Devil's Island"* (New York and London: G. P. Putnam's Sons, 1930). Nitti was the nephew of former Prime Minister Francesco Saverio Nitti. On the escape, see also Garosci, *Storia dei fuorusciti* [4], 55–56.

Notes

14. For more on Giustizia e Libertà, see Garosci, *Storia dei fuorusciti* [4] and *Vita* [1] esp. I, 159–243 and II, 289–352; Salvemini [1]; Barbara Allason, *Memorie di un'antifascista* (Florence: Stabilimenti Grafici Vallecchi, n.d. but shortly after 1945), 87–181; and Delzell [12], 60–75.

15. Sion Segre Amar, "Sui 'fatti' di Torino del 1934 Sion Segre Amar ci ha scritto," *Gli ebrei in Italia durante il fascismo* [6], II, 126.

16. For more on Carlo Levi, see H. Stuart Hughes, *Prisoners of Hope: The Silver Age of the Italian Jews 1924–1974* (Cambridge, Mass.: Harvard University Press, 1983), 65–73.

17. Allason [14], 157–58; Delzell [12], 137 and 357; and Formiggini [4], 112. Natalia Ginzburg [4] mentions Foà several times, for he was a friend of her brother Alberto.

18. Formiggini [4], 181–84.

19. Caizzi [4]. See also various references to Adriano in Ginzburg [4], esp. 143–44. Adriano was married to Natalia and Mario's sister Paola, and he brought Natalia the news of her husband Leone's arrest in Rome in November 1943.

20. Nello Rosselli's best known works are *Mazzini e Bakunin: 12 anni di movimento operaio in Italia, 1860–1872* (Turin: Fratelli Bocca, 1927) and *Carlo Pisacane nel Risorgimento italiano* (Turin: Fratelli Bocca, 1932).

21. Garosci, *Vita* [1], II, 499–515; Salvemini [1], 66; and Delzell [12], 155–61.

22. Formiggini [4], 217–19; and Delzell [12], 56–60.

23. Guido Lodovico Luzzatto [6], 38.

24. Ibid.

25. Delzell [12], 56–59, 178–80, 205, and 394. See also Vera Modigliani, *Esilio* (Milan: Garzanti, 1946).

26. Terracini to Formiggini [4], 413–18.

27. As seen in chapter 3, footnote 4, Zionism was never strong in Italy before 1938.

28. Marina Sereni, *I giorni della nostra vita* (Rome: Edizioni di Cultura Sociale, 1955); Formiggini [4], 406–13; and Bondy [9], 3–11, 41, 49–50, 69–71, 97–98. Marina Sereni was Emilio's wife. Enzo Sereni is discussed later in this chapter.

29. Delzell [12], 92, lists twelve nonjurors, without indicating which were Jewish. Guido Lodovico Luzzatto [6], 44, mentions three Jewish nonjurors but adds a fourth, Fabio Luzzatto, who does not appear on Delzell's list. Fabio Luzzatto may have been among the younger professors who, in the years following 1931, acquired university positions and were asked to sign the oath.

30. Formiggini [4], 97–98; and Gemma Volli, "Gli ebrei nella lotta antifascista," *Emilia*, anno VII, n. 8–9, August–September, 1955, 226–30.

31. Formiggini [4], 111–12.

32. Pino Levi Cavaglione, *Guerriglia nei Castelli Romani* (Rome: Giulio Einaudi, 1945).

33. Emanuele Artom, *Diari: gennaio 1940–febbraio 1944* (Milan: Centro di Documentazione Ebraica Contemporanea, 1966), esp. 28–30.

34. *Ebrei in Italia: Deportazione, resistenza* [12], 20 and 49–50, quotes the official citation to Calò at the time his gold medal was awarded, and describes his life briefly. See also Formiggini [4], 283–89; Jona [12], 24; and Giuseppe Mayda, *Ebrei sotto Salò: La persecuzione antisemita 1943–1945* (Milan: Giangiacomo Feltrinelli, 1978), 150. Mayda refers to Calò's wife as Caterina. The facsimile of the official list of prisoners transported from Fossoli to Auschwitz, reproduced in *Ebrei in Italia: Deportazione, resistenza*, 21, refers to her as Carolina.

35. Giancarlo Sacerdoti, *Ricordi di un ebreo bolognese: Illusioni e delusioni 1929– 1945* (Rome: Bonacci, 1983), 166. On Jacchia generally, see *Ebrei in Italia: Deporta-*

zione, resistenza [12], 52; Formiggini [4], 310–15; Jona [12], 24–25; and Volli [30], 226–30.

36. Memo Bemporad, *La Macine: Storia di una famiglia israelita negli ultimi 60 anni di vita italiana* (Rome: Carucci, 1984), 75.

37. From a tribute to Forti on the tenth anniversary of his death, quoted at length in Formiggini [4], 307–8. See also *Ebrei in Italia: Deportazione, resistenza* [12], 51–52.

38. *Ebrei in Italia: Deportazione, resistenza* [12], 52–53; Formiggini [4], 316–21, including a long letter to the author from Rosani's commanding officer; and Jona [12], 25–26.

39. Sacerdoti [35], 79.

40. Alfredo M. Rabello, "In memoria di Franco Cesana, 'il più giovane partigiano d'Italia,'" *Gli ebrei in Italia durante il fascismo* [6], III, 140–45.

41. Eugenio Curiel, *Scritti 1935–1945*, ed. Filippo Frassati (Rome: Riuniti, 1973), especially the preface by Giorgio Amendola, xi–lx. See also Formiggini [4], 293–301; *Ebrei in Italia: Deportazione, resistenza* [12], 51; and Jona [12], 24.

42. Fabio Della Seta, *L'incendio del Tevere* (Trapani: Editore Celebes, 1969), 191. See also Formiggini [4], 290–93; *Ebrei in Italia: Deportazione, resistenza* [12], 50–51; and Jona [12], 25.

43. For Giorgio Diena, see his "La rivoluzione minimalista," 113–19, and Edmondo Rho, "Ricordo di Giorgio Diena," 120–21, in *Gli ebrei in Italia durante il fascismo* [6], II. For more on Paolo and the parents, see A. Cauvin and G. Grasso, *Nacht und Nebel (notte e nebbia): Uomini da non dimenticare (1943–1945)* (Turin: Casa Editrice Marietti, n.d. but after 1980), 22, and Formiggini [4], 104–5. Ada Gobetti Marchesini Prospero, *Diario partigiano* (Turin: Giulio Einaudi, 1956), 235, wrote of Paolo on October 17, 1944, the day she learned of his death, "I remember . . . the joyful vitality that his child-like face expressed under the blaze of red hair: so strong, so merry, so alive! I absolutely cannot think about his mother."

44. Formiggini [4], 116–18.

45. From Tesoro's own account, quoted at length in Formiggini [4], 418–21.

46. Formiggini [4], 358.

47. Bondy [9], 241.

48. Ibid., 123.

49. This account of Sereni's capture, imprisonment, and death is from Bondy [9], 223–41. For more on Sereni, see *Per non morire: Enzo Sereni: Vita, scritti, testimonianze*, ed. Umberto Nahon (Milan: Federazione Sionistica Italiana, 1973); Clara Urquhart and Peter Ludwig Brent, *Enzo Sereni: A Hero of Our Times* (London: Robert Hale Limited, 1967); and Carlo Leopoldo Ottino, "Cenni sull'esperienza sionista e antifascista di Enzo Sereni," *Gli ebrei in Italia durante il fascismo* [6], II, 67–85.

50. The one exception I have found is mentioned, with few details, by Lucien Steinberg, *Not as a Lamb: The Jews against Hitler*, trans. Marion Hunter (Farnborough, Hants, England: Saxon House, 1974), 73–74. It involves Raffaele Jona, who set up a Resistance group near Ivrea and funneled money from Jewish charities in Switzerland to Jews in hiding in Italy. In another case, not of a network but of a Jewish partisan deliberately and directly aiding Jews, Steinberg, 75–77, mentions Vito Volterra, who organized a raid, with Royal Air Force support, on an internment camp near Servigliano, in the province of Ascoli Piceno, where Jewish inmates were about to be deported.

51. Formiggini [4], 102.

52. As seen in chapter 8, one exception occurred in Asti, where a small fraction of the Jewish community reported voluntarily to an internment center.

Notes

13 / Conclusion

1. While the Bulgarian king and semi-independent Parliament agreed to racial laws and to the deportation of over 11,000 Jews from newly acquired Macedonia and Thrace, they never agreed to the deportation of Jews from Old Bulgaria. Unlike their actions in Denmark (see conclusion, footnote 23) and Italy, the Germans never forced the issue, and most Bulgarian Jews survived. The Nazis had far more success in Hungary, but there again, unlike their actions in Denmark and Italy, they never acted without extracting agreement from the increasingly subservient regime. For Bulgaria, see Martin Gilbert, *The Holocaust: A History of the Jews of Europe during the Second World War* (New York: Holt, Rinehart & Winston, 1985), 541–47; and Raul Hilberg, *The Destruction of the European Jews* (New York: New Viewpoints, 1973), 473–84. (A revised and definitive edition of Hilberg's book was published, under the same title, by Holmes & Meier in New York in 1985.) On Hungary, see conclusion, footnotes 3 and 18.

2. The first deportations were to Chelmno from the Wartheland, in the part of western Poland annexed to the Third Reich. Thousands of Polish Jews had already been killed, however, in random violence during the first six months of occupation. Another half a million are estimated to have died from such violence and from "natural causes," such as starvation and disease, during the ghettoization period from May 1940 to the end of 1941. See Lucy S. Dawidowicz, *The War against the Jews, 1933–1945* (New York: Holt, Rinehart and Winston, 1975), 397.

3. Thousands of Jews living in Hungary had died before April 1944, in other ways. At least 11,000 stateless Jews were massacred by German SS *Einsatzgruppen* in August 1941, when Hungarian officials forced them out of the country and into the German-occupied Ukraine. About 30,000 to 40,000 more died from cruelty and neglect during forced labor service. Another 25,456 of the 37,200 Jews sent with the Hungarian army to fight in Russia in 1941 were killed, wounded, or missing, while several thousand Serbs and Jews were massacred in Hungarian-annexed areas of Yugoslavia. Then in July 1944, roughly another 50,000 Jews from western Hungary were deported before Horthy finally stopped the deportations. Several thousand more died before the end of the war from starvation, disease, bombing raids, and slave labor service. See Hilberg [1], 509–54; Dawidowitz [2], 379–83; and Helen Fein, *Accounting for Genocide: National Responses and Jewish Victimization during the Holocaust* (Chicago: University of Chicago Press, 1979), 108–10.

4. Memo Bemporad, *La Macine: Storia di una famiglia israelita negli ultimi 60 anni di vita italiana* (Rome: Carucci, 1984), 102; Luciano Morpurgo, *Caccia all'uomo!* (Rome: Casa Editrice Dalmatia S.A., 1946), 189.

5. Bemporad [4], 75–128; Giancarlo Sacerdoti, *Ricordi di un ebreo bolognese: Illusioni e delusioni 1929–1945* (Rome: Bonacci, 1983), 108–63.

6. For fascinating accounts of Jews who survived in Nazi Germany through various combinations of passing and hiding, see Valentin Senger, *No. 12 Kaiserhofstrasse: The Story of an Invisible Jew in Nazi Germany,* trans. Ralph Manheim (New York: E. P. Dutton, 1980); and Leonard Gross, *The Last Jews in Berlin* (New York: Simon and Schuster, 1982).

7. For an excellent description of Polish Jews, see Nechama Tec, *When Light Pierced the Darkness: Christian Rescue of Jews in Nazi-Occupied Poland* (New York and Oxford: Oxford University Press, 1986). On p. 12, Tec relates that in a Polish census in 1931, only 12 percent of the Jews surveyed declared that Polish was their native language. Seventy-nine percent mentioned Yiddish, and the rest, Hebrew. Even Jews who looked Polish and spoke the language perfectly, without tell-tale Yiddish expressions, were often unfamiliar with Polish customs. Tec describes on pp. 34–39

the detailed religious instruction necessary to teach Jewish children to pass as Christians, as well as the efforts of adult Jews to learn to eat and drink like non-Jews.

8.   Tec [7], 42, 44, and 45, shows that it was not unusual in Poland for Jewish parents to urge children who looked and spoke Polish to escape, while they and their more Semitic-looking children did not even try. They knew, after all, that if they were caught in hiding, they would be shot immediately—a fate in itself more visible than in Germany and Italy, where Jews captured while hiding were discreetly deported for private execution, but rarely executed on the spot.

9.   Bemporad [4], 57–59.

10.   Ibid., 73, and Carlo Modigliani, *Una croce e una stella: Dal mio diario* (Milan: Gastaldi, 1959), 40–42.

11.   Enzo Levi, *Memorie di una vita (1889–1947)* (Modena: S.T.E.M. Mucchi, 1972).

12.   For analysis of the behavior of Dutch Jews during the Holocaust, see B. A. Sijes, "Several Observations Concerning the Position of the Jews in Occupied Holland during World War II," *Rescue Attempts during the Holocaust: Proceedings of the Second Yad Vashem International Historical Conference, Jerusalem, April 8–11, 1974,* eds. Yisrael Gutman and Efraim Zuroff (Jerusalem: "Ahva" Cooperative Press, 1977), 527–53. For personal accounts of Jews who for various reasons obeyed official summonses to report for "resettlement," see Gross [6] for Germany; Aranka Siegal, *Upon the Head of the Goat: A Childhood in Hungary 1939–1944* (New York: Farrar, Straus and Giroux, 1981) for Hungary; and Hana Demetz, *The House on Prague Street: A Haunting Story of a Girl's Survival* (New York: St. Martin's Press, 1970) for Czechoslovakia. Also, Hilberg ([1], 541) quotes an SS observer of deportations in Hungary who commented with surprise on how easy it could have been for Jews to hide in nearby forests and mountains, and to escape during long marches when guards were few.

13.   Tec [7]; and Peter Hellman, *Avenue of the Righteous: Inspiring True Stories of Heroic Christians and the Jews They Saved from the Holocaust* (New York: Bantam Books, 1981), 167–264.

14.   Gross [6].

15.   On French anti-Semitism, the unpopularity of foreign Jews in France during the 1930s, and the Vichy regime's anti-Jewish measures and eventual agreement to the actual deportation of foreign Jews (an agreement that Mussolini never made before occupation), see Michael R. Marrus and Robert O. Paxton, *Vichy France and the Jews* (New York: Basic Books, 1981). On French rescuers of Jews, see Philip Hallie, *Lest Innocent Blood Be Shed: The Story of the Village of Le Chambon and How Goodness Happened There* (New York: Harper and Row, 1979); Anny Latour, *The Jewish Resistance in France (1940–1944),* trans. Irene R. Ilton (New York: Holocaust Library, 1981); and Hellman [13], 107–66.

16.   Belgium was unique in producing a rescue organization, the *Comité de Défense des Juifs* (CDJ), which not only united nearly all pre-existing Jewish associations (including Zionists, Communists, and Socialists; natives and foreigners), but also worked closely with non-Jews and formed an integral part of the Belgian Resistance. See Lucien Steinberg, *Not as a Lamb: The Jews against Hitler,* trans. Marion Hunter (Farnborough, Hants, England: Saxon House, 1974), 131–51; and by the same author, "Jewish Rescue Activities in Belgium and France," *Rescue Attempts* [12], 603–15.

17.   Tec [7], 58, cites one such murder, and learned of another attempt from a rescuer who narrowly escaped death. Of course, not all Polish partisans acted in such a way. Many actively helped Jews.

18.   Hungary allied with Germany in order to annex areas of Czechoslovakia, Rumania, and Yugoslavia—for the most part, regions lost after World War I. Hungary joined the Tripartite Pact on November 20, 1940, and Hungarian troops participated

Notes

in the German invasion of Russia in June 1941. However, Admiral Horthy firmly resisted German demands for general mobilization, and by mid-1942 Prime Minister Miklos Kallay was attempting to extricate the army from Russia. In August 1943, after Mussolini's overthrow, Kallay actually broadcast a peace speech. See Dawidowitz [2], 379. Mussolini, in contrast, continually supported the war and urged Hitler to employ Italian troops.

19. The political "irrelevancy" of practicing Italian Catholics was insured when Vatican officials declared in 1871, in the wake of the loss of Rome to the newly unified Italy, that it was "not expedient" for Catholics to vote in parliamentary elections. Pope Pius IX confirmed the ruling in 1874. Strictly observant Catholics withdrew from political life. The *non-expedit*, somewhat relaxed for elections in 1904, 1909, and 1913, when Socialist candidates seemed likely to win in many constituencies unless Catholics were able to vote against them, was not formally canceled until 1919.

20. Memo Bemporad's father, a textile manufacturer with several factories near Florence, experienced major labor difficulties before and, especially, after World War I. His life was threatened, and he moved his wife and children out of town for a time. Yet striking workers apparently never referred to their employer's Jewishness. See Bemporad [4], 12–35.

21. Tec [7], 99–109, describes some rescuers who were actually anti-Semitic, but admits that the phenomenon was rare.

22. Carlo Brizzolari, *Gli ebrei nella storia di Genova* (Genoa: Sabatelli, 1971), 321–22.

23. During the first two and a half years of the German occupation of Denmark, the Danish king and his government, unlike Mussolini, refused all Nazi demands for anti-Jewish legislation. The Nazis scheduled a nationwide roundup for the night of October 1–2, 1943, to be executed, like the Rome roundup at about the same time, without Danish knowledge or cooperation. Georg Ferdinand Duckwitz, a courageous German attaché for shipping affairs at the German legation in Copenhagen, warned Danes of the raid. They in turn convinced the Jews to hide. The SS caught 477 Jews, less than 10 percent of a community of about 6,000. In the month that followed, Danes at all levels of society united in a spectacular rescue operation to ferry remaining Jews to Sweden. See Hilberg [1], 357–63; Harold Flender, *Rescue in Denmark* (New York: Simon and Schuster, 1963); Leni Yahil, *The Rescue of Danish Jewry, Test of Democracy* (Philadelphia: Jewish Publication Society of America, 1969); and Leni Yahil, "The Uniqueness of the Rescue of Danish Jewry," *Rescue Attempts* [12], 617–25. In his article in *Rescue Attempts*, 624, Yahil describes Jewish rescue in Denmark as definitely not the work of the Jews themselves, calling them among the most passive in Europe. This is a clear contrast to the Italian case.

24. Reported by Daniel Carpi in *Rescue Attempts* [12], 599.

25. See variants of this theme in CDEC, Milan, 9/2: *Medaglie d'oro: Riconoscimento ai benemeriti,* f. Benemeriti (medaglie d'oro), s.f. Tiburzio Giuseppe, letter from Tiburzio, March 30, 1955, and s.f. Zuccolin Gr. Uff. Marcello, letter from Zuccolin, March 28, 1955.

26. An explanation of why some people are altruists is beyond the scope of this work. In her study of the problem, Tec [7], 115–93, finds that Polish rescuers cannot be differentiated along political, religious, or class lines. She does find, however, that they shared certain characteristics, including individuality or separateness from others in the society, independence or self-reliance in pursuing personal values, a tendency to downplay the exceptional heroism of rescue work, a long previous history of helping the needy, an unplanned beginning to their rescue activities, and what she calls universalistic perceptions of the needy.

27. For discussion of these cases, see chapter 10.

28. While Polish rescuers, when caught, were usually executed on the spot along with the Jews in their care and, sometimes, all members of their own families, captured Italian rescuers were usually deported to concentration camps, not extermination camps. As seen in chapter 10, however, there were dreadful exceptions.

29. For societal disapproval in Poland, see Tec [7], 52–69. Because Italian altruists did not operate in defiance of their society as did the Poles, they may as a group exhibit slightly less individuality and independence than Tec's rescuers (see footnote 26). They may fall into the category Tec describes, 152, as "normative altruism" (helping behavior supported and honored by society) rather than "autonomous altruism" (helping behavior opposed by society). Nevertheless, while Italian rescuers, like the Danes, did not defy their peers, they certainly, unlike the Danes, defied their government, which had been instructing them on anti-Semitism since 1938. And as in all nations, the risks were enormous.

30. *Rescue Attempts* [12], 652.

31. See chapter 7.

32. See chapters 5 and 9.

INDEX

Action party, 250–52
Alatri, Lionello, 104
Alessandria: destruction of synagogue in, 285; forced labor in, 62
Allers, Dietrich, 185
Almansi, Dante, 26, 65, 106–7, 109, 114, 300n18
Almansi, Renato J., 300n18
Ambrosio, General Vittorio, 86
American Joint Distribution Committee, 65, 66, 88, 93, 210
Ancona, 147; escape of Jews of, 154–55
Anticoli, Lazzaro, 193, 312n15
Anti-Semitism, xvi, xviii, 16, 20, 22–23, 25, 73, 95, 96, 114, 136, 165, 174–76, 278, 279, 282–84; Catholic, 292n14; Danish rejection of, 281; in France, 97, 276; in Poland, 276, 278; violence and, 58–60; see also Racial laws
Apparuti, Primo, 69
Arab-Israeli War, 162
Arbe, 79
Ardeatine Caves massacre, xv, 145, 192–93, 299n2, 300n27, 311n5
Artom, Emanuele, 20, 21, 48, 59, 61–63, 72, 247–48, 261
Artom, Isacco, 15
Aryanization program, 39, 47, 292n27
Ascarelli, Ada, 268–69
Ascarelli Castelnuovo, Silvana, 108, 144
Ascoli, Max, 251–52
Assisi, rescue of Jews in, 215
Asti, 64, 164; detention of Jews in, 179–80; refugees in, 57
Athens, 80; deportations from, 81; Italian occupation of, 97–98
Auschwitz, xv, 8, 9, 57, 67, 79, 80, 89, 92, 117, 119, 122–26, 130, 137, 158,

160–62, 164, 165, 168, 171–74, 179, 180, 184–87, 189–90, 197, 200, 221, 224, 229, 262, 302nn51, 57, 303n58, 308n15, 309nn17, 18, 310n43, 318n34
Avanti! (newspaper), 266
Avenia, Giacomo, 220, 221
Avvenire d'Italia, L' (newspaper), 224

Babudieri, Brenno, 217
Badoglio, Marshal Pietro, 3, 4, 6–8, 67, 70–73, 87, 88, 100, 140, 141, 247, 251, 257, 259, 272, 306n21
Bagni di Lucca internment camp, 169
Balbo, Italo, 26, 39
Banfi, Don Carlo, 238
Bank of Italy, xiii, xv
Baptism, involuntary, 14
Barale, Monsignor Vincenzo, 208, 211, 213, 314n18
Barani, Aristide, 68
Barbieri, Ostillo, 220, 221
Barzilai, Salvatore, 17
Basilica of Saint Paul Outside the Walls, 194
Bassani, Giorgio, 43–46
Bassi, Giacomo, 219
Beccari, Don Arrigo, 216
Belgium, 274, 279; deportations from, 8, 273; rescue of Jews in, 276–77
Belgrado, Rabbi Fernando, 307n47
Belzek, 128, 185
Bemporad, Memo, 38, 49–50, 159, 264, 274, 275, 322n20
Benedetto, Father Maria, 115, 209–10, 213, 298nn28, 40, 301nn36, 37

324

Index

Index

Index

Graziani, Marshal Rodolfo, 3, 151, 153
Greece, Italian occupation of, 3–4, 8, 75, 80–82, 96–98, 100
Gries concentration camp, 183–84, 189, 190, 270, 310n41
Grini, Graziadio Mauro, 195, 197, 313n22
Gross, Leonard, 320n6
Guardia Nazionale Repubblicana (GNR), 150–52, 193, 198, 212, 258, 284, 306n25
Gubbio, murders in, 197–198

Haage, SS Sergeant Major Hans, 180, 181
Hias-Ica Emigration Association (HICEM), 65
Hilberg, Raul, 292n29, 296n46, 321n12
Himmler, Heinrich, 109, 111, 112, 300n28, 301n29
Hirschl, Julia, 76–77, 80, 297n7
Hitler, Adolf, *xvi*, 25, 29, 33, 134, 153, 175, 195, 273, 274, 303n69, 322n18
Hochhuth, Rolf, 303n72
Hofer, Gauleiter Franz, 148
Horthy, Admiral Nicholas, 278, 320n3, 322n18
Hudal, Bishop Alois, 129, 130
Hungary, Nazi occupation of, 273–74, 278

Interlandi, Telesio, 29, 30, 34, 71
Internment camps, 52–54, 56, 66
Ischia, Marco, 160
Istituto La Casa, 212
Istituto Palazzolo, 238
Italia libera, L' (newspaper), 126
Italian Academy, 31, 35
Italian African Police (PAI), 150, 193
Italian Constituent Assembly, 258, 259
Italian Foreign Ministry, 75, 77, 79, 83, 86, 298n46
Italian General Staff, 78, 79, 81
Italian Maritime School, 32
Italian Military College, 116–20, 136
Italian Ministry of the Interior, 35, 38, 86, 96, 150
Italian Red Cross, 121
Italian Social Movement, 306n28

Jabotinsky, Vladimir Zwed, 32
Jacchia, Mario, 262–63, 266
Jacchia, Valeria, 263
Jani, Emilio, 178
Jesi, Bruno, 61
Jesuits, 34
Jewish Community, 143, 146; of Pisa, 198; of Rome, 106, 113–16, 207, 258; of Turin, 156; of Venice, 139
Jewish Council, 104
John XXIII, Pope, 22
Jona, Giuseppe, 139–40
Jona, Raffaele, 319n50
Jona, Salvatore, 20–21, 289n4, 292n18, 308n60
Josephus, 12
Judenrat, 276
Jung, Guido, 26, 292n27

Kabiglio, Alberto, 311n46
Kalk, Israele, 294n2
Kallay, Miklos, 322n18
Kaltenbrunner, Ernst, 112
Kappler, SS Lieutenant Colonel Herbert, 109–13, 117, 126, 127, 135, 300n27, 302nn40, 43
Katz, Robert, 125, 300n18, 302n51, 303n64, 304n74, 305n89
Kessel, Albert von, 303n69
Kibbutz Givat Brenner, 268–69
Klarsfeld, Serge, 298n29
Knochen, SS Colonel Dr. Edward, 86
Koch, Pietro, 148
Koch band, 148–49, 155, 193, 194, 266, 284, 306n22
Kohn, Ora, 21–23
Kostoris, Leopoldo, 225
Kuliscioff, Anna, 243

Lächert, Elsa, 183
Lambert, Erwin, 184
Laqueur, Walter, 304n73
La Risiera concentration camp, 184–87, 195, 197, 311n46, 313n22
Latis, Giorgio, 267
Lausanne, Treaty of, 288n4
Laval, Pierre, 83, 289n8
Leonardi family, 68

Index

Index

Index

332

Index